San Diego Christian College
2100 Greenfield Drive
El Cajon, CA 92019

CHILDHOOD
AND
CHILDREN'S
BOOKS
in Early
Modern Europe,
1550–1800

CHILDREN'S LITERATURE AND CULTURE

Jack Zipes, Series Editor

Children's Literature Comes of
Age Toward a New Aesthetic
by Maria Nikolajeva

Sparing the Child Grief and
the Unspeakable in Youth
Literature About Nazism and
the Holocaust
by Hamida Bosmajian

Rediscoveries in Children's
Literature
by Suzanne Rahn

Inventing the Child Culture,
Ideology, and the Story of
Childhood
by Joseph L. Zornado

Regendering the School Story
Sassy Sissies and Tattling
Tomboys
by Beverly Lyon Clark

A Necessary Fantasy? The
Heroic Figure in Children's
Popular Culture
edited by Dudley Jones and Tony
Watkins

White Supremacy in Children's
Literature Characterizations of
African Americans, 1830–1900
by Donnarae MacCann

Ways of Being Male
Representing Masculinities in
Children's Literature and Film
by John Stephens

Retelling Stories, Framing
Culture Traditional Story and
Metanarratives in Children's
Literature
by John Stephens and Robyn
McCallum

Pinocchio Goes Postmodern
Perils of a Puppet in the
United States
by Richard Wunderlich and
Thomas J. Morrissey

Little Women and the Feminist
Imagination Criticism,
Controversy, Personal Essays
edited by Janice M. Alberghene
and Beverly Lyon Clark

The Presence of the
Past Memory, Heritage,
and Childhood in
Postwar Britain
by Valerie Krips

The Case of Peter Rabbit
Changing Conditions of
Literature for Children
by Margaret Mackey

The Feminine Subject in
Children's Literature
by Christine Wilkie-Stibbs

Ideologies of Identity in
Adolescent Fiction
by Robyn McCallum

Recycling Red Riding Hood
by Sandra Beckett

The Poetics of Childhood
by Roni Natov

Voices of the Other Children's
Literature and the Postcolonial
Context
edited by Roderick McGillis

Narrating Africa George Henty
and the Fiction of Empire
by Mawuena Kossi Logan

Reimagining Shakespeare for
Children and Young Adults
edited by Naomi J. Miller

Representing the Holocaust in
Youth Literature
by Lydia Kokkola

Translating for Children
by Riitta Oittinen

Beatrix Potter Writing in
Code
by M. Daphne Kutzer

Children's Films History,
Ideology, Pedagogy, Theory
by Ian Wojcik-Andrews

Utopian and Dystopian
Writing for Children and
Young Adults
edited by Carrie Hintz and Elaine
Ostry

Transcending Boundaries
Writing for a Dual Audience of
Children and Adults
edited by Sandra L. Beckett

The Making of the Modern
Child Children's Literature
and Childhood in the Late
Eighteenth Century
by Andrew O'Malley

How Picturebooks Work
by Maria Nikolajeva and Carole
Scott

Brown Gold Milestones of
African American Children's
Picture Books, 1845–2002
by Michelle H. Martin

Russell Hoban/Forty Years
Essays on His Writing for
Children
by Alida Allison

Apartheid and Racism in South
African Children's Literature
by Donnarae MacCann and
Amadu Maddy

Empire's Children Empire and
Imperialism in Classic British
Children's Books
by M. Daphne Kutzer

Constructing the Canon of
Children's Literature
Beyond Library Walls
and Ivory Towers
by Anne Lundin

Youth of Darkest England
Working Class Children
at the Heart of Victorian
Empire
by Troy Boone

Ursula K. Leguin Beyond
Genre Literature for
Children and Adults
by Mike Cadden

Twice-Told Children's Tales
edited by Betty Greenway

Diana Wynne Jones The
Fantastic Tradition and
Children's Literature
by Farah Mendlesohn

Childhood and Children's Books
in Early Modern Europe,
1550–1800
edited by Andrea Immel and
Michael Witmore

CHILDHOOD
AND
CHILDREN'S BOOKS
in Early Modern Europe, 1550–1800

Edited by

Andrea Immel and **Michael Witmore**

Routledge
Taylor & Francis Group
New York London

"Adopted Children in Shakespeare's Romances and Constructions of Heredity, Nurture. and Parenthood" is a condensed version of Chapter 3 from *Reading Adoption: Family and Difference in Fiction and Drama*, by Marianne Novy, The University of Michigan Press, © by the University of Michigan 2005, and appears with permission.

Figures 8.1, 8.2, 8.3, 10.1, 10.2, 13.2, 14.1, 14.2, and 14.3 appear courtesy of the Cotsen Children's Library. Department of Rare Books and Special Collections. Princeton University Library.

Published in 2006 by
Routledge
Taylor & Francis Group
270 Madison Ave,
New York NY 10016

Published in Great Britain by
Routledge
Taylor & Francis Group
2 Park Square, Milton Park,
Abingdon, Oxon, OX14 4RN

© 2006 by Taylor & Francis Group, LLC

Routledge is an imprint of Taylor & Francis Group

Transferred to Digital Printing 2008

International Standard Book Number-10: 0-415-97258-2 (Hardcover)
International Standard Book Number-13: 978-0-415-97258-1 (Hardcover)
Library of Congress Card Number 2005030498

Library of Congress Cataloging-in-Publication Data

Childhood and children's books in early modern Europe, 1550-1800 /
   [edited by] Andrea Immel and Michael Witmore.
       p. cm. -- (Children's literature and culture ; v. 38)
   Includes index.
   ISBN 0-415-97258-2 (acid-free paper)
   1. Children--Books and reading--Europe--History. 2. Children's
literature, European--History and criticism. 3. Children in literature.
   4. Children--Europe--History. I. Immel, Andrea. II. Witmore, Michael.
   III. Series: Children's literature and culture ; 38.

Z1037.A1C457 2005
028.5'5094--dc22   2005030498

informa
Taylor & Francis Group
is the Academic Division of Informa plc.

Visit the Taylor & Francis Web site at
http://www.taylorandfrancis.com

and the Routledge Web site at
http://www.routledge-ny.com

Contents

Series Editor's Foreword   VII

1   Introduction   1
    Andrea Immel
    Michael Witmore

2   Learning to Laugh   19
    Erica Fudge

3   "Oh that I Had Her!"   41
    Michael Witmore

4   Adopted Children and Constructions of
    Heredity, Nurture, and Parenthood in
    Shakespeare's Romances   55
    Marianne Novy

5   "Pretty Fictions" and "Little Stories"   75
    Claire M. Busse

6   The Godly Child's "Power and Evidence"
    in the Word   103
    Michael Mascuch

7   "In the Posture of Children"   127
    Kristina Straub

8   Curiosity, Science, and Experiential
    Learning in the Eighteenth Century   153
    Cynthia J. Koepp

9   "GOVERNESSES TO THEIR CHILDREN"   181
    Jill Shefrin

10 SPECTRAL LITERACY   213
    Patricia Crain

11 SOLACE IN BOOKS   243
    Jan Fergus

12 PERFORMANCE, PEDAGOGY, AND POLITICS   261
    William McCarthy

13 OTTO'S WATCH   277
    Arianne Baggerman
    Rudolf Dekker

14 THE SCHOOL OF LIFE   305
    Jürgen Schlumbohm

CONTRIBUTORS LIST   329

INDEX   335

Series Editor's Foreword

Dedicated to furthering original research in children's literature and culture, the Children's Literature and Culture series includes monographs on individual authors and illustrators, historical examinations of different periods, literary analyses of genres, and comparative studies on literature and the mass media. The series is international in scope and is intended to encourage innovative research in children's literature with a focus on interdisciplinary methodology.

Children's literature and culture are understood in the broadest sense of the term children to encompass the period of childhood up through adolescence. Because the notion of childhood has changed so much since the origination of children's literature, this Routledge series is particularly concerned with transformations in children's culture and how they have affected the representation and socialization of children. Although the emphasis of the series is on children's literature, all types of studies that deal with children's radio, film, television, and art are included in an endeavor to grasp the aesthetics and values of children's culture. Not only have there been momentous changes in children's culture in the last fifty years but also there have been radical shifts in the scholarship that deals with these changes. In this regard, the goal of the Children's Literature and Culture series is to enhance research in this field and, at the same time, point to new directions that bring together the best scholarly work throughout the world.

Jack Zipes

INTRODUCTION

Little Differences: Children, Their Books, and Culture in the Study of Early Modern Europe

ANDREA IMMEL
MICHAEL WITMORE

There has been no shortage of writing about children and childhood since Philippe Ariès advanced the controversial hypothesis in *L'enfant et la vie familiale sous l'ancien régime* (1960) that the idea of childhood did not exist until the early modern period.[1] Since then, the substance of Ariès's argument has been refuted: clearly there was something like a distinct phase of life called childhood (*l'enfance, das Kindheit, pueritas*) in the European Middle Ages that was recognized and accommodated in various regions of medieval culture.[2] But even if some of Ariès's claims no longer stand, his underlying assumption—that childhood and its subculture are always, in some sense, made and not found—has become more compelling over the years.[3] Indeed, the notion that different constructs of childhood emerge in multiple spheres of social and cultural activity has spurred a great deal of scholarship in the last half century.[4] Ariès's legacy can be traced across disciplinary lines in the work of historians, literary critics and art historians who, regardless of their position on Ariès's specific historical claims, have put his methodological assumption of "historical constraint" to a new, broader use.

Indeed, the next chapter in the "history of the history of childhood" reads something like a romance tale. The itinerary here is not quite a wandering one, but it has a certain expansiveness that has come to mark scholarship within children's studies over the last twenty years. As Ariès's findings continue to be debated among revisionists in different fields, the study of children and their culture has moved out of the relatively enclosed spaces of the nursery and the school onto more public stages where children had substantially more than walk-on parts to play. In the case of Reformation studies, scholars have documented the manifold ways in which the domains of childhood, adolescence, and adulthood overlapped in the lives of individuals. The 1522–1532 correspondence of the Nuremburg apprentice Michael Behaim, for example, reveals how this teenaged boy struggled to insure his future livelihood as a merchant, clashing with an obstructive master and a mother whose remarriage he feared would jeopardize his paternal inheritance.[5] A more surprising convergence of child and adult roles has been documented in studies of several female prophets who were active in England during the mid-seventeenth century. A godly Puritan girl such as eleven-year-old Martha Hatfield, the subject of James Fisher's *The Wise Virgin*, acquired real spiritual authority when her wondrous utterances and extraordinary physical sufferings engaged debates about the afterlife and the ideal relationship between church and community.[6] In eighteenth-century studies, moreover, we find representations of children in portraits, conversation pieces and genre paintings being discussed as sites for the articulation of ideas about the family, moral education, and socialization.[7] Analyses of the circulation and reception of children's books, whether their focus is a massive picture encyclopedia, the materials for young readers available at circulating libraries, or the earliest attempts to write critical histories of children's books, try to cast new light on the dissemination of cultural values within the public sphere.[8] And the study of early modern children's books—which has traditionally focused on the emergence of children's books as an autonomous literary genre and distinctive publishing market—has been integrated into major national book history projects such as the *Histoire de l'édition française* and *Cambridge History of the Book in Britain*.[9]

Drawn from an expanding, multidisciplinary field, this new scholarly work is exemplary in its holistic treatment of children and their relationship to the broader culture, an approach mirroring approaches

to the study of children in modern society, such as the one proposed
by Gertrud Lenzer, founder of the interdisciplinary Children's Studies
Program at Brooklyn College. In addition to highlighting the role
children play in the maintenance of class structures, Lenzer contends
that the experiences of individual children can help us understand
broader contemporary social dynamics.[10] We would argue that a similar intellectual agenda is appropriate for the investigation of children
in the past. Although much of recent historical work has thrived on
isolating the culture of childhood's unique qualities at a given time, it
is just as important to connect those issues of particular relevance to a
child's situation to those circulating in the wider culture. Children's
studies cannot be an island, although it may have sometimes seemed
so during the years following the publication of *Centuries of Childhood*,
as revisionist critics worked to establish the distinctness of children as
a sociohistoric group.

It is thus significant that many of the writers in this collection go
out of their way to link early modern representations of children and
their experiences to broader intellectual, economic, and social trends.
Claire Busse, for example, presents a nuanced view of the boy actor's
economic circumstances within the early-seventeenth-century theater
company, correlating his status as his employer's "property" with the
dramaturgical function of the roles he played. A different type of early
modern child actor emerges in the essays by Michael Mascuch and
Michael Witmore, who investigate the ways in which the extraordinary
behavior of children possessed either by the Holy Spirit or demonic
forces was made intelligible within broader evidentiary schemes of
value. In such seemingly disparate situations, the actions of children—
whether subject to a divine or diabolical force—are shown to have
been convincing or self-authenticating precisely to the degree that they
seemed spontaneous or uncontrolled, an unexpected twist on the old
idea that children lack credibility and authority because they are not
entirely in control of their own behavior.

Such "lateral moves" within children's studies have been enabled by
recent methodological shifts in the humanities and social sciences.
Perhaps the most important of these has been the impulse to "histori-
cize" within literary and cultural studies (not to mention historiography), an impulse that leads scholars to situate particular elements of a

given culture within broader networks of symbolic and material practices. Within this historicist perspective, developments in one part of a culture are rarely seen as isolated, but instead linked to other cultural domains, which in turn form a broader network of influences. Thus, in this volume, Kristina Straub argues that the tendency in eighteenth-century England to consider household servants as children regardless of their chronological ages can best be explained by appealing to ideas about the proper relationships between parent and child, master and servant, household and market, and household and state. The synthetic nature of Straub's work demonstrates that there is usually a public aspect to dealings with children within the private sphere (however constructed), and, thus, that it is also reasonable to look for the ways those dealings may resonate in other discursive contexts.

This tendency to see the boundary between children's subculture and the wider social environment as fluid has, moreover, compelled scholars to move beyond simple oppositions between childhood and adolescence or childhood and adulthood that were so important in the early stages of research in the social history of childhood. A broader range of categories must be introduced, since it is usually a bundled set of associations—childishness with, say, servitude or femininity—that structures action and perception at any given time. For example, Erica Fudge demonstrates how early modern discussions of a child's laughter helped shape crucial early modern philosophical distinctions about "human-ness" at a time when adult faculties were systematically opposed to those of animals and children. From those distinctions, Fudge then shows how teaching a child to regulate his outbursts of laughter was an essential part of the educational process. In doing so, she provides an important new context for thinking about the role of pleasure in Reformation theories of education. Similarly, William McCarthy shows how the pedagogical strategies adopted by three late Enlightenment teachers for individual pupils reflect a key distinction between the teachable and the unteachable, one that continues to inform contemporary pedagogical debates.

This type of work owes an obvious debt to Michel Foucault, who advocated broad analysis of discourses and institutions on the assumption that they were elements in some larger "episteme" or reservoir of knowledge that could itself be identified and studied. (Ironically,

Foucault himself did not write about children, even in a work such as *Discipline and Punishment,* in which some extended consideration of their situation would have been relevant.) Equally applicable is Pierre Bourdieu's work on the forms of social authority and privilege that attach to particular symbolic and institutional practices, as are sociological approaches that question the universality of categories like "childhood" and so look for its distinctiveness in more local webs of social interaction.[11] Although not all the contributors to this volume would characterize themselves as exponents of these writers' ideas, the assumption of mutual interaction among the cultural domains (and so, different academic disciplines) is a near constant in the work on offer here.

Indeed, among scholars who have favored an integrative approach to the study of early modern Europe, the child's amphibious nature has become an engaging source of interest. Whether considered as individuals or as members of groups, children almost by definition straddle important early modern social, economic, and philosophical categories. As young people gradually relinquish the prerogatives of childhood (the license that comes from freedom from adult responsibilities) to assume more adult privileges (those powers granted at a designated age or when deliberation and self-restraint can be exercised rationally), the process of maturation inevitably raises basic questions about the nature of agency, reason, and knowledge in societies that want to prescribe, cultivate, and regulate all three. If cultural historians and critics since Francis Bacon have increasingly assumed that certain kinds of truth can only be found in unusual situations or cases, then the child or the stages of childhood become obvious "places" to look for knowledge of the broader culture.[12] As liminal beings, children are per force among those "special cases" of humanity with the potential to reveal deeper truths about the social structure. Thus, Marianne Novy's comparison of children's treatment by their birth-parents and foster-parents in Shakespeare's late plays offers unexpected insights into Renaissance views of the roles of nature and nurture. Her essay also demonstrates how fictional representations of adults who turn over their children to surrogates may have resonated in a society where such separations were more routine than in our own.

Alongside this tendency to see deeper social truths at the margins (*in extremis veritas*) we find increased interest in reconstructing the experiences of people traditionally ignored as historical subjects—the so-called silent populations, whether those of workers, of women, of the subaltern, or, most recently, the disabled.[13] Work on silent populations has been motivated, in part, by the desire to bring a historically informed perspective to bear on the contemporary situations of such groups. Children too have often qualified as another silent population by virtue of their necessary subjection to adult authority. But it may not be as simple to "retrieve" the place and experiences of children as a marginal group as it has been for other groups like workers, subalterns, or women because, unlike these other groups, children have always suffered from being too intelligible to those who wish to understand their condition. It is assumed that since everyone was once a child, therefore anyone can intuitively grasp the nature of childhood experience. Along with this persistent presumption of transparency we must recognize another set of methodological challenges posed by recent attempts to write history "from below." The concept of "below" has been defined largely in Marxist historical terms and so this subspecies of history has concentrated almost exclusively on subjects that are not directly relevant to young children, such as labor history or the documentation of the working class's sociopolitical activities. Likewise, it has proven difficult to adapt the Marxist model and its key categories in the study of the preindustrial world.[14] Although early modern children may have been marginalized because of their subordination to parents, teachers, or masters, it does not necessarily follow that their situation is so similar to those of workers or slaves that the same models will serve for all.

Alternative models of social subordination would surely facilitate more subtle analyses of children's relationships to authority figures (to mention but one of many important topics); such models may emerge through methodological reflection, but are perhaps most likely to follow from our ongoing attempts to synthesize large bodies of new information. Like any socially marginal group, children may not command those resources of a culture's symbolic power that are most readily documented in the historical record. But children can leave traces in a variety of other sources that have yet to be explored. Thus, we agree with Hugh Cunningham that new work in the field should put a high priority on finding raw data about as many aspects of childhood as possible, data that must then be carefully weighed and imaginatively contextualized.[15] New evidence can alter our current perspectives on what we know, affording us greater opportunities to hear other voices from the past and to situate children over the *longue durée*. Jill Shefrin's chapter in this volume about aristocratic mothers is exemplary in this respect. Lawrence Stone characterized the relationship between the well-born mother and her children during the eighteenth century as one in which the woman could exercise the prerogative to delegate (or abdicate) maternal responsibilities to subordinates due to the obligations and pressures of social life.[16] Shefrin's extensive archival research about a group of prominent English aristocratic mothers who carefully supervised their daughters' educations suggests why Stone's view of upper-class mothers must be qualified. What emerges from her analysis of these women's correspondence is not just a richly detailed and fascinating portrait of a network of real women that included the influential teacher Jeanne Marie Le Prince de Beaumont (better known as the creator of *Beauty and the Beast)*. This essay might also serve as an outline for a new chapter in the development of child-centered education, an important concept whose history is still imperfectly understood in spite of its centrality to modern pedagogy.

Other contributors to this volume have discovered unpublished library sources about young people that have similarly challenged key assumptions about early modern children, their experiences, and their responses to their surroundings. Jürgen Schlumbohm, for example, has combed through German autobiographical writings for descriptions of those skills that the authors born into peasant families recalled having mastered in the "school of life." In the process he uncovers a vital form of learning distinct from the book-centered instruction that took place within the model classroom or in the sheltered confines of the bourgeois family circle—the usual focus of discussions about late Enlightenment education. Two other chapters examine sources in which children speak for themselves, as opposed to reflecting on the significance of their childhood experiences long after the fact as adults. Jan Fergus's analysis of a provincial bookseller's account books establishes that the boys at Rugby School were willing to spend their own money on the slickly packaged children's books of John Newbery, which runs contrary to the prevailing view in that eighteenth-century children did not choose to read such books but had them foisted upon them by anxious adults.[17] Arianne Baggerman and Rudolf Dekker show how certain entries in the diary of a Dutch boy, Otto van Eck, reflect fundamental shifts in the conception of time during the Enlightenment. Otto's diary is, in its own way, just as remarkable as the manuscripts relating to the trial of Menocchio, the sixteenth-century heretic miller who is the subject of Carlo Ginzburg's *The Cheese and the Worms*. The way Otto describes his anxiety when his watch goes missing and his palpable relief at its discovery outdoors (none the worse for exposure to the winter weather) speaks volumes about the way in which children internalized larger cultural concerns with time management, concerns that are still percolating down to younger members in our society.

Another invaluable source for the study of early modern childhood that remains largely unexplored are children's books themselves, as authors in this volume demonstrate. As Mitzi Myers once observed, these works continue to be sequestered from the broader interests of early modern culture because of the remarkable staying power of the Romantic construct of childhood, which condemns the authors of many children's books for ruthlessly attempting to repress the imaginations of young readers. Some literary critics have stigmatized Enlightenment children's books as too crudely didactic to sustain serious critical attention. But there is far more to be found in such texts, as Myers insists (and as her own recovery of Maria Edgeworth's "wee-wee stories" demonstrates), arguing that we ought to treat these texts as "a historically constituted locale within a complex web of power relationships and signifying practices, something we have to come at through words written by somebody at a particular moment for a particular purpose."[18] Cynthia Koepp's essay on the first international children's best-seller, the Abbé Pluche's *Spectacle de la nature*, bears out Myers's point, showing how a text traditionally dismissed as a routine venture in the popular transmission of the new science was in fact highly affiliative, dialogic, and egalitarian. This is especially clear as Pluche experiments with different ways of presenting information to young readers, inventing a series of lively conversations between a cast of fictional characters of different ranks, old and young, male and female. The orphan Goody Two-Shoes's rise from rags-to-riches, argues Patricia Crain, reflects the new and highly complex notion of literacy as a kind of intellectual property that emerged at the same time that the concept of property as a form of capital underwent a radical reconfiguration. Both these chapters put to rest the notion that a text simple enough for a child to understand is a straightforward read for the critic. Indeed, just the opposite might be the case.

These developments in historiography, literary, and cultural studies have been underway for some time now, and so it should not be surprising that their effects can be glimpsed in contemporary children's studies in other periods. One reads, for example, in James Shultz's book, *The Knowledge of Childhood in the German Middle Ages, 1100–1350*, that the knowledge of childhood "is the culturally constructed meaning of childhood, as articulated in discourses, practices and institutions."[19] This trio of "discourses, practices and institutions" represents a reservoir of "knowledge" that the historian can retrieve and then use to illuminate the broader patterns of meaning that knit together the texts of medieval German aristocratic writers. Carolyn Steedman's book, *Strange Dislocations: Childhood and the Idea of Human Interiority, 1780–1930* also takes an integrative approach, arguing that during the nineteenth century, the child came to represent the intrinsic "historicity" of the self.[20] Here, too, the child is seen not simply as a type of person but as a figure with broader cultural meaning. That meaning is symbolic and discursive, which is to say, it circulates within and among texts as a means of understanding basic social categories like the self and identity—categories that cultural historians find indispensable for explaining how people act and understand themselves at a given time and place. Even the realm of intellectual history is being invigorated by the study of children and children's culture. A recent exhibition catalogue from the Bibliothèque nationale, *Le printemps des génies: Les enfants prodiges*, collects essays from a number of historians illuminating the role of the child-genius as writer, performer, and artistic ideal from antiquity to the present.[21] This work is not simply a history *of* childhood: it is also cultural history *as* the story of the child's changing place in different intellectual and cultural arenas.

This tendency to work through the child to what are the nominally "adult" concerns of social, cultural, and intellectual history represents an unmistakable trend within the various fields that take children and childhood as a subject of inquiry. What is less often remarked in discussions of this work, however, is the degree to which fields such as social, cultural, and intellectual history might themselves be altered by their encounter with this marginal group—much as they have in the case of working-class history, the history of women, or, most recently, disability studies.[22] Ultimately, continued work in "history of childhood"—if we are to keep Ariès's term—must also illuminate the manifold ways in which dominant cultures appropriate or rely on marginal groups for their own sense of privilege and authority. This dynamic might be obvious in parent-child relations or in the rough justice of the early modern schoolroom, but it is also apparent in the "self-evidence" attached to various historical forms taken, for example, by the market, commodities, knowledge, the self, the household, humanity, agency, sensibility, and good taste—all of which are, at some point or another, defined with reference to children and their "distinct" behaviors or abilities. If this volume accomplishes anything within the confines of this larger scholarly conversation, we hope it draws attention to the two-way traffic between the culture of childhood and the broader social categories that have shaped the more "elevated" realms of European culture.

A number of significant themes or areas of inquiry have emerged from the essays collected here, one of which is the growing sophistication of books designed for children between the years 1550 and 1800. As we move into the seventeenth and eighteenth centuries, we find these books offering surprisingly complex and imaginative strategies to young people navigating the "flat world" of the page. Such strategies are often overlooked because they, like reading habits themselves, must be painstakingly reconstructed from textual prompts and contextual clues. As new evidence about text production, circulation, and reading habits is contextualized, however, a number of new voices emerge, deepening our sense of how adults hoped to assist children in the acquisition of knowledge and values. Cynthia Koepp and William McCarthy, in their respective discussions of the Abbé Pluche's *Spectacle de la nature* and Anna Leticia Barbauld's *Lessons for Children*, show how the format and organization of these texts expressed new ideas about curiosity, the importance of give-and-take between teacher and pupil, and immersive education—what in the later eighteenth century was sometimes called the education of the moment. While innovative authors for children have always hoped to make it easier for their readers to learn how to make meaning, they cannot guarantee results because young readers are no more homogenous an audience than one of adults. Just as contemporary critics of children's books understand that young people, like adults, have the ability to interpret texts in different ways, so too studies of the reception of children's books in the past should be expected to turn up multiple readings of texts. In her chapter on the circulation of fiction at Rugby School, for example, Jan Fergus tries to relate the boys' embattled subjectivities to their preference for a particular book, suggesting that they might have coped with the psychic and physical rigors of public school by identifying across gender lines with the sturdy, cheerful, upwardly mobile heroine of *The History of Goody Two-Shoes*. Bibliotherapy, it would seem, is not a modern invention. Patricia Crain's analysis of the same text, on the other hand, recontextualizes its free-wheeling blend of elements from genres ranging from the fairy tale to the language of contemporary advertising. In doing so, her reading underscores the story's modernity while uncovering a number of unexpected elements that help account for its appeal in the English-speaking world well into the nineteenth century.

But was print as important to lower and working class children as it seems to have been to those in the middle and upper classes? In his chapter on the "practical and symbolic" education of German peasant children, Jürgen Schlumbohm engages Neil Postman's argument that children were excluded from the adult world, insofar as that world was structured around print instead of oral communication. Schlumbohm shows that autobiographers repeatedly stress the importance of work, not print, in creating bonds of inclusion within peasant families and within their communities, a factor Postman overlooked. That this testimony comes from authors, who in real life rose like Goody Two-Shoes from humble origins into the professional classes, is somewhat unexpected. Equally intriguing is the fact that these highly literate adults, for whom books had been passports both to imaginative realms and to better lives, stood back and questioned the wisdom of protecting children by having them acquire experience through reading rather than interaction. We might well ask if this is a typically German response to the expanded role of reading in children's lives, or if late-nineteenth-century authors in other countries (whether autobiographers, reviewers, or educators) expressed similar reservations. In each of these chapters, we see that the "difference" children make raises interesting questions for the broader field of book history.[23] To what extent, for example, might children be seen as a symbiotic "extension" of print culture itself, serving as a paradigmatic audience for a progressive program of philosophically-minded reform? Do child readers, with their marginal facility with words and their connotations, also represent difficulties of adult writers in the period as they struggle to communicate their own concerns to a rapidly expanding reading public composed of individuals whose skills, competencies, and interests varied considerably from class to class?

Another thread connecting these essays is agency, itself a vibrant issue in the seventeenth and eighteenth centuries as philosophers and moralists began to consider the possibility that impediments to positive human action such as vice and error could be eliminated through the universal cultivation of reason. The actions of children could pose troubling dilemmas in early modern discussions of agency: children might be subordinate to adults because of their limited command of language or right to command others, but it did not follow that they were powerless. The ability to communicate by means other than words, for example, could confer a special form of spiritual power upon a child, as in the case of the girl-minister Sarah Wight. A young evangelical who was active during the mid-seventeenth century, Wight was highly literate, as evidenced by her extraordinary familiarity with scripture and an highly emphatic declamatory style. Yet the display of these competencies was not the most important factor in her success as a spiritual guide, as Michael Mascuch argues. It was rather her affecting presence and her physical sufferings that created "sensations" of grace in those who listened to her. Likewise the suspension of normal speech patterns gave the "testimony" of bewitched children in early modern witchcraft trials an eloquence which exceeded that of a simple utterance. In so-called "experimental" investigations into witchcraft, children's perceived cognitive inferiority allowed their bodies to function as "signs" of supernatural activity, elements in a spontaneous and therefore truthful language of a different kind. This gift of non-verbal communication was not bestowed just on extraordinary children in highly unusual circumstances, nor were its possessors invariably mute. The skill was exercised regularly in the streets, when small rude boys laughed at passersby, behavior that confirmed their half-civilized status in the eyes of many adults. Because a child's laughter could be a form of wordless mockery, as Erica Fudge's analysis of late sixteenth-century discussion of Aristotelian theories of the soul shows, it was imperative to teach a child to restrain his thoughtless, scornful mirth in order to widen the gap between boy and beast.

Empowered children were thus often viewed as unruly figures who needed to be broken and then reined in, a belief that was not simply the distillation of Calvin's doctrine of original sin. Claire Busse explores these contradictions in her essay on the agency of early seventeenth-century child actors. At first it would seem that child actors were on the same footing as apprentices, being their master's property (in this case, the management of the theatrical company). The boys' lack of agency as workers is doubly confirmed by the fact that child actors were regarded in much the same light as performing animals, learning without thinking to mimic the behavior and gestures of the adult roles they played. Like schoolboys challenging the master's authority in the classroom, boy actors could (and apparently did) willfully and knowingly rebel against their lot by departing from the carefully memorized script and subverting the performance, a kind of power playwrights such as Ben Jonson ruefully and hilariously celebrated. Kristina Straub makes a similar point in her chapter about the situation of English servants vis-à-vis their employers. Although servants were necessary to the smooth functioning of a household, they were nevertheless regarded with considerable suspicion as potentially disruptive forces who might steal, corrupt the children, and tempt the master and sons instead of attending to their work. Thus when English writers represented their servants as children, they tended to erase servants' value as commodities or labor and instead drew them into the moral and affective life of the family in order to teach them their duty, both for their own benefits, as well as their employers'. In each of these essays, the child's subordinate status as agent leads directly to larger issues within the domains of spirituality, knowledge, and economic activity.

Taken together, these essays raise a number of provocative questions. Why is it, for example, that some of the powers that seem characteristically to belong to adults—powers of rational self-inhibition usually associated with modern subjectivity—can best be grasped in relation to those of children? If the concept of agency can be defined comprehensively through a set of strategic contrasts between children, animals, and social subordinates—does it make sense to think about children or adults possessing inherent or intrinsic powers at all? To what degree has the "obvious" marginality of children impeded our ability to see adults exercising a similarly middling kind of power?

The case studies that are the focus of several chapters in this volume illustrate some of the benefits of focusing on individuals in order to make new generalizations or refine old ones. The relationship between the general and the particular is always an issue in any historical analysis, but it becomes even more pressing when dealing with children because of the paucity of evidence. The children discussed by Mascuch and Witmore could be regarded simply as freaks or charlatans, but it is quite helpful to regard them as privileged witnesses to supernatural phenomena, as emblems of a sort which allow us to gain insights into the physical shock of evangelical or demoniacal testimony. In their chapter on the diaries of Otto van Eck, Rudolf Dekker and Arianne Baggerman show how Otto's increasingly sophisticated sense of time helps us understand how this child's routine was structured by the progressive ideas to which his parents subscribed, but also how his evolving concern with efficiency could shape his narrative mode of recollection. Similarly, the memories of growing up in a peasant family of Friedrich Paulson—the professor of pedagogy discussed at length in Jürgen Schlumbohm's chapter—highlight his own sense that participation in a family economy was an education in local social dynamics superior to anything he would have obtained through reading. Paulson's implicit critique of the more privileged city child's book-centered experience reminds us that in our attempts to understand where, how, and what children learn, we cannot focus exclusively on books with a progressive social agenda like Pluche's *Spectacle de la nature*, ingenious new educational toys like the jigsaw puzzles Lady Finch introduced into the royal nursery, and a brilliant teacher's strategies like the ones Itard developed while instructing Victor the wild

boy of Aveyron, however important they may be. Nor can we overlook as evidence the fictional "lives" of child characters, whether that
of Goody Two-Shoes or of the roles played by seventeenth-century
boy actor Salomon Pavy, as another means of correlating constructions of childhood and actual data about young people. Such individual cases raise intriguing methodological questions. To what degree
are children as a group particularly susceptible to analysis by "case"?
We have already seen the ease with which they can become symbols
and objects of affection. Is there a similar "ease" with which they are
seen (deliberately or inadvertently) to become conduits or traffic points
between our own scholarly concerns and those of the cultures we study?

The last theme in the collection emerges across rather than within
the individual chapters. Although the writers of these chapters are
not always in direct dialogue with one another, the interconnections
between them suggests that an international approach to children and
childhood is becoming more and more important. Particularly in the
context of print, which circulates beyond national or regional boundaries, it is clear that "child lore" and materials destined for children's
hands are dispersed across multiple national traditions. One senses an
implicit parallel here between the mobility of children as cultural symbols and the portability of print—its ability to enter the public sphere
and reproduce perceptions in multiple social contexts. As we learn
from Marianne Novy's discussion of "lost" children in Shakespeare's
late romances, the child is often a shuttle between multiple plots and
scenes of interaction. Extending the analogy, we might say that the
study of children and childhood in Europe has its own meandering
logic, bringing together multiple locations and far-flung regions of
cultural activity. Perhaps it is only through comparative study, or at
least the consultation of multiple national traditions, that we can piece
together the culture of childhood in this period—a culture that is, in
every sense, co-extensive with early modern culture writ large.

Notes

We owe a particular debt of gratitude to Peter Hanns Reill, Director
of the Center for 17th- and 18th-Century Studies at the University of
California at Los Angeles, for introducing us in 2000. It was he who suggested that we jointly organize a conference about the history of childhood

in Europe, which proved to be the genesis of this volume. The essays contained herein are based on papers presented at the conference "Seen and Heard: The Place of Children in Early Modern Europe 1550–1800" (April 18–20, 2002), which was sponsored and hosted by the Cotsen Children's Library, Princeton University. We would also like to thank the Department of English at Carnegie Mellon University for all manner of support during the creation of this collection, as well as the Cotsen Children's Library's publication fund for underwriting the costs of the illustrations.

1. Philippe Ariès, *L'enfant et la vie familiale sous l'ancien régime* (Paris: Plon, 1960). The English translation followed two years later under the title *Centuries of Childhood: A Social History of Family Life*, trans. Robert Baldick (New York: Vintage, 1962).

2. See, for example, Urban T. Holmes, "Medieval Children," *Journal of Social History* 2 (1969): 164–72; Shulamith Shahar, *Childhood in the Middle Ages* (New York: Routledge, 1990); James Shultz, *The Knowledge of Childhood in the German Middle Ages, 1100–1350* (Philadelphia: University of Pennsylvania Press, 1995); and Nicholas Orme, *Medieval Children* (New Haven: Yale University Press, 2001).

3. According to Adrian Wilson, Ariès historicized the family "at a stroke." See Adrian Wilson, "The Infancy of the History of Childhood: An Appraisal of Philippe Ariès," *History and Theory* 19 (1980): 136. Some thought-provoking critiques of Ariès's procedures can be found in Lawrence Stone, "The Massacre of the Innocents," *The New York Review of Books* (1974): 25–31; Peter Laslett, "The Character of Familiar History, Its Limitations and the Conditions for Its Proper Pursuit," *Journal of Family History* 12, 1–2 (1987): 263–289, and Linda A. Pollock, *Forgotten Children: Parent-Child Relations from 1500–1900* (Cambridge: Cambridge University Press, 1983).

4. See, for example, Ilana Krausman Ben-Amos, "Adolescence as a Cultural Invention: Philippe Ariès and the Sociology of Youth," *History of the Human Sciences* 8:2 (1995): 69–89, or Patrick H. Hutton's "Philippe Ariès and the Secrets of the History of Mentalités," *Historical Reflections* 28:1 (2002): 1–19.

5. *Three Behaim Boys: Growing Up in Early Modern Germany: A Chronicle of Their Lives*, ed. Steven Ozment (New Haven, London: Yale, 1990).

6. Nigel Smith, "A Child Prophet: Martha Hatfield as the Wise Virgin," in *Children and Their Books: A Celebration of the Work of Iona and Peter Opie*, eds. Gillian Avery and Julia Briggs (Oxford: Oxford University Press, 1989): 79–93. *The Wise Virgin*, it also should be noted, was probably intended for both young and mature readers.

7. Recent examples include James Steward Christen's ambitious exhibition catalog *The New Child: British Art and the Origins of Modern Childhood 1730–1830* (Berkeley: University Art Museum and Pacific Film Archive, University of California, Berkeley in association with the University of Washington Press, 1995) or Chapter VII, "The State of the Child," in Marcia Pointon's *Hanging the Head: Portraiture and Social Formation in*

Eighteenth-Century England (New Haven and London: Yale University Press, 1993), 177–226.

8. For recent reception studies of early modern children's books, see Anka te Heesen's *The World in a Box: The Story of an Eighteenth-Century Picture Encyclopedia*, trans. Ann M. Hentschel (Chicago: University of Chicago Press, 2002), M. O. Grenby, "Adults Only? Children and Children's Books in British Circulating Libraries 1748–1848," *Book History* 5 (2001): 19–38 and Andrea Immel, "James Pettit Andrews's "Books" (1790): The First Critical Survey of English Children's Literature," *Children's Literature* 28 (2000): 147–163.

9. The monumental three-volume *Handbuch zur Kinder- und Jugendliteratur* co-edited by Theodor Brüggeman, Hans-Heino Ewers, and Otto Brunken remains the most ambitious enumerative bibliography of European children's books in any language, whereas Marjorie Moon's bibliographies of the early-nineteenth-century English children's book publishers John Harris and Benjamin Tabart have done much to advance understanding of the art and business of publishing children's books. For national book history projects that include chapters on children's books, see Dominique Julia's "Livres de classe et usages pedagogiques" in *Histoire de l'edition française*, 2:468–497 and Andrea Immel, "Children's and School Books" in the *Cambridge History of the Book in Britain*, Volume 5, forthcoming.

10. Gertrud Lenzer, "Children's Studies: Beginnings and Purposes," *Lion & the Unicorn* 25: 2 (April 2001): 182–183.

11. See Pierre Bourdieu, *Distinction: A Social Critique of the Judgment of Taste* (Cambridge: Harvard University Press, 1987) and the essays in *Constructing and Reconstructing Childhood: Contemporary Issues in the Sociological Study of Childhood*, eds. A. James and A. Prout (London: Falmer Press, 1997).

12. On Bacon's predilection for "special cases," see Lorraine Daston and Katharine Park, *Wonders and the Order of Nature: 1150–1750* (New York: Zone Books, 1998), Ch. 6, and Michael Witmore, *Culture of Accidents: Unexpected Knowledges in Early Modern England* (Stanford: Stanford University Press, 2001), Ch. 5.

13. For a comprehensive survey of the pioneering work on the physically handicapped, see Catherine J. Kudlick, "Disability History: Why We Need Another Other," *American Historical Review* 108:3 (June 2003): 763–793.

14. Jim Sharpe, "History from Below," in *New Perspectives on Historical Writing*, ed. Peter Burke (University Park: University of Pennsylvania Press, 1992), 25–27.

15. Hugh Cunningham, "Histories of Childhood," *American Historical Review* 103:4 (1998): 1196.

16. Lawrence Stone, *The Family, Sex and Marriage in England 1500–1800* (Harmondsworth: Penguin, 1979), 286.

17. See, for example Geoffrey Summerfield, *Fantasy and Reason: Children's Literature in the Eighteenth Century* (Athens: University of Georgia Press, 1985).

18. Mitzi Myers, "The Erotics of Pedagogy: Historical Intervention, Literary Representation, the 'Gift of Education' and the Agency of Children," *Children's Literature* 23 (1995) 3.
19. Shultz, *Knowledge of Childhood*, 10.
20. Carolyn Steedman, *Strange Dislocations: Childhood and the Idea of Human Interiority, 1780–1930* (Cambridge, Harvard University Press: 1995), 12.
21. *Le printemps des génies: Les enfants prodiges.* ed. Michéle Sacquin (Paris: Bibliothèque Nationale/Robert Laffont, 1993).
22. For a thoughtful appraisal of the impact of feminist history on the profession, see Joan Scott, "Women's History" in *New Perspectives on Historical Writing*, 42–66.
23. On book history and the history of the book, see *The Book History Reader*, eds. David Finkelstein and Alistair McCleery (New York: Routledge, 2001).

2

LEARNING TO LAUGH

Children and Being Human in Early Modern Thought

ERICA FUDGE

In their *Godly Forme of Houshold Government* of 1603, John Dod and Robert Cleaver wrote "it were better for children to be vnborne than vntaught."[1] Almost sixty years later, this dictum was repeated by Thomas Fuller, who termed it "our English proverb."[2] For Fuller, the phrase seemed to sum up a position that held national and, because of its source, possibly religious connotations. The statement sounds somewhat overblown, a puritanical threat in an age in which sport and so many other activities were perceived to reduce a human to the status of a beast, and in which there was, according to C. John Sommerville, a "pre-occupation" with children.[3] However, this chapter takes Dod and Cleaver's statement seriously; it uncovers a possibility that in some theological and philosophical ways it was logical, in late-sixteenth and early-seventeenth-century England, to say that "it were better for children to be unborne than untaught." The chapter will not make a case that the uneducated masses were treated and lived so poorly that their existence was perceived by many to be animal-like (however far that might be the case); rather, it will look particularly at the question of the nature of the child. In addressing this question, I hope to show not merely that Puritan writers were interested in children, childhood, and education in ways that previous generations of writers had not been (Sommerville and others have already done that extremely clearly)[4] but that the concept of the child formed under the influence of Aristotle and Calvin allows us to think about the status of children in somewhat different, perhaps more extreme ways.

The first question is an apparently simple one: what, in early modern England, is a child? The obvious answer is that a child is an immature human, but this statement creates problems, problems that require another question. What is a human? This chapter will answer that question in the first instance with the application of some Aristotelian logic; that is, it will examine what it is that makes a child—and I am initially thinking about the infant—a human. It will then trace the ways in which an answer to that question might allow us to think about the ways in which children were educated and trained in late-sixteenth and early-seventeenth-century England.

Middle Terms

Jonathan Barnes offers a brief and useful guide to one form of Aristotelian logic, the logic of causes: "the fact that we are trying to explain," he writes, "can be expressed in a simple subject-predicate sentence: S is P. The question we ask is: Why is S P?" He turns to what he calls the "middle term" (M) that offers the link between S and P, and that allows for the statement S is P because of M.[5] So, if we take the infant as the subject (S) and the human as the predicate (P) what we are looking for is the middle term (M) that offers the causal link. We look, in fact, to what are termed the "properties" of humanity. The question "why is S P" becomes then: what qualities does an infant share with the adult that would allow us to think of the infant as human? In early modern England, a list of properties of humanity could be drawn up: it would include speech, reason, memory, judgment, dreams, prophetic powers; all of these things are presented as proper only to humans.[6] But the focus here is on the early modern child or, more particularly at this point, the infant (the infant matures as the chapter progresses) so it will begin with some of these properties of humanity to see to what extent they form a middle term between infant and human.

In 1631, Daniel Widdowes wrote: "All Creatures are reasonable, or unreasonable. They which want reason, are Beasts, who live on Land or in Water. Those which live on the earth, moove on the earth, or in the ayre."[7]

This is clear and to the point. There are two sides to this debate: reason and unreason, human and beast. Widdowes's designation of difference is not, of course, new in the mid-seventeenth century: classical thought was premised, in many ways, on the fact that reason was the property of humans. Or, to put it another way, that humans were unique in their ability to reason abstractly.[8] Animals, by contrast, could only reason simply, relying on the presence of immediate stimuli. What this distinction allows for is the easy and, apparently, unquestionable demonstration of the superiority of humans.

But, if the human is defined as a "rational animal," an infant displays none of the qualities that might be understood to come under the heading of reason in early modern thought—intellect, memory, judgment—therefore, it cannot be said, following this, that an infant is a human. Likewise, it is hard to assume that an infant can communicate through speech, or experience prophetic dreams, something else that is, according to Artemidorus, the father of dream-divination, particular to humanity. In the 1606 edition of *The Judgement, or exposition of Dreames* he wrote:

> what is ther more honest, more holy, & that comes neerer to Diuinitie, then that a humane spirit may support, know, and vnderstand a part of future things without offending God, only by the meanes of causes & significations præcede[n]t, which are sent to vs by him, which is onely proper to man, who hath alone the vse of reason, whereby he may discerne, and iudge of things to come ...[9]

Perhaps the simplest way of representing the deficiency of animals is to turn to the issue of temporality. Widdowes wrote, following convention, that "Memorie calling backe images preserved in former time, is called Remembrance: but this is not without the use of reason, and therefore is onely attributed to man."[10] In similarly conventional terms, the Jesuit Thomas Wright argued that "beasts regard only or principally what concerneth the present time, but men forecast for future euents; they knowe the meanes and the end, and therefore comparing these two together, the prouide present meanes for a future intent."[11] Animals have only a present; they cannot conceive (remember) a past, and they cannot imagine (forecast) a future. The world of the non-human is always materially present, always limited, always driven by urges that the human can transcend.

However, the distinction of human from animal is not always as simple as these texts might appear to present it. According to William Kempe, writing in 1588, and following classical convention, "because youth is forgetfull, not greatly moued with regard of things past, or things to come, but wholy caried away with that which is before their face."[12] Eleven years later, Wright wrote of children that "they lacke the vse of reason, and are guided by an internall imagination, follow-ing nothing else but that pleaseth their senses, euen after the same maner as bruite beastes doe."[13] Like animals, youths are only con-cerned with what is in front of them, with what is present, and not with the past or the future, or what is absent or remembered. A sheep, according to discussions of memory, can recall that it is scared of a wolf only when the wolf stands before it; it cannot actively recall a wolf in its absence and scare itself by imagination.[14] Active recall—reminiscence—is the property of humanity. Kempe is saying the same thing of youths, and if, following J. A. Sharpe, we see "youth" in the early modern period as the stage between fourteen and twenty-eight years of age, the issue of present-mindedness might well be even clearer when thinking of infants and children.[15] These are creatures who live only in the now.

So how can the first question—what is a child?—be answered? If a child fails to display the so-called properties of humanity, is a child human? The answer might have to be "no." But there is one property, deliberately ignored in the discussion so far, that does offer an answer: laughter. In *De partibus animalium* Aristotle wrote that man is "the only animal that laughs,"[16] and this argument became a commonplace for two millennia, repeated by, among others, Porphyry, Galen, Boethius, Erasmus, Vives, and Castiglione.[17] Here the subject-predicate rela-tionship finds its middle term: a child is a human because laughter is proper only to humans, and a child laughs. An infant, whose language capacity or ability to exercise reason is limited, is able to laugh, and is therefore revealed as human. A dog (even an adult dog) can never laugh—dog laughter is something I come back to—because a dog is never ever human.

Laughter, then, provides a middle term between human and child. It also, in early modern conceptions, offers a link between mind and body; between the immaterial and the material.[18] And it is this that provides a way in to taking Dod and Cleaver's statement seriously.

Belly Laughs

According to M. A. Screech, Aristotle's writings on laughter are "the pillar on which whole edifices of thought were raised."[19] And in *De partibus animalium,* Aristotle sets out the basis for all early modern interpretations. He turns to the midriff. This, he writes, is present in all "sanguineous animals," and divides "the region of the heart from the region of the stomach." As such, this "partition-wall and fence" separates the "nobler from the less noble parts": the heart from the liver. As well as having this vital physiological function, the midriff also serves as a site of a further, and more generally important, division. Aristotle argues "[t]hat heating of [the midriff] affects sensation rapidly and in a notable manner is shown by the phenomena of laughing. For when men are tickled they are quickly set a-laughing, because the motion quickly reaches this part, and heating it though but slightly nevertheless manifestly so disturbs the mental action as to occasion movements that are independent of the will." The shared physiology of man and animal with which Aristotle begins this section breaks down with the impact of heating the midriff. He writes, "[t]hat man alone is affected by tickling is due firstly to the delicacy of his skin, and secondly to his being the only animal that laughs." What also breaks down is the importance of the human will in the establishment of the human as a separate and particular being. Will—an immaterial, reasoned capacity—is overwhelmed by the body.[20]

In early modern versions, this bodily power of laughter is frequently repeated. In 1579 the surgeon to the French King, Laurent Joubert, following the convention, argued that laughter "is common to all, and proper to man." He outlines the physical effect of laughing:

> Everybody sees clearly that in laughter the face is moving, the mouth widens, the eyes sparkle and tear, the cheeks redden, the breast heaves, the voice becomes interrupted; and when it goes on for a long time the

veins in the throat become enlarged, the arms shake, and the legs dance about, the belly pulls in and feels considerable pain; we cough, perspire, piss, and besmirch ourselves by dint of laughing, and sometimes we even faint away because of it.[21]

Pissing oneself, it seems, is proper to humans.[22]

He goes on, and looks beyond the apparent, visible manifestation of laughing on the body to its internal operation. The pericardium, "the sheath or cover of the heart," he writes, "pulls on the diaphragm to which it is thoroughly connected in men, quite otherwise than in animals. ... And this is (in my opinion) the reason, or at least one of the principal ones, why only man is capable of laughter."[23] The diaphragm is moved via the convulsion of the heart in the pericardium, and it is this that causes what Erasmus terms a kind of "fit," otherwise known as laughter.[24] Once again, it is the human anatomy, this time the fact that in humans the pericardium is connected to the diaphragm, that causes laughter.

But, of course, laughter that is due to mere anatomy is limited. Being tickled does provoke laughter, but this is termed "bastard laughter" as it is a purely bodily response, requiring no operation of the mind. The other "untrue" version of laughter is "dog laughter," or the "*cynic spasm*" as Joubert terms it. This is false, and emerges either through willed contortion of the face ("angry and threatening dogs have this look"), or injury (a knife to the diaphragm): it is therefore potentially both reasonable (willed) and unreasonable (bodily).[25] In the *Schoole of good manners* (1595) William Fiston simplifies this distinction, writing: "some laugh so vnreasonably, that therewith they set out their teeth like grinning dogs."[26] The lack of reason and the overwhelmingly bodily response turn a man into an animal. It is, perhaps, for this reason that one of the earliest signals of the possession of one of the Warboys children discussed by Michael Witmore in this volume was the "exceeding laughter," "the exceeding hearty and immodest laughter" of one of the daughters of the household.[27] It is her laughter that signals the child's loss of human status.

There is, however, an alternative form of laughter that is based on physiological factors—the possession of the link between pericardium and diaphragm—but that goes beyond the merely material. The true laugh (as opposed to the bastard or dog laugh) calls on the workings of the immaterial, the mind, and it is this laugh that is truly the property of humanity. Joubert writes, following Aristotelian convention, that all passions—the appetites of the mind, such as joy, hate, anger and so on—"proceed ... from the sensitive appetite." He goes on:

> This [sensitive] faculty necessarily precedes the movement of the heart. And yet we say that one does not covet the unknown, for in imagining an object, and judging it good or bad, the humors, agitated by our noticing it, affect the heart, which as though hit and struck, is moved, desiring or disdaining the object.

What follows this natural—and inevitable—movement (from eye, to brain, to heart) is a struggle between rationality and physicality. The danger is that the will will be overwhelmed by the motions of the heart; that the rational soul will be taken over by the sensitive. Joubert's image to illustrate this point comes from Plato: the will's relation to the heart, he writes, "is like a child on the back of a fierce horse that carries it impetuously about, here and there, but not without the child's turning it back some, and, reining in, getting it back on the path."[28] He goes on to emphasize that, despite this battle, reason can rule the heart through something akin to "civil or political [power] where with authority one points out obligations." (This is opposed to another form of power that is used by reason as a last resort wherein it "simply commands.") The will, therefore, is "free ... to choose or refuse the right thing." The power of movement, which is voluntary, is always at the command of the will; the power of the sensitive appetite, however, "does not obey immediately, and often contradicts the will, employing long arguments and various thoughts, after which it sometimes happens that the diverted will yields to the emotions." The fact that laughter can resist the will, that we can laugh—and sometimes feel we *have* to laugh—in spite of ourselves, shows that laughter cannot be "under the rational ... faculty": that it must be, Joubert writes, of the "sensitive faculty" which humans share with animals.[29] This sharing of a form of perception has wider implications, however. As Thomas Wright notes, in the "alteration which Passions woorke in the witte, and the will, wee may vnderstand the admirable metamorphosis and change of a man from himself when his affects are pacified, and when they are troubled. *Plutarch* said they changed them like *Circes* potions, from men into beasts."[30]

It is because of the conflict between mind and body that is innate to laughter that it becomes an important aspect of being human. In fact, a true laugh becomes a necessary exhibition of human-ness.[31] Quentin Skinner has recently shown in great detail a key understanding of the nature of laughter in Renaissance thought.[32] Again, the precedent is classical: according to Quintilian, laughter "has its source in things that are either deformed or disgraceful in some way."[33] In this Quintilian is following Socrates who proposed that laughter is a "combined" emotion. Socrates argued "when we laugh at the ridiculous qualities of our friends, we mix pleasure with pain."[34] But Joubert goes even further: in the experience of joy, he argues, the heart expands, whereas in the experience of sorrow it shrinks. One can die of joy (the heart can burst), but one cannot die of laughter, because laughter is a dilation and contraction of the heart, is a movement between joy and sorrow. For this reason, laughter is perceived to proceed from "a double emotion": "laughable matter," Joubert writes, "gives us pleasure and sadness."[35]

This innately contemptuous quality of laughter uproots any links to joy that might be assumed to be inherent in this human expression, and the scornfulness is repeated by numerous early modern thinkers including Baldessare Castiglione, Thomas Wilson, Robert Burton (who of course takes on the persona of Democritus, the laughing philosopher, in his *Anatomy of Melancholy*), Sir Thomas Browne, and Thomas Hobbes.[36] Joubert writes, "inasmuch as laughter is caused by something ugly, it does not proceed from pure joy, but has some small part of sadness."[37] The link between joy and sadness gives the laugher a particular sense of themselves: as Hobbes put it, "the passion of Laughter is nothyng else but a suddaine Glory arising from suddaine Conception of some Eminency in our selves, by Comparison with the Infirmityes of others, or with our owne formerly."[38] In laughing, humans simultaneously acknowledge an exterior failure and their own success. Laughing as such is a moment of self-reflection as well as self-aggrandizement. It is where, as Screech has shown, the dictum *nosce teipsum*—know thyself—is put to work.[39] Without self-knowledge, how could one recognize the deformity of others?

This is where we shift from viewing laughter as a purely bodily (and therefore unwilled) phenomenon to laughter as something that invokes and requires the will. To laugh is ideally to perform an act of judgment, is to discriminate, and this is yet another reason why animals cannot laugh. Not only is the pericardium not linked to the diaphragm in any animal other than the human, only the human has the judgment that is required to truly laugh.

So the "true" laugh is simultaneously of the body and of the mind. One of the crucial things about it is that it cannot be faked; a true laugh is always true of the body, not quite willed (and therefore unfalsifiable), but is also, paradoxically, willed and therefore of the mind. A good laugh is a laugh in which mind and body agree: in which what the intellectual faculty regards as "deformed" is in parallel with the bodily movement.[40] A *loud* laugh, however, does not show the absolute agreement of body and mind: quite the contrary. Richard Greenham writes "a foole when hee laugheth liftes vp his voyce, but the wise man is scarse heard."[41] A wise man exercises control over his body; his almost silent laugh reflects the power of his mind. Plato, like Christ, never laughed.[42]

For this reason, laughter becomes a vital property of humanity. It is a place where mind and body are brought into potential conflict. True laughter, it might be said, is when the mind takes control of something that is potentially, and powerfully, out of its control; is when judgment is not overwhelmed by the animal-body but actually overwhelms it. This is evidence of powerful reason. The laugh may be of the body, but the true laugh is certainly of the mind.

The Laughter of a Child

This dangerous conflict between will and body that is central to laughter, however, makes the laughter of a child somewhat problematic. According to Aristotle and, following him, Pliny, an infant laughs only after its fortieth day (Charles Darwin observed his children and found that they laughed on their forty-fifth and forty-sixth days).[43] Until that point, according to my logic, the infant is not human, it is a mere animal being: it does not have the discrimination to laugh, and so we get something else. Joubert, having cited Pliny and Aristotle, writes that not only are the muscles of infants incapable of the kinds of convulsions necessary to laughter, but that they "do not conceive the laughable in their minds since they only know during the first months what is necessary for life, just as do animals." With time, however, the infant does begin to laugh, but, as Joubert notes, there are still problems: "the laughter of small children is counterfeit and illegitimate, like dog laughter."[44] There seems to be some confusion here between Joubert's categories of bastard and dog laughter: dog laughter implies fakery (a willed state), whereas bastard laughter involves nothing more than the body. To say that a child can fake a laugh is to imply, I think, that a child can produce a true laugh, something that Joubert would want to deny.

But, if we accept that the child's laugh (whatever else it is) is not a true laugh we can begin to trace a logic. If true laughter is about making judgments—Laurel L. Hendrix has called laughing "an act of reading"[45]—then a young child cannot truly laugh. An infant does not judge the world around him or her: in Aristotelian terms (and these were the most common in the early modern texts I am looking at) the fact that the world is completely new means that a judgment beyond the "that's new" is impossible and therefore concepts of good, bad, true, and false are problematic. An infant lives, in fact, in a world of the immediate and of wonder: it has an incapacity to judge and therefore is merely astonished by its new place.[46] This wonder may cause the heart to convulse, and therefore cause a form of laughter, but the lack of will involved in wonder means that this is not laughter in its true sense: Joubert writes, "astonishment does not cause laughter, but only holds the mind in suspense."[47] Albertus Magnus, following Aristotle, argued that this suspension is not the end, rather it is the beginning of philosophy: "wonder is the movement of the man who does not know on his way to finding out."[48]

This, in a sense, is the more positive model of the child's laugh. It is a laughter of innocence that proclaims the purity of the child itself. Adam and Eve, of course, did not learn the distinction between good and evil until they ate the fruit of the tree of knowledge. A child, laughing in wonder, is like the first parents, conversing naked without shame. Dressing oneself, for Jacques Derrida, is one potential property of humanity;[49] it is a property that emerges only after the Fall, only after the need to discriminate, and therefore only after the possibility of laughter. An infant, like its prelapsarian parents, does not dress itself, nor can it judge beyond its natural instincts. Discrimination has not yet entered to change joyous wonder into scornful cackling.

But there is, of course, another way of interpreting the laughter of a child, and this is the one that is held by most of the writers in early modern England whose work I am looking at here. Although they follow key aspects of Joubert's theory, they differ on one particular issue: the status of the child. The Fall, again, plays its part. For Robert Burton, it was the cause of human misery and lack of innate self-knowledge. On page 1 of *The Anatomy of Melancholy* he wrote:

> But this most noble Creature, ... O pittifull change! is falne from what he was, and forfeited his estate, become *miserablilis homuncio,* a cast-away, a catiffe, one of the most miserable creatures of the World, if he be considered in his owne nature, an vnregenerate man and so much obscured by his fall (that some few reliques excepted) he is inferiour to a beast. *Man in honour that vnderstandeth not, is like vnto beasts that perish,* [marg: Psal. 49.20] so *David* esteemes him: a monster by a stupend Metamorphosis, a beast, a dogge, a hogge, what not?[50]

In this, Burton is following a well-established Reformed tradition in which emphasis is placed on human corruption and closeness to the beast. Thomas Morton, writing in 1596, argued that postlapsarian humans are "carnal and worldly minded men," who, "beholding the glorious creatures of God, are no more affected then are the brute beastes, which never once lift vp their eies to heauen."[51] Leicester divine John Moore proposed "mutability" as a quality innate to man, going on to argue that, where God was truly immutable, man had both the "power of standing, and the possibility of falling: power of standing he had from God his creatour: possibility of falling from himselfe, being a creature."[52] We can will our own destruction; this is a product of the Fall.

It is not only that "man," the adult, is differently judged in Reformed theology, however. Calvin's infamous denigration of the child (a being previously held by the Roman church to be incapable "of mortal sin until the age of seven")[53] gives the infant's laughter a new meaning. The "depravity"[54] (Calvin's term) of the infant means that its laughter is

merely revelatory: it shows the infant's innate and unexceptional sinful-
ness. In fact, it shows the infant to be controlled by the body. There is
no judgment (no act of reason)—this is in agreement with Joubert's
more positive (Catholic) model of children's laughter—there is only
body. And the only wonder for a Calvinist would be that adults might
think that the infant is innocent. It is that lack of judgment that
reveals a mind held in suspense; reading Calvin, we could argue, offers
the route from suspension to belief. How to acknowledge the corruption of the child, the need for judgment, and moderation of the bodily
response, is central to conceptualizations of children and forms a cor-
nerstone, I think, of many attitudes towards education in the period.

Christian Laughter

According to the Elizabethan Calvinist William Perkins, the first
stage in parental care of the infant is baptism,[55] and here godparents
make declarations on behalf of the child, declarations that the child,
as it matures, is expected to make for him or herself. The reason for the
intercession of the godparents is simple: Richard Jones asked "Whether
maie fooles, mad men, or children bee admitted to the Supper of the
Lord?" His answer is clear: "*No, for they cannot examine themselues.*"[56]
The godparents stand in to examine the child on his or her behalf.[57]

Following baptism, parents are expected to continue with their
children's godly education, and the catechism—the rote learning of
key religious questions and answers—emerges as a primary form of
indoctrination. C. John Sommerville has noted that catechitical
"memorization ... was to make orthodoxy the child's second nature."[58]
What had been external is made internal: what was culture begins to
appear as nature. As well as this, the catechism is a display of key
properties of the human memory and speech. And the latter, according to Dod and Cleaver, could precede the former: "let him haue the
words taught him when he is able to heare and speake words, and
after, when he is of more discretion, he will conceiue & remember the
sense too."[59] Parroting precedes speaking: animal, as ever, comes before
human. In learning the catechism (parents were fined if the child had
not learned it by the age of eight)[60] the child was displaying its entry
into the human community as well as into the Christian community:

in fact, the two—human and Christian—seem inseparable in this context. But speech, like Christian doctrine, needs to be overseen with care. Fiston advises his boy reader that, on hearing ribald speeches by superiors, he should "make semblance, as though [he] heard them not."[61] Feigned ignorance (an act of will) is more appropriate than bastard laughter, as bastard laughter gives priority to the body, and returns the human to its (dangerously natural) animal status.

But laughing itself—whether true, bastard, or dog—is also problematic. For divines, the Scriptural evidence would seem to point away from laughing at all. Christ never laughed: "he wept three times," wrote William Perkins, "at the destruction of Ierusalem, at the raising of *Lazarus,* and in his agonie: but we neuer reade that he laughed."[62] As if this were not warning enough, the Old Testament also presents laughter as dangerous. II Kings 2:23–25 records the story of the children who laughed at Elisha's baldness. Verse 24 reads, "And [Elisha] turned back, and looked on them, and cursed them in the name of the LORD. And there came forth two she bears out of the wood, and tare forty and two children of them." Screech writes of this, "God intended to fix irrevocably in men's minds the respect due to elders and to his ministers, who are in *loco parentis.* They must not be laughed at."[63] He is, of course, right; but an even more general warning is also recorded in this passage: laughter itself is dangerous. In 1595, Fiston noted that "Too earnest & violent laughter, is seemly for no age: but most vnseemly for children."[64] Richard Greenham referring, perhaps, to Psalm 111, "The fear of the LORD is the beginning of wisdom," states "When a man is most merrie, he is nearest danger. ... The way to godlie mirth, is to feele godlie sorrow."[65]

But these writers did not refuse laughter altogether. William Perkins wrote, somewhat pragmatically: "As for laughter, it may be vsed: otherwise God would neuer haue given that power and facultie vnto man." He goes on, however, to speak what is a Reformed commonplace: "but the vse of it must bee both moderate and seldome, as sorrow for our sinnes is to be plentifull and often."[66] So, even as Elisha's curse seems to call for silence, there is a place wherein laughter can be used. Following Thomas Aquinas's belief that "sparing" laughter works as a useful relief to the mind,[67] Perkins proposes that two kinds of jesting are "tolerable" to Christians: the first "is moderate and sparing mirth, in the vse of things indifferent, in season conuenient, without the least scandall of any man, & with profit to the hearers. The seco[n]d is that which the Prophets vsed, when they iested against wicked persons, yet so, as withall they sharply reproued their sinnes."[68] Religious laughter requires self-examination. A sin is risible only if the laugher recognizes it as a sin. In doing this, the laugher not only distances him or herself from the sinner but from the sin as well. Scorn, once again, is self-awareness, and it is this that the child must gain. A Christian education must include, therefore, teaching the child to laugh.

Learning to Laugh

In *The Education of a Christian Prince*, Erasmus famously argued that morality should be "pressed in, and rammed home" through parables, analogies, and epigrams, and should be placed constantly before the child by being "carved on rings, painted in pictures, inscribed on prizes." He goes on: "When the little pupil has enjoyed hearing Aesop's fable of the lion being saved in his turn by the good offices of the mouse ... and when he has had a good laugh, then the teacher should spell it [i.e., the moral] out."[69] Laughter here precedes learning; it is, in fact, the means by which the lesson is learned. The bitter pill of education is sweetened with pleasure.

This sense of the importance of laughter and pleasure in the classroom can be traced in many English writings on education in the late sixteenth and early seventeenth centuries. In his dialogue on the correct forms of godly learning, Bartholomew Batty states simply that "pleasure & delight" are key.[70] And Perkins, too, proposes that "the first instruction of children in learning and religion, must be so ordered, that they take it with delight."[71] Fiston takes the link between learning and pleasure into slightly different territory, writing "learning is but sport and play to such as haue willing minds."[72]

In a work that we might term predominantly humanist rather than Reformed, however, a slightly different notion of laughter emerges. In his *Positions* (1581), Richard Mulcaster presents laughter as a form of exercise. He writes "can there be any better argume[n]t, to proue that it warmeth, then the rednesse of the face, and flush of highe colour, when one laugheth from the hart, and smiles not from the teethe?" In his terms laughter is a medicine: "it must needs be good for them to vse *laughing,* which haue cold heades, and cold chestes, which are troubled with melancholie, which are light headed by reason of some cold distemperature of the braine, which thorough sadnesse, and sorrow, are subiecte to agues. ..." These people, he suggests, should "suffer themselues to be tickled vnder the armepittes, for in those partes there is great store of small veines, and litle arteries, which being tickled so, become warme themselues, and from thence disperse heat thorough out the whole bodie." What is clear in Mulcaster's representation of laughter is that this is not "true" laughter in the sense outlined by Joubert. Indeed, the laughter that Mulcaster promotes is bastard laughter, purely bodily, from the heart, and due to the tickling of the armpits. Like the Reformed writers, however, Mulcaster, too, emphasizes moderation: "But as moderate *laughing* is holesome, & maketh no too great chaunge, so to much is daungerous, and altereth to sore."[73]

But it is not only as the sugaring of the pill of learning that laughter operates in Reformed writings. It has a more significant role to play than that. If laughing is, as I have argued, a moment when body and mind are in potential conflict, and if one of the properties of being human is the exhibition of reason (the control of the mind over the body), then laughing must be brought under control as part of the process of becoming human. Just as the human must control the bodily urges of lust, greed, and so on in order to be virtuous and therefore truly human, so the urge to laugh must likewise be controlled.

There are two elements to the Reformed education, then: learning doctrine, and learning human-ness. These are both addressed in the notion of "pleasurable" learning. The fact that the infant laughs at so early a stage in its development signals not only, as Aristotle had said, that laughter is natural—of the body—but that it needs to be modified, controlled: rationalized. The rationing of laughter—making it modest and directing it at things indifferent—was not merely mannerly nor, I would argue, a part of what Norbert Elias termed "the regulation of instinctual life."[74] Its function was part of a wider and potentially even more significant process: not that of becoming civilized, but that of becoming human.[75] Now, of course, civilization and human are often in the early modern period interchangeable terms:

what lacks civilization—a New World native, for example, lacks human status. Robert Gray, for one, argued: "The report goeth, that in *Virginia* the people are sauage and incredibly rude, they worship the diuell, offer their young children in sacrifice vnto him, wander vp and downe like beasts, and in manners and conditions, differ very little from beasts, hauing no Art, nor scice, nor trade, to imploy themselues, or giue themselues vnto ..."[76] In this context, the perceived "beastliness" of the natives allows for the civilized (Christian) English to lay a claim to the land: it is not theft if that which is taken is never owned. However, the missionary endeavor, the fact that one of the claims of the Virginia Company was the need to spread the Christian doctrine in the barbarous New World,[77] meant that a concept of "monogenesis" must be in place.[78] If the natives were not always-already human, how could they be converted to the true faith? Underlying Gray's apparent species distinction persists a recognition of sameness.

In distinction from Grey and others writing about the encounters with the natives, I am using "human" here in what might be termed more of a species than a civil sense: I am arguing that the human as a species was being made, implicitly and sometimes explicitly, in the process of the regulation of laughter. In this sense, Dod and Cleaver's short, sharp dictum "it were better for children to be vnborne than vntaught" signals a very real understanding of the status of the child. It might sound like puritanical overstatement, but I think that it frames a fear, a fear that the infant, the child, even the youth may not after all become human without help. Learning to laugh is learning to give the mind dominion over the body, and this is why a child's laughter is important.

What can be traced in early modern theories of laughter, then, is not only scorn (a mixture of joy and sorrow) but also self-knowledge. If children cannot receive the sacraments on their own behalf because, in Richard Jones's phrase, "*they cannot examine themselues,*" then a true laugh—a regulated, learned laugh—represents evidence of self-examination. So learning with "delight" can be interpreted as being a double-layered entry into human status. Not only are moral and religious truths of society made natural, alongside this pleasure itself is a control of the body by the mind, is a learned enculturation of the body, and this is central to the process of becoming human. In this sense, the reinsertion of Aristotle in the Renaissance canon, and the predominant inclusion of his ideas within theories of laughter, and Calvin's new assessment of the child means that when we look at the conceptualization of the human in early modern texts, not only do we find those texts peopled with animals, we also find that those animals might actually be children, children who are being taught to laugh.

Notes

1. John Dod and Robert Cleaver, *A Godly Forme of Houshold Government* (London: Thomas Man, 1630), R2v. A version of this chapter appeared in *Textual Practice* 17:2 (2003), 277–294. I am grateful to the editors for allowing me to reproduce the essay here.
2. Thomas Fuller, *The History of the Worthies of England* (1662), quoted in David Cressy, *Education in Tudor and Stuart England* (London: Edward Arnold, 1975), 43.
3. C. John Sommerville, *The Discovery of Childhood in Puritan England* (Athens and London: University of Georgia Press, 1992), 19 and passim.
4. As well as Sommerville, see Patrick Collinson, "The Protestant Family," in his *Birthpangs of Protestant England: Religion and Cultural Change in the 16th and 17th Centuries* (Basingstoke: Macmillan, 1988), 60–93; Ian Green, "'For Children in Yeeres and Children in Understanding': The Emergence of the English Catechism under Elizabeth and the Early Stuarts," *Journal of Ecclesiastical History* 37:3 (1986), 397–425; Philip Greven, *The Protestant Temperament: Patterns of Child Rearing, Religious Experience and the Self in Early America* (New York: Meridian, 1979); Christopher Hill, "The Spiritualization of the Household," in Hill, *Society and Puritanism in Pre-Revolutionary England* (1964, reprinted Harmondsworth: Penguin, 1986), 429–466; Leah Sinanoglou Marcus, *Childhood and Cultural Despair: A Theme and Variations in Seventeenth-Century Literature* (Pittsburg: University of Pittsburg Press, 1978); John Morgan, *Godly Learning: Puritan Attitudes Towards Reason, Learning and Education, 1560–1640* (Cambridge: Cambridge University Press, 1986); Robert V. Schnucker, "Puritan Attitudes Towards Childhood Discipline, 1560–1634," in *Women as Mothers in Pre-Industrial England: Essays in Memory of Dorothy McLaren*, ed. Valerie Fildes (London and New York: Routledge, 1990), 108–121; Keith Thomas, "Age and Authority in Early Modern England," *Proceedings of the British Academy* 62 (1976), 205–248; Thomas, "Children in Early Modern England," in *Children and their Books: A Celebration of the Work of Iona and Peter Opie*, eds. Gillian Avery and Julia Briggs (Oxford: Oxford University Press, 1989), 45–77.
5. Jonathan Barnes, *Aristotle* (Oxford: Oxford University Press, 1982), 53.
6. Jacques Derrida has argued that such a list reveals one thing: "it can attract a non-finite number of other concepts, beginning with the concept of a concept." The unsatisfactory infinity of this list leads Derrida to propose

an alternative property of humanity: bestiality. This, he writes, "can never in any case be attributed to the animal or to God." It need not be expressed here what would happen to the status of humanity if its position as the "bestialising animal" was to become a commonplace. Jacques Derrida, "The Animal That Therefore I Am (More to Follow)," *Critical Inquiry* 28 (2002), 374 and 409.

7. Daniel Widdowes, *Natvrall Philosophy: Or A Description of the World, and of the severall Creatures therein contained* (second edition, London: T. Cotes, 1631), p. 64.

8. Richard Sorabji has argued that Aristotle's denial to animals of "reason (*logos*), reasoning (*logismos*), thought (*dianoia*), intellect (*nous*), and belief (*doxa*)" was "not peripheral, but central to Aristotle's concerns." Sorabji, *Animal Minds and Human Morals: The Origins of the Western Debate* (London: Duckworth, 1993), 14 and 15.

9. Artemidorus, *The Iudgement, or exposition of Dreames, Written by Artimodorus, an Auntient and famous Author, first in Greeke, then Translated into Latin, After into French, and now into English* (London: William Jones, 1606), The Epistle Dedicatory, n.p.

10. Widdowes, *Natvrall Philosophy*, 51–52.

11. Th. W. [Thomas Wright], *The Passions of the Minde* (London: VS for WB, 1601), 312.

12. W. K. [William Kempe], *The Education of Children in learning: Declared by the Dignitie, Utilitie, and Method Thereof* (London: Thomas Orwin, 1588), Fr.

13. [Wright], *Passions of the Minde*, 12.

14. See, Aristotle, *De Memoria et Reminiscentia*, in *Aristotle on Memory*, ed. Richard Sorabji (London: Duckworth, 1972). An early modern version of this argument is in Gulielmus Gratorolus, *The Castel of Memorie … Englished by Willyam Fulwood* (London, Rouland Hall, 1562), Fvv-Fvir.

15. J. A. Sharpe, "Disruption in the Well-Ordered Household: Age, Authority, and Possessed Young People," in *The Experience of Authority in Early Modern England*, ed. Paul Griffiths, Adam Fox, and Steve Hindle (Basingstoke: Macmillan, 1996), 188.

16. Aristotle, *De partibus animalium*, Book III, Chapter 10.

17. See Helen Adolf, "On Medieval Laughter," *Speculum* 22 (1947), 252; M. A. Screech, *Laughter at the Foot of the Cross* (London: Penguin, 1997), 1–3; M. A. Screech and Ruth Calder, "Some Renaissance Attitudes to Laughter," in *Humanism in France at the End of the Middle Ages and in the Early Renaissance* (Manchester: Manchester University Press, 1970), 219; Juan Luis Vives, *The Passions of the Soul: The Third Part of De Anima et Vita*, trans. Carlos G. Noreña (Lampeter: Edwin Mellen Press, 1990), 59; Baldesar Castiglione, *The Book of the Courtier*, trans. George Bull (London: Penguin, 1976), 155.

18. Vladimir Propp proposed that "We do not laugh now as people once laughed … a definition [of the comic and of laughter] can only be historical." Cited in Stephen Halliwell, "The Uses of Laughter in Greek Culture," *Classical Quarterly* 41:2 (1991), 279.

19. Screech, *Laughter*, 13.
20. See Katherine Park, "The Organic Soul," in *The Cambridge History of Renaissance Philosophy,* ed. Charles B. Schmitt and Quentin Skinner (Cambridge: Cambridge University Press, 1988), 464–484.
21. Laurent Joubert, *Treatise on Laughter* (1579), trans. Gregory David De Rocher (Tuscaloosa: University of Alabama Press, 1980), 17 and 28.
22. This begs the question, where would it be deemed inappropriate for an animal to piss? The answer, inevitably, is that it is inappropriate for an animal to piss within the domain of the human. This is a capacity that must be learned, and which the animal may often fail in, and therefore reveal itself as animal. By implication, a wild animal can never evacuate inappropriately.
23. Joubert, *Treatise,* 46 and 47.
24. Cited in Screech, *Laughter,* 216.
25. Joubert, *Treatise,* 76.
26. W. F. [William Fiston], *The Schoole of good manners* (London: I Danter for William Ihones, 1595), B8r.
27. *The Most Strange and Admirable Discoverie of the Three Witches of Warboys* (London, 1583) cited in Sharpe, "Disruption," p. 199.
28. Joubert, *Treatise,* 32. See Plato, *Phaedrus,* 246A–247C and 253D–254E.
29. Joubert, *Treatise,* 33, 34 and 35.
30. [Wright], *Passions of the Minde,* 100.
31. I hyphenate the term human-ness to signal the separation of the quality (in this instance, laughter) from the species being, and to highlight the fact that in many discussions from this period—as with others—the quality comes to stand for the species. It is, in Derridean terms, the true "supplement." See Jacques Derrida, "... That Dangerous Supplement ...," in Derrida, *Of Grammatology,* translated by Gayatri Chakravorty Spivak (Baltimore and London: Johns Hopkins University Press, 1974), 141–164.
32. Quentin Skinner, "Why Laughing Mattered in the Renaissance: The Second Henry Tudor Memorial Lecture," *History of Political Thought* 22:3 (2001), 418–447.
33. Quintilian, *Institutio oratoria,* cited in Skinner, "Why Laughing Mattered," 428.
34. Plato, *Philebus,* 50A-B, translated by Harold N. Fowler (Loeb Classical Library) (London: William Heineman, 1962), 339.
35. Joubert, *Treatise,* 44.
36. All are cited in Skinner, "Why Laughing Mattered," passim.
37. Joubert, *Treatise,* 39.
38. Thomas Hobbes, *The Elements of Law,* cited in Skinner, "Why Laughing Mattered," 423. On Hobbes, see R. E. Ewin, "Hobbes on Laughter," *The Philosophical Quarterly* 51:202 (2001), 29–40.
39. Screech, *Laughter,* 69.
40. As Screech has shown, deformity is not limited to the physical—although this is certainly an unpleasant possibility—it is also intellectual deformity. Erasmus's laughter, Screech notes, was often directed toward theological ignorance. Screech, *Laughter,* 161ff.

41. Richard Greenham, *The Workes of the Reverend and Faithfull Servant of Jesus Christ M. Richard Greenham* (London: Felix Kyngston for Robert Dexter, 1601), "Of Joy and Sorrow," 350.

42. Plato's lack of laughter is according to Diogenes Laertius, cited in Marjorie O'Rourke Boyle, "Gracious Laughter: Marsilio Ficino's Anthropology," *Renaissance Quarterly* 52:3 (1999), 717.

43. J.Y.T. Greig, *The Psychology of Laughter and Comedy* (London: George Allen & Unwin, 1923), 25.

44. Joubert, *Treatise*, 114 and 119.

45. Laurel L. Hendrix, "'Mother of laughter, and welspring of blisse': Spenser's Venus and the Poetics of Mirth," *English Literary Renaissance*, 23 (1993), 119.

46. Writing of Columbus's wondering, Stephen Greenblatt states that "European culture experienced something like the 'startle reflex' one can observe in infants: eyes widened, arms outstretched, breathing stilled, the whole body momentarily convulsed." Stephen Greenblatt, *Marvelous Possessions: The Wonder of the New World* (Oxford: Oxford University Press, 1991), 14.

47. Joubert, *Treatise*, 96.

48. Albertus Magnus, *Commentary on the Metaphysics of Aristotle*, cited in Greenblatt, *Marvelous Possessions*, 81.

49. Derrida, "The Animal That Therefore I Am," 373.

50. Robert Burton, *The Anatomy of Melancholy* (Oxford: John Lichfield and James Short for Henry Cripps, 1624), 1.

51. [Thomas Morton], *A Treatise of the threefolde state of man* (London: R. Robinson, 1596), 34.

52. John Moore, *A Mappe of Mans Mortalitie* (London: George Edwards, 1617), 7.

53. Schnucker, "Puritan Attitudes," 114.

54. John Calvin, *The Institutes of the Christian Religion*, trans. Henry Beveridge (London: James Clarke & Co, 1949), II, 215.

55. William Perkins, *Of Christian Oeconomie* in *The Works of that Famous and Worthie Minister of Christ in the University of Cambridge, Mr William Perkins* (London: J. Legatt, 1616–18) III, 694.

56. Richard Jones, *A Briefe and Necessarie Catechisme* (London: Thomas East, 1583), Cvir.

57. See Erica Fudge, *Perceiving Animals: Humans and Beasts in Early Modern English Culture* (2000, reprinted Urbana and Chicago: University of Illinois Press, 2002), 40–46.

58. Sommerville, *Discovery*, 136.

59. John Dod and Robert Cleaver, *A Treatise of Exposition Vpon the Ten Commandments* (London: Thomas Man, 1603), 8r.

60. Sommerville, *Discovery*, 145.

61. [Fiston], *Schoole of good manners*, D5r.

62. William Perkins, *A Direction for the Government of the Tongve According to Gods Word*, in *Works*, I, 448.

63. Screech, *Laughter*, 35.

64. [Fiston], *Schoole of good manners*, B8r.

65. Greenham, "Of Joy and Sorrow," 348.
66. Perkins, *Direction*, 448.
67. Screech, *Laughter*, 136.
68. Perkins, *Direction*, 448.
69. Desiderius Erasmus *The Education of a Christian Prince*, ed. Lisa Jardine (Cambridge: Cambridge University Press, 1997), 10 and 12.
70. Bartholomew Batty, *The Christian mans Closet* (London: Thomas Dawson and Gregory Seton, 1581), 8r.
71. Perkins, *Of Christian Oeconomie*, 694.
72. [Fiston], *Schoole of good manners*, C5r.
73. Richard Mulcaster, *Positions* (London, 1581), 63. On Mulcaster's place in humanist education, see Alan Stewart, "'Traitors to Boyes Buttockes': The Erotics of Humanist Education," in Stewart, *Close Readers: Humanism and Sodomy in Early Modern England* (Princeton, NJ: Princeton University Press, 1997), 84–121.
74. Norbert Elias, *The Civilizing Process* (1939) translated by Edmund Jephcott (Oxford: Blackwell, 1994), 140. Skinner argues that the "civilizing process" had an impact on laughing that was "an obvious instance of an uncontrolled reaction that needed, in polite society, to be governed and preferably eliminated." Skinner, "Why Laughing Mattered," 445.
75. Anthony Fletcher has argued that in early modern ideas masculinity was not given at birth but had to be attained; my argument about the attainment of humanity echoes his ideas but takes them into the realm of species rather than gender: Fletcher, "Manhood, the Male Body, Courtship and the Household in Early Modern England," *History* 84:275 (1999), 419–436.
76. Robert Gray, *A Good Speed to Virginia* (London: Felix Kyngston, 1609), C2v.
77. 'The *Principall* and *Maine Ends* ... weare *first* to preach, & baptize into *Christian Religion*, and by propagation of that *Gospell*, to recouer out of the armes of the Diuell, a number of poore and miserable soules, wrapt vpp vnto death, in almost *inuincible ignorance;* to endeauour the fulfilling, and accomplishment of the number of the elect, which shall be gathered from out all corners of the earth. ... Secondly, to prouide and build vp for the publike *Honour* and *safety* of our *gratious King* and his *Estates* ... some small Rampier of our owne.' Anon., *A Trve and Sincere declaration of the purpose and ends of the Plantation begun in Virginia* (London: I. Stepneth, 1610), 2–3.
78. See Margaret T. Hodgen, *Early Anthropology in the Sixteenth and Early Seventeenth Centuries* (Philadelphia: University of Pennsylvania Press, 1964), especially 207–253.

3

"Oh that I Had Her!"

The Voice of the Child in a Body Possessed

MICHAEL WITMORE

Some of the most celebrated cases of witchcraft in England involve children who are both victims of "diabolical practice" and witnesses for its prosecution. Perhaps the most notorious case of this kind occurred in the town of Warboys, Huntingdonshire, in the winter of 1589, one that was recognized by subsequent demonologists as a nearly unimpeachable example of witchcraft at work. The story of the Witches of Warboys begins with the strange fits of a ten-year-old girl, Jane Throckmorton, who in November of that year is suddenly taken ill with fits of "very loud and thick" sneezing, followed by a trance-like state of silence. When she wakes, Jane's family is terrified to find that her belly has swollen and begun to heave so violently that she cannot be held in one place. What looks like a "running palsy" travels across her body, one leg shaking and then falling motionless as the disturbance travels from limb to limb, moving to the arms and ending finally in her head. Like the mysterious shaking that spreads through her body, the distressing news of Jane's fits spreads out across the town of Warboys, drawing neighbors into the Throckmorton home so that they can witness a spectacle that continues for several days. One onlooker, an old woman named Alice Samuels, is singled out by Jane for her grizzled looks. "Did you ever see," declares the child, "one more like a witch than she is? Take off her black thrummed hat, for I cannot abide to look on her." Three years later, "Mother Samuels" and her family

41

will be executed as witches, almost entirely on the basis of the fits (and accompanying testimony) of Jane and her sisters.[1]

What made Jane and her sisters so convincing? In the narrative account of the case published in 1593, entitled *The most strange and admirable discoverie of the three Witches of Warboys*, the Throckmorton children become vessels for voices that are not properly their own, voices that foretell future events and identify antagonists with an uncanny clarity of purpose. Toward the end of their nearly three-year ordeal, the children declaim emphatically on the need for the accused witches (Alice Samuels, her husband, and their daughter Agnes) to confess their crimes in sermons lasting over a half an hour. These hortatory displays alternate with more vatic, but also more descriptive, utterances in which the children "repeat" what is told to them by an attendant spirit. Throughout their trials, Joan, Elizabeth, Mary, and Jane claim to be hearing something called "the thing" that tells them about the precise movements of their absent siblings, the nature and frequency of their future fits, and the activities of Mother Samuels. In making such pronouncements, the Throckmorton children stand outside the usual course of nature and, like other early modern prodigies such as monstrous births or portents in the heavens, suggest some kind of divine or—in this case—diabolical meddling in the world.[2]

But the Throckmorton children also represent a convergence of assumptions about speech, possession, and the body, that compels those who hear them to explore and ultimately believe their extraordinary claims. These assumptions, which we find present at almost every turn in the case, create a rhetorical situation in which the children are believable precisely to the degree that their speech is understood to be involuntary, more of a physical symptom than a symbolic act. Witchcraft makes the bodies of the Throckmorton children vibrate with the wrong sounds, and when those sounds issue into the public space of an investigation, they acquire a rhetorical power every bit as gripping as the children's physical distress.

As in France and Germany, the culture of witch lore in England encouraged investigations into maleficium, just as it provided tests that confirmed or disproved accusations of diabolical activity.[3] The published account of Warboys represents a significant development in the English tradition, because this text's self-avowedly "experimental" dissection of the causes of the children's fits provides later generations with a yardstick for future performances. Indeed, to the degree that this and other cases of possession are marked by a number of characteristic signs—heaving of the body, trance-like states of inattention, shrieking, speaking in inappropriate voices, foretelling future events, convulsions on hearing scripture—the entire venture of publicizing, authenticating, and debunking cases of diabolism seems ultimately to have standardized the marks of possession, making them portable from one context to the next.

Later demoniacs were situated within a tradition that treated the child as a receptacle for diabolical activity, and the Throckmorton case appears to have provided a powerful image of the fit-plagued child who has become a hollow vessel for some occupying force. The famous counterfeiter William Somers, for example, was given a copy of the Warboys pamphlet when he began to manifest symptoms similar to those of the Throckmorton children in the late 1590s. Somers, whose possession and subsequent exorcism was itself the subject of a celebrated pamphlet that Shakespeare consulted for *The History of King Lear,* first began to show signs of possession when he was fourteen years old—at the upper threshold of childhood by early modern standards.[4] Whereas Somers's most convincing performances took place in his late teens, his sense of the "role" was clearly patterned on the performances of other child demoniacs. Under the supervision of the Puritan exorcist John Darrel, Somers was reputedly taken to observe the thirteen-year-old Thomas Darling of Burton-on-Trent, whose fits provided a blueprint for Somers's subsequent performances.[5]

Darling's performance recalled the symptoms witnessed at Warboys, creating the appearance of a total loss of physical control that, by a strange logic of negation, subordinated the will of the young victim to the autonomous, wayward powers of his body. Even his speech had a repetitive, mechanical quality as he was heard to chant "heaven openeth, heaven openeth" and "Wild horses ... Wild horses." In his *A Guide to Grand-Jury Men* (1627), Richard Bernard notes all of these signs:

> He had strange fits, and seemed therein deaf and dumb: he could writhe
> his mouth aside, roll his eyes, as nothing but the white would appear,

and his head shake as one distracted. He usually would cast up his meat, vomit pins, rags, straw, wrest and turn his head backward, grate with his teeth, gape hideously with his mouth, cling and draw on his belly and guts; groan and mourn pitiously; tell of the apparition of a spirit after his fits, seeming like a black bird.[6]

This impressive list of symptoms is clearly conventional by the early seventeenth century, leading jurists like Bernard to note that "there is nothing almost in things of this nature so really true, but some can so lively resemble the same" (30). The hint of skepticism in Bernard's remark betrays a growing sense that child demoniacs are virtuoso performers instead of diabolical victims, something James I (himself once an ardent witch hunter) begins to suspect after encountering several bewitched children whom he personally certifies as fakes.[7] The Throckmorton case, however, never seems to elicit the doubts that overshadow later instances of child bewitching and possession, in part because the children's prophetic powers (their knowledge, for example, of what Mother Samuels is doing at all times) cannot be explained.

In all of these cases, the possessed child's performance—inspiring awe in some, skepticism in others—gains rhetorical force when it crosses the body and the voice, making one the vehicle or representative of the other. About two months after the first outburst, three of the Throckmorton children are gathered in the parlor by their uncle, Gilbert Pickering, who is conducting "experiments" designed to pinpoint the cause of the fits. As soon as Mother Samuels and her friend Cicily Burder are led into the room, all three girls fall to the floor in violent convulsions, "strangely tormented." The writer of the pamphlet, perhaps Pickering himself, describes a pattern in which a disturbance beginning in the body culminates in an enigmatic declaration. If they were allowed to continue in their fits, readers are told, the children:

> would have leaped and sprung like a quick pickerel newly taken out of the water, their bellies heaving up, their head and their heels still touching the ground as though they had been tumblers; and would have drawn their heads and their heels backwards, throwing out their arms with great groans most strangely to be heard, to the great grief of the beholders (246).

Like animals (another common victim of witchcraft), the children become "simple," nondeliberating creatures, uttering shrieks and groans as family members struggle to restrain them.[8] Without any specific content, these first utterances appear to be a physical response to some violent, phatic contact with another signifying realm. Here the present fact of the body—its susceptibility to pain and uncontrollable passions—becomes its own truth, an index of an overriding supernatural agency, that is organizing the scene. That agency will literally dictate how the children's troubles are interpreted by those around them.

What initially began as a series of shrieks now begins to take shape in words. Jane, who has been spirited away into a neighboring parlor by Pickering, is soon discovered frantically scratching at her bedcover, repeating the phrase: "Oh, that I had her! Oh, that I had her!" (247). The words are an occasion of "great admiration" for Pickering, as they "disclose some secret whereby the witches might be by some means or token made manifest and known." Acting on this clue, he leaves the parlor to retrieve Mother Samuels who has been waiting in the adjoining room, no doubt alarmed at what is happening. Placing his own hand in the child's, Pickering waits to see if she will continue her scratching, but Jane does nothing to his hand, just as she does nothing to that of a second test subject, a Mistress Andley. Finally, Mother Samuels's hand is forced into Jane's, resulting in a fierce scratching and "extraordinary passion," which halts only when another hand is interposed between the child's and the older woman's. Moving into an adjoining parlor, Pickering encounters a second Throckmorton child who makes an identical declaration. She, too, will not be satisfied until she is allowed to scratch at the hand of one of Mother Samuels's accomplices, Cicily Burder.

Scratching begins to serve as an alternate "language" or cipher in the Throckmorton case, allowing an enigmatic declaration of desire ("Oh that I had her") to be glossed by a more concrete form of action. Pickering is initially skeptical of this well-known test, whereby the victim's suffering is relieved when he or she scratches the witch; in his deposition at the Huntingdon Assizes, he says that it was employed "only to taste by this experiment whereto the child's words would tend" (247). It is clear even from Pickering's reluctant affirmation that the words of these children mark out a semantic trajectory whose origin and destination are unclear. Thus the value of the test. But if such kinetic metaphors for intention (the uncertain "drift" of speech) are common in this period, they are particularly significant when applied to a child, as they engage fundamental doubts about children's ability to originate and govern their own actions.[9] In the legal system, these doubts surface as anxieties about the veracity of child testimony. According to the seventeenth-century jurist Matthew Hale, children are not allowed to give testimony in court until they reach the age of fourteen (the age of discretion), because it is only then that they are thought to understand the meaning of an oath.[10] Early modern children are also associated with mimicry, frequently receiving the vaguely insulting tag of "ape" or "parrot." Many of the children's theater companies in London capitalize on this association, presenting performances by young "scholars" who exemplify the child's native powers of mimicry in elaborate rhetorical declarations.[11]

Returning to the child's pronouncement in the Throckmorton case, it is not clear where this declaration comes from and how it ought to be interpreted. "Oh, that I had her!" Does this declaration signify a desire directed at some object? Is it an index of some physical ailment, obtaining the same evidentiary status as, say, the urine samples that were sent to Cambridge in order to identify the natural cause of the children's distemper? Is it an involuntary ejaculation, like the sneezes that preface the beginning of the fits, as much a physical event as a deliberate communicative act? Or is it a mystical instruction, a spiritual form of *prosopopoeia* that makes an insensible "object" of the child, only to make her "admirably" speak? In developing these questions, I want to suggest that there is something demonstrably physical about the language that is spoken in the Throckmorton case, and that this physicality both enhances the children's rhetorical effect on spectators and shifts the possible interpretive frames in which their language is understood. By suggesting some limitation on the speaker's deliberate intent, this physical rhetoric provides a means of signifying and so authenticating the fact that the speaker is now subject to another force—another voice—that she does not strictly own. This voice does not come from the realm of nature, even if it emerges from a body whose ailments might be diagnosed in medical terms.

The sense that the children are temporary vessels or conduits is reinforced by the sudden manner in which they repossess their bodies (and resume their customary manners) once the trouble is gone. After several extraordinary episodes of heaving, convulsing, and weeping, spectators are shocked to see the Throckmorton children suddenly stand up, wipe their eyes, and resume their daily activities as if nothing had happened. Although the children often claim to be repeating what "the thing" has told them, the vehemence of their declarations can at times seem preternatural, far exceeding the capacities of the body that produces it. In one instance late in the proceedings, the youngest daughter Mary is told by "the thing" that she must scratch the young witch, Agnes Samuels, who has now become a suspect along with her mother and father. Agnes is brought to Mary, who begins hurling insults and clawing at the young woman's face, scraping off a shilling's breadth of skin. When the episode is over, Mary is brought downstairs into one of the parlors by the maid, where she is suddenly overcome by a "wondrous" sorrow. She did not want to attack the young woman, Mary says, but the thing commanded her to do it, stretching out her fingers "whether I would or not" (286). The witness at this point, a local minister named Doctor Dorington, states later that anyone who knew Mary would say that she had been "overruled in this action; for she was carried with such vehemency and cruelty for the time against the maid [i.e., Agnes] as that it appeared to be altogether besides her nature" (286). This same scene is repeated almost exactly by Mary's sister, Elizabeth, who scratches Agnes's hand fiercely when given the opportunity and, sobbing, declares the young woman to be a witch. Soon afterward, Elizabeth stops crying and begins to exhort Agnes, "lifting up her voice with such vehemency and desire for her amendment as that we may verily think the like was never heard to come forth of a child's mouth" (287).

In each of these instances, spoken words are not so much a deliberate communication between speaker and her audience as they are a compass needle, pointing automatically toward the guilty party. This kind of verbal "pointing"—detached from the deliberate will of the one who is speaking—works in the reverse direction as well, as is apparent in the final witch test employed by the presiding Assize justice, Edward Fenner, in April 1593. Bringing the members of the Samuels family into the presence of the troubled children, Fenner charges them to utter what we might now call a diabolical performative, which for legal purposes serves as a "confession." In their trial at Huntingdon, the Samuels are charged with complicity in the death of Lady Crumwell, who had became ill and died soon after a confrontation with Mother Samuels at the Throckmortons' home. Arraigned on this charge, the aged John Samuels is brought into the presence of Jane, who is at that moment fully in the throes of a fit, and is commanded in court to utter the following sentence: "As I am a witch and did consent to the death of the Lady Crumwell, so I charge the devil to suffer Mistress Jane to come out of her fit at this present" (291).[12] No sooner are the words spoken than Jane stands up and wipes her eyes, recognizing her father who has been standing there (unnoticed) all along and asking his blessing. This same formula—apparently suggested by the children themselves—is also employed out of court with Agnes Samuels in the presence of the oldest Throckmorton daughter, Joan, with similar wondrous effects.

Faced with this outcome, the courts choose to condemn John, Alice, and Agnes Samuels for their role in Lady Crumwell's death and their practice of witchcraft. All three are hanged in 1593. Although the evidence obtained through these final performative "confessions" seems hopelessly arbitrary, there can be little doubt that it harmonizes with the broader principles of interpretation that govern the Throckmorton case. Faced with child victims of an uncertain deliberative status, doctors, magistrates, and family members credit evidence that—like the bodily actions of these children—seems free-standing, detached from the will, and so perhaps beyond interpretation. This is not to say that those who deal with the children simply ignore canons of probability and testimony (although they do this as well), but, rather, that the specific statements of both witch and bewitched have to be sealed with some kind of embodied event or confirmation. What becomes "other" for those who encounter the Throckmorton children, to use the vocabulary of Michel de Certeau, is not simply the diabolical genius that seems to be animating them, but the capacity of the body to act on its own—to tear the reins from the rider of consciousness and, in doing so, disclose some hidden truth.

When they try to understand the Throckmorton children's mysterious fits, family members, preachers, and doctors are struggling not just with witches and devils but also with problems of demonstration and knowledge. The autonomous power of the body in this case, aligned as it is with the cognitive simplicity of the child, becomes a paradigm for an ideal situation in which the truth (of diabolism, of witchcraft, of the causes of things) "speaks for itself." Although the case illustrates a lethal collision between childish improvisation and community strife, it also should be viewed in the context of a growing intellectual and cultural interest in forms of demonstration that persuade by necessity rather than by deliberate rhetorical appeal.[13] One model for this form of demonstration is clearly the experiment, which in the 1620s will emerge as a fully formed intellectual program, but which in the 1590s remains an appeal to experience rather than textual authority or logical deduction. When the word "experiment" is used in this and other cases involving bewitched children, for example that of Mary Glover (1602) or the Fairfax children of York (1621), it does seem to indicate precisely the sort of deliberately "contrived" experience that early modern natural philosophers such as Francis Bacon thought would lead to reliable knowledge.[14] Another model might be self-persuading or in-artificial proofs from rhetoric, which comprise evidence given under torture, confessions, written contracts, oaths, and, suggestively for this case, conversations overheard by children. Appeals using evidence of this sort involve no art, according to the ancient authorities, which is why they are so effective inside and outside the courtroom.[15] Such forms of demonstration exemplify a poetics of simplicity or "indifference" in the acquisition of knowledge, one that will become more powerful in England as natural philosophers embrace the ideal of direct, unmediated observation or witnessing of nature under experimental trial.[16]

Those gathered in the parlors, gardens and inns in Huntingdonshire may not be certain what kind of truth they are looking for, but they are willing to trust the evidence of their senses. One can see the bodies of these young children tormented, hear the voices that those bodies produce, and leave convinced—how else could such things come about?—that witchcraft is the cause. Such convictions are strengthened by legal proceedings that take the tortured body of the child and, in a grim command performance, make it speak the finality of the witch's guilt. The irony of the situation is that the very signs that seem to testify to the artlessness of the child "victims" in the Throckmorton case are those most easily simulated by subsequent imposters.[17] As possessed children turn up in Burton, Nottingham, and Leicester over the next two decades, spectators become less likely to credit the authenticity of convulsions, weeping, heaves, and "hollow voices." In the hands of a skeptic such as Samuel Harsnett, these "outward signs" of diabolical activity become the clever simulations of child performers, creatures who are acting on their own or others' devices. The fits of the Throckmorton children thus serve as a pattern or digest for future deception, one that allows skeptical investigators to read through hysterical trials of the body, back to some originating plan or pretense. Many more witches will be identified and killed, however, before this kind of skepticism becomes widespread. English witch hunters and demonologists learn too late that the body is never artless, nor does it ever really speak for itself.

Notes

This chapter first appeared in *Textus,* Special Issue: Discourses on/of the Body, eds. Vita Fortunati, Stephen Greenblatt and Mirella Bill 13 (2000), 263–276. The author wishes to thank Barbara Johnstone and Holger Schott Syme for valuable comments.

1. The main record we have of the Warboys case is a narrative account that begins at the first onset of the fits and continuing over the course of several years to conclude with the trial at the Huntingdon Assizes in 1593. The book, which some suspect was written by the children's uncle Gilbert Pickering, is entitled *The most strange and admirable discoverie of the three Witches of Warboys, arraigned, convicted, and executed at the last assises at Huntington, for the bewitching of the five daughters of Robert Throckmorton Esquire, and divers other persons, with sundrie divellish and grievous torments: And also for the bewitching to death of the Lady Crumwell, the like hath not been heard of in this age.* (London: 1593), reprinted in Barbara Rosen, *Witchcraft in England, 1558–1618* (Amherst: University of Massachusetts Press, 1991), 239–97. Parenthetical references in the text are to Rosen's modernized edition.

2. At least two physicians at Cambridge testified to the lack of a natural cause for Jane's fits after examining her urine and finding that a prescription for worms had no effect. The fallback explanation was witchcraft. On the association of prodigies with intrusions of the supernatural, see Lorraine Daston and Katharine Park, *Wonders and the Order of Nature: 1150–1750* (New York: Zone Books, 1998) and their "Unnatural Conceptions: The

Study of Monsters in Sixteenth- and Seventeenth-Century France and England," *Past and Present* 92 (1981), 20–54. On the split between natural (medical, psychological) explanations of witchcraft and supernatural ones in the famous case of possession in Loudun, France, see Michel de Certeau, *The Possession at Loudun,* trans. Michael B. Smith (Chicago: University of Chicago Press, 2000), Chs. 8 and 9. Stephen Greenblatt analyzes a similar tension emerging in English witchcraft theory, in which skeptical writers such as Reginald Scot oppose the possibility of real diabolical action with other explanations (like melancholia or theatrical illusion), in his "Shakespeare Bewitched" in *New Historical Literary Studies: Essays on Reproducing Texts, Representing History,* ed. Jeffrey N. Cox and Larry Reynolds (Princeton, NJ: Princeton University Press, 1993), 108–135, esp. 115–119.

3. Alan Macfarlane provides an analysis of the various gradations of proof and presumption in witchcraft, noting European precedents, in *Witchcraft in Tudor and Stuart England* (London: Routledge & Kegan Paul, 1970), 18–20.

4. Schemes for classifying the "ages of man" during this period are notoriously fluid, but most tend to place the end of childhood (and onset of adolescence) at either fourteen or twenty-one. See Philip Ariés, *Centuries of Childhood: A Social History of Family Life,* trans. Robert Baldick (New York: Vintage, 1962), 18–30. Early modern references to children in English texts (i.e., "boy" and "girl") apply mostly to individuals in their early teens, although such terms are regularly applied to servants who are much older.

5. Darling, too, had been influenced by swirling lore about the devil's hold on children: the boy began to suspect that he had been bewitched only after overhearing several neighbors discussing the possibility. (See ed. Rosen, 243.) On Darling's knowledge of the Warboys case, see Ronald Seth, *Children Against Witches* (London: Robert Hale, 1969), 142.

6. Richard Bernard, *A guide to grand-jury men* (London, 1627), 32. I have modernized the spelling. On Darling's exclamations during his fits, see [Jesse Bee] *The most wonderfull and true storie, of a certaine Witch named Alse Gooderige of Stapen hill ... As also a true report of the strange torments of Thomas Darling ...* (Printed at London for I.O.: 1597), 29–30.

7. James was eventually quite bold about declaring the spurious nature of possession. In 1616, a thirteen-year-old boy from Lancashire named Smythe or Smith accused six women of causing his convulsive fits. Here there is evidence that someone around the boy had read the Throckmorton case, as the witches were made to repeat the phrases that were used to identify the Samuels as witches (see later). Apparently, James happened through Leicester on a progress when the trial was taking place, examined the boy, and sent him to Lambeth for further examination. Both James and George Abbot, Bishop of Canturbury, declared the boy an imposter, but only after he had had nine women hanged. Six more awaiting their verdict were released from prison. See D. P. Walker, *Unclean Spirits: Possession and Exorcism in France and England in the Late Sixteenth and Early Seventeenth Centuries* (Philadelphia: University of Pennsylvania Press, 1981, 82) and

ed. Rosen, 332. Two other children were found counterfeiting in cases of diabolism during James's reign: Grace Sowerbutts (14), a witness in the Lancashire witch trials of 1612 and William Perry (12), the possessed Boy of Bilston, who was active in 1620. James's son also detected a counterfeiting witness, Edmund Robinson (11) of Lancashire, who had styled his 1634 testimony on events of the 1612 trial.

8. Harsnett makes this analogy between the possessed and animals clear in his *A discovery of the fraudulent practises of John Darrel bacheler of artes* (London, 1599), 62, in which he suggests that the possessed individual is lashed to an exorcism chair like a "Beare to the stake."

9. There is a long tradition of thinking of children as "simple" or nondeliberating, reaching back to Aristotle's comparison of children and animals in the eighth book of the *History of Animals*. The proverbial simplicity of children is criticized by Richard Hooker who objects to the widely held opinion that "childish simplicitie [is] the mother of ghostly, and diuine wisdome." (Richard Hooker, *Of the lawes of ecclesiastical politie*, 3rd ed. [London, 1611], Bk. 3, p. 98). On the development of this theme through the Middle Ages into the sixteenth century, see Leah Marcus, *Childhood and Cultural Despair: A Theme and Variations in Seventeenth Century Literature* (Pittsburgh: University of Pittsburgh Press, 1978), 10–25.

10. Matthew Hale, *Historia placitorum coronae: The History of the Pleas of the Crown*, vol. 2 (London: E. and R. Nutt, and R. Gosling, 1736), 278–279.

11. Several of the children's theater companies around the turn of the seventeenth century were attached to grammar schools. Their actors or "schollars" were prized for their ability to reel off difficult passages in the prevailing rhetorical style. See Michael Shapiro, *Children of the Revels: The Boy Companies of Shakespeare's Time and Their Plays* (New York: Columbia University Press, 1977). One fourteen-year-old witness in the Lancashire witch trials of 1612 is repeatedly referred to as a young "scholler." See Thomas Potts, *The Wonderfull Discoverie of Witches in the Countie of Lancaster* (London, 1613), M2v–M3v. Harsnett uses the term repeatedly, and with the same connotation, in his *A Declaration of egregious popish impostures* (London, 1603), 38.

12. Significantly, this transaction takes place in open court rather than in a private interview with the Assize Judge (the more likely venue for such a sensitive inquiry). Jane is "set in the Court before the Judge" and "Old Samuel" is "brought from amongst the other prisoners to the upper barre, near unto the place where the Clerkes sate: where also stoode the said Jane." These details do not appear in Rosen's edited version of the pamphlet. See *The most strange and admirable discoverie*, N3v–0r. The author of the pamphlet claims, at one point, that Jane's fits were witnessed by "five hundred men."

13. I have written about the appeal of "accidental events" in this larger epistemological context in *Culture of Accidents: Unexpected Knowledges in Early Modern England* (Stanford: Stanford University Press, 2001).

14. To the extent that cases of witchcraft and possession were treated in a juridical context, it is not surprising to see something like the epistemology of experiment emerging here. On the linkages between early modern law

and the Baconian notion of "experiment," see Julian Martin, *Francis Bacon, the State, and the Reform of Natural Philosophy* (Cambridge: Cambridge University Press, 1992). On the origins of English notions of experiment in a theory of "contrived" or exceptional experiences, see Peter Dear, "Miracles, Experiments, and the Ordinary Course of Nature," *ISIS* 81 (1990): 663–683. The Yorkshire poet Edward Fairfax, who daily chronicled the bewitching of his own children a manuscript written in 1621, sounds like one of the Baconian investigators in Solomon's House when he discusses the value of observing witchcraft in the "extremities" of his children's behavior. The document (BL Add. MS. 32496) is transcribed as *A Discourse of Witchcraft. As it was acted in the Family of Mr. Edward Fairfax of Fuystone in the County of York in the year 1621*, vol. 5, *Miscellanies of the Philobiblon Society* (London: Charles Whittingham, 1858–59). See p. 6 ibid. and Edward Fairfax, *Daemonologia: A Discourse on Witchcraft as it was acted in the family of Mr. Edward Fairfax, of Fuyston, in the country of York, in the year 1621.*, ed. W. Grainge (Harrogate: R. Ackrill, 1882), 34. Reference to "experiment" in the case of Mary Glover can be found in Stephan Bradwell, "Mary Glovers late woefull case, together with her joyfull deliverance," British Library, MSS. Sloane 831 (1603), 27v.

15. Cicero, in his *Topics,* gives a variety of examples of particularly credible evidence that is given of "necessity" or inadvertently, for example, when children give important information without knowing its pertinence, when one makes incriminating statements while someone else is listening through a wall, or when one talks while drunk or in one's sleep. See Cicero, *De Inventione, De optimo genere oratorum, Topica,* trans. H. M. Hubbell (Cambridge, MA: Harvard University Press, 1976), §74–75. On inartificial or nontechnical modes of persuasion, see Aristotle, *The Rhetoric and Poetics of Aristotle,* trans. W. Rhys Roberts and Ingram Bywater (New York: McGraw-Hill, 1984), 24. On inartificial proofs in the context of Renaissance dialectic, see R. W. Serjeantson, "Testimony and Proof in Early-Modern England," *Studies in History and Philosophy of Science* 30, no. 2 (1999): 195–236, esp. 203.

16. On the foundational importance of acts of witnessing in the work of the Royal Society, see Steven Shapin and Simon Schaffer, *Leviathan and the Air-Pump: Hobbes, Boyle, and the Experimental Life* (Princeton, NJ: Princeton University Press, 1989).

17. This is in keeping with the larger trend in the skeptical literature on exorcism produced by Samuel Harsnett and others, which—as Stephen Greenblatt has shown—work within prevailing assumptions about the theater to show that "what seems spontaneous is rehearsed; what seems involuntary, carefully crafted; what seems unpredictable, scripted." See his "Loudun and London," *Critical Inquiry* 12, no. 2 (1986): 338.

4

Adopted Children and Constructions of Heredity, Nurture, and Parenthood in Shakespeare's Romances

MARIANNE NOVY

Near the end of his career, Shakespeare wrote three plays that conclude with the reunion of parents with children separated from them when very young. These three plays, often called romances, are full of comments about the contrast between the transplanted child and her or his surroundings and the similarity revealed when she or he meets hereditary family. In two of these plays, girls are born and grow to sixteen or so; the third includes two youths of twenty-two and twenty-three, always referred to as boys, their younger sister, and her husband, whose orphaned childhood is a key factor in his characterization. In these characters' relationships with their parents and foster-parents, their relative youth is salient, and their childhood experiences are frequently mentioned throughout the play.

Literary children raised in families different from those into which they are born are always likely to raise questions of where they belong and which set of parents they resemble most. How important is nurture in determining behavior, and how important is nature, and how much of nature is heredity? To which sets of parents are the children more closely bound? In recent years, some discussion of these issues has gone beyond dichotomous answers; do the romances anticipate such complexity at all? How do these plays define parenthood and family?

In many of Shakespeare's plays, parents and children are heart-breakingly alienated from one another, in spite of a common heredity. As Miranda points out in the romance that directly follows these, *The Tempest,* "Good wombs have borne bad sons."[1] However, the plays I consider here present a mythology of blood as identity and love. In the happy endings of both *Winter's Tale* and *Pericles,* a long-separated daughter miraculously recreates her apparently dead mother before her father's eyes. In *Cymbeline,* a sister and the brothers kidnapped twenty years earlier are mysteriously drawn to each other when they meet.

The mythology of blood in these plots has sometimes been taken for granted. Nevertheless, it is not the only element in their family dynamics. All of them present nurturing by foster-parents, and it could even be argued that all of them also present family as a construction. The plots always define the birth-parents as the real parents, and some foster-parents in two of the plays are murderous, but the plays all present alternative images of foster-parents as actively benevolent.[2]

A belief in "blood" was part of the Renaissance worldview, even though there were conflicting views about how heredity worked. The writings of Aristotle, Hippocrates, and Galen, with their differing views of "seeds" and "blood," were still influential.[3] But early modern people also knew that, on the one hand, children were often very different from their parents, and, on the other hand, good or bad nurture had a significant impact on how children developed.[4] Nurture was often discussed with regard to both teachers and wet-nurses (who were thought to transmit moral qualities very literally with their milk), and the concept is clearly relevant to the foster-parents of these plays.[5] There was no formal legal procedure for adoption in this period; the terms *foster* and *adoptive* could be used interchangeably. The family of early modern England was fluid. There was a high parental death rate and frequent remarriage, and many children experienced substitute parents not only during wet-nursing but later in service, apprentice-ship, and other kinds of child exchange.[6] Later, this chapter will turn to the implications of this demography in relation to the plays, but first let us consider the plays themselves.

The relative benevolence of the foster-parents in comparison to the biological parents increases from the earliest of these plays to the latest. *Pericles,* written first, clearly poses evil foster-parents against good biological parents. Thinking his wife Thaisa is dead, Pericles gives the newborn Marina to his friends Cleon and Dionyza to raise— emphasizing that they should give her education according to her noble rank; because she outshines their daughter in weaving, sewing, and singing, Dionyza plots Marina's murder, and only the chance kidnapping by pirates saves her—to be sold to a brothel. She is skillful enough to escape the brothel by her talents at sewing, singing, and persuasion to chastity, and at the end of the play is reunited first with her father and finally with her mother, who turns out to be still alive in a temple of Diana.

Cleon and Dionyza exemplify evil foster-parents—although the term "parent" or "foster-parent" is never used to refer to the relation they have to Marina. The key word is "nurse." Pericles plans to leave his daughter "at careful nursing" (3.1.80). When Dionyza thinks about how she will tell Pericles that his daughter is (as she thinks) dead, she says, "Nurses are not the fates;/ To foster is not ever to pre- serve" (4.3.14–15). This usage both connects the couple to the common practice of wet-nursing, and points up their opposition to Marina's good foster-parent—her nurse Lychorida.[7] The murder plot occurs after Lychorida's death; Dionyza tries to gain Marina's confidence by saying, "Have you a nurse of me" (4.1.25).

Lychorida is a shadowy figure who appears only in the scene in which Marina is an infant, but she is credited with passing on to Marina the story of her birth, and an admirable image of her father's courage and patience.

> My father, as Nurse says, did never fear,
> But cried, "Good seamen!" to the sailors,
> Galling his kingly hands, hailing ropes;
> And clasping to the mast, endured a sea
> That almost broke the deck (4.1.55–59).

The nurse's repetition of memories about Marina's parents and ancestry is a significant contrast to earlier versions of the Pericles story.

In the ninth-century *Apollonius of Tyre,* it is only when the nurse is dying that she tells Marina's prototype her ancestry: the girl exclaims, "If any such thing had happened to me before you revealed this to me, I should have been absolutely ignorant of my ancestry and birth."[8] Similarly, in Twine's *The Patterne of Painefull Adventures* (1594), which Shakespeare used, and in George Wilkins's *The Painful Adventures of Pericles, Prince of Tyre* (1608), a novelized version of Shakespeare's play, written by his most likely coauthor, the girl thinks of the murderous surrogates as her parents until the nurse, at the point of death, enlightens her.[9] This alteration by Shakespeare gives more emphasis to the nurse as a purposeful bearer of family memory.

Heredity is dominant over environment in *Pericles,* but environment is not as weak an influence as generalizations sometimes assume. Not only is the nurse's image of Marina's parents important, but also nurture and nature must combine to produce Marina's superlative musical skills: Pericles was a musician, and Cleon teaches her.[10] We might read the supremacy of nature over nurture in the way Marina's goodness escapes the bad influence of Cleon and Dionyza, as well as in the way she shows the courage and patience that the nurse has told her her father exemplified, but we also could credit Lychorida's influence. None of these points is explicitly made—the spectators can analyze Marina's virtues and talents however they wish.

In *Cymbeline,* the distribution of good and evil between biological and surrogate parents is somewhat more ambiguous than in *Pericles.* Is Cymbeline, Imogen's father, good or bad as a parent? He has brought up the orphaned and admirable Posthumus in his household, but on Posthumus's marriage to Imogen, and his own to his new wife, Cymbeline banishes him, and rages at his daughter. Is Belarius, who has been raising Cymbeline's sons (Imogen's brothers) as his own in the pastoral setting of Wales, good or bad as a foster-parent? Belarius criticizes the insincerity of the court world, and gives the boys training in religion and morality. He is a kidnapper, but, on the other hand, his kidnapping is in retribution for Cymbeline's injustice to him. In general, he seems morally superior to Cymbeline. When he says that the boys "take" him for "natural father" (3.3.107), there is also a pun on the way he is raising them with the virtuous discipline of living in nature.

Posthumus, Guiderius, and Arviragus are all presented as virtuous by both heredity and nurture. Characters are more emphatic about the power of heredity here than in *Pericles*. Belarius believes that his boys' true identity appears in their ambition and desire to fight. "How hard it is to hide the sparks of nature! … their thoughts do hit / The roofs of palaces, and nature prompts them / In simple and low things to prince it much / Beyond the trick of others" (3.3.79, 83–86). As Susan Baker has noted, however, the fact that Belarius himself knows they are princes can be seen as influencing his upbringing of them, and so one can argue that it is he who so prompts them, not nature—but Baker is countering scores of critics who emphasize "blood" with this reading.[11]

Good heredity in this play is much more associated with the male side than with the female. There are strong suggestions that women's hereditary influence is either lacking or bad. These suggestions are developed further—and perhaps finally exorcized—in Posthumus's odyssey away from and back to belief in his ancestry. When Posthumus loses faith in Imogen, he loses faith in his mother and in his connection to "that most venerable man, which I / did call my father" (2.5.3–4). He proclaims himself a bastard, and rails against what he calls, "the woman's part in me." However, when he repents of his plot against his wife, he regains faith in his parents. After his heroic performance in battle, his deceased family appears to him in a dream vision praying to Jupiter on his behalf. His mother finally appears, and speaks about his painful birth. His father, confirming the restoration of Posthumus's heredity, says, "Great nature, like his ancestry, / Molded the stuff so fair, / That he deserv'd the praise o'th'world, / As great Sicilius' heir" (5.4.48–51). As Meredith Skura has pointed out, "Posthumus cannot find his parents in the flesh; he must find the idea of his parents … he must make what he can of the past, recreate his family in his dreams."[12]

Other characters in the play do find their family in the flesh, but through a confused and gradual process. When Imogen, in masculine disguise, meets her kidnapped, unknown brothers, all three at once feel a strong, although unclear, connection, as does her father, in meeting the disguised Imogen later.

In the final recognition scene, after Imogen's identity has been clarified, Belarius eventually confesses his kidnapping. When he says to

Cymbeline, "First pay me for the nursing of thy sons" (5.5.326), he alludes to the practice, discussed in John Boswell's chapter on Roman law in *The Kindness of Strangers*, of requiring the father of an exposed child to pay the expenses of the parents who had raised the child before returning him to the original family.[13] Ultimately Belarius's wrong in kidnapping the children is easily forgiven; Cymbeline says to him, "Thou art my brother"(403), and Imogen echoes, "you are my father too" (404). Blood relations are important in this play, but, as in *Pericles*, the blood tie does not lead to clear recognition without additional evidence, and good adoptive relations are not erased.

The Winter's Tale is ambivalent about the adoptive father, referred to only as Shepherd, in a different way than *Cymbeline* is, and it is even more ambivalent about the birth-father, Leontes. Unlike any other father in the romances, Leontes threatens his infant child with death and commands her to be abandoned, because of his suspicion about her parentage. When the Shepherd finds the baby, he seems a highly preferable father. Unlike his counterpart in the source, Greene's *Pandosto*, the shepherd at once decides to take up little Perdita, even before he knows that gold has been left with her. His compassion for her is refreshing in comparison to Leontes's condemnation: "They were warmer that got this than the poor thing is here" (3.3.73–74). For a while, he is—unusually for a father in Shakespeare—so unconflicted about his daughter's choice of husband he doesn't even pretend to create obstacles, although a skeptical reader might think this is because he guesses that the shepherd Doricles is really Prince Florizel in disguise.[14] His pastoral world seems, emotionally, a better environment for child-rearing than the cold and suspicious world of the court, and this helps to present his nurturing of Perdita, even more clearly than Belarius's raising the boys, as an act of nature as well as of adoption.

The shepherd's evocation of his dead wife, Perdita's adoptive mother, as a hostess, shows a remarkable appreciation of her energy and sociability. Nevertheless, Perdita does not follow him in citing this adoptive mother as a precedent at the sheep-shearing feast; she simply says, "It is my father's will I should take on me / The hostess-ship o' the day"(4.4.71–72).

Thus, imaginatively the play makes still tenuous the role of the shepherd's wife in nurturing Perdita; Hermione's place is to be left unfilled until the very end. And the shepherd's benevolence to Perdita disappears when he sees that Polixenes, Florizel's father, and the old friend whom Leontes mistakenly accused of adultery with his wife, is angry about the apparently cross-class betrothal. He shows Polixenes the birth tokens he found with Perdita, and this fear-motivated virtual disowning helps bring about the happy ending, as the shepherd, his son, Polixenes, and, in a different boat, Florizel and Perdita, all meet at Leontes's court, and Leontes and Perdita are reunited.

Critics have seldom noted that in the report of the recognition, Leontes "thanks the old shepherd, which stands by like a weather-bitten conduit of many kings' reigns" (5.2.55–57), and that, after this depersonalizing image, there is, nevertheless, a brief dialogue between the shepherd and his son after this scene, suggesting utopian possibilities of an extended cross-class family of biological and adoptive parents: the son says, "the King's son took me by the hand and called me brother; and then the two kings called my father brother; and then the Prince my brother and the Princess my sister called my father father; and so we wept" (5.2.141–45). But clearly Perdita has been restored to Leontes as *his* daughter, and in the next scene, as he discovers that his wife is still alive, the shepherds are not mentioned as present and are given no lines. In a similar situation, Belarius could be acknowledged, but here, whether because of class bias, desire for dramatic concentration after *Cymbeline*'s diffuseness, or both, the final emphasis is on the family of birth and the aristocrats bound with them in friendship and marriage.

Descriptions of Perdita by observers often hint at the influence of heredity by suggesting that she is superior to her surroundings: Florizel's father, himself a king in disguise, says, "Nothing she does or seems / But smacks of something greater than herself, / Too noble for this place" (4.4.157–159). Although in other plays of Shakespeare aristocratic heredity does not inevitably produce intelligence or moral nobility, the standard reading of this scene stresses the influence of Perdita's heredity over her environment. Nevertheless, the shepherd knows about her aristocratic birth, because of the clothes and gold left with her, and though he has not told her, he might be imagined as having influenced her by having higher expectations of her.[15]

Many speeches in *Winter's Tale* explicitly emphasize heredity in commenting on physical resemblance—and although the issue of marital fidelity is in *Pandosto,* this emphasis on resemblance is not.[16] After Leontes is first reunited with Perdita, but before he knows that Perdita is his daughter, he says that he thought of Hermione, "Even in these looks I made [admiring Perdita]" (5.1.228). Observers of the father-daughter reunion stress "the majesty of the creature, in resemblance of the mother" (5.2.36–37). In several earlier comments, Leontes makes father-child physical resemblance the test of a mother's fidelity to her husband. At the beginning, he is worried about whether his son looks enough like him to prove Hermione's faithfulness ("They say we are / Almost as like as eggs. Women say so, / That will say anything" 1.2.129–131). He greets Florizel for the first time by saying, "Your mother was most true to wedlock, Prince, / For she did print your royal father off, / Conceiving you" (5.1.124–126).

A textual emphasis on physical similarity, such as is found in *Winter's Tale* and *Pericles,* has a complicated effect in the theater. Anne Barton remarked of Shakespeare's *Twelfth Night* that it would be an extremely rare theater company that would have two actors as similar as Viola and Sebastian are supposed to be. So too, in many cases of family resemblance in these plays, the play's language is in tension with the stage picture in which the actors are not really identical, and given this problem, it is interesting that Shakespeare sometimes added such emphasis to his sources.[17] Perhaps the issue is analogous to the issue of how the Elizabethan audience saw boy actors as female characters: most of the time most of them focused on the female character, but for some of them most of the time and most of them some of the time (cued by textual self-consciousness) awareness of the actor's sex might surface occasionally. The plays are providing much material today for reflections on gender as a construction; they may provide material for reflections on the construction of family relationships as well.[18] The audience, guided by the dialogue and the plot, will want Marina to look like Thaisa, and Perdita to look like Hermione, and will probably imagine that they look similar, if this is at all possible. Sometimes these mothers and daughters are doubled in performance, which means that the experience of the hereditary resemblance in the reunion scene with the father is less of an imaginative construction; but then the audience would still have to use its imagination about the other figure who is brought into the play to perform the mother in middle age.

One moment in *The Winter's Tale* particularly exemplifies the ideology of resemblance as a sign of family relationship: the moment when Paulina enumerates all the details in the baby girl's face that are like Leontes's to prove Hermione's faithfulness. When Paulina refers to the baby as having "the trick of's frown, his forehead, nay, the valley, / The pretty dimples of his chin and cheek, his smiles, / The very mold and frame of hand, nail, finger" (2.3.101–103), she is describing details that the audience must find impossible to see; indeed, most likely the baby would have been "played" by a doll, not a live baby at all. This passage briefly pictures Leontes as himself an infant (there is no other passage I know of in Shakespeare where the "pretty dimples" of an adult male are mentioned); more significantly here, it evokes the persistent tendency to *look for* details of resemblance between family members, and to imagine them into existence, especially in relation to babies. Clearly it is part of the dominant ideology that babies are supposed to look like someone else in the family, and if that resemblance is not obvious it will still be imagined. In the theater, the question of whom members of the audience believe about the baby's similarity to Leontes could be like the question of whether they believe the idealistic Gonzalo or the villainous Antonio about the island in *The Tempest*. Paulina may be credible in her description to the extent that she seems to be morally reliable in general; yet already in Jacobean times it must have been obvious that even if the baby were not as identical to Leontes as she claimed, it would not necessarily have meant that Leontes did not beget it. Some might well consider any exaggeration on Paulina's part justifiable as an attempt to save the baby and Hermione from Leontes's rage. This would then suggest how the desire to preserve a child—not just by confirming its paternity, as here, but also by flattering parents' frequent desire to see themselves recreated—may generate the ability to imagine resemblances between child and parents. Ultimately, Leontes's recognition of Perdita as his daughter takes place off-stage and the play subordinates the question of whether Perdita looks like him; the emphasis on her resemblance to her mother, which has nothing to do with fidelity in marriage, testifies to the fact that Leontes has regained his belief in Hermione.

The recognition scenes of these plays in general tend to develop the perspective of the genetic fathers much more than the perspective of anyone else in the large family constellation. There is no attention to how Perdita, Guiderius, and Arviragus feel about discovering a different set of parents, or how they come to terms with those they earlier thought of as their only parents. (In his rewritten last act of *Cymbeline*, George Bernard Shaw imagines that Guiderius would say "We three are fullgrown men and perfect strangers. / Can I change fathers as I'd change my shirt?" and then refuse to inherit the throne.)[19] Nor are these plays much concerned with the feelings of the foster-parents, although the foster-fathers receive somewhat more attention than the foster-mothers. With the exception of the shepherd's wife and Euriphile (significantly both deceased, as is Lychorida after only a few speeches), foster-mothers are characterized in a way congruent with the general cultural prejudice against stepmothers.[20] And although birth-mothers are recovered in two of these plays, the final reunion is clearly seen from their husbands' points of view, not theirs.

Many of Shakespeare's plays can be discussed with reference to an absent mother. Romance is the genre in which he gives mothers, comparatively, the most attention, and an idealized image of motherhood is evoked most vividly in the return of Hermione in *The Winter's Tale*.[21] In her words of affection and attention to Perdita, suggesting that it is through concern for her daughter alone she has preserved herself, she is the mother that any separated daughter would want.[22] The fact that Hermione speaks only to Perdita, and indeed says that it was because of hope to see her that she remained alive, appeals to the fantasy that any child might have, that it was she her mother loved best after all. When she asks, "Where hast thou been preserved? Where lived?" (5.3.124), she is, in a sense, the perfect mother, because she wants to know about the other family without criticizing them, giving her daughter room to assimilate the complexity of her experience.

The idealized birth-mothers Hermione and Thaisa contrast sharply to the evil foster-mothers, Dionyza and *Cymbeline*'s nameless queen. Although Stephen Collins relates the negative view of stepmothers in the Renaissance to a general misogyny, these plays show that misogyny could be part of a polarized view of women.[23] Hermione and Thaisa, in their return, are as idealized as a dead or absent mother is likely to be by a child who lives with an unsatisfactory substitute. And indeed they are accompanied in the romances by a third idealized birth-mother, appearing only in a dream-vision, Posthumus's mother, who died at his birth.[24] Perhaps the point is to focus dramatic attention on the birth-mother (recovered at the end of *Pericles* and *The Winter's Tale*) by removing motherly competition from her. When women do foster maternally in Shakespeare—Lychorida, Paulina—they are no threat to the prerogatives of the birth-mother; indeed, they present her or her memory to her daughter.

The recognition scenes of all these plays emphasize bodily connections in the family. Embraces are indicated by the characters' words. Rediscovered characters are introduced to each other as "Flesh of thy flesh" (Pericles says this of Marina to Thaisa, 5.3.47) or "The issue of your loins ... and blood of your begetting" (Belarius thus returns Cymbeline's sons, 5.5.333–334). The plays are full of the imagery of birth, pregnancy, and conception—most often in literal references to characters' origins.[25] This imagery reinforces the plays' mythology of "blood" and their emphasis on biological relatedness. But it is often used metaphorically—and sometimes the point of the metaphor is to make the reunion of parents and children into a rebirth or a reconception. Pericles, seeing Marina, says, "I am great with woe, and shall deliver weeping" (5.1.109). Cymbeline, recognizing his sons on Belarius's proof, says, "O, what, am I/ A mother to the birth of three? Ne'er mother / Rejoiced deliverance more" (5.5.372–374). And Pericles welcomes Marina as "Thou that beget'st him that did thee beget"—using of her generative power a word primarily used of male actions. These images stand out because of the intense moments in which they are uttered, but birth/pregnancy imagery is also used at other times—Camillo alludes to folklore about pregnancy when he describes his desire to see "Sicilia" (a name that refers to both his king, Leontes, and his country) as "a woman's longing" (4.4.671) and Imogen describes her desire to see Posthumus by saying, "Never long'd my mother so/ To see me first, as I have now" (3.4.2–3). Although good mothers here are largely absent or dead, imagery of biological maternity is frequent in the words of both male and female characters.[26] Concern with the link between generations is so strong that images of pregnancy and childbirth appear frequently partly because they are the most vivid way to picture that link, and occasionally images of begetting also figure. But the plays also show, and use for images, child-rearing as well as child-bearing. A memorable line when the young Pericles declares his love of Thaisa puts "fostering" and "blood" together and suggests fostering may be seen as just as basic.

> Simonides: What, are you both pleased?
> Thaisa: Yes, if you love me, sir.
> Pericles: Even as my life my blood that fosters it (2.5. 88–90).

In each of these plays, the characters raised in a second family are described by others as extraordinary. Marina and Perdita speak exceptionally well and outshine others in beauty and talents; Guiderius and Arviragus are brave, ambitious, yet gentle and civil. Marina transcends the brothel and Perdita surpasses all expectations for shepherdesses. Belarius comments on the boys that he has raised, "How hard it is to hide the sparks of nature," and many critics have analyzed these plays in terms of the supremacy of heredity. The tendency of the romance genre to idealize its central characters (found also in the portrayal of Imogen and Miranda, raised by the fathers who begot them), here uses the lost child theme among its strategies. But in spite of all the blood and birth imagery, much of the play's presentation of heredity could be seen as a construction mediated by the good foster-parent. Belarius knows the boys are princes, the Old Shepherd infers that Perdita, found with fancy clothes and gold, comes from a wealthy and perhaps aristocratic background, and Lychorida passes on to Marina the image of Pericles's bravery. Perhaps each of them makes a connection comparable to Paulina's emphasis on the similarity between Leontes and his infant. Does one need modern psychology to imagine this? Only the notion of the self-fulfilling prophecy, a dynamic arguably exemplified in many of Shakespeare's plays. Nevertheless, none of these plays makes this aspect of the foster-parent's role explicit, and only the dead Lychorida receives tribute for the memories she has passed on.

The family separations and reunions in Shakespeare's plays have many possible relations to early modern family psychology. Although adoption was not part of the legal code under that name in Renaissance England, there were many different ways in which children were raised by people who did not give birth to them, and the word might even be used, as it is when the Countess in *All's Well That Ends Well* says, "Adoption strives with nature, and choice breeds / A native slip to us from foreign seeds" (1.3.142–43).[27] The word was familiar from various biblical passages, especially in the Epistles of Paul, where Christians are referred to as adopted children of God.[28] But the events in the plays also connect with everyday family experience in Shakespeare's time. Gail Paster writes in *The Body Embarrassed* that Perdita's experience is "a version, romantically heightened, of what happened soon after birth to countless babies in the wet-nursing culture … inexplicable extrusion from the birthing chamber, enforced alienation from the maternal breast, and a journey to the unknown rural environment of a foster family lower in station than its own. Even though the birth parents knew where they had placed their baby and occasionally visited it, the physical and social separation of the two environments was virtually as complete as it is here."[29] A similar analysis could be made, although with more qualifications, of Marina's, Guiderius's, and Arviragus's experiences. Perhaps these events glamorize also the many other family separations common in Shakespeare's culture; from about ten years of age on, upper-class children might be sent to other families to learn manners and to bond dynasties, middle-class children to learn trades and professions, and children of all classes to become servants.[30] Here these ordinary separations are transformed into the more dramatic separations of abandoning, kidnapping, and shipwrecking. Perhaps these romance plots also provided a fantasy transformation for the more permanent separations caused by frequent mortality, which was much higher than ours for both parents and children, and highest, it seems, in London, where the plays were performed. At the beginning of the seventeenth century, the life expectancy is London was only 22.3 years, and "by age twenty forty-seven percent of women born in London had suffered the death of their fathers."[31] Furthermore, infant and child death rates were, in general, high in early modern Europe. "An infant in the first four months of life had in general a 20 to 40 percent chance of dying before his or her first birthday … the chances of surviving to age twenty were in general no better than fifty-fifty."[32]

Members of the original audiences in different family circumstances probably differed to some extent in their responses to these plays, just as do members of the audience in different circumstances today. Paster has argued, for example, that the emphasis on the difference in behavior between Perdita and her foster family and on characters' identification of her with nobility "offers a powerful counternarrative for the specific fears and repressed anxieties of the wet-nursed child."[33] We could imagine that the play also could soothe anxieties of parents of wet-nursed children.

And what of the many audience members whose parents had died early and who had been raised by stepparents? How important was it to them to emphasize their connections with their deceased parents? How much did their stepparents take on parental roles in their imagination? How much does the orphaned Posthumus's alienation from his dead parents dramatize anxieties of the time? For some members of the audience, who could never hope for a reunion in real life, Posthumus's dream-vision of his family could have served as a reassurance of their continued connection with their family, but Posthumus's marriage to Imogen reconnects him with his foster-father Cymbeline as well as with her.

Adults raised by stepparents could have enjoyed the wish-fulfillment of the reunions with birth-parents presented in these plays, but they also might have drawn another kind of satisfaction—as could parents who were raising stepchildren—from the fact that actors seldom have as much similarity as the characters they are playing are supposed to have. The doubleness of effect—characters are biologically related, and the text tells us to see them as similar, actors are not related, and probably don't look very similar—is analogous to the doubleness in the meaning of family terms such as "father," "mother," that stepfamilies and adoptees have to deal with. The term "role" is used in connection with parenthood, in ordinary language today, almost as much as it is used in relation to sex and gender. Is there a theatrical aspect to parenthood? Or is this usage a sign of inauthenticity? What are the strengths and limitations of the formulation "The real parents are those who act like parents"? Leontes does not act like a parent when he commands Perdita to be exposed; does Pericles when he leaves Marina at Tharsus? For much of the rest of both plays, penance is the only way these fathers have of acting like a parent.

The plots of these plays are largely structured to limit a family to one "real" set of parents, male and female, and the conclusion of

Pericles—following the play in which the good foster-parent, Lychorida, appears only briefly and the wicked foster-parents are more vivid—stays closest to this model. But knowing something about the frequent uses of nursing, fostering out, and other varieties of child care beyond the nuclear family in Renaissance England, as well as the high infant death rate, may help to explain one of the most vexed aspects of this play: why is Pericles not only grief-stricken but also virtually immobilized and apparently also in need of prolonged penance after he hears about his daughter's death from Dionyza, when he acted in good faith believing that she and Cleon were responsible people?

It may well be that parents whose children died while in someone else's house had a particularly complicated sense of self-blame—they were following the accepted pattern in their society, but was that why their child had died? Within England, Gottlieb notes, although wet-nursing was often criticized, sending children away after seven was not openly questioned—but at least one Italian observer felt that this showed "the want of affection in the English."[34] When Pericles assumes that he must give Marina to others to raise in their home, instead of taking her and Lychorida or another nurse with him—when the years he stays away pass quickly in Gower's act 4 Chorus—those whose children had died, or who feared their children might, when away, had particular reasons for interest in his story. Both the death of children and their boarding out might have been especially frequent in 1608–1609, the probable first year of *Pericles* was peformed; plague closed the theaters part of that time.[35] Perhaps it is because such ordinary behavior on his part—rather than the insane jealousy of Leontes, for example—seems to have brought about disaster, that *Pericles* was one of the most popular Shakespearean plays of its day.[36]

Notes

1. This and all quotations from Shakespeare are taken from *William Shakespeare: The Complete Works*, ed. David Bevington, updated 4th ed. (New York: Longman, 1997). This one is from *Tempest* 1.2.120. An expanded version of this chapter appears in Marianne Novy, *Reading Adoption: Family and Difference in Fiction and Drama* (Ann Arbor: University of Michigan Press, 2005).
2. Barbara Estrin, *The Raven and the Lark: Lost Children in Literature of the English Renaissance* (Lewisburg: Bucknell University Press, 1985), while

noting that such plots in literature "predicate that the biological parents are superior to the adoptive ones," also writes that "the good of art appears in the adoptive sections where the supremacy of inheritance is superseded by the idealization of the replacement" (14).

3. See Thomas Laqueur, *Making Sex: Body and Gender from the Greeks to Freud* (Cambridge, MA: Harvard University Press, 1990), 25–43, and his explanation on 55–57 of how the encyclopedist Isidore of Seville, still influential in the Renaissance, simultaneously holds "that only men have sperma, that only women have sperma, and that both have sperma" (55). See also Janet Adelman, "Making Defect Perfection: Shakespeare and the One-Sex Model," in *Enacting Gender on the Renaissance Stage,* ed. Viviana Comensoli and Anne Russell (Urbana: University of Illinois Press, 1999), 23–52, and François Jacob, *The Logic of Life: A History of Heredity,* trans. Betty E. Spillman (1973; Princeton, NJ: Princeton University Press, 1993), 25. Use of the term "blood" for biological kinship comes from the ancient belief that "seeds," whether of male or female, are refined blood; see Laqueur, 38. But see also Aristotle's belief that the fetus feeds on menstrual blood, which accounts for the resemblance of children to their mothers, in Ian Maclean, *The Renaissance Notion of Woman* (Cambridge: Cambridge University Press, 1980), 37. For a classic, influential text of another dimension of belief in "blood," the natural love of parents for their children, combined with a description of how Nature uses women's blood to feed the seed, see Plutarch, "On Affection for Offspring," in *Moralia,* 16 vols., trans. W. C. Helmbold (Cambridge, MA: Harvard University Press, 1970), 6: 343–353. For still other Renaissance notions of "blood," see Gail Kern Paster, *The Body Embarrassed: Drama and the Disciplines of Shame in Early Modern England* (Ithaca, NY: Cornell University Press, 1993), 64–112.

4. Children's difference from their parents was sometimes explained as the influence of the maternal imagination; see Clara Pinto-Correia, *The Ovary of Eve: Egg and Sperm and Preformation* (Chicago: University of Chicago Press, 1997), 128–130. For other explanations related to the condition of both parents at conception, see Paster, *The Body Embarrassed,* 167–172.

5. For the early modern comparison of teachers to gardeners, see Rebecca Bushnell, *A Culture of Teaching: Early Modern Humanism in Theory and Practice* (Ithaca, NY: Cornell University Press, 1996), 73–116. On the influence of wet-nurses, see Valerie Fildes, *Breasts, Bottles, and Babies: A History of Infant Feeding* (Edinburgh: Edinburgh University Press, 1986), 168–178. See also Paster, *Body Embarrassed,* 197–201, on early modern wet-nursing and its transformations in drama.

6. Beatrice Gottlieb, *The Family in the Western World from the Black Death to the Industrial Age* (New York: Oxford, 1993), 160; these customs are discussed with specific reference to the late sixteenth and early seventeenth century in Ivy Pinchbeck and Margaret Hewitt, *Children in English Society, Vol. 1* (London: Routledge and Kegan Paul), 1969), 25–26. Lawrence Stone discusses what he calls a "mass exchange of adolescent children, which seems to have been peculiar to England," in *The Family, Sex, and Marriage in England 1500–1800* (New York: Harper & Row, 1977), 107.

Lori Humphrey Newcomb discusses *WT*'s source, *Pandosto,* in relation to the widespread institution of adolescent service in "The Romance of Service: The Simple History of *Pandosto*'s Servant Readers," *in Framing Elizabethan Fictions: Contemporary Approaches to Early Modern Narrative Prose,* ed. Constance Relihan (Kent, Ohio: Kent State University Press, 1996), 117–139. I am grateful for a prepublication copy of this essay, now expanded into *Reading Popular Romance in Early Modern England* (New York: Columbia University Press, 2002). In another chapter in this volume, "'Pretty Fictions' and 'Little Stories': Child Actors on the Early Modern Stage," Claire Busse discusses the exchange of children as well as child mortality in relation to the children's theater groups popular close to the time of Shakespeare's romances.

7. Dionyza's words resonate ominously with some contemporary cases of infanticidal nursing, mostly of illegitimate children; see Keith Wrightson, "Infanticide in Earlier Seventeenth-Century England," *Local Population Studies* 15 (1975): 10–22. Thanks to Frances Dolan for sending me a copy of this article.

8. See Elizabeth Archibald, *Apollonius of Tyre: Medieval and Renaissance Themes and Variations* (Bury St. Edmunds: D. S. Brewer, 1991), 145.

9. See Geoffrey Bullough, ed., *Narrative and Dramatic Sources of Shakespeare,* VI (New York: Columbia University Press, 1966), 396–405, 445–453, 518–529. Wilkins's Pericles alone motivates this secrecy, by telling the nurse that Marina should be "brought uppe as the daughter of Cleon and Dyonysa, lest that the knowledge of her highbirth, should make her growe prowd to their instructions" (524).

10. F.D. Hoeniger, "Introduction," in *Pericles,* ed. Hoeniger, Arden Edition (London: Methuen, 1963), lxxviii, notes that Pericles' role as music-teacher is emphasized in the sources.

11. Susan Baker, "Personating Persons: Rethinking Shakespearean Disguises," *Shakespeare Quarterly* 43 (1992): 312.

12. See Meredith Skura's "Interpreting Posthumus' Dream from Above and Below: Families, Psychoanalysts, and Literary Criticism," in *Representing Shakespeare,* ed. Murray Schwartz and Coppélia Kahn (Baltimore: Johns Hopkins University Press, 1980), 212–215.

13. John Boswell, *The Kindness of Strangers: The Abandonment of Children in Western Europe from Late Antiquity to the Renaissance* (New York: Vintage, 1988). Such a requirement is also present in a number of the newly dis-covered private adoption contracts in early modern France discussed by Kristin Elizabeth Gager, *Blood Ties and Fictive Ties: Adoption and Family Life in Early Modern France* (Princeton, NJ: Princeton University Press, 1996), 101–102.

14. On his lack of possessiveness, see Carol Thomas Neely, *Broken Nuptials in Shakespeare's Plays* (New Haven, CT: Yale University Press, 1985), 202.

15. Baker makes this suggestion.

16. Fawnia's "natural disposition did bewray that she was borne of some high parentage"—Robert Greene, *Pandosto,* in Bullough, 175, but specific resemblances do not, for example, strike her father, and thus he pursues her without suspecting his love is incestuous. Shakespeare also added

discussion of the Bastard's physical resemblance to his father to his historical source for *King John*. See Phyllis Rackin, *Stages of History: Shakespeare's English Chronicles* (Ithaca, NY: Cornell University Press, 1990), 187, 190.

17. Anne Barton, "*As You Like It* and *Twelfth Night:* Shakespeare's Sense of an Ending," *Shakespearian Comedy*, Stratford-upon-Avon Studies 14, ed. D. J. Palmer and Malcolm Bradbury (New York: Crane, Russak and Co., 1972), 176.

18. The tension between seeing actors as identical characters, as the text suggests, and as different, also might be compared to the tension between seeing actors in children's companies as adults, as the text suggests, and as children: see Busse, this volume, and her discussion of "dual-consciousness."

19. Shaw, "*Cymbeline* Refinished" (1937), quoted in Ann Thompson, "*Cymbeline's* Other Endings," in *The Appropriation of Shakespeare*, ed. Jean Marsden (New York: St. Martin's, 1992), 213.

20. On that prejudice, see Stephen Collins, "'Reason, Nature, and Order': The Stepfamily in English Renaissance Thought," *Renaissance Studies* 13 (1999): 312–324; see Neely, 174, on the desexualization and sanctification of mothers in the romances through real and mock deaths. The foster-mother in *Pandosto* begins as a misogynist caricature who threatens to cudgel her husband "if hee brought any bastard brat within her dores," although eventually she nourishes "it so clenly and carefully as it began to bee a jolly girle, in so much that they began both of them to be very fond of it," Greene, *Pandosto,* in Bullough, 174, 175.

21. See Janet Adelman, *Suffocating Mothers* (New York: Routledge, 1992), 9–10 and passim, for a detailed analysis of the varying roles of mothers and fantasies about mothers in Shakespeare's canon. Hermione and Thaisa are less idealized early in the play than after they reappear. Only two other plays include mother-daughter relationships—*Romeo and Juliet* and *Merry Wives of Windsor;* in both those relations are rather cool and distant, to tragic effect in *R & J*.

22. Paster, *Body Embarrassed*, 179.

23. Collins, "'Reason, Nature, and Order.'" 320–321. On polarization in views of women, see, for example, Mary Beth Rose, *The Expense of Spirit* (Ithaca, NY: Cornell University Press, 1988), 4–5.

24. Compare the presence of the idealized mothers Ceres and Juno in the masque of *The Tempest*.

25. Doreen Delvecchio and Antony Hammond give a list of examples in *Pericles;* see their "Introduction" to *Pericles, Prince of Tyre*, ed. Delvecchio and Hammond (Cambridge: Cambridge University Press, 1998), 47–49. See also Neely, *Broken Nuptials,* 191–192, and Marianne Novy, *Love's Argument* (Chapel Hill: University of North Carolina Press, 1984), 171–174.

26. For an interpretation of the cross-gendered imagery emphasizing male nurturance, see Novy, 174; for the view that it involves male appropriation of female procreative power that excludes women, see Adelman, *Suffocating Mothers,* 197–198 (which also emphasizes the repression of sexuality)

and Marilyn Williamson, *The Patriarchy of Shakespeare's Comedies* (Detroit: Wayne State University Press, 1986), 165.

27. Bevington glosses this passage as referring to grafting, a metaphor also used of adoption in some twentieth-century writing, such as *Perspectives on a Grafted Tree,* ed. Patricia Irwin Johnston (Indianapolis: Perspectives Press, 1983).

28. See Galatians 4: 5–7 and Romans 8:12–17. Gager has speculated that, in spite of clerical hostility to adoption discussed by Jack Goody in *The Development of the Family and Marriage in Europe* (Cambridge: Cambridge University Press, 1983), 99–101, "the Christian theology of 'adoption through baptism' might very well have aided in sustaining adoption traditions for families interested in having a non-natal child to stand as their heir" (*Blood Ties,* 69; see also 44–46). Perhaps some ambitious historian will discover records notarizing adoption in England as Gager has done in France.

29. Paster, *Body Embarrassed,* 273.

30. Gottlieb, *The Family in the Western World,* 160, claims that apprenticeship often began around seven, but Ilana Krausman Ben-Amos finds that ten, twelve or later were much more likely ages, although younger children could be boarded out for reasons such as schooling, outbreaks of plague, poverty, or parental death; see her *Adolescence and Youth in Early Modern England* (New Haven, CT: Yale University Press, 1994), 54–64. Her view of apprentices' age is supported by Paul Griffith, *Youth and Authority: Formative Experiences in England 1560–1640* (Oxford: Clarendon Press, 1996), 33.

31. Heather Dubrow, *Shakespeare and Domestic Loss: Forms of Deprivation, Mourning, and Recuperation* (Cambridge: Cambridge University Press, 1999), 162. She deals with the relation of the romances to the threat of parental death on 166, 189–193. See also her comments on parental death, stepparenting, and theatricality on 165 and 170. I am grateful for a pre-publication copy of this chapter, which is expanded from "The Message from Marcade: Parental Death in Tudor and Stuart England," in *Attending to Women in Early Modern England,* ed. Betty S. Travitsky and Adele F. Seeff (Newark: University of Delaware Press, 1994).

32. Gottlieb, *The Family in the Western World,* 133. Frances E. Dolan, *Dangerous Familiars: Representations of Domestic Crime in England 1550–1700* (Ithaca, NY: Cornell University Press, 1994), 168, has argued that *Winter's Tale* in particular is a displaced, aestheticized resolution of anxiety about infanticide.

33. Paster, *Body Embarrassed,* 276.

34. Daniele Barbar, *Italian Relations* (1551), in Molly Harrison and O. M. Royston, eds., *How They Lived,* vol. 2 (Oxford, 1963), pp. 267–268; in Gottlieb, *Family in the Western World,* 162. She notes criticism of this pattern eventually developing in England, beginning with William Penn, and argues that "some people were genuinely puzzled by why they were doing what was expected"(161).

35. See Hoeniger, "Introduction," xxv.

36. Hoeniger notes that "There are few plays by Shakespeare for which as much evidence is available to testify to their popularity on the stage during the early decades of the seventeenth century," "Introduction," lxvi–lxvii. Portions of this essay previously appeared in "Multiple Parenting in *Pericles*," in *Pericles: Critical Essays*, ed. David Skeele (New York: Garland, 2000), 238–248; it is revised from "Multiple Parenting in Shakespeare's Romances," in *Domestic Arrangements in Early Modern England*, ed. Kari Boyd McBride (Pittsburgh: Duquesne University Press, 2002), 188–208.

5

"PRETTY FICTIONS" AND "LITTLE STORIES"

Child Actors on the Early Modern Stage

CLAIRE M. BUSSE

Written about a child who, while a public figure, held no social prestige, Ben Jonson's "Epitaph on S[alomon] P[avy], A Child of Q[ueen] El[izabeth's] Chapel" appears out of place amidst the satirical depictions of social vices and laudatory tributes to virtuous noblemen in Jonson's 1616 *Epigrams*.[1] For Salomon Pavy was merely a young child actor who performed in a number of Jonson's plays, including *Poetaster* and *Cynthia's Revels* and died at the age of thirteen. Unlike the majority of the epigrams, which focus on contemporary social behaviors and relationships, Jonson's "Epitaph on S.P." is more fiction than actuality, presenting the boy's death as the result of the fates mistaking Pavy for one of the old men he so convincingly portrays and accidentally taking him before his time. Despite his seeming insignificance, Pavy's identity as a child actor, and even as a child, places him within the network of material relations that structured early modern English life; he thus possesses a close kinship with several of the other children discussed in this collection, figures who have similarly been shown to be part of broader material and social networks. Indeed, children in the period were frequently considered the property of their parents or the masters to whom they were apprenticed.[2] The child actor was no exception, as much the property of the theater for which he performed as other children were of the adults they served under.

"Epitaph on S.P." belongs to a triad of poems in Jonson's collection that tell tales of the deaths of children in what can only be described as material terms. The other two poems are striking for their personal nature, for they convey the grief of Jonson and his wife over the loss of their children, Benjamin and Mary.[3] Poignant as they may be, all three poems employ metaphors that depict the children as objects to be lost more than as individuals to be mourned. Evoking period concerns about the kind of markets in which the child commodity could be circulated, the three poems highlight the status of these children as property, with each of them functioning as objects in different systems of exchange. In epigram 22, Jonson's daughter Mary is presented as a "gift" received from heaven that ultimately must be returned. Rather than becoming a possession of the new owner, this gift represents an obligation to reciprocate, a form of exchange that Georges Bataille identifies as existing in "primitive economic institutions."[4] Although it is precapitalist, this type of expenditure nevertheless indicates the beginnings of commerce. In these transactions, social obligations are formed through the transmission of objects.[5] As Patricia Fumerton has argued, such systems of exchange were not uncommon in the period, for early modern practices of child-fosterage functioned as a form of gift exchange that benefited the children's families. Jonson's poem invokes such practices. Much like the children of the nobility who were sent from family to family as a means of solidifying relationships between adults and adding to the value of the children, Mary is given from heaven to her parents, then sent back to serve in the "virgin train" of "heaven's Queen."[6] The description of Jonson's son Benjamin, the subject of epigram 45, describes a financial transaction more pressing to the citizen classes. Benjamin is a loan, an investment into which Jonson has placed "too much hope" but must now "pay" back.[7]

The portrayals of Mary and Benjamin's deaths, for all the public display of the poems, merely hint at and cover the larger, private grief of their parents.[8] Benjamin may be figured as Ben Jonson's "best piece of poetry," as epigram 45 "On My First Son" sadly avows, yet the essence of this poem, Jonson confirms, lies buried underground, with only an acknowledgement of it written on the gravestone above. Salomon Pavy, however, is different. Unlike Mary and Benjamin, whose deaths are private matters to be mourned by their

parents, Pavy's "story" is marketed to the public. Jonson's tale of
Pavy's death invites the reader to join him in his mourning, to:
"Weep with me all you that read / This little story" (1–2). Much like
today's celebrities, Pavy's life belongs to the public, granted none of
the privacy alluded to by Jonson in the poems about his offspring.
Mary and Benjamin may be commodities, but they are commodities
traded within closed systems of exchange: Jonson receives the children from heaven, and must return them back, either as gifts or with
interest.[9] The unfortunate Salomon Pavy, however, exists within
less controlled market conditions. Instead of functioning as a link
between two individuals in an economic exchange, young Salomon
is a commodity on an open market. Unlike Mary and Benjamin, who
belong to their parents, it is unclear who is responsible for Pavy.
Instead, heaven and nature "strive" over "which owned the creature."
With no particular adults watching over him, Pavy is at the whims of
the market and the law.

Early modern relations between children and adults, no matter how
affectionate, could not entirely escape cultural understandings of children as property. For Jonson, as for many other dramatists of the early
seventeenth century, children not only were a source of aesthetic inspiration, but more importantly a means and embodiment of literary
production—and by extension, a potential means of financial prosperity. Benjamin may have figuratively been his father's "best piece of
poetry," but, as an actor, Salomon Pavy literally embodied Jonson's
dramatic creations, receiving praise for having "played [them] truly."[10]
Although literary figures such as the deceased Benjamin manifest
adult hopes and desires, child actors such as Salomon were physically
and legally forced into their service as vehicles for the author's representations. As unpaid workers, supplied only with room, board, clothing, and occasionally a basic education, the boy actors were a valuable
resource for the private theater companies, bringing in revenue for little
expense. In fact, the adults running the children's companies in which
actors like Pavy performed had the legal right to impress boys to perform in their theaters.[11] Conscripted into an occupation still considered suspect by much of society, with few opportunities for career
advancement, the children of the theater companies would seem to
have little room for rebellion.

Jonson's portrayal of S.P. may depict a figurative loss, but it also emphasizes the literal and material transactions of the theater that surrounded and, in this case, ultimately consumed the young actor. The story told in "Epitaph of S.P." is supplemented by language that invokes the material forces controlling young Pavy; young Salomon may be the "stage's jewel" figuratively, but in reality he is essentially a possession of the theater. Not a young man, but a "creature" to be "owned," by age thirteen, Pavy had become the property of the theater in which he performed. Jonson's image of heaven and nature "striving" to determine "which owned the creature" evokes the suspected competition between rival theater companies to acquire boy actors. The depiction of the fates mistakenly taking young Salomon away after being deceived by his believable performances of old men serves a dual function. For while it offers a defense of the quality of the children's companies—affirming that, although the children are young, they can nevertheless be convincing in their roles—it also recalls the practice of abducting young actors off the streets and spiriting them into the theater companies.[12] As David Riggs indicates, despite Jonson's praise for the young actor's skills, the poem also hints at the darker side of Pavy's fate:

> This extravagant compliment disguises (even as it alludes to) the painful truth that hovers around the edges of this epitaph. Sall was old before his time; his life was a performance wherein he was doomed to play a part devised by cynical adults.[13]

The tension between praise for the child actor and awareness of his lack of agency that Riggs identifies in Jonson's poem is not unexpected, for Jonson's involvement with the children's companies made him complicit with the plight of the child actor.

Although the child actor was an object to be employed for the benefit of the author, adult actors had the ability to negotiate their position in the theater. Actors in the adult companies not only earned a wage for a job they chose, but by the time of Pavy's death could potentially invest in the companies in which they performed.[14] We can see the differences in Jonson's perceptions of the objectified and commodified child actor and the paid adults performing within the public theaters by examining "Epitaph on S.P." in light of another epigram written about an adult actor, epigram 89, "To Edward Alleyn."[15] Even the titles of the poems reveal a shift in perception of their subject. Whereas Salomon, Benjamin, and Mary are each the subject of a Jonson poem, figures to be written about, Alleyn receives a poem addressed "to him." Of course, it would be remiss not to point out the obvious fact that Alleyn, as a living subject, can receive the poem whereas the dead children can merely be discussed.[16] However, there is something more to be said about the positioning of the children as objects to be written on, exchanged as "little stories" between poet and audience. The differences suggest a passivity for the children that does not exist in Jonson's portrayal of the adult Alleyn. Although Pavy is continually acted on, Alleyn acts. Pavy, as the "stage's jewel," is glorified as a valuable possession of the stage. Alleyn is an actor who gives the work of the dramatist its value, winning glory for the stage. Jonson can choose to write about young Salomon for the pleasure of his readers. When he represents Alleyn, however, it is in order to repay him for the benefits he has brought to the stage. Jonson enters into an exchange with Alleyn, offering that "tis just that who did give/ So many poets life, by one should live" (13–14). Although Pavy can bring the characters on stage to life, his actions are limited to the space of the theater. Alleyn's deeds, however, move outward to the world, bringing to life the poets themselves, not just the speeches they have constructed for others.

Despite Jonson's distinctions between them as poetic figures, the real Pavy and Allen did, however, have something in common. For both were popular actors with name recognition. The child actor, while financially disempowered, could find security in his own popularity. For it is the actor, not the playwright, who engages the audience in theatrical performance. As Nora Johnson has argued, the circumstances of the early modern theater created a "logic of celebrity" in which "theatrical practice … created an appetite for individual figures who could, as individuals, promise theatrical pleasure."[17] Thus, the relationship between author and actor becomes one of negotiation:

For a player to become known on stage is to become known for working around the script, playing off the controlling authority, developing a

personal reputation while playing a series of roles devised by others. For a
dramatist to achieve a reputation is similarly to work around the authority
of the players, establishing a presence in negotiation with them (79).

Child actors might be possessions of the theater, but they form the
relationships with the audience on which a production's success rests.
Just as adult actors could manipulate their popularity on stage, so could
the child actor.

Rather than an empty vessel speaking others' words, the child here
acquires a power unavailable to the playwright—indeed, a particular
power over the playwright. For the playwright relies on the child to
convey his intentions without distorting or undermining them. But
unlike the adult actor who may benefit financially from his mutual
relationship with the author, the child actor is as likely to use this
celebrity against the success of the production as he is to use it in favor
of it. Children as property are expected to behave. But children on
the stage have every opportunity not to. Thus, rather than presenting
"little stories" told to an admiring audience, in his plays, Jonson depicts
child actors as independent and potentially disruptive forces.

Jonson was not alone in drawing attention to this facet of the child
actor. In the early seventeenth century, a number of plays appeared in
which child actors perform the roles of child actors. Plays including
Cynthia's Revels (1600), John Marston's *Antonio and Mellida* (1599/
1600) and *Jack Drum's Entertainment* (1600), and John Day's *Isle of
Gulls* (1606) begin with inductions in which the child actors enter the
stage playing themselves. Francis Beaumont took the practice one step
further and, in *The Knight of the Burning Pestle* (c. 1607–1611), created a play which not only presented the boy actors as themselves but
also undermined the distinctions between theatrical spaces on and off
stage and theatrical identities within and outside of performances.[18]
In all of these plays, the child actors threaten to take over and potentially undermine the productions. Rather than resisting the power
of the children's celebrity, the authors use it to their advantage by
enticing their audiences with a theater of uncertainty rather than
predictability.

Although twentieth-century critics have frequently overlooked the
child actors, early modern playwrights revealed a much stronger interest

in the boys, their abilities as actors, their status as unpaid laborers, and their behavior as children.[19] This interest became particularly acute in the first decade of the seventeenth century, a moment marked by the return of the children's companies to a theatrical world increasingly dominated by the adult companies of the public theaters. We have little historical evidence of the daily lives of the boys or their perceptions of their status in the theater, yet examination of theatrical representations of the boy actors can at least provide, if not an accurate record of their lives, insight into how their society and the adults who worked within the theater perceived them.

Boys Will Be Boys: The Child Actor and the Induction

Somewhere between 1597 and 1600, the children's companies reappeared on the London stage after an almost ten-year break. Their return coincided with a moment when playwrights were emphasizing the importance of their work to theatrical productions and attempting to claim status as a central component of the theaters. Emerging from a tradition of children appearing in court performances that dates back several centuries, the commercial companies, the Children of Paul's and the Children of the Chapel Royal, gained popularity in the 1580s, offering performances of plays by popular authors (including John Lyly, George Peele, and Christopher Marlowe) to the public for a price, only to disappear from the records throughout the 1590s. Although there is no certainty about the reason for their absence, theatrical historians speculate that the companies were shut down for performances that fed into the Marprelate controversy, a public and satirical dispute started by attacks on the Anglican bishops who were defended by a number of authors, including several writing for the children.[20] In the ten-year period in which the children were out of commission, the adult companies of the public theaters thrived, creating strong rivals for the children when they appeared back on stage. To return successfully to the theatrical world of the early seventeenth century, the companies needed to carve a space for themselves within a much more crowded and competitive theatrical milieu.

The reappearance of the children is frequently tied to a moment in which satire took hold of the English stage. As much as it focused outward on the foibles of society, satire of the early 1600s also took an inward turn, to mock the styles and conventions of the theater and even of particular authors. Ben Jonson, John Marston, and, to a lesser degree, Thomas Dekker—the three playwrights identified with what has been commonly called "the War of the Theaters"—were particularly culpable of this type of satire, writing a series of plays that mocked each other's styles and credentials as playwrights and poets.[21] Although the satire is harsh and unflattering, it seems to have done little damage to their personal and professional relationships, for the playwrights collaborated on later plays. Reavley Gair suggests that the War of the Theaters was a "seventeenth century publicity strategy to control taste," a marketing strategy used to bring audiences to the private theaters. I would add that it was also a strategy employed to emphasize the importance of the poet/playwright. The common critical focus on the engaging nastiness of the satirical representations often detracts our attention from a theme common to all the plays, the importance of the figure of the author to society. By depicting the author as a subject fit for theatrical performance and controversy, the plays enhanced the author's status.

Critical attention to the drama by Jonson and Marston in this period frequently emphasizes the material produced for the War of the Theaters, overlooking another body of works performed a year or so before the satires that also emphasized the importance of the author. If the plays in the poetomachia legitimize the author's place in society, Marston's *Antonio and Mellida* (1599/1600), *Jack Drum's Entertainment* (1600), and Jonson's *Cynthia's Revels* (1600) turn inward to examine the relationship between the author, actor, and audience during the theatrical performance, with the child actor playing a prominent role. All three plays begin with an "Induction" in which the child actors appear on stage as themselves and address the audience about the work they are about to perform. Through the inductions the authors present the benefits and drawbacks of their young performers, using the boys to provoke audience sympathies. As the first performances of the reestablished children's companies, the plays offered a space through which the playwright could imagine the impact of this particular medium of representation (child actor) and the possibilities it offered for the conditions of performance.[22]

It is not a coincidence that Jonson and Marston used the newly opened children's companies for the performances of their plays.[23] Neither fully subject nor fully object, commodity nor agent, the child actor presented authors with an indeterminate identity through which they could offer their representations to their audience. The ambivalent status of the child enabled the authors to manipulate audience perceptions of what they were viewing on stage. And, where better to employ this strategy than a theatrical moment that was equally liminal, the induction? Unlike the other elements that frame productions, the prologue and epilogue, the induction is distinct in that it is a staged dialogue to be performed, rather than a speech to be recited.[24] Existing in a space external to the plot of the play, yet internal to the theatrical production, inductions provided authors with a means of influencing their audience's reactions to the play that was to follow.[25]

What is unique about these inductions is their attempt to undermine the distinction between the theatrical space, which includes audience, actors, and stage, and the space of the performance. The child actors appear in scripted moments meant to seem as if they are unscripted. By using the indefinable child actor within the context of the shifting boundaries of the induction, playwrights are able to destabilize theatrical boundaries and break down the distance between the audience as spectator to the performance and the audience members as individuals participating in the theatrical enterprise. In doing so, they create a space in which the audience is as accountable for its reception of the production as the author is for his script, and the actor for his performance.

A common argument about the inductions in the children's companies has been that they were used by early modern playwrights as a means of flattering their audience, drawing attention to their status as spectators in the more expensive, and by extension more exclusive, private theaters.[26] In *Children of the Revels: The Boy Companies of Shakespeare's Time and Their Plays,* Michael Shapiro identifies this as one of many strategies embraced by the children's companies as a means of creating a dual-consciousness, what Shapiro defines as the audience's ability to move between their recognition of the individuals on stage as characters in a plot and as actors on a stage. Authors employed this dual-consciousness in order to "expose the artificiality

of the play world" and to "[emphasize] the reality of the spectators'
visions of themselves."[27] By highlighting the audience's presence in a
theatrical space, Shapiro argues, the children's companies could flatter
the audience for attending this more elite form of dramatic entertainment.[28] The theatrical world and the world of its audience would
remain distinct and separate. Yet, rather than dividing audience and
actor, the inductions of the children's companies conflate the space of
the audience and the stage to the point at which the audience is
unable to discern that which is fictional from that which is not. This
is particularly true of the induction to Ben Jonson's *Cynthia's Revels.*
No longer spectators removed from the action, the audience is recognized as another element of the performance, complicit with the
actions appearing on stage (for at times the actors in it directly address
the audience, bringing them into the debates occurring on stage).

Jonson's induction emphasizes that, much as this is a staged event,
it is also a live performance that depends on the use of young actors he
depicts as theatrical commodities that are uncontrollable. On the one
hand, the image of children as empty vessels, waiting to be filled and
"seasoned" with the words and ideas taught to them by adults, for
which they were not culpable, dominated early modern conduct manuals and found their way into other cultural productions, as a number of
essays in this collection reveal.[29] This image of the vessel, frequently
used to describe the educational practices of the time, which relied on
rote memory, can easily be applied to the training of young actors.
However, as Michael Witmore shows in his discussion of early modern
witchcraft cases, early modern adults were aware that children working
with adults also could use assumptions of their artlessness as a means
of deception.[30]

Jonson uses this dual vision of the child to his advantage. Thus, the
first audience to see the induction to *Cynthia's Revels* must have been
uncertain about whether the actions they were seeing on stage were a
scripted performance or a moment of childish misbehavior. The induction begins with three of the child actors walking on stage arguing
over which one of them will have the opportunity to speak the prologue, settling the matter only after drawing lots for the right to play
the part. Unhappy with the outcome, one of the losing boys decides to

spite the author and proceeds to give away the entire plot of the play, potentially ruining its novelty.[31] Jonson depicts the children as actively undermining the company, author, and production. His induction draws on the audience's belief in the possibility that the children may turn on the company and act out of control, creating a moment of theatrical instability. This is, of course, a clever move, for the scripted nature of this induction provides perhaps the ultimate moment of authorial control, one in which the author is able to manipulate the audience's perceptions of reality and fiction.

The competition between the boys over their "rights" to speak the prologue quickly reveals that there are competing forces within the theater that determine how a play is to be performed. The first child claims the right to speak the prologue based on his possession of the cloak used to designate the speaker of the prologue. The second child argues that the part is his through seniority, for he was the one to study it first. The third child adds his piece and claims that he is the author's choice for the role, and thus deserves it. With the cloak indicating the expensive costuming theaters depended on,[32] the second child's studies highlighting the company masters responsible for training the boys for performance, and the third child's claims invoking the author's intentions, Jonson draws attention to the most crucial elements of a theatrical performance, and places the audience in the position of considering which of these elements should take precedence. By invoking these elements within a space of competition, the discussion serves the dual purpose of indicating the material circumstances the theater is built on and emphasizing the instability of this environment.

Despite the emphasis on these theatrical forces, their hold over the children is quickly discredited. An interruption by an adult voice offstage locates the children outside of theatrical systems of control. As the children are debating who will speak the prologue, a voice interrupts, chastening: "Why Children, are you not asham'd? Come in there" (Ind. 11). Emphasizing the actors' youthful status, the voice attempts to contain the children within a moral sense of responsibility. Their actions should cause shame; the comment on their actions should cause them to behave. Yet the children ignore the voice, continuing with their conversation as if there had been no interruption. This is not to say that there is no effect; for, two lines later, the first child quickly offers to turn to the audience for the solution to their problem. The other children, however, suspect the first child's motivation to be his popularity with the crowd, and are unwilling to take this risk. Instead, they turn to the more equitable solution of drawing lots that ends by reestablishing the prologue that had started the play. By chance rather than through authority, the results reaffirm the desires of the audience as well as what had seemed to be the intention of the theater company: the first child regains his right to speak the prologue.[33]

Children are presented as both the material through which this play is performed and the unstable force that can potentially undermine the performance. Although the child actors are as much the property of the theatrical companies as the costumes are, Jonson's induction emphasizes that the child actor has an agency that cannot entirely be controlled. Unlike adult actors, who are paid wages for their performances, the children receive no monetary compensation for their work, and thus lack accountability. They are at once essential and disruptive. The children's size and youth marks them as vulnerable and manageable, yet their ability to control the performance requires adults to negotiate and form alliances with them.[34]

Rather than claiming the boys as allies, Jonson depicts himself as a target of their mischievous actions. Surprisingly, these actions come from the boy who seems most likely to defend the author, the third child, who asserts his rights to the prologue because of the author's support for his reading of it. Despite the author's support, this child shows no loyalty, attempting to sabotage the play and its author:

> Slid, I'll do somewhat afore I go
> in, though it be nothing but to revenge my self on the
> Author: since I speak not his Prologue. I'll go tell all
> the argument of his play aforehand, and so stale his invention
> to the auditorie before it come forth (Ind. 33–37).

The boy's spiteful decision to announce the plot of the play may impact the audience's perception of the entire production, but his target is clearly the author. And, there is motivation for this spite. At a later point in the induction another of the actors accuses the author of having little investment in the children:

> We are not so officiously befriended by him,
> as to have his presence in the tiring-house,
> to prompt us aloud, stamp at the book-holder,
> swear for our properties, curse the poor tire-man, rail
> the music out of tune, and sweat for every venial
> trespass we commit, as some Author would, if he had such fine
> engles as we. Well, tis but our hard fortune (Ind. 160–166).

The boys performing *Cynthia's Revels* describe themselves as being in a state of neglect. They expect the author to train them for their performance and intervene in their favor against the other adults running the theater. Abandoned by their author, the children rebel. The author, these lines suggest, cannot take the allegiance of his performers for granted.

By creating a fictional distance between the children performing his plays and himself, Jonson is then able to criticize the audience in an attempt to sway them toward a proper response to his play. For, later in the induction the children mimic and mock the behavior of their typical audience members, criticizing their vanity, ignorance, drunkenness, and all-around foolishness. By presenting this critique of the audience within the children's playful, albeit spiteful, actions, Jonson attempts to limit the potentially negative reaction of his audience, while instructing them in their proper response to the play. Indeed, the third child's synopsis of the plot does not destroy it but provides the audience with the proper way to interpret the actions. Similarly, the children's imitation of their spectators provides the audience, which may very well find itself satirized in the play that is to follow, with the proper response for this unflattering imitation. The audience is to endure criticism graciously, as one of the boys offers, because there is no way to respond to unflattering imitations, except to accept them humbly. There is no other way "to get off with any indifferent grace" (Ind. 218–219).

The creation of an induction that undermines the audience's ability to distinguish events and comments that have been scripted by the author from activities outside of the author's direction provides Jonson with the ability to satirize and attempt to reform his audience while at the same time displacing the responsibility of these actions onto the youthful disruptions of the boy actors. Although Jonson attempts to assert an authorial control over his performance, his dependence on the audience's responses to this performance—especially the audience's recognition of the unstable nature of the child actor—underscores instability in theatrical production that cannot be controlled by the author. Even at the moment in which he is most in command of this instability (by scripting it), Jonson remains aware that the theatrical space is unstable and uncontrollable, for it depends on the audience's response and the behavior of actors who receive no compensation for their performance.

As much as Jonson seems to desire a theatrical world that is entirely controlled by the author, he is unable completely to imagine the possibility. The ambivalence about this control, which Jonson presents in the induction, is echoed in the plot of *Cynthia's Revels,* which highlights the theatricality of society itself, presenting courtly behavior as a form of acting that can be taught, learned, and then employed. The play invokes early modern educational practices, yet challenges their ability to create moral subjects. Individuals within the play echo sentiments that character can be acquired through study. Disreputable figures believe that one can easily adopt "the particular and distinct/ face of every your most noted species of persons, as your/ merchant, your scholar, your soldier, your lawyer, courtier, / &c" (2.3.16–19). Appearances are believed to carry far more weight in society than substance:

> For, let your soul be assur'd of this
> (in any rank, or profession what-ever) the more general,
> or major part of opinion goes with the face, and (simply)
> respects nothing else. Therefore, if that can be made exactly,
> curiously, exquisitely, thoroughly, it is enough (2.3.53–57).

More noble figures attempt to use theater as a space of education and reform by placing unruly characters in noble roles with the hopes that, although taking on a different identity may not entirely transform an individual, the appropriation of a noble character will serve to control and restrain that person's immoralities and excesses:

yet the most of them
(Being either courtiers, or not wholly rude)
Respect of majesty, the place, and presence,
Will keep them within ring; *especially*
When they are not presented as themselves,
But masqu'd like others (5.5.23–28, emphasis mine).

In the end, attempts to reform through theater are not entirely successful. Although the resolution of the play seems to confirm this belief in
the reformative power of performance—for the rebellious members of
Cynthia's court are reformed—there is a moment of doubt inserted
into the scene. Although the goddess Cynthia seems successful in her
attempts to stage this performance, she questions whether the appropriation of these virtuous roles has the power to change the individuals
involved, or undermines the power of the virtues invoked:

how much more doth the seeming face
Of neighbor virtues, and their borrow'd names,
Add of lewd boldness, to loose vanities (5.11.56–58).

Rather than purifying the kingdom by creating virtue, Cynthia fears
that these performances are an infectious wound in the body politic
and determines that "we must lance these sores, / Or all will putrefy"
(5.11.67–68).[35]

The circumstances surrounding the performance in *Cynthia's Revels*
reflect the induction that precedes the play. Like the courtiers performing in the revels, the children seem wild and unruly until the play
begins and they are placed in roles that enact a taming of their insub-
ordination. In both cases, the actors' seditious behavior is a means to
a larger plan for societal reform. Cynthia identifies the danger of the
insubordinate courtiers in order to reform them; Jonson draws on the
potential for instability of the child actors as a means of reforming his
audience. Nevertheless, the two situations reveal a concern that theatrical spaces may be ultimately uncontrollable, for its participants may
have competing agendas.

Dismissing the conventional traits of the "ceremonious epilogue,"
which asks for the audience's favor, the epilogue to *Cynthia's Revels*

once again underscores the tenuous control the author holds over his actors. The young actor playing "Epilogue" appears, explaining:

> The Author (jealous, how your sense doth take
> His trauailes) hath enjoyned me to make
> Some short, and ceremonious epilogue;
> But if I yet know what, I am a rogue:
> He ties me to such lawes, as quite distract
> My thoughts; and would a year of time exact.
> I neither must be faint, remiss, nor sorry,
> Sowre, serious, confident, not peremptory:
> But betwixt these (3–11).

The child speaking Jonson's epilogue reveals that his behavior happens only under duress. Ironically, the same speech in which he stresses his obedience is one in which he seems to be misbehaving. The author has sent him out to satisfy the audience with an epilogue; instead, the child relates the author's instructions to him. Where he was to defend the play, the boy challenges the author, expressing his frustration with his acting duties, which "distract" his own thoughts and take up far too much of his time. No empty vessel to be filled, the boy's frustrations overflow to take over the conclusion of the play. Through the epilogue and induction, Jonson creates a frame narrative that suggests that although he, as author of the play, determines the play's content, the nature of the performers of his play creates an unstable force which, unless kept in check by strict laws and thorough instruction, is always on the edge of quickly spinning out of control.

Acting on Request: Boy Actors and Their Audience

Inductions depicting child actors, such as the one to *Cynthia's Revels,* served as models for a number of plays that followed. The elements of the inductions that once may have created confusion between the spaces outside of the performance and those within became conventions. Later plays stopped attempting to undermine the boundaries between audience and performance. Instead, they represented this process on-stage, reaffirming a space between audience and performer.

No longer a participant in the induction, the audience sees itself mirrored on stage—with some actors playing themselves and others playing audience members. Once the focus of an author and actors working to please, the audience of later plays such as *The Malcontent* (1604),[36] John Day's *The Isle of Gulls* (1606), and Francis Beaumont's *The Knight of The Burning Pestle* (c. 1607–1611) find themselves targeted by inductions that mimic their taste and perceptions.

These later inductions move their attention from unruly children to unruly audiences. Depictions of child actors shift from presenting them as threatening the success of the play to a vision of the children as the disciplined force attempting to save the theater from its audience. For it is the audience depicted in the induction that now threatens to take over the play. This possibility is alluded to in the induction to John Day's *The Isle of Gulls*, but it comes to full fruition in Francis Beaumont's *The Knight of the Burning Pestle*. Beaumont's play begins with an induction that mocks the audience's desire to influence the content of the play. In contrast to Day, who places his interchange between actors and audience in a clearly defined space external to the plot of his play, the induction of *The Knight of the Burning Pestle* (as well as the audience members introduced in it) quickly begins to take over until it dominates the entire play. Where traditionally the induction precedes the prologue, Beaumont allows his audience to hear three lines of the prologue before interrupting it with faux audience members, a citizen grocer named George and his wife Nell, who climb onto the stage. The couple demand that the boy sent out to speak the Prologue find them chairs and then insist that the child actors perform on a topic of their choice, in this case a play about a "grocer errant." No longer on the periphery of the drama, the induction elbows its way into the plot. Like the induction, other elements of the performance that would normally be considered external to the main narrative such as the interludes (traditionally filled with music and dancing) and the epilogue become extensions of the plot. Within the span of the performance, there is no clear division between the production of the play and its content. Characters move freely between the (fictional) realm of the audience and the space of the play.

Throughout the play, the actors are interrupted numerous times by the grocer and his wife, who seem to be unable to maintain any one perspective on the performance and its actors—perhaps as a result of seeing too many inductions. At times the audience members address the actors, asking about their welfare and demanding changes in the plot. At other moments, the citizens forget that they are watching a fictional production and converse with the characters of the play, asking them about their well-being and attempting to help them by providing information about actions that have happened in previous scenes. Frequently, the interruptions reveal an inability to read the play properly—for the wife and her grocer husband continually align themselves against the hero and heroine of *The London Merchant*, the play the children are performing. At other times, they take control of the performance, insisting that the children's play be replaced by one more to their taste acted by their servant Rafe.

The boy actors become the only force standing between the success of the play and the inferior plots demanded by the grocer and his wife, for the author figure is noticeably absent from *The Knight of the Burning Pestle*.[37] The boys function as enforcers of theatrical conventions and genres, attempting to forestall the dramatic inconsistencies conjured up by their audience. The children originally concede to George and Nell, allowing their man Rafe to perform his scenes during the interludes external to the boys' performance, but begin to resist when asked to allow Rafe to enter into their production. The children respond that such actions "lie contrary" to their play and will "hazard the spoiling" of the plot they are to perform (2.264–265). Later requests from the audience for imitations of popular plays glorifying the citizen classes like *The Travels of the Three English Brothers* and *The Four Prentices of London* are also resisted on the basis that they are "stale" and may alienate much of the audience. The style of closure asked for by the citizens (who want Rafe's comedy to end with his death) is also rejected on the grounds that it is inappropriate, for it does not fit the genre. Although the intrusions of the grocer and his wife are opposed for aesthetic reasons, the boys invoke more practical issues as well. A "spoiled play," the actors assert, will not only lead to a poor response from the audience but also a financial loss for the theater. As one of the boys warns Nell, her actions will "utterly spoil our play,/ and make it be hissed, and it cost money" (3.239–295).

Yet, the children are no match for the demands of George and Nell. Instead, they become the means through which the audience changes the play intended by the author. For, the young actors of *The Knight of the Burning Pestle* are vulnerable to the desire of the adults surrounding them. The children's obligations to the author and theater company fall by the wayside when they are faced with the demands of the physically proximate (and most likely physically stronger) grocer and his wife. Indeed, the desires of those closest to them on-stage take priority over those of the remainder of the audience sitting off-stage. The children reveal an awareness of this when they apologize to the rest of their audience for the path their play is to take, offering the excuse: "it is not our fault" (4.45–51).

At the same time, the children's deference to the grocer and his wife works to their advantage, for they profit from the venture. The grocer and his wife have paid more to acquire their on-stage seats than the general audience and thus have a larger investment in the performance. The financial relationship between the children and the citizens is emphasized by transactions in which the boys receive money from their on-stage audience. There are a number of instances in the play where the grocer and his wife either directly supply the child actors with money or are duped into providing money for the characters in the plot. It is not surprising, then, that the children turn against the instructions of the author and company (who do not provide them with any financial incentive) to follow the demands of the citizen and his wife who do.

George and Nell may have a flawed understanding of generic and theatrical conventions, yet their interruptions reveal a clear sense of the status of the child actor. Throughout the interruptions, the actors, even those playing adult characters, are frequently addressed and referred to as "boy" and "youth." Nell frequently seems more interested in nurturing the children than viewing the performance. Over the course of the play, Nell admires some of the children, worries about the health of others, provides one with money to buy frivolities, and even attempts to comfort and soothe a character who has recently been beaten on-stage. But the wife is also clearly aware that these children are performers who may not be working in the theater by choice. In fact, Beaumont uses the wife's interruptions to point to one of the more troubling circumstances surrounding the child actors, the abduction of children to perform in the theaters. The first indication of this practice is somewhat subtle, arising when the wife, admiring one of the boys, wonders about his origins:

> Sirrah, didst thou ever see a prettier child? How it behaves
> itself, I warrant ye, and speaks and looks, and pert up the
> head?—I pray you brother, with your favour, were you
> never none of Master Monkester's scholars? (1.94–97).

The wife's belief that the boy was once a scholar at Mulcaster's school reveals more sinister practices than a first glance might suggest. Although there is no certain evidence, historians of the children's companies indicate that some children were stolen from rival theater companies—Nell's particular emphasis on Mulcaster's school, St. Paul's (source of the Children of Paul's) suggests that this may have happened to this boy. That Nell is aware of such practices becomes clear in the next act when she remarks that Rafe's acting is so impressive that she'd be surprised if he was not also conscripted into the theater: "and he be not inveigled by some of / those paltry players, I ha' much marvel" (2.202–203).[38] For all of Nell and George's difficulty with theatrical decorum, they are nevertheless cognizant, albeit uncritical, of the practices used by the theaters to acquire their actors.

References to the unstable economic and social status of children in *The Knight of the Burning Pestle* are not limited to the interactions between the audience and actors, but permeate the intertwining stories acted by Rafe and the children. Indeed, the play's framing mechanism as well as its plots highlight the vulnerable and economically dependent condition of children in a number of social settings including the family, the workplace, and the theater. Even Nell, for all of her maternal instincts, reveals a notion of children as objects that can be easily replaced, rather than as irreplaceable individuals. Recalling a time when her child wandered off and almost drowned, the wife remembers Rafe as being particularly comforting for he offers to replace the child with "another as good" (2.344–349). The wife's comment once again reveals her inability to interpret properly, for she fails to recognize the lascivious implications of Rafe's offer. However, it also reveals a clear insight into the early modern status of children as commodities.

This understanding of children is not limited to Nell, but also can be seen in the plot of *The London Merchant*, the play originally slated to be performed by the children, which arises out of a tradition of plays in which children designated as their parents' property rebel against their parents' wishes. The Merchant's daughter, Luce, is twice identified as a possession that can be "stol'n away." Links between children and property are even internalized by the children, for Jasper, the hero of the play, admits that every drop of his blood "belongs" to his parents. Nevertheless, these children plot to liberate themselves from their parents' possession, with the play supporting their attempts.

By juxtaposing representations of children as commodities with commentary on the boy actors, Beaumont draws attention to the economic and cultural forces that enable the productions of the children's companies, revealing an awareness of the theater's own complicity with these practices. Like Jonson, Beaumont creates a plot that depends on the audience's recognition of the child as both property and agent. The transactions throughout the play in which the children receive money emphasize that this unpaid source of labor has no obligation to the company, and is an unstable force. Beaumont's play expresses the fear exposed by all the induction dramas: although children are expected to perform the parts supplied for them by the theater company, they can choose to do otherwise when offered a better incentive. Authors may attempt to control children by representing them on-stage, but can never be certain that their efforts will prevail.

Cultural ambivalences about children, which viewed them as both static vessels to be filled and untamed individuals impossible to control, enabled early modern authors to challenge audiences and attempt to position themselves as central forces controlling the theater. The child actor offered the audience a novel thrill—the possibility that some unexpected rebellion, some childish misbehavior, could erupt on stage. It is not surprising, then, that authors and theatrical companies capitalized on this potentially disruptive force. Yet in doing so, they created the very real possibility that the popularity of individual child actors, enhanced into celebrity by their portrayals in these inductions, would enable such children to control the production. We will probably never know whether or not the child actors took advantage of this power. But as the induction dramas suggest, it was always possible that the stage's jewel could steal the show.

Notes

1. Ben Jonson, *Epigrams,* in *Ben Jonson: A Critical Edition of the Major Works,* ed. Ian Donaldson (Oxford: Oxford University Press, 1985), 221–281. Epigram 120, "Epitaph on S. P." appears on page 270.

2. For an extended discussion of early modern conceptions of children as property see my article "Profitable Children: Children as Commodities in Early Modern England," in *Domestic Arrangements in Early Modern England,* ed. Kari Boyd McBride (Pittsburgh: Duquesne University Press, 2002), 209–243.

3. *Epigrams,* 22 "On My First Daughter" (229) and 45 "On My First Son" (236).

4. Georges Bataille. "The Notion of Expenditure," in *Visions of Excess: Selected Writings, 1927–1939,* ed. and trans. Allan Stoekl with Carl. R. Lovitt and Donald M. Leslie, Jr. (Minneapolis: University of Minnesota Press, 1985), 118–123.

5. Bataille's qualification that these "unproductive expenditures" must entail "a loss that must be as great as possible … to take on its true meaning" seems particularly relevant in this poem which emphasizes the loss faced by Jonson and his wife (118).

6. Patricia Fumerton, *Cultural Aesthetics: Renaissance Literature and the Practice of Social Ornament* (Chicago: University of Chicago Press, 1991). See Chapter 2, "Exchanging Gifts: The Elizabethan Currency of Children and Romance." Fumerton posits that such exchange works not only to solidify relationships between adults and noble families but also to add value to the child. Fumerton argues "gift exchange fashioned living trivialities into meaning-filled ornaments as valuable as jewels. Faced with the child's disconnection or detachment from civilized society, the Renaissance made of the child a kind of aesthetic artifact whose very detachedness *in the form of circulation* rendered it immensely precious" (37). Mary's value, Fumerton's argument would suggest, lies in the exchange between her father and the Virgin. Like Benjamin and S.P., Mary functions in a system in which children mediate social, economic, and artistic relations between adults.

7. Bataille views the return of the gift with interest as a sign of primitive potlatch, noting that usury is an element of the potlatch (121). However, the transaction Jonson describes here seems to be more rooted in images of early capitalist ventures. This description of a loan into which one has unwisely invested too much hope, and must suffer a personal loss when it is due, also appears in Shakespeare's *Merchant of Venice,* with the depiction of the troubles caused by Antonio's merchant ventures. Like Jonson, Antonio has placed too much hope in an uncertain means of profit (shipping ventures) and must pay back a loan at great cost.

8. See Fumerton, Chapter 3, for a discussion of the "Double Elizabethan Self," which conceals a private self "withheld from the cultural whole" amid the ornamentation of a public self, revealed through aesthetic production.

9. This type of controlled exchange invokes one of the ways in which early modern authors attempted to deal with the problems of defining children as commodities: children could be exchanged, but only within controlled market systems (see the discussion of Stockwood and Gibbon in Busse, "Profitable Children" 220–231).

10. David Lee Miller argues that the children of Jonson's poems are caught up in literary systems of exchange between the poet and his readers. Miller's language invokes a theatrical relationship of children performing the scripts adults have drafted for them when he describes young Benjamin and Salomon as figures who, even after their deaths, are coopted to fulfill the poet/playwright's aesthetic needs. Miller turns to the last line of "On My First Son" to argue that even when the son appears to speak posthumously in the poem, it is the father's voice we hear "tell[ing] a dead child what to say on that inconceivable occasion when it will 'speak'" See David Lee Miller, "Writing the Specular Son: Jonson, Freud, Lacan, and the (K)not of Masculinity," in *Desire in the Renaissance: Psychoanalysis and Literature*, ed. Valeria Finucci and Regina Schwartz (Princeton, NJ: Princeton University Press, 1994), 240–241.

11. Writs of impressment date back to the Middle Ages and were originally granted to the masters of the choir schools at St. Paul's and the Chapel Royal so that they could fill the choir with able singers. As the choir schools mutated into training grounds for stage performances, the masters used their powers to acquire actors as well. Although the strongest documentation we have of the practice of impressment, a 1601 lawsuit filed by Henry Clifton in response to the forcible seizure of his son Thomas to perform for the Children of the Chapel at Blackfriars (the company for which Pavy performed), condemns the practice, it was entirely legitimate and royally authorized. Salomon Pavy was one of the many children listed in the Clifton suit as having been abducted by Nathaniel Giles to act on stage at Blackfriars. By 1606, perhaps in response to the Clifton suit, masters were prohibited from impressing boys to act on stage. See Harold Newcomb Hillebrand, *The Child Actors: A Chapter in Elizabethan Stage History* (New York: Russell and Russell, 1964), esp. 196–197, and Charles William Wallace, *The Children of the Chapel at Blackfriars: 1597–1603* (Lincoln: University of Nebraska Press, 1908) esp. 60–72.

12. There are interesting links to the Clifton suit here, for Clifton's suit had validity only in that the directors of the company, Nathaniel Giles and Henry Evans, mistakenly took the son of a gentleman. The abduction of the child was not a problem; the identity of the abducted child was. The image of the fates mistaking Pavy for an old man, who could legitimately be taken, and the desire to keep this acquisition after the mistake is discovered seems to invoke the concerns raised by the Clifton suit, where the theater directors originally refused to return the boy, even after learning of his identity (see Wallace 77–83).

13. David Riggs, *Ben Jonson: A Life* (Cambridge, MA: Harvard University Press, 1989), 92.
14. See Gerald Eades Bentley, *The Profession of Player in Shakespeare's Time* (Princeton, NJ: Princeton University Press, 1984), 25–63 for a discussion of sharers in the theater companies.
15. *Epigrams* 252.
16. That Jonson was aware of the differences and using them for distinct purposes becomes clear through the three epigrams written for Lucy, Countess of Bedford. Of the three poems, two are titled "To" the countess and directly address her (Epigrams 84 and 94, pp 250 and 255). The other epigram (76, which appears first in the collection) is titled "On Lucy, Countess of Bedford" and depicts the countess as the ideal subject for Jonson's poetry the "kind of creature I could most desire/ To honour, serve and love, as poets use" (247). In this epigram, Lucy functions much as the children do, as the inspiration for Jonson's poetry.
17. Nora Johnson, *The Actor as Playwright in Early Modern Drama* (Cambridge: Cambridge University Press, 2003), 20.
18. John Marston, *Antonio and Mellida*, in *The Malcontent and Other Plays*, ed. Keith Sturgess (New York: Oxford, 1997), 3–55. *Jack Drum's Entertainment: or The Comedy of Pasquill and Katherine*, in *The Plays of John Marston*, ed. H. Harvey Wood, vol 3 (Edinburgh: Oliver and Boyd, 1939), 175–241. John Day, *The Isle of Guls: A Critical Edition*, ed. Raymond S. Burns (New York: Garland, 1980). Francis Beaumont, *The Knight of the Burning Pestle*, ed. Michael Hattaway (New York: Norton, 1991). All citations to these works in this article are from these editions and are cited hereafter in the text.
19. The failure to do more than cursorily mention the children performing in these companies, as much a result of a neglect or lack of interest as it is of a paucity of sources, has not only created a significant gap in our understandings of the early modern theater, but has led to misconceptions about the status of the child actor. The reasons for dismissal of the children as insignificant are specious, for they frequently rely on a conception of child actors as aberrations, curiosities particular to an infant stage of the early modern theater. The problem, of course, is not only theoretical but also practical. The children's lack of authority and inability to participate in the economies of the theater means that there are few records concerning them, leaving historians and literary critics with scant evidence for their discussions. Thus, even promising titles, such as Reavley Gair's *The Children of Paul's: The Story of a Theatre Company, 1553–1608* (Cambridge: Cambridge University Press, 1982), Wallace's *The Children of the Chapel at Blackfriars: 1597–1603*, Hillebrand's *The Child Actors*, and Michael Shapiro's *Children of the Revels: The Boy Companies of Shakespeare's Time and Their Plays* (New York: Columbia University Press, 1977) fail to provide detailed discussions of the children, instead focusing on the institutional structures of the companies and the plays they performed. Despite its promising title and purpose, the more recent *A New History of Early English Drama*, with its stated goal "to provide the most comprehensive account yet available of early English drama," lists only eight pages under

the index heading "Actors, boy," with five of those pages devoted to boys acting in women's roles. John D. Cox and David Scott Kastan, eds., *A New History of Early English Drama* (New York: Columbia University Press, 1997).

20. See Hillebrand 143–150; Gair, 110–112; and G. K. Hunter, *English Drama 1586–1642: The Age of Shakespeare* (Oxford: Clarendon, 1997), 280 n 3.

21. "The War of the Theaters" is also referred to as "the poet's quarrel" and the "poetomachia." For discussions of the quarrel, and the plays which are classified as belonging to the debate see Alfred Harbage, *Shakespeare and the Rival Traditions,* (New York: Macmillan, 1952), 90–119; Riggs 63–85; and Hunter 299–300.

22. Designating Jonson and Marston as "the founding fathers of the new drama," G. K. Hunter notes their similar "avant-garde" projects, which "hope to obliterate the past with an explosion of novelty," using the boy companies as "the appropriate launching pad for their ambition" (283).

23. Hunter suggests that Jonson and Marston's interest in the boys was grounded in their ability to control them: "No doubt both of them relished the opportunity to impose themselves on boy actors trained to subservience (as were all Elizabethan children)" (285). Elizabethans may have attempted to train their children into subservience, but were constantly forced to acknowledge the limitations of this training. Indeed, what seems to interest Jonson and Marston most about the boys in the inductions is the possibility that the boys are an uncontrollable force.

24. The inductions of the early 1600s took a new and distinct form from earlier inductions. Unlike the "causal inductions" popular in the 1580s which were "used ... to introduce the motives or external causes of the main action of the drama," later inductions served to emphasize the motives surrounding the production of the drama. For discussion of the causal induction see Robert Y. Turner "The Causal Induction in Some Elizabethan Plays," *Studies in Philology* 60.2 (1963): 183–190, esp 183. Lynn Humphrey Elliott defines the induction as "an independent action, involving two or more speaking roles, which, although it occurs prior to the main action, creates a link, usually thematic, into the main action." See Elliott, "Engagement and Detachment: The Function of the Induction in Ben Jonson's Plays" (Ph.D. diss, University of California Santa Barbara, 1972), 9. I find Elliott's definition of inductions appealing; however, I am particularly interested in the ways inductions work outside of the context of the plays that follow. For, as much as they are a link into the play, they are also an action external to it.

25. In this way, inductions function much like prefaces to Renaissance printed works. Like the prefaces that Wendy Wall examines in *The Imprint of Gender: Authorship and Publication in the English Renaissance* (Ithaca, NY: Cornell University Press, 1993), inductions "mark the threshold of the work" and "form a lens through which the [audience] views the text, and assesses its relationship to its public audience" (174).

26. See Elliott and Shapiro.

27. Shapiro, 109.

28. Discussing the induction to *Jack Drum's Entertainment*, Shapiro writes "these inductions remind the spectators that they are watching actors in a fashionable private theater, a fact which they 'always knew,' confirming their sense of participation in a courtly or aristocratic ritual" (112). The foundation of Shapiro's argument however, that the audience of the private theaters was an elite audience, has been contested by Gair who argues that records showing servants and middle class individuals attending performances at Paul's are not surprising, as it would be cheaper for residents living near Paul's to pay the higher entrance fees than for them to pay travel costs to attend the cheaper public theaters across the Thames (72–73).

29. See Michael Witmore's essay "'Oh that I had Her!' The Voice of the Child in a Body Possessed" and Michael Mascuch's "The Godly Child's 'Power and Evidence' in the word: Orality and literacy in the Ministry of Sarah Wight," in this volume. In his description of a child minister, Mascuch argues that the child herself becomes less significant than the events that happen to her. He marks the transition of Sarah Wight from a child speaking words supplied by God to a young woman ministering to others as the transition of Wight into adulthood, implying that agency in word and deed is a mark of adulthood.

30. Witmore's language indicates the theatrical nature of the imitations of the Throckmorton children in later witchcraft cases.

31. Although this actor has commonly been identified as Salmon Pavy, Matthew Stuggle has recently offered the compelling premise that Pavy actually played the boy who speaks the prologue, "a persona much more in line with his reputation as 'the stage's jewel'" ("Casting the Prelude in *Cynthia's Revels" Notes and Queries* 248.1 (2003): 62–63).

32. Bentley suggests that costumes were most likely the "greatest expense" for theater companies (88).

33. If Matthew Stuggle is correct in identifying this actor as Pavy, this moment can be viewed as Jonson acknowledging the importance of an actor's celebrity, while trying to harness its power for his own purpose.

34. Of course, we must be careful not to fall into a reading of this induction that believes the children to be actively disrupting the play. For, of course, Jonson's induction is scripted and controlled. The negotiations of the induction are completely fictional.

35. Cynthia's concern that theatricality can harm the body politic echoes a similar fear expressed by antitheatricalist Stephen Gosson: "if private men be suffered to forsake their calling because they desire to walk gentleman-like ... proportion is so broken ... and the whole body must be dismembered and the prince or head cannot choose but sicken" (*Plays Confuted in Five Actions*, 1582, pref. Arthur Freeman [New York: Garland, 1972] G7r-v).

36. I am referring her to the version of *The Malcontent* amended by John Webster for the King's Men's performance of Marston's earlier version of the play. Webster adds an induction that mimics the style of those performed by the boys. In doing so, he highlights the fact that this play has

been stolen from the children's companies. *The Malcontent,* ed. W. David Kay (New York: Norton, 1998).

37. Roy J. Booth offers that: "Beaumont is either too aloof to imagine himself as a dramatized dramatist horrified by what the actors and audience are doing to his plot, or represents an age of theater in which such authorial self-consciousness is still developing" ("'Down With Your Title, Boy!' Beaumont's *The Knight of the Burning Pestle* and its Insurgent Audience," *QWERTY: Arts Litteratures and Civilisations du Monde Anglophone* 5 (1995): 56). Although I would agree with Booth that Beaumont is writing in a time in which this "authorial self-consciousness" is coming into being, I hesitate to use this as an explanation for the lack of the author's presence, particularly as the authorial presence is so clearly alluded to in inductions by Jonson and Marston.

38. Michael Hattaway's notes on the play draw attention to these practices and identify Mulcaster as the master of Paul's.

6

THE GODLY CHILD'S "POWER AND EVIDENCE" IN THE WORD

Orality and Literacy in the Ministry of Sarah Wight

MICHAEL MASCUCH

It has long been an uncontested and largely unqualified commonplace of historiography that the story of the Protestant Reformation is a story of reading and writing. This is a corollary of the equally unchallenged view of Christianity as a religion of the book.[1] Not surprisingly, both opinions owe their popularization to the Protestant Reformation itself, whose controversialists and publicists routinely exploited and touted print as an evangelical instrument. Besides the blatant message of the numerous esoteric works of biblical commentary and interpretation from this period that established reading and writing as a pillar of piety and 'true' religion, we can find in a popular text such as John Foxe's *Book of Martyrs* (1563) both a documentary archive of the acts of Christian martyrs and a monument to writing itself, which was the sine qua non for the martyrs' renown. But if we look beyond the words of clerics and other learned advocates to the experience of laypersons, especially the experience of illiterate women and children, the Reformation story bears a somewhat different moral. In the practice of the less educated laity we find the persistence of a culture whose religious knowledge and authority remained rooted in speech and oral modes of communication.

The account of the ordeal of Sarah Wight, an adolescent girl troubled by sin whose attempted suicide left her in a coma from which she awoke after eleven weeks, attributing her recovery to a visitation by Christ, affords a glimpse of this other culture. All that we know about Sarah Wight derives from the Protestant "best-seller"[2] tract composed for the press and first published in 1647 by the Baptist/Independent minister Henry Jessey, *The Exceeding Riches of Grace Advanced by the Spirit of Grace, in an Empty Nothing Creature, viz. Mistress Sarah Wight.*[3] As this title suggests, Jessey's book presents a sort of religious conversion narrative that anticipates John Bunyan's now better-known example, *Grace Abounding to the Chief of Sinners,* in both its concept and execution. Like *Grace Abounding* and other works of its kind, *The Exceeding Riches of Grace* is concerned with an imminent spiritual reality that obviated regard for worldly posterity. Consequently, Jessey does not tell us much more about Sarah Wight than what is necessary to his purpose in publishing, as he put it, "her precious Evangelicall expressions," (2) which was "for great refreshing to many sad, troubled, disconsolate souls," (A8v) and "exalt[ing] and commend[ing] *the LORD*" (A3). Yet despite a paucity of personal detail, it is possible to piece together a rudimentary picture of Sarah Wight and her milieu. Wight was celebrated in her day, not as Martin Luther was, for being an author, a bearer of texts, but rather like a charismatic saint of old, for the performance of a miracle and her powers of healing. In the figure of Sarah Wight, the "child" symbolizes not so much a body's physical immaturity as an intellectual disposition toward religious knowledge and authority, that of the "common" or "simple sort" of person in whose experience reading and writing and the habits of thought that inhere in such skills occupied a relatively minor place. In the child-like mentality of Sarah Wight and her similarly disposed communicants, embodiment and gesture are the dominant modes of religious practice and understanding.

The principal events related by Jessey occurred several months before Wight's sixteenth birthday; the book containing the relation appeared just a month or two after. Wight was the child of Mary Wight, a widow whose latest husband, Sarah's father, had been a clerk in the office of the auditor and the exchequer. Jessey describes Mary Wight as a "gracious *Matrone*" (A2), residing "in *Lawrence Pountney*-Lane near *Caning-Street*, in *LONDON*," (5) within a Tower Hill parish that Jessey frequented as a preacher. When Wight was nine years old, her mother suffered her own "deep afflictions of Spirit, and sore Temptations," (6) during which time Sarah was briefly placed in her paternal grandmother's custody, until, with Jessey's ministerial assistance, Mary Wight found Christ, not long after. By her "godly faithfull" grandmother, according to Jessey, Sarah was *well trained up in the Scriptures*"; in her "faithfull" (5) mother's house, the girl "gave her selfe much to read and study the *Scriptures*," which "she then understood not aright" (6). This misunderstanding no doubt exacerbated a predisposition to despair. Jessey reports that "[f]rom her childhood, [Sarah Wight] was of a *tender* heart, and oft afflicted in Spirit" (6).

However, Wight's "more violent Temptations" began at age eleven (7). At the instigation of a superior, she stole some trivial thing. A month or so later, she lied to her mother about the whereabouts of an article of clothing. Afflicted in her conscience by these two misdeeds, Wight became "terrified ever since, that she was shut out of Heaven, and must be damn'd, damn'd" (7). Living "in a grievous horrour day and night" (8–9), she commenced a string of unsuccessful suicide attempts, seeking to die, in turn, "by drowning, strangling, stabbing, [and] … beat[ing] out her braines" (7–8). She meanwhile consulted with several godly ministers both in London and beyond, to little or no avail. Ultimately Wight's unrest and self-destructive behavior drove her exhausted mother to hire an additional maid, whose sole duty was to act as Sarah's bodyguard, in order "to prevent her mischieving her selfe" (13).

The servant, a woman named Hannah Gay, came to assume her place in the Wight household on the evening of April 6, 1647. On arrival, she found her new charge already in distress, "weeping most bitterly, & wringing her hands grievously, saying, *I am a Reprobate, a Castaway, I never had a good thought in all my life. I have been under sinne ever since I can remember, when I was but a childe*, &c" (14). Wight's condition rapidly escalated from bad to worse. According to Jessey, who was not then present but took the testimony of Gay and Mary Wight verbatim,

Her hands and feet were clunched, so as shee could not stand. She was tempted to blaspheme God and die. And when shee was urged to speak, her tongue was smitten. Afterward she being laid down, she said to her Mother, *Ile lye still, and heare what God will say to me: He will speak Peace, Peace. If God will speak a word of Peace at the last moment, I should be contented.* Then she desired them that none might trouble her, but that shee might lie in peace. And she lay still, as in a sleep, or as in a trance rather (15).

She stirred only occasionally, to drink a few cups of water. Here, from Jessey's standpoint, at least, Wight's story truly begins, for, in the minister's words, "… this was the time of love, when the exceeding riches of Grace was advanced" (15).

Besides her lameness, Wight was found to be "struck blind and deafe" (15). She lay abed in this state, eating nothing and drinking little, for four days. On the fourth day, about midnight, according to Jessey, Wight started to come to her senses, and "began to expresse the first expressions of comforts" (15), or "speeches of Grace" (3), which she continued to do, sporadically, in the presence of her mother, stepbrother, Hannah Gay, Mr. Simpson the parish minister, and Jessey, for about two weeks. During this period, word spread of Wight's condition. After public offerings of prayer in her name both in her own parish church and in those of the adjacent parishes, a steady stream of "diverse neighbors and loving friends" headed down the lane and up the stairs to Wight's bedside, desiring "to hear her speake, being much taken and greatly refreshed with what they had heard of her" (35). *The Exceeding Riches of Grace* records the exact words of twenty-three separate conferences Wight had with visitors during her seventy-day convalescence—roughly, one every three days. The attendees at these bedroom assemblies ranged in number from one to as many as twelve persons at a time, comprising an extended congregation whose social composition included lords and ladies of the lower nobility, the local gentry, and most frequently, common servants. Wight graciously entertained such guests, lying with a sheet of linen over her weak eyes, speaking to her company typically "with a low voyce, in a humble, modest, melting manner, her teares sometimes stopping her speech" (35). According to Jessey, who was the most frequent bedside visitor outside the Wight household, "He and the rest, listened, and were greatly affected in hearing her" (35), being moved "even to admiration, in hearing a child so speak" (38). In fact, Jessey apologized, in one aside, "It cannot affect so much in hearing it at second hand, as if you had heard it her self, with such brokennes of heart uttering it" (35).

Nevertheless, the minister sought out and scrupulously transcribed nearly every word Wight was heard to utter, as well as those of her interlocutors, on a daily basis (55). At first, Jessey intended his transcript merely to provide some exemplary and edifying "golden sayings" and "last words," as it appeared to everyone that Wight was gradually starving herself to death. Early modern evangelicals of both the radical and moderate sorts highly valued the last words of persons deemed to have died gracefully, as Wight was thought likely to do. Besides a memorial function, the preservation of such discourse served a practical purpose, by exemplifying how to live and die in a godly way, and thereby to anticipate salvation. Ministers accordingly catered to popular expectation, collecting and then publishing pious utterances by means of the preached and occasionally printed funeral sermon seasoned with sayings. Throughout her ordeal, Sarah Wight proved to be an "exceedingly rich" source of such seasoning. However, after the abrupt and unanticipated full recovery of her senses and appetite nearly two months since she began her public interviews, Jessey ended up producing instead of a funeral sermon a quasi-biographical book, a written documentary testament of Wight's "deliverance," which he believed to be a "marvellous" (A6v) and "wonder[ful]" (A7) work of God's "tender-Mercie" (A2v), worthy of remembrance through magnification in print (A2v).

Although a publication such as *The Exceeding Riches of Grace* was not unknown to early modern England—it is regarded today as a specimen of the small but important prophet/prodigy/portent division of the large "wonderfull and strange news" class of early modern English printed texts, and as such likely found a ready audience within a cultural horizon of expectation defined by providential occurrences[4]— it remains nevertheless remarkable for its painstaking exactness in preserving and promoting the experience and pronouncements of an otherwise unremarkable individual, a female and an adolescent, to boot.

Jessey's apparent effort to position this "empty nothing creature" center stage in his account, making her its authority, while relegating his own presence in the text to the marginal role of amanuensis and advocate, is untypical of relations describing the spiritual experience of women and children. Even less typical is the work's brief but intense popularity: it went to seven editions in the first ten years of publication, with two more in the next ten. The total numbered twelve before the end of the seventeenth century.[5] It is fair to say the Wight phenomenon stirred significant and unparalleled contemporary interest, in both its live and recorded performances.

Recently, scholars have cottoned to the figure of Wight as an example of the exceptional power of the female "prophets" of seventeenth-century England.[6] For instance, Nigel Smith considers Wight's speeches within the context of radical puritan religious prophesy of the 1640s and 1650s, noting that by her confessional discourse Wight "gains the authority of an inspired and wise woman within the community who may be consulted for spiritual advice."[7] Barbara Ritter Dailey, who focuses on Jessey's printed account as an example of texts in the longstanding *ars moriendi* tradition, attributes the power of Wight's "lay preaching" to the credence seventeenth-century evangelical Protestants, like their Roman Catholic forebears, habitually accorded to the last dying words of the godly.[8] Taking the work of these predecessors as a point of departure, Katharine Gillespie accords Wight the symbolic status of a "girl-king" in her account of early modern women's participation in the cultural formation of what Gillespie calls the "sovereign individual."[9] Wight's profile has been elevated further by a rising tide of scholarly interest in the experience of early modern children. In her account of Wight's prophetic power, Susan Hardman Moore stresses Wight's social position as a child, over and above her femaleness. She poses the difficult question, "how could a child leap so dramatically from the periphery to the centre, from inferiority to authority[?]" in order to propose that Wight epitomizes the vulnerable spiritual character that early modern contemporaries attributed to children, which formed the basis of the fascination she engendered.[10] This is, I believe, a plausible position, though it cries out for further research into the beliefs of seventeenth-century evangelical Protestants about children's emotions and spirituality. In what follows, I will develop an alternative explanation for the popular interest in Wight, which focuses on the girl's religious insight and communicative practice, rather than on her role as a woman, a dying Christian, or a child.

Certainly, Moore is correct to insist on Sara Wight's role as a child. Although, according to long tradition, the age of legal adulthood in various contexts of early modern English society hovered around fifteen, the seventeenth century saw numerous attempts to retard youth's attainment of legal maturity. Religious "adulthood" was also delayed, to the extent that, as the historian Keith Thomas reports, in early modern England, "The full Christian life was not for adolescents."[11] In keeping with these trends, Jessey repeatedly used the term "child" to express both Wight's worldly and spiritual immaturity, above all other likely means of describing her. By such usage Jessey intended a figurative meaning as well, in which Wight as "child" epitomized a specific relation to scripture that corresponded to the understanding of many who knew of her story, either by reading it themselves or hearing tell of it by others: that of the unlearned and/or inexperienced soul. In making this association Jessey drew upon a linkage commonly made in the titles and introductions of early modern catechisms, which indicate that childhood and ignorance of Christian knowledge were synonymous.[12]

But we can be even more precise than Moore has been in refining our description of Wight: rather than as a child-prophet, the girl was in fact presented to her audience as a child-"minister." In displaying Wight thus, Jessey merely endorsed Wight's own self-description, which emerged in the dramatic culmination of her ordeal. On day seventy-five by Jessey's reckoning, June 10, to be exact, at about 10 o'clock at night, Wight experienced a manifestation of divine presence, which "came in, as if it had been whispered to her soule from God" (134). The voice instructed her, Wight later said, "as ... Paul," to "*Rise, and stand upon thy feet: For I have appeared to thee for this purpose, to be a Minister and a witness. ...*" "So," Jessey explained to his readers, "God had bid her *Arise* ... that she might be a *Witness* of the Grace of God, to *minister* to others, what he had *administered* unto her. And that as *Paul should be a witnes, both of the sufferings of Christ for him, and of his own sufferings for the Name of Christ: So shee* should be a witness of both in like manner. ... and now shee must testifie and minister that Grace of God that shee had received, unto others" (135). Such a concept of Wight's role was underwritten by the book's reference to nine other scripture-places "of *ministering to others*," which "were brought into her besides that of *Paul*" (136–137). By this spectral inundation of vocalized scriptural authority, according to Jessey, "a full perswasion was given to her therewith, that so it should be with her selfe" (137). Wight's conversion and subsequent vocation, it seems, was the palpable experience of a calling by the voice of the spirit: it addressed her in a manner that she and Jessey both interpreted as a divine ordination or sacred commission, endorsed by holy writ, to minister the exceeding riches of the Christian god's grace to others.

After daybreak the next morning, Wight directed her maid to find and read aloud from scripture the actual chapter and verse places that sounded out to convince her in the night, and then, speaking with "*power* and evidence," not in the feeble manner of the days before, asked for some broiled fish (138). She ate it, miraculously, "not finding the least distemper or inconvenience at all thereby" (138), then dressed, "and *arose*, and *stood* on her feet" (139). Fifteen days later she was able to walk unassisted (143). Five days after that she left her house for the first time, to attend a monthly fast at nearby Great Allhallows (147). Immediately following the service, Wight traveled about a mile to call on "two women, that were in deep despaire, for refreshing them by the comforts shee had received, being greatly affected with their sad conditions." The next day, she traveled another mile, to visit another sad soul; meanwhile, many others still "resorted to" her at home "daily … who would draw out expressions from her" (147–148). By appearances, Wight was conducting, as one recent scholar puts it, "a regular day clinic" for despairing women.[13] Jessey reports that Wight found herself so in demand that she had to remove temporarily to the country, "that she might be more *retired*, and recover strength, for further service among the little ones, that are afflicted &c" (148). The importance and necessity of Wight's activity to Jessey seems clear: without reservation, he praises the "notable and marvailous … work" of God in delivering Wight from perdition and enabling her "so to improve and make use of the *Holy Scriptures*, to despairing soules, and otherwayes" (150–151).

To be sure, Wight's "ministry" was hardly conventional. Given the prohibitions placed upon both women and children in early modern English civil society, ecclesiastical authorization of her sacred commission would have been unthinkable. However, Wight was divinely ordained during the heady days of the Interregnum, when sectarian interests held sway politically, and all sorts of unorthodox religious practices flourished. Had her manifestation occurred at some other time, she might not have found the favor of such an eloquent and enthusiastic advocate as Jessey, who cautioned readers with "no experience of such kind speakings of the Spirit ... or of such manner or measure of Faith as here is mentioned," not to *decry, or cry down what thou knowest not*" (157). Even so, there were limits to what pretensions to power might be allowed of laypeople, especially the underage. As the historian Anne Laurence notes, despite the leveling tendencies of many sectarian congregations at this time, "it is far from clear how widespread was the belief that ministerial gifts might be found in anyone, and that they must be given the freedom to exercise them."[14] Although uneducated "mechanic" men might gain authority as ministers, women, even articulate, somewhat educated women of middling or better social status, such as Sarah Wight, who appears to have acquired at least the grammar school basics (she could write as well as read), were largely excluded from church organization by the sects, to the same degree that they were by the Church of England.[15] Children were so beyond the pale in this respect that despite their ubiquity in society—at the middle of the seventeenth century, children under fifteen made up roughly 35 percent of the population[16]—little or no mention whatsoever is made of their ministerial qualifications in the early modern controversies over ecclesiastical authority. We might expect such silence, as the sects continued to respect differences of age even after they set aside most other marks of social distinction, evidence of the degree to which the practice of early modern society adhered to its traditional gerontocratic ideal.[17] Indeed, to the best of my knowledge, there is virtually no evidence of child ministers in evangelical Protestantism before the mid-nineteenth century. To the extent that children were seen or heard at all in early modern England, they appear most frequently as perpetrators of disorder. On the whole, children were subject, and hardly equal, to the authority of adults.[18] The same can also be said of the relation between the unlettered laity and the lettered, especially the lettered clergy.

In this light, Wight's personal spiritual authority was as remarkable as her deliverance from despair and imminent death. However, *The Exceeding Riches of Grace* cautions against paying undue attention to Wight's person. It admonishes readers to "Exalt the Lord the Creator alone, and not the Creature: Say not, *What a one is shee?* but, *What a God is he?* in all reading, or speaking, of her, or to her. For the Lord is jealous of his glory, and will not give it to an image of him" (156). In keeping with this warning, Jessey limited his work to establishing the legitimacy of Wight's ministry, explaining the child's "power and evidence" in the word as yet another divine gift. Anticipating that many would "*hardly beleeve*" that Wight's discourse "*should flow from a* childe, *not sixteen years old*" (A6v), he listed the names of the child's more socially prominent visitors and other reputable witnesses "for better satisfying some, that would know many particulars distinctly" (A). Furthermore, in the second edition's epistle to the Christian reader, Jessey explained that

> *If some yet say;* How is it possible, that one so young, and never under-
> standing to purpose till now, should be able so to speak? *Tis answered;*
> This is the Lord's work and it is marvellous in our eyes: who out of the
> mouths of babes and sucklings, hath ordained strength, & perfected
> praise. ... *And hath promised to his, to* power out of his Spirit in the last
> dayes, upon them, and upon their children, their sons and daughters. ...
> *Our Lord* Jesus *promised to his Disciples, that his* Holy Spirit *should bring to
> their remembrance, what he had said to them. ... This* good Spirit *brought to
> her remembrance now, when it was most usefull, what she had read and heard
> formerly, and opened her heart to understand them: and opened her mouth to
> utter them in an* humbling, melting *manner; as he opened to her; even* her
> bodily eyes and ears were held ... (second edition, London, 1647, Av).

But Jessey could not simply wield the sword of holy writ to dictate how others should regard this marvel. Despite its manifold reference to scriptural precedent as the grounds of the girl's activity, in order for Jessey's book's bid to legitimate Wight's ministry ultimately to succeed, its subject's performance had first to be deemed credible by the local community of believers, the majority of whom were of the simple sort.

There reputation was established first and foremost by eye- and ear-witness. For this reason Jessey situated his transcriptions of Wight's twenty-three conferences with visitors in *The Exceeding Riches of Grace* to underwrite, literally as well as figuratively, Wight's positive reception among her neighbors and friends. The interviews show how many and diverse guests, including physicians and ministers who minutely examined her physical and theological condition, were moved to affectation and admiration by Wight. The book authorizes Wight's ministry on the one hand by describing and documenting the personal functions and effects of Wight's work within the local community, her ad hoc congregation, and on the other by stamping the community's embrace of her with the imprimatur of scripture.

Moreover, although as far as can be told she returned to her parish church to assume her place within its body as a regular communicant, Wight also appears to have maintained a special, independent status as, to apply a revised version Nigel Smith's phrase, an inspired and wise child-minister within the local community, to whom many resorted for spiritual advice, fellowship, and solace. This is the most plausible way to understand Jessey's concept of Wight as a "minister to others," because private meetings of laypeople, with or without a formally ordained minister present, held in a domestic setting, for mutual edification, were common among evangelicals of all stripes at this time. There are clues to the fact that Wight's private ministry was no fleeting phenomenon, like the sudden, stellar, and quickly spent reputations of two other mid-century child prophets whose experiences were magnified in printed books, the eleven-year-old Martha Hatfield and the fifteen-year-old Anna Trapnel. One clue to Wight's longevity is the printing in 1656, nine years after her manifestation of grace, of a "pleasant and profitable letter" Wight wrote to an anonymous friend, "expressing the joy [that] is to be had in God in great, long, and sore affliction" (t.p.). This original work of Wight's hand—the only one known to survive—was written on the occasion of Wight's elder stepbrother's death, and allegedly published by one "R.B." without the author's knowledge and consent, suggesting that Wight's name and discourse were still current in wider London, and perhaps even provincial, evangelical circles.[19] Another clue to Wight's active presence is the continued popularity of Jessey's book, every edition of which prominently displayed the location of her home and parish church to would-be pilgrims, right up until the Restoration, when political forces beyond both Jessey's and Wight's control moved to put an end to sectarianism and independency in religion. As a result, the sort of gatherings around Wight that were depicted in Jessey's book, of persons "over and above those of the same Household," to pray, read, preach, or expound scripture together, were explicitly deemed by the 1664 Conventicle Act as instances of unlawful assembly.[20] Taken together, these clues strongly suggest that Wight stayed active and effective as a local itinerant minister well beyond the time of her miraculous recovery, at least until the Restoration, and possibly after.

If we can thus accept as fact the legitimacy of Wight's unorthodox ministry, it remains to consider the grounds of her evangelical power and evidence, as it was experienced by her contemporaries. Such consideration returns us to the difficult question posed by Susan Moore about Wight's case, concerning a child's dramatic leap from inferiority to authority. Moore's suggestion, that in Wight adults appreciated a child's extreme spiritual ingenuousness, and thus perhaps a kind of authenticity or capacity to discover truth,[21] is a start at an answer. However, this approach doesn't account for the peculiarity of Wight's case in comparison to those of other marvelous children, such as the aforementioned Trapnel and Hatfield. These two were mere prophets: they testified while others listened, observed, located signs of a divine message, and rendered meanings, thus ending the performance, which was short-lived and largely out of the children's hands. Their authority remained negligible at best, and the duration of their interest to others brief. Wight, by contrast, despite her simplicity, administers: her experience and words refresh many sad, troubled, disconsolate souls individually, and her activity is, despite Jessey's efforts, self-authorizing. The more Wight comes into contact with others, it seems, the more others want to come into contact with her. Her ministry is the embodiment of a self-fulfilling prophecy. Whereas the child-prophets are merely mediums of a divine message broadcast indiscriminately, Wight the child-minister constitutes a message in herself. And that message, I propose, is herself; or rather, it is her gracefully affecting physical presence. This was a performance to which Wight's youthfulness certainly contributed. However, it derived its force essentially from the girl's resort to physical gesture, and her manner of conversing with others who, like herself, were unfulfilled by their limited and confusing experience with scripture as text.

Despite its obvious confidence in writing, *The Exceeding Riches of Grace* makes much of embodied communication. It appears that in publishing the book, Jessey, who would later pen the landmark *Catechisme for Babes* (1652), deliberately exploited print's potential to "reinvigorate" and inspire oral culture, a process that has been well documented in recent scholarship.[22] The majority of Jessey's text is presented as a dialogue, to emphasize speech rather than writing. All of Wight's words are printed in italics, to suggest their spoken resonance. Curiously, perhaps, given that Jessey was a Cambridge graduate, a Hebrew scholar who projected a revised translation of the Bible, and was widely recognized for his minute and accurate knowledge of scripture, his book routinely places aspects of concrete physical sensation over metaphysical verbal semiotics. This priority is apparent, for example, in Wight's personal concept of "grace," which is central to both her ministerial rationale and Jessey's attempt to legitimate it. When questioned by a "good *Lady*," a worthy patron of piety, in the company of other such ladies and ministers at Wight's bedside, as to how Wight's spiritual "refreshings" came in to her, whether "by discourse, or in prayer, or how was it," Wight replied, *"By visions of God, as he pleased to come in, filling me with admiration for the free love of God."* God, Wight said, *"reveal'd to me Jesus Christ crucified for my sinnes, I saw it ..."* (86).[23] The lady next inquired whether because Wight experienced God's love in such manner, does she now "less esteem the written word?" Wight answered, *"The word is the letter of the Spirit, and types out him, therefore not to be the less esteemed"* (86). This reply indicates Wight's general endorsement of the bible; moreover, it coheres with the hermeneutic inclinations of many learned evangelical Protestants of the time, who practiced "typology" as a means of understanding scripture's potential prophetic and allegorical meanings.[24] Wight similarly endorsed learned evangelical practice in her response to a question about "the Ordinances"—public religious exercises such as sermons, lectures, fasts, conferences, and communions. Therefore, despite her own reliance on feelings stimulated by sensory data, Wight clearly esteemed abstract literate knowledge and practice. Yet ultimately, for Wight, literate knowledge alone proved insufficient for the personal experience of grace.

On the same occasion just noted, after the lady had finished her queries, Wight was next approached by Mr. Sprigge, a minister, whose inquiry into the basis of Wight's understanding was more direct. He asked, "which way the Lord came in to refresh you?" Wight said, *"It was revealed to me, that Christ was crucified for me, even for me, the chiefest of sinners. I never had a glimpse of Christ before, and then I admired him. I saw it plainly"* (89). "Plainly" in this instance means directly, by her own physical sense, without the mediation of, say, a literary commonplace, a book, or a learned minister's interpretation. Next Mr. Sprigge, recounting, as Jessey did for readers earlier in the text, that prior to her confinement to bed, Wight "usually every morning ... was wont to read alone above twenty chapters [of the Bible], ... so ... to have stilled her Temptations; but was not a jot the better," asked, "You knew the Scriptures before, that comfort you now: wherein then is your comfort?" Wight answered that *"The Letter did but kill, it could not comfort, but God hath refreshed me in his love. God was the same to me in his love formerly, that he is now. But in the fulnes of time, he manifested that, which was before"* (89). From this particular interview—which is, unlike any other save for a proximate one with Mr. Cogge, a physician, more an examination than a conference, and therefore a set-piece argument in the drama—readers discover that to Wight, God appears as a "manifest" presence, one "plainly" known through the senses, and thereby made evident to the intellect. Scripture, sermons, services, and the like—the stuff of ecclesiastical organization and oversight—are but verbal "similitudes of him," which serve perhaps to prepare tortured souls to apprehend Christ intimately, but which in themselves can neither occasion nor constitute such sensation, which formed the basis of the belief of the people to whom Wight ministered. To this end Wight tells a troubled visitor, tired out by reading and gadding to sermons, "Desire he would but speak the word, and manifest it to your soule" (100). In Wight's understanding of grace, God is manifest as a living, present, and therefore a true, loving *voice*, seen and heard plainly. In depicting this *The Exceeding Riches of Grace* reflects a conspicuous division of labor between two sorts of ministry:

on the one hand, Wight's own broken- and tender-hearted exchanges with "little ones" in despair of their souls, demonstrating a ministry of mutual intimacy and solace tantamount to "love"; and, on the other, Jessey's massive critical apparatus of scriptural commonplaces, demonstrating a ministry of literate, learned, and comparatively impersonal conviction achieved via the letter. Whereas through the book Jessey the writer and scholar performs the ministry of the literate learning, composing and scripturally supporting the documentation of Wight's activity, Wight as both a literary and actual phenomenon projects and promotes the ministry of love, of real presence. By virtue of having experienced, through seeing and hearing, the exceeding riches of grace in the flesh, Wight becomes herself graceful: she embodies the gnosis, the grace, of the word in the flesh. Thus the title page proclaims that, "in and by this Earthen Vessell [i.e., Wight]; [the Lord] holds forth his Own eternall love, and the Glorious Grace of his dear Son, to the CHIEFEST of SINNERS."

It is perhaps too easy for us, technologically mature producers and consumers of writing, to appreciate Jessey's ministry, and thus to overlook or undervalue the meaning of Wight's encounters with her little ones. The letter, after all, is what we confront most directly in *The Exceeding Riches of Grace*—not only in the graphic aspect of the book as a material object but also in its text's copious referencing of scripture. In the first edition, Jessey's "Table of the Places of holy Scripture, that in this Book are opened, illustrated, and applied," lists over 180 different chapter-and-verse citations of the bible in what is an 159-page octavo text; the second edition, which appeared only a few weeks after the first, whose title page advertises "added proofs," lists in its table over 280 different places, in a book of identical format and page length. But these reflect Jessey's priorities, of copious and accurate scriptural knowledge and inter-textual reference and documentation of spiritual transactions. By contrast, what seems fundamental to Wight in her relations with her humble and certainly less textually oriented neighbors was sensory data. For immature laypeople such as Wight, in seeking to know God, words alone, no matter their divine inspiration, possessed inherent limitations: as Wight told one maid, "*My earthly tongue cannot express, what I felt, its beyond expression*" (54). In stressing this aspect of the text I am not arguing that scripture, or writing in

general, for that matter, had no place in Wight's ministry, or, by association, in the spiritual life of others like her—to insist on that would
contradict the obvious contemporary value of both the printed bible
and books such as *The Exceeding Riches of Grace*. Rather, I am suggesting that a religious practice chiefly determined by a literate orientation to knowledge, an alphabetical religion of textual semiotics, so to
speak, was for Wight and probably for many of her contemporaries
itself inadequate to their need. Scripture was a starting point, the
beginning and ground of spiritual life. The full achievement of grace
was beyond reading and writing, in the physical sensation of interper-
sonal reciprocity.[25]

Sympathetic gesture is Wight's peculiar talent and the basis of her
charisma or grace in her contact with her flock. To these seekers she
offers no text, no sermon, but feeling itself, in the form of conversation. As Wight told a visitor, *"My tongue was not able to tell the misery
I was in before continually and now my tongue is not able to tell what love
and mercy hath been shewed to me, I can never enough express his Name"*
(40–41). Yet she is compelled to speak, despite her own infirmity and
the evident deficiency of language. As the various interviews Wight
conducts with troubled souls demonstrate, what edifies best is not
so much verbal signs of redemption but the immediate exchange of
sympathy that physical expressions of comfort make possible. Those
to whom Wight administers, principally lost and lonely souls like one
whose "heart will not be wrought upon" (76), come not to gawk or
witness but to conduct together with Wight an improvised, spontaneous exchange whose verbal contents are less important than the
multiple physical sensations evoked by lively conversation. In this
manner they feel or imbibe and derive sustenance from Wight, as
Wight herself took in Christ. "I am full," Wight had said during her
confinement; *"Jesus Christ feeds me,"* despite her refusal of foodstuff
(26; 56). "I am not able to express how sweet that word is," Wight
explained, of her vision of Christ (30). In imitation of Christ, Wight
offers her interlocutors what Jessey described as *"succoring Answers* for
upholding and *refreshing [the] weary soule"* (48). She is even able "to
put out fit questions" in order to "gain in" upon reticent parties (73).
As speech, words in Wight's ministry become significant not as signs
but as sensations, with the potential to relieve the body of the key

symptoms of spiritual angst, emptiness, and loneliness. In this regard Wight's communicants apprehend her voice "in itself," as the literary critic Roland Barthes has put it, feeling "everything in the voice which overflows [linguistic] meaning."[26] The "grain of the voice," says Barthes, can only be described through metaphors, which Jessey attempts to do when he characterizes her speech as "tender-hearted" (28). Elsewhere Jessey notes that Wight's voice was "very low; *and oft whispering, (it could be heard by none, but that were very neer her) uttered in an humble, melting manner, stop'd sometimes with teares or sighs*" (3). By these approximate verbal means, the text signifies the palpable sustaining pleasure or *jouissance* of actual conversation with Sarah Wight.

Another dimension of the extra-linguistic aspect of Wight's discursive ministrations is her physical bearing or deportment. In *The Exceeding Riches of Grace* readers find Wight performing a subtle manipulation of the complex "politics of touch and openness," both in her habit of receiving guests in her bedchamber and her mode of addressing and speaking with them.[27] Throughout the early modern period, much as today, one's social respectability and integrity depended in part on the defense of personal space as a dimension of social identity. By surrendering nearly all of this space, exposing herself to neighbors and strangers alike in a highly private location, Wight made herself unusually accessible to others. In her sickbed, appearing weak, vulnerable, and insignificant—the "empty nothing creature" of the book's title—Wight was able to take in those who believed, as she herself once did, that they are the chief of sinners, and therefore alone in the world. Further, by engaging and holding the lonely in dialogue, Wight was able to express sympathy and thereby offer solace. Consider for instance the following excerpt of a conversation Wight had with a "maid" who came to her, "*in deep despair*":

> Maid. I am without God, an enemy to him.
> S. Well, let it be so, you are without God in the world, a stranger, an enemy: yet such hath he reconciled by the death of his Son: all the want is, you cannot see it.
> ...
> Maid. But I have rejected him.

S. You can doe nothing els, but reject him: but your greatest
rejecting is, to reject a promise from God when he holds
one out to you, then you say, it is not to me. Thus I find, as
you do, in rejecting promises, and that was my greatest sin.

Maid. Your sin was not like mine.

S. No sin was like mine, as I judged. Mine was against such
light, that I judged I had sind against the Holy Ghost.

Maid. That word terrifies me, that was said to me, Repentance
is hid from thine eyes.

S. That word when I read it, I was ready to teare it out of my
book. There were three other Scriptures that were terrible
to me. He that believes not, is condemned already, was one:
Another was, He that beleeveth not the Son,—the wrath
of God abides in him. A third was, He that made them,
will not have mercy on them: no mercy, none at all. But
above all this, Repentance is hid from mine eyes.

Maid. Was it so with you? And then said, The Discoveries of
Christ, and promises, are more terrible to me, then the
curses of the Law.

S. Sometimes it was so with me; salvation was turned into condemnation to me: promises that were ever so sweet, were
terrible to me (105–107).

Perhaps the most remarkable detail in this passage is the terror
scripture produced in both girls: this is not the way we have been led
by our study of early modern evangelical commentary to think of scripture's function. But is easy to imagine how a simplistic, too literal interpretation could result in such an effect, which would only be amplified
were one to read by oneself, in relative isolation, or in the company of
other unsophisticated students—those who are "children" in understanding, if not in years, who read, as Jessey explained of Wight's own
early unfortunate study of scripture, "not aright." Apparently the
terror was so extreme that whoever felt it could only imagine herself
alone in torment, suffering the desperate fate of the chiefest of sinners.
That is one way to grasp what Wight may have intended by her use
of the trope, "the letter did but kill, it could not comfort," in response
to the lady questioner quoted previously. In any case, to sufferers of

despair, Wight could offer tangible, credible sympathy, having herself directly experienced both the terror and the deliverance. In this exchange, which is typical, the maid insists at first that Wight is "not like" her. But Wight works to, as contemporary evangelicals would have put it, 'open' and 'melt' the resistant conviction of her conversant. The maid's question, "Was it so with you?" may be read as a sign of her surprise and relief to find in Wight another person who felt what she had been feeling. It is an opening, a crevice, through which Wight seeps in. If to describe the relation Wight establishes here as "communion" stretches the limits of plausible interpretation, at least we can observe that the maid now begins to find her isolation less extreme. The conversation draws to a close thus:

> Maid. If I could weep day and night, I should find some ease, but I cannot.
> S. What if you could! Yet the Law and all your doings are weak; but you have not what you would in your selfe, that you must not rest short of Christ. You would not else desire the riches of Grace to such a one. Are you not weary and sorrowfull?
> Maid. I am.
> S. He will satiate the weary soul: and he will replenish the sorrowfull soule.
> The maid having further heard by this Gentlewoman, how sad her condition had been; and that yet the Lord had been so gracious to her, shee said: Mine was not sadder than yours hath been: but onely that I had sind against greater light. How long were you in that sad condition?
> S. Four years and above, since I was little more then eleven yeeres old: But the last half yeer and above before the Lord delivered me, I was full of terror night and day; and at last, I had no rest at all, being violently tempted against my life.
> Maid. Then I may have some hope that the Lord may deliver me; because I have not been above two moneths so violently troubled (112–113).

Wight's sympathy is not the antidote to physical torment—only Christ can provide that remedy. Indeed, the maid departs from the interview still somewhat self-obsessed, deriving hope from a precise comparison of the duration of her own trouble with that of Wight, which keeps the two personalities conceptually apart and neglects the more fundamental feeling of affiliation Wight attempted to establish. Nevertheless, in their exchange Wight has performed a meaningful ministerial function, offering her interlocutor a kind of "succor," in the form of real presence, that a book is unable to provide such persons, no matter how long they stay with it. In fact, the reciprocal sympathetic feeling that Wight extends to her guest can only be achieved in the flesh, between one body and another, and never from an inanimate object such as a book. Likewise, the achievement of grace is an effect of animate gesture, whether real, as in what Wight administered directly to others, or imaginary, as in what Wight felt Christ administered to her, when he showed her "*a glimpse of his love,*" in which Wight "*saw myself crucified with Christ, that my sins pierced him …*" (53–54). Touch, reciprocal sympathy, the palpable grain of the voice, not only or even primarily the letter, is the medium and bond of communion among godly people such as these.

In yet another and perhaps the most decisive repetition of embodied communication, *The Exceeding Riches of Grace* presents the example of Sarah Wight herself, a lonely child surrounded by family, friends, neighbors, ministers, and others seeking to comfort her, but with whose love she was unable to connect or, in the language of the text, "refresh" herself. In fact, ashamed of her own loveless and apparently forsaken condition, she strove to remove herself further from others' affection, in several suicide attempts. On sending herself into convulsions with the last suicidal gesture, she found herself confined in a bedroom that became a kind of laboratory of love, in which Wight was convinced, through the exchange of sympathetic gesture with the hundreds who visited her, that she was capable of being loved, and of giving love in return. Arguably the most compelling instance of these convincing exchanges was the first one to occur after Wight regained consciousness, between the daughter and her mother, whom, let us recall, Wight had deceived and sinned against. Mentally alert, but still blind and deaf, Wight commenced to murmur of pardon, and called for her mother, "to testifie that shee had pardond" her daughter. Mary Wight then came to her, and took her daughters hand, and put it on her own neck, where her daughter felt a skare that was there, through the enemy: whereby her daughter knowing her, cast her head into her mothers bosome, and wept greatly, and kissed her, and stroaked her face, and said, *I know you mother; and I love you with another love then I loved you before* (24–25).

The visitation of Christ that occurred two months after this exchange can be taken as a psychic reenactment and confirmation of this decisive moment, in which a troubled girl received sympathy from the body best able to offer it. The affiliation felt between Mary and Sarah Wight through this gesture is manifest, not abstract, since the sign that Wight knew her mother by was a scar made "by the enemy," meaning that it was the physical trace of the mother's own desperate, self-destructive response to isolation. They possessed more than genealogy in common. The recognition of this common possession, and the genuine, spontaneous feeling of love it produced, reversed Wight's determination to destroy her body and set in motion a process of bodily attention that led to its full recovery and an appreciation of its capacity to heal others. The stream of bedside visitors in the interim, between the mother's touch and the visitation of Christ, served merely to reinforce the sensation of love achieved by this initial sympathetic gesture.

Given all that *The Exceeding Riches of Grace* makes available to us, which I have lightly touched on here, it is unreasonable to assert that because she was a child, Sarah Wight possessed an inherent capacity or advantage for sympathetic gesture. If anything, we might presume that a body lacking the kind of self-knowledge characteristic of intellectual maturity would be incapable of the genuinely sympathetic expression published in Jessey's book. It is probable, therefore, that Wight's childhood finally terminated in her newfound capacity for sympathetic gesture. In this regard, Jessey's learned literate writing proves to be less exact than modern scholarship demands, as his use of the word "child" to describe Wight does not do justice to the level of spiritual and psychological understanding her actions demonstrate. But to be fair, monitoring the limits of childhood was not Jessey's chief concern in composing the book. Jessey presented Wight's case in the manner of sacred biography, a literate instrument to construct and certify a holy person's corporeal charisma. As I hope to have shown, for sophisticated readers such as ourselves it succeeds brilliantly in this objective. For Wight, and for other spiritually immature contemporaries like her, the book may have been treated as merely a record of events and feelings that transpired by other means than reading and writing. *The Exceeding Riches of Grace* displays a system of power and knowledge ideally suited to children in years and understanding—people whose knowledge of or faith in the letter is limited, and inadequate to their spiritual and physical needs.

Notes

1. For a recent account of both views, see Brian Cummings, *The Literary Culture of the Reformation: Grammar and Grace* (Oxford, 2002), Chapter 1.
2. According to Ian Green, *Print and Protestantism in Early Modern England* (Oxford, 2000), 416, there were about nine editions in twenty years.
3. The full title is, The exceeding Riches of GRACE ADVANCED By the Spirit of Grace, in an Empty Nothing Creature, viz. M^tris SARAH WIGHT, Lately hopeles and restles, her soule dwelling as far from Peace or hopes of Mercy, as ever was any. Now hopefull, and joyfull in the LORD, that hath caused LIGHT to shine out of DARKNESS; that in and by this Earthen Vessell, holds forth his Own eternall love, and the Glorious Grace of his dear Son, to the CHIEFEST of SINNERS. Who desired that others might hear and know, what the LORD hath done for her soul, (that was so terrified day & night:) and might neither presume, nor despair and murmure against God, as shee hath done[.] Published for the Refreshing of poor souls, by an Eye and Ear-witness of a good part thereof, HENRY JESSE, a servant of Jesus Christ. London, 1647. Subsequent citations of this text will appear in parentheses in the body of the paper.
4. Alexandra Walsham, *Providence in Early Modern England* (Oxford, 1999), Chapter 4, esp. 212–213.
5. Among works of its kind, only Philip Stubbes's *A Christal Glasse for Christian Women*, his verbatim account of the last dying words of his wife Katherine, first published in 1591, was more popular, appearing in an estimated thirty editions to the end of the seventeenth century.
6. For an overview, see Phyllis Mack, *Visionary Women: Ecstatic Prophecy in Seventeenth-Century England* (Berkeley and Los Angeles, 1992).
7. Nigel Smith, *Perfection Proclaimed: Language and Literature in English Radical Religion 1640–1660* (Oxford, 1989), 46.
8. Barbara Ritter Dailey, "The Visitation of Sarah Wight: Holy Carnival and the Revolution of the Saints in Civil War London," *Church History,* 55 (1986), 438; but compare the reading of Carola Scott-Lukens, who finds in Jessey's text "convincing evidence of an evolving 'female' tradition

of *ars moriendi*," in Carola Scott-Luckens, "Propaganda or Marks of Grace? The Impact of the Reported Ordeals of Sarah Wight in Revolutionary London, 1647–52," *Women's Writing*, 9 (2002), 223.

9. Katharine Gillespie, *Domesticity and Dissent in the Seventeenth Century: English Women Writers and the Public Sphere* (Cambridge, 2004), 191.

10. Susan Hardman Moore, "'Such Perfecting of Praise Out of the Mouth of a Babe': Sara Wight as Child Prophet," in *The Church and Childhood*, ed. Diana Wood (Oxford, 1994), 314, 323. For other studies of early modern child prophets, see Nigel Smith, "A Child Prophet: Martha Hatfield as *The Wise Virgin*," in *Children and Their Books: A Celebration of the Work of Iona and Peter Opie*, eds. Gillian Avery and Julia Briggs (Oxford, 1989), 79–93; Alexandra Walsham, "'Out of the Mouths of Babes and Sucklings': Prophecy, Puritanism, and Childhood in Elizabethan Suffolk," in *The Church and Childhood*, 285–299. For related studies, see J. A. Sharpe, "Disruption in the Well-Ordered Household: Age, Authority, and Possessed Young People," in *The Experience of Authority in Early Modern England*, eds. Paul Griffiths, Adam Fox, and Steve Hindle (New York, 1996), 187–212; Elizabeth A. Foyster, "Silent Witnesses? Children and the Breakdown of Domestic and Social Order in Early Modern England," in *Childhood in Question: Children, Parents, and the State*, Anthony Fletcher and Stephen Hussey, eds. (Manchester and New York, 1999), 57–73.

11. Keith Thomas, "Age and Authority in Early Modern England," *Proceedings of the British Academy*, LXII (1977), 225. For the delayed age of maturity, see 221ff.

12. For examples, see Ian Green, *The Christian's ABC: Catechisms and Catechizing in England c.1530–1740* (Oxford, 1996).

13. John Stachniewski, *The Persecutory Imagination: English Puritanism and the Literature of Religious Despair* (Oxford, 1991), 42.

14. Anne Laurence, "A Priesthood of She-Believers: Women and Congragations in Mid-Seventeenth-Century England," in *Women in the Church*, W. J. Shiels and Diana Wood, eds. (Oxford, 1990), 359.

15. Laurence, "Women and Congregations," 363. For a historical consideration of the role of women in Baptist congregations, including that of Henry Jessey, see B.R. White, *The English Baptists of the Seventeenth Century* (Didcot, 1996), Chapter 4, especially 145–155.

16. Wrigley and Schofield, *The Population History of England, 1541–1871* (London, 1981), 218.

17. Thomas, "Age and Authority," 209.

18. Keith Thomas, "Children in Early Modern England," in *Children and Their Books*, ed. Avery and Briggs, 45–77.

19. *A Wonderful Pleasant and Profitable Letter Written by M^{ris} Sarah Wight, To a Friend* (London, 1656). Dailey, "Visitation of Sara Wight," 453, speculates that R.B. is Robert Bacon, a religious radical.

20. Patrick Collinson, "The English Conventicle," in *Voluntary Religion*, W. J. Shiels and Diana Wood, eds. (Oxford, 1986), 223.

21. In "A Child Prophet," 85, Smith finds that the Hatfield case is "an early Puritan version of the later and more widespread attitude that the

innocence of children gives them a special insight into reality." Lorraine Daston has argued that the "purity" of innocence was essential to the distinction between the evidence of "true" and "false" miracles during the first half of the seventeenth century, see Lorraine Daston, "Marvelous Facts and Miraculous Evidence in Early Modern Europe," in *Wonders, Marvels, and Monsters in Early Modern Europe*, Peter G. Platt, ed. (Newark, 1999), 92–93.

22. On the "dynamic continuum" of oral and literate culture, see Adam Fox, *Oral and Literate Culture in Early Modern England 1500–1700* (Oxford, 2000), p. 50, passim; on Jessey as catechist, see Barbara Ritter Dailey, "Youth and the New Jerusalem: The English Catechistical Tradition and Henry Jessey's *Catechism for Babes* (1652)," *Harvard Library Bulletin*, 30 (1982), 25–54.

23. Vision is the principal means of apprehension. To another on an earlier occasion she explained that "Jesus Christ was presented to me, as crucified for my sins. I saw it: and my selfe crucified with him: and when I saw a glimpse of his love, then I mourned bitterly for my sins ..." (54). Cf. 53, 67.

24. Thomas M. Davis, "The Traditions of Puritan Typology," in *Typology and Early American Literature*, Sacvan Berkovitch, ed. (Amherst, MA, 1972), 11–45.

25. In her essay, "'Communion of the Saints': Spiritual Reciprocity and the Godly Community in Early Modern England," *Albion*, 27 (1995), 19–41, Diane Willen describes how "spiritual relationships based on strong emotional bonds" (23) were established and maintained among the learned gentry through epistolary exchange. The habit Willen describes represents the attempt to employ the novel technology of letter-writing to accomplish the effects of what had thus far been an embodied practice.

26. Roland Barthes, *The Grain of the Voice: Interviews 1962–1980*, tr. Linda Coverdale (Berkeley, 1991), 183–184.

27. Laura Gowing, *Common Bodies: Women, Touch and Power in Seventeenth-Century England* (New Haven and London, 2003), Chapter 2.

7

"IN THE POSTURE OF CHILDREN"

Eighteenth-Century British Servants and Children

KRISTINA STRAUB

This chapter is about the rhetorical effects of writing about domestic servants as if they were children, effects that shape representations of both servants and children as pedagogical subjects within the domestic sphere. Eighteenth-century British domestic servants spanned a broad range of ages including many whom we would join in characterizing as "children," and many whom we would not. Many children entered service through the institution of apprenticeship and remained in service as adults. As Bridget Hill has argued, domestic service became, increasingly over the course of the century, more a lifetime vocation and less the temporary role of the older child or adolescent.[1] Domestic servants, young and old, straddle the public and domestic spheres as objects of discipline in both realms, sharing with many of their counterparts among the working poor subjection to the public discipline of an emergent, modern criminal justice system and subjection to—as well as the benefits of—philanthropic and educational institutions such as the Charity school movement. What distinguishes the subjection of servants from that of other, predominantly poor people is their particular relation to the family. Throughout the eighteenth century, domestic servants were represented as analogous to children; in Defoe's words, servants were thought of in "the Posture of Children,"[2] a position that naturalized their subordination within the family hierarchy and erased the problem of differing economic interests between master and servant. It also helped to create and sustain a concept of the family as a powerful means of regulating the agency of adult servants and children of both classes within it.

The analogy between servants and children came readily to the imagination of eighteenth-century British readers because it fused seamlessly with the material state of most of their past and many of their present servants. As Ann Kussmaul demonstrates, "Most youths in early modern England were servants; that so few are now is one of the simplest differences between our world and theirs."[3] As a period of transition from life-cycle to professional service, the eighteenth century saw the elaboration of a family ideology that constructed servants as children, a condition that may or may not have meshed with the particular servant's actual chronological age.[4] This rationalization of servants' subjection within a patriarchal family hierarchy persists—and even grows more strident—up through Sarah Trimmer's fictionalized model servants in the late eighteenth and early nineteenth centuries. It perhaps came all the more readily to hand because of what Hugh Cunningham calls the "dominant patriarchalist theory of the seventeenth century": "the obedience which children owed to their parents was the foundation of political order." Cunningham sees this theory persisting into the late eighteenth century in the form of organized philanthropy and poor laws.[5] It also informed the literature on relations between masters and servants from the seventeenth and well into the nineteenth century.

The foundations of a domestic order linking servant and child are to be found at least as early as the seventeenth century. Literature on the linked institutions of service and apprenticeship urges readers to think of masters and servants, respectively, as fathers and children. Defoe exhorts his readers, to "put the Master entirely upon the Father's Place, and the Servants in the Posture of Children."[6] Masters should guard the health of their servants as they would that of their own children, a late-seventeenth-century conduct manual insists;[7] the same text calls for masters to discipline their servants as they would their children: "And what will the Discipline of a Family be, when Youth are left to the Liberty of their own Inclinations, without the Apprehension of any to question or control them?"[8] A 1674 pamphlet characterizes the master as "Guardian," not having the same "power as a Lord hath over a Slave," but rather as a "Discipliner, or Teacher, with authority of using moderate Correction as a Father, not as a Tyrant, or otherwise."[9] Masters of apprentices (many, of course, who *were* children) are urged to function *in loco parentis*.[10] Kearsley, writing in the last quarter of the eighteenth century, still maintains that "A boy, on his being put apprentice, ought to consider that his parents, or his friends, have for his advantage devolved their authority on his master; whom he should regard as deputy of those who gave him being."[11] In conjunction with what we might call the paternalization of the master, servants were represented as children under the protection of their master. George Rosen notices a prevalent tendency to look on apprentices as child-like, despite the fact that many entered the state in their teens and remained well into their twenties.[12] The fiction of the servant/child is matched by the fiction of the paternal master. That many masters deviated grossly from the fatherly ideal is frequently commented on,[13] and it was broadly recognized that the reality of apprenticeship and service was that masters often worked young people purely to extract their labor, with little or no regard to their vocational, let alone their religious and moral, training.[14] The literature on domestic service and apprenticeship does not ignore the probability that the relationship between master and servant was primarily an economic one, which held contradictory interests for both. The literature written for the instruction of servants themselves, however, strongly counters this probability with an affective, pedagogical resolution to "the servant problem."

It is difficult to know how many servants actually read the many conduct books that discuss the servant's duties using the second personal pronoun. In her late-eighteenth-century educational tracts, Sarah Trimmer's fictionalized Tom and Betty spend their evenings perusing books such as *Serious Advice and Warning to Servants,* but whether or not historical Toms and Bettys did so is hard to say. Jan Fergus's work on servants' reading habits suggests that while servants could claim a fair percentage of literacy by the mid-eighteenth century, they, like other more-or-less literate groups, did not confine themselves to such "useful" reading matter, including a range of fictional texts, especially plays, in their literary fare.[15] I focus my claims about the pedagogical literature that directly addresses a servant reader, on the rhetorical and ideological importance of its idealized models for master/servant relations. However servants may have read these texts—if they did, indeed, read them—their representations of the servant as a child rather than as an adult worker are consistent and relentless enough to make them hard to ignore. The servant as child in need of education forms an important part of the horizon of ideological possibility, the other side of the "servant problem" coin. Whether or not servants took from this literature the propensity to think of themselves as children (and it seems rather unlikely to me that they did), the instructional literature on domestic service evinces a clear need on the part of writers to imagine domestic affective relations in which servants and children alike are willingly subordinate to the masters' and mistresses' economic and moral authority.

These roles, and the pedagogy that produces them, parallel quite closely the roles and the pedagogy of literature directed toward children. In Defoe's *Family Instructor,* for example, dialogues between parents and children and masters and servants are bundled together in a work that sees each individual servant and child playing a harmonious and subordinate role in the perpetuation of a patriarchal ideal of progress; families prosper, both spiritually and economically, because their children and their servants alike willingly do the work of religion and capitalism.[16] Always ahead of his time, Defoe forecasts the work of reformers such as Sarah Trimmer, late in the century, who carries on his vision of both servants' and children's key roles within economically productive and religiously principled families. Like many of her contemporaries, Trimmer urged her readers to teach servants the values and ideals of middling domesticity as if they were children; thus, integrity and industry in the pedagogical literature for servants and children alike, are grounded in the affective, familial relations of a discernible middle class.[17]

Early eighteenth-century conduct manuals for servants prepare the imagination for the analogy of servant as child by rationalizing the domestic servant's submission to familial authority through an implicit model of childhood as removed from the economic and political cares of adulthood. William Fleetwood consoles servants for their lack of autonomy:

> The State of Servitude is accounted the meanest and the most miserable of all others, but yet it is to be made easie, though not eligible. Servants may have more of the Labours of Life, but then they have less of the Cares, than other People; their Bodies are more fatigu'd and exercis'd, but their Minds are less perplex'd: They are only concern'd in one matter, to do the work that lies before them, whilst others have a world of things to think on, and look after. They have their Masters only to please; their Master, may be, are to court and humour all they deal with: They, generally speaking have themselves alone to provide for; their Masters have Wives and Children, and Relations. Whatever scarcity or dearness happens, they find but little Alteration; what-ever publick mischiefs oppress a Nation, they feel but little of them.[18]

Writing later, in 1743, Eliza Haywood reiterates the economic responsibility of masters and the child-like, carefree state of their servants:

> The exorbitant Taxes, and other Severities of the Times, have, for some Years past, reduced our middling Gentry, as well as Tradesmen, to very great Straits; and the Care of providing for you, and paying your Wages, is much more than an Equivalent for your Care of obliging them, and doing your Duty by them. It often costs many a bitten Lip and aking Heart, to support the Rank they have been accustomed to hold in the World, while you, entirely free from all Incumberances, all Distraction of Mind, have only to do your Duty quietly in the Stations God has placed you. Whatever Changes happen in public Affairs, your Circumstances are unaffected by them. Whether Provisions are dear or cheap is the same Thing to you. Secure of having all your real necessities supplied, you rise without Anxiety, and go to Bed without Danger of having your Repose disturbed. And as to your Labour, if you consider the Difference of Education, it is no more to you than those Exercises which are prescribed to your Superiors for the Sake of Health.[19]

Jonas Hanway's Farmer Trueman advises his daughter not to envy the superior state of her mistress, for "Little dost thou know of the anxiety which attends the condition of many a master and mistress, to support their rank, in the maintenance of their servants."[20] The construction of service as a sort of prolonged economic childhood, contained within the protective frame of the domestic sphere, prepares the ground for interpolating the servant into the disciplinary structure of the ideal family. Like the child, the servant's labor is, literally, taken out of public circulation; servants' economic agency, like that of the child, is ideally understood within the terms of domestic, not public, exchange. This is not to deny the obvious: both children, especially the children of the poor, and servants worked—and played, at times—in highly public ways. Servants, like other workers, sold their labor to the highest bidder, a practice increasingly noted (and decried) in the urban context of London. The ideological separation of domestic labor relations from the public sphere offered, however, a compensatory fantasy, even, occasionally, the reality of a safe haven from the social antagonisms caused by masters' and servants' conflicting interests. Buttressing the construction of child and servant labor as domestic training rather than work, the servant's relation to the family is represented as affective and emotional rather than economic.

Despite the many expressions of distrust directed at greedy, unfeeling servants by the polemical literature on "the servant problem," many of the conduct and advice books addressing servants offer them affective relations with masters as incentive to give up their relative social mobility and economic agency. As Hecht explains, "The harshness of this state was presumed to be greatly mitigated by the emotional or sentimental tie binding master and servant; for it was supposed that what was in the first instance a contract would develop into a truly family bond, characterized by mutual devotion."[21] Eliza Haywood intones on the inevitability of the servant's filial affection for the master: "Methinks, if you would thoroughly weigh the Comforts of your condition, you could not help having an Affection for those under whose Roof and Protection you enjoy them, especially when they behave to you with any tolerable Degree of Affability and Sweetness; for then not to love them would be the highest Ingratitude."[22] Servants should give up the power to "give warning" in exchange for the rewards of this Affection: "Nothing is so comfortable and creditable to all parties, as when a servant lives many years in the same family. Such servants never want a real friend."[23] The family in which the servant was supposed to form these affective bonds is, increasingly as the century wears on, the "middling" sort that employs two or three servants, not the "great house" with dozens.[24] The affective language tying servants to families intertwines with an antiaristocratic strain that gathers force over the course of the century. Sarah Trimmer's model servant Thomas compares the parental care of his master and mistress to the callousness of Lord and Lady Townley, who simply cast off on the public charge any servants who can no longer work for them because of age or disability.[25] The ties that bind servants to masters are, increasingly over the course of the century, the affective relations of middling domesticity.

As naturalizing as this familial construction of servant/master relations is, it is accompanied by explicit indications that good servants—like good children—do not come naturally but must be made through a laborious process of early and ongoing education. In this process, the master is primary teacher, the family is the key pedagogical unit, and the servant/child analogy is often literalized: the servant often IS a child who must, in the absence of his parents, be educated by the master and his wife. Educating the servant is not merely a matter of teaching him or her to do the job but also a moral and religious obligation. This obligation is particularly strong in relation to apprentices. One of Defoe's fictionalized fathers tells the master of his son, "he is under your Family Care, as to his Body, he is your Servant; but as to his Soul, I think, he is as much your Son as any Child you have."[26] But Defoe extends this spiritual responsibility to all the servants of the household, who, in his ideal family, attend regular prayers and services lead by the master of the house.[27] In the words of one manual on domestic service, "Every Master is a Priest in his own Family; and I have often thought this Obligation to teach and govern his Servants, is much greater than that of a Minister to any particular Family in his Charge."[28] In addition to making sure that his servants attend prayers, Defoe's good masters are responsible for complete moral surveillance: "His Time is yours, and you ought to know how he spends it; if any of his Time is employ'd out of your Business, you ought to exact an Account of it from him, how it has been disposed of, as much as you would of Money that you had trusted him with, how he had paid it."[29] *The Family Instructor* places particular emphasis on policing servants' Sundays, making sure that they attend church instead of walking in the fields around London or, worse, attending one of its places of public amusement. Defoe, writing in the second decade of the eighteenth century, anticipates the culture of surveillance and self-discipline that is evident in children's, as well as servants', pedagogy by the late eighteenth century. Like the good child, the good servant is the servant whose discipline exceeds the limits of "eye-service," the master's direct observation. As with children, this self-discipline depends on subjection to domestic authority; loosened from that authority, the servant became a dangerous point of contact between domestic relations and corrupt social conditions that result, at least in part, from servants' control over their labor, their ability to sell their services to the highest bidder.

The other side of the child-like servant is the corrupt and degenerate servant who brings nothing but trouble to the family. The figure of the London servant, in particular, crystallized a moral degeneracy that was loosely associated with several laboring groups generally drawn from the ranks of the working poor or lower artisanal class: the male servants of the upper classes, particularly liveried footmen, butlers, and valets, female servants and apprentices in a range of domestic positions, and male apprentices whose work supported a private estate or household, such as cooks or grooms. The London servant summed up not only what was NOT child-like about servants but also what was, indeed, blatantly threatening to children. Throughout the century, servants may be seen as analogous to children, but they also are seen as dangerous to the latter's eventual development into a proper adulthood. Andrew O'Malley notes an anathema to servants' "plebian" influence on children's education from Locke up through the radical camps of late-century reformers such as William Godwin and Mary Wollstonecraft.[30] Mitzi Myers argues that although Maria Edgeworth may see servants as sharing with children a theoretical perfectibility, she also sees them as sharing and, indeed, magnifying, a practical recalcitrance to "improvement." Servants embodied not only the "bad" influence of the plebian classes, but the contaminating practices of the aristocracy; Myers observes that "Domestics symbolized not only the unenlightened ignorance of the old wife, but also upper-class artifice."[31]

I would argue that although class-stereotyping certainly plays a role in the idea of domestic servants as dangerous to children, the specific contexts of changing labor relations between masters and servants in the eighteenth century aggravated paranoia over the contaminating influences of servants on children. Insofar as servants are NOT like children—as they circulate as adult agents who sell their labor in the public sphere—they threaten the affectively conceived domestic sphere on which the child's proper education depends.

Over the course of the century, a moral polarity emerges between good servants who function like their childish counterparts in the domestic sphere, and bad servants who circulate in public, even sometimes criminal, ways. The "good" servant shares—so the theory, at least, goes—with the child an ideological disconnect from the public sphere subject. Eighteenth-century London servants emerge as evil counterparts to the child-like "good" servant in large part because they were perceived as having a relatively greater degree of economic mobility within changing urban economic relations. Urban conditions allegedly gave servants an agency that cut them free from domestic hierarchy and allowed them to act in the public realm in ways that many writers, from Defoe on, found threatening to the social order.

When domestic servants came to London, at least according to the polemical literature on service, they found their social positions redefined in three ways: First, their relations with their masters were framed as contractual and economic, not familial and moral. Instead of the almost filial position of the servant to his master, the London servant was taken on purely for labor, a motivation that, according to writers such as Swift and Thomas Seaton, led to the family's moral pollution: Swift's *Directions to Servants* is rife with images of physical pollution: cooks spit in their employer's food, hair and bodily secretions are served up with the family's dinner, and forced bodily contact occurs between manservant and mistress: "If you are a young sightly Fellow, whenever you whisper your Mistress at the Table, run your Nose full in her Cheek, or if your Breath be good, breathe full in her Face; this I have known to have had very good Consequences in some Families."[32] The family is physically assaulted by its servants, and metaphors of disease are common in imagining the effects of bad servants on family life. Seaton blames this contamination not on some lower-class essence but on the new framing of master/servant relations as contractual and material: "but we have Masters that choose Servants as they do their Horses; if they be strong, and able for their Work, they mind no more: though you would not bring a scabbed Sheep into your Flock; yet are there not those that bring in druncken, swearing Servants, with the Plague of Profaneness upon them, into their Houses, and lay the infected Wretches with their dear Children and other Servants?"[33] The bad, polluting servant and the injured or infected child signal the family's corruption by a materialist, commercial culture.

The contractual, economic reframing of master/servant relations also allowed for the second change that London wrought on the servant's position: their ability to "give warning" and find a new place in a context of relative anonymity gave them more economic autonomy than was possible in smaller, more intimate communities. As a result of this ability, they were able to act in their own interests in ways that did not necessarily support those of the servant-employing family. The relative ease with which it was supposed that London servants could find new places when dissatisfied with their old allegedly gave them an agency that was almost universally seen as a desecration of the family, as defined by its right to privacy. Defoe complains that the "custom of warning" early in the century leads to "a great inconvenience to masters and mistresses," leaving them "at the mercy of every new comer to divulge your family affairs, to inspect your private life, and treasure up the sayings of yourself and friends."[34] Servants with economic agency become intruders on the family instead of its subordinates. George Kearsley sums up the cruel truth: the family's economic interests were not one, united front, but divided in two by the different economic interests of master and servant:

> To expect attachment from a servant is idle, and betrays an ignorance of the world. Servants will now and then affect it, in order to gain the confidence of their employers, and thus forward their own interest; but if we suppose them in our interest, it is because we do not thoroughly know them. Economy in a family, servants do not like. The more extravagant a master or mistress is, they [sic] better they live, and the more they can purloin; and should, what they call, a generous master of mistress fail in the world, owing to a waste or an inattention to domestic concerns,

they will cry to their fellow-servants, 'It is a pity! He was a good-natured generous man!—Come let us go look for another place!' This being considered, we are to expect nothing from them, but a performance of their duty, keep them whilst they do it, and discharge them when they neglect it.[35]

Cold-blooded economic relations between employer and employee lead to a Hobbesian nightmare of conflicting self-interests. Parasitical servants move freely from family to family, leaving a trail of domestic ruin.

What Kearsley accepts as a matter of social reality—the separate and even conflicting economic interests of master and servant—Defoe struggles with, campaigning for a family pedagogy that will fuse these interests. Another rhetorical tactic, taken most often in the late seventeenth and early eighteenth century, is the attempt to reconcile the servant's economic interests with his or her master's. One of the most frequent warnings to maidservants over the course of the century is that a "rolling stone gathers no moss."[36] Conduct guides for servants seek to inculcate in their readers the idea that "moss," literally, capital, is best accumulated by not exercising the most obvious economic agency open to domestic servants: the right to "give warning" and change places. For the most part, conduct literature directed at teaching servants their "place" tends to stress the alleged economic benefit of stable employment—room, board, and steady employment conducive to accumulating savings—whereas the polemical literature on "the servant problem" tends to stress the divided economic interests of master and servant.[37] In the ideal families presented as models by Daniel Defoe at the beginning of the century and Sarah Trimmer at the end, the good servant willingly gives up his or her economic agency to the larger goal of an economically healthy family, assured that his or her own security lies in a combination of strong familial bonds and personal thrift.

Despite, however, the powerful pedagogical discourse denying the reality of any division in family economic interests and suppressing the servant's agency, the latter emerges disturbingly in texts such as Kearsley's and, most pointedly, in Jonathan Swift's satiric *Directions to Servants,* which savagely parodies the pedagogical literature directed at servants by inverting this literature's message of cheerful subordination within the family:

> If you find yourself to grow into Favour with your Master or Lady, take some Opportunity, in a very mild Way, to give them Warning, and when they ask the Reason, and seem loth to part with you, answer that you would rather live with them, than any Body else, but a poor Servant is not to be blamed if he strives to better himself; that Service is no Inheritance, that your Work is great, and your Wages very small: Upon which, if your Master hath any Generosity, he will add five or ten Shillings a Quarter rather than let you go: But, if you are baulked, and have no Mind to go off, get some Fellow-servant to tell your Master, that he had prevailed upon you to stay."[38]

As in *The Beggar's Opera,* and its myriad of imitators, economic agency is a leveler that transforms traditional hierarchies of value into relations of pure economic interest and greed. In the case of domestic servants, that leveling reaches deep inside the domestic sphere. The servant, focused on his or her own financial gain rather than the welfare of the master's family, becomes in Swift's satire on conduct books for servants a sexual threat to the young people of the family. Swift advises his footman that he may "sometimes pick up a Fortune, perhaps your Master's Daughter";[39] the maid is advised to encourage her young lady in clandestine amours by which she might gain "five or six hundred Pounds for disposing of her."[40]

Finally, the same, relative anonymity that led servants to "give warning" allowed them to use their economic agency for vertical movement—or at least its appearance—within the social hierarchy. The maid and footman who dress like and are even mistaken for their "betters" are common in conduct and polemical literature on servants from Defoe on, and are well-worn figures of ridicule on the stage. In the case of both male and female servants, a dangerous sexuality saturates such transgressions. In the case of female servants, economic agency, combined with sartorial masquerade, makes Defoe's maid a whore, "slippery in the tail," and able to rove "from bawdyhouse to service, and from service to bawdyhouse again, ever unsettled and never easy, nothing being more common than to find these creatures one week in a good family and the next in a brothel. This amphibious life makes them fit for neither, for if the bawd uses them ill, away they trip to service, and if their mistress gives them a wry word, whip they are at a bawdyhouse again, so that in effect they neither make good whores nor good servants."[41] Much of the century's discourse on servants, including Richardson's *Pamela*, struggles over the proper means to contain the maid's sexual "slipperyness" or to at least inoculate the family from its contagion.

The economic agency of London male domestics, particularly footmen, is as susceptible to sexualization as the London maid turned whore, and Defoe's sexually amphibious maid has her counterpart in the opportunistic footmen of Defoe, Eliza Haywood, and Jonathan Swift. Swift's footman, for example, is a sexual magnet "with whom all the maids are in Love." More disturbingly, his sexuality is intertwined with the economic and social mobility attributed to London servants. His dress signals a disturbing confusion of class hierarchy, for he "is sometimes a Pattern of Dress to your Master, and sometimes he is so to you." A morally dangerous love of finery is a trait shared by both servants and children, according to the polemical and pedagogical literature of the period. Robert Dodsley, in his *Footman's Friendly Advice to his Brethren of the Livery,* jokes that he need not admonish his "brethren" too much about neatness in dress, given the footman's chronic attentiveness to the niceties of dress.[42] Wollstonecraft lumps together children and servants for their innate love of finery;[43] whereas children may be educated out of this dangerous distraction from more solid occupations, servants presented a more difficult task for the pedagogue. Unlike children, servants circulated out of the hothouse of domestic pedagogy and into the realm of public sphere ideology, giving them a mobility in both geographical space and in social institutions that made them recalcitrant subjects to family ideology.

The urge to regulate servants who had not crossed the line into overtly criminal behavior ultimately came up against the ideology of egalitarianism. In the public sphere, servants are defined as adults before the law. Even the laws regulating relations between masters and servants were framed in terms of equal protection:

In the Infancy of our Constitution the Common People of England were little better than Slaves. But since the Abolition of Vassalage, Knight's

Service, and Homage, the Tyranny of the Nobility is restrained; the Commonality are upon the same Footing, as to Liberty and Property, as the Gentry; and Servants of the lowest Class, being under the protection of the Laws, if mal-treated, have the same Remedy and Redress as their Masters. Nevertheless, the wise Legislature which established those Protections in behalf of this inferior Order of English Subjects, judged it also highly expedient to lay them under proper Restrictions.[44]

The language of equal protection in this quotation (*The Laws Relating to Masters AND Servants,* my emphasis) is not, of course, the language of equality, and William Godwin reminds us forcefully late in the century that even equal protection for master and servant is often illusory. The point is that servants' agency, whether real or illusory, was a part of the horizon of ideological possibility. What to do with that agency within the cross-hatching discourses of social hierarchy and social egalitarianism is a concern that came home to the family as the perfect unit—at least in theory—for encouraging voluntary submission to discipline.

Practically, however, the family did not seem to many to be doing its job. Complaints that masters fail in their duties are as, if not more, common than praise for those who attain the ideal. Often, the lament takes a gently nostalgic or antiaristocratic form, as exemplified in Hanway's Farmer Trueman's commentary: "I do not find that it is a custom or fashion among the gentry to say any thing at all about devotion, neither as it relates to themselves, nor their servants. ... My master used sometimes to give his sentiments in company, in a rational and familiar manner, like a man and a christian, as I thought: but I am sorry to tell thee Mary, his acquaintance, who were otherwise sober people, were generally as silent as the grave."[45] Urban fashion, in particular, undermines the paternal master's teaching of his servant/child. By 1815, Thomas Broughton complains, "As these great Cities entertain, so they ruin no small number of Servants; who soon exchange the simplicity of the country, for the foppery of the town; and the evil communications thereof too easily corrupt their manners. ... Thus the Town proves a school of corruption to them, wherein they learn every thing that is evil. ... With this wretched furniture of vices, how can they make good Servants?"[46] Both Broughton and, earlier, Defoe couch their critiques of domestic labor markets in terms that revealingly evoke the teaching of children; Defoe's "Nurseries" and Broughton's "schools" point towards a pervasive cultural tendency to think of the urban migrants who came seeking work in domestic service as children in need of a better education. George Kearsley displaces the metaphor of schooling with that of disease, but sustains the idea of a vulnerable, child-like "class" exposed to the wrong influences: "London is so much the sink of vice, that the lower class of people are very much corrupted. Those brought from the country are soon infected with the dissolute manners of town-servants, and become equally bad with them."[47] The infection that corrupts urban servants is linked, for Jonas Hanway, to the destabilizing effects of urban, economic goals on domestic service. His Farmer Trueman, himself a former servant of the old school, advises his daughter on going to service, "In these days of pleasure and dissipation, Mary, the most part of the nobility and gentry of this island carry their families to London, where servants entertain each other, with accounts of profitable places; as how much wages some have more than others. These do not consider so much the comfort and peace, the safety, and good treatment they enjoy, as how much they may get; I say may get, for it is not the lot of one in a thousand to be in such services as are represented to them!"[48]

The family's failure to educate new entrants into urban domestic service is commonly a primary rationale for the large output of texts such as Hanway's "advice" to a female teenager first entering service. Whether these texts were actually read by servants or not, the corrupting "Nursery" of London service seems to have called forth considerable prose in the service of putting right what urban economic conditions had made wrong. Print production of conduct manuals, how-to books, and polemical pamphlets on the subject of domestic service, written for both masters and servants as readers over the course of the century, is evidence of a large-scale pedagogical project directed at modeling relations in service as something other than an exchange of labor for wages. Despite—or because of—frequent admissions of the family's failure in its pedagogical task, pedagogy was directed at children as potential servants, bringing the ideology of domestic pedagogy into the broader field of social management.

Given the power of the analogy of servant-as-child, it is not surprising that the pedagogical literature for servants and for children—especially the children of the poor—are closely intertwined. Defoe bundles together, without comment, dialogues between parents and children and masters and servants; later reformers like Trimmer recognize that educating poor children is tantamount to educating future servants. Many children among the working poor, it was recognized, were unlikely to receive the kind of early education that would make them good servants. John Waugh, in "A Sermon Preach'd at the Parish Church of St. Bridget, alias Bride, August 24th, 1713. Being the Festival of St. Bartholomew; At a Meeting of about 1400 Persons of both Sexes. Being part of those who had been Educated, and afterwards put out to Trades and other Services, by the Trustees of the Charity-Schools, in and about the Cities of London and Westminster," flatters his audience that, "The true Reason why the Children of the poorer sort, who are born Servants, do not discharge their Duty as they should, is the Want of those Advantages which you have had. They were never acquainted with the Ways of God and Religion; their Minds never seasoned with Divine Things; but from their Infancy they were bred up in Ignorance and Sloth, and a total Neglect of all those Qualifications which are required to make a good Servant."[49] He praises his audience's education for the sense of "obligations" which will set them above the "many slothful and dishonest, stubborn and treacherous Servants, who create so great Trouble, and do so much Mischief to Families."[50] Some families, it is clear, are the right kind of pedagogical unit and some are not. Poor children, most likely to be "born Servants," are least likely to receive the religious and social education that would lead to domestic industry and a proper sense of "obligations." The economic and social identity of "the family" is being consolidated within an economically-based social hierarchy that still allows interpellation of the working poor into domestic ideology. What enables this trans-class project of educating individuals into the "right" form of familial relations is the figure of the educable child, whose theoretical perfectibility holds out hope for anchoring the dangerous instability of the domestic servant.

The social project of educating servants is thus, not surprisingly, intertwined with educational agendas directed at poor children. Defoe's confidence in the power of paternalistic pedagogy to reclaim both straying children and servants within the private family seems almost touchingly naïve in comparison with social reformers' bleak view of what happens when those "born Servants" enter the families of those born to employ them. Sarah Trimmer remarks in 1787, "It is a general complaint that domestic servants are not attached to their masters and mistresses, but act towards them from selfish and mercenary motives; ... This may justly be imputed to their being sent into the world without a proper sense of the duties of their station."[51] But Trimmer shares with Defoe a commitment to the model of family pedagogy, although she sees that it must be supplemented by social reforms such as Sunday and charity schools:

> If our servants are profane and immoral for want of our admonition, we shall be called to a strict account for it: It is unreasonable to complain of their dishonesty and corruption, if we take no pains to instruct them, and allow them no time for divine worship: a kind of Sunday-evening-school in every family would be a likely mean of reforming many and is a very necessary succedaneum to Sunday-schools for children; the benefit of which may be rendered ineffectual to the most important purposes of life, if religious instruction ceases as soon as young people are dismissed from the schools. Many servants may be adverse to receiving these instructions; but, if they persist in refusing them, they certainly should be dismissed, as improper members of a Christian family: many others will accept them with thankfulness, and repay their kind benefactors with gratitude and affection.[52]

The "Christian family" is implicitly the family who employs servants, a category that excludes poor people, not fit to perform the family's pedagogical functions: "The education of youth" is "so indispensable, that, without it, punishment becomes not only useless, but cruel. Children should first be taught what is right, before they are corrected for doing what is wrong: poor infants are most likely to learn the latter, from their necessitous, negligent, and perhaps wicked parents, and should therefore be totally removed from them at a very tender age; certainly not later than ten; and apprenticed to all inhabitants in the parish, of good characters, who have occasion for servants."[53] If the poor cannot or will not educate their children properly, the solution, according to Trimmer, is to make them servants. As in Waugh's sermon, "children of the poor" and "servants" fuse into one, hopefully educable, cohort.

The naturalizing of servants as children, then, was accompanied by, indeed, inextricably linked to, the pedagogical project of educating the poor into a proper sense of "obligation." The affective relations of the middle-class family, realized through the servant's idealized role in that family, helped to suppress the problem of servants' and masters' contradictory economic interests. This project is more complex and extensive than the simple inculcation of "false consciousness." It involves the management of servant's agency, not through the repression of that agency, but through its installation into particular models of character. Literacy is key to this expansion from the domestic to the social. Reading is imagined as simultaneously bridging and sustaining the gap between servants and masters. The nineteenth-century mavens of conduct literature for servants, Sarah and Samuel Adams, offer "Hints on Self-Improvement" to the footmen, who were often considered highly problematic because of their detachment from productive labor: "we may observe that no situation admits of more opportunities for self-improvement than that of the Footman. He has much leisure time which cannot be better employed than in reading profitable books, by which we mean such as will amuse and at the same time instruct him, and thus open to him innumerable enjoyments, which must be quite unthought of by those whose education has been neglected in their earlier years. ... by industry and economy, many servants have secured an independence, or in some cases of legacies from their late masters to reward them for past integrity." The hope of economic improvement is dangled before the male servant, but the main purpose of his literacy is making him happy in his place: "Books, however, are now so cheap, and good as they are cheap, that every servant who studies his own enjoyment will strive to possess a few volumes, which will often keep him out of bad habits and altogether render him a better informed and more useful member of society."[54] Writing is also approved, in some of the literature on service, as a means by which servants can be both happier and more useful. Hanway, notably, recommends that women servants be taught to write because it would extend their usefulness in matters of household management.[55] The happy, productive servant shares many skills, values, even pleasures, with his or her master. The pedagogy that sustains this commonality also, however, sustains the social hierarchy of difference between masters and servants by subordinating the latter's implied agency. Imagining servants as children, the objects of family pedagogy, helped to sustain family hierarchy. In "the posture of children," servants could participate in domestic ideology without claiming equal status to their masters; they could be "part of the family" without challenging economic and social hierarchy.

The education of servants and apprentices is a key concern of writers on domestic service from the late seventeenth century up through the Sunday school social reformers of the late eighteenth and early nineteenth centuries. What kind of literature servants should consume is a large part of the discussion. Plays are the most widely distrusted genre in Samuel Richardson's generation, with novels assuming a comparable role by the end of the eighteenth century. Richardson advises keeping apprentices away from the theater because certain popular dramatic forms encourage too much identification with and sympathy for criminals:

> now the horrid Pantomine and wicked Dumb Shew, the infamous Harlequin Mimicry, introduc'd for nothing but to teach how to cozen, deceive, and cuckold; together with the wretched Group of Rogues, form'd from the Characters of Shepherd, Jonathan Wild, Blueskin, and in fine, from every Rogue that has made a Noise in the World by his superlative Wickedness, has yielded the principal Characters exhibited, and that not for the Sake of Poetical Justice, in their Execution, but to divert the Audience by their Tricks and Escapes; and if they have been brought to Justice at last, it has been in such a Manner, as to move the Pity of the Audience for them.[56]

Servants should not identify with the criminals who were often, as Peter Linebaugh and Lincoln Faller demonstrate, heroic figures to poor Londoners.[57] Richardson's one exception is, not surprisingly, *The London Merchant,* a play performed throughout the century as a Shrove Tuesday "treat" for London apprentices: "I know but of one Instance, and that a very late one, where the Stage has condescended to make itself useful to the City-Youth, by a dreadful Example of the Artifices of a lewd Woman, and the Seduction of an unwary young Man; ... I mean, the Play of George Barnwell, which has met with the Success that I think it well deserves; and I could be content to compound with the young City Gentry, that they should go to this Play once a Year, if they would condition, not to desire to go oftener, till another Play of an equally good Moral and Design were acted on the Stage."[58]

Given the ubiquitous presence of servants in the London theaters, drama is critical to the historical processes of imagining servants' social and sexual agency. The theater, as both a social and a representational space, offered male servants, in particular, alternatives to the child-like role of the asexual *tabula rasa,* the subject of the pedagogical project. Footmen, especially, made up a significant—and often powerfully disruptive—part of the theatrical audience for the first half of the century, and there is another story to tell about their most un-child-like behavior within London theaters.[59] Richardson's imperative to keep servants out of the theater can be read as an early part of an effort that builds momentum over the century to contain servants as subordinates within domestic hierarchy—literally, to keep them at home, with the children.

During the second half of the century, anxieties about servants' literary consumption seem to shift emphasis towards the novel. At the century's end, Sarah Trimmer's ideal servants eschew novels and instead pour over conduct manuals such as *A Present for Servants, Serious Advice and Warning to Servants,* and Hanway's *Domestic Happiness Promoted.*[60] In Trimmer's imaginary ideal family, a suspect new cook introduces "a history," but the servants Thomas and Kitty "found it full of nonsense about lords, and ladies, and 'squires, falling in love with one another, and running away from their parents, and shooting themselves, and sort of stuff, as neither he nor Kitty at all liked, for it would not teach them any thing of their duty either to God or man."[61] Trimmer perhaps inadvertently suggests some of the subversive potential of servants' reading texts that shed none-too-flattering a light on the aristocracy; class difference in the texts approved by Trimmer is both a more prosaic and insidious system than that imagined in the romance novel. It involves moral, aesthetic, and religious standards that are shared by masters and servants even as it locks them into their respective positions of "duty."

One can almost say, by the early nineteenth century, that a full-blown imagined subjectivity was circulating in the literature written specifically for servants' consumption. *The Servant's Magazine,* a mid-nineteenth century compilation of stories, poetry, and practical advice for servants, offers not just instruction on how to be a good servant but also models of aesthetic experience and intellectual aspiration that are suitable for one in service. Not coincidentally, many of these models couple the servants' education with that of the children. One recurring feature is "The Nurse Maid Walks Out with Her Children"; the only point that I can discern in its discussions of birds and plant life is how the maid might help cultivate in herself and her young charges a proper aesthetic and scientific appreciation of nature. This feature tellingly links the subordinated agency of children with that of the maidservant. The latter shares with her employer's children forms of subjective experience that are deemed "healthy"; both learn not just rules for behavior (though the conduct literature is full of these, too), but a sensibility, the means to subjective pleasures that in no way threaten the social or familial order, while offering the assurance of cross-class participation.[62]

The evocation of the child in the context of "the servant problem," of labor relations increasingly defined by economic exchange, points toward what gets suppressed in the child's construction as pedagogical subject: that the child's "best interests" are determined by the social and economic agendas of adults. Without this construction, it may not have been possible to reframe economic struggles between groups defined by their labor, not their age, as pedagogy, the benign care of the helpless. The nineteenth- and twentieth-century moral imperative of the modern child who must be protected from the brutalizing effects of industrial labor may, ironically, have its roots in the eighteenth-century impulse to reframe emergent labor relations in the domestic sphere as affective rather than economic, essentially erasing conflicting interests and exploitation of weaker parties within the domestic sphere. Our "protection" of children is, too often in history, a cover story for what is too hard for us to bear. The analogy of the servant as child is one trope in the historically persistent fiction of the family as the child's safe haven from exploitation.

Notes

1. Bridget Hill, *Servants: English Domestics in the Eighteenth Century* (Oxford: Clarendon Press, 1996).
2. Daniel Defoe, *The Family Instructor in Three Parts; I. Relating to Fathers and Children. II. To Masters and Servants. III. To Husbands and Wives*, 2nd edition (London: Eman. Matthews, 1715); facsimile reproduction (Delmar, NY: Scholars' Facsimiles & Reprints, 1989), 275.
3. Ann Kussmaul, *Servants in Husbandry in Early Modern England* (Cambridge: Cambridge University Press, 1981), 3.
4. Ilana Krausman Ben-Amos notes the tendency to look at London apprentices as childlike, despite the fact that an increasing number entered the state in their late teens. See *Adolescence and Youth in Early Modern England* (New Haven, CT: Yale University Press, 1994), 84–85.
5. Hugh Cunningham, *The Children of the Poor: Representations of Childhood since the Seventeenth Century* (Oxford: Blackwell, 1991), 18–9.
6. Defoe, *Family Instructor*, 275.
7. *Instructions for Masters, Traders, Laborers* (1699), 10.
8. *Instructions*, 19.
9. *The Cities Great Concern, in this Case or Question of Honour and Arms, Whether Apprentiship Extinguisheth Gentry?* (London: William Godbid, 1674), 32.
10. J. Jean Hecht, *The Domestic Servant Class in Eighteenth-Century England* (London: Routledge & Kegan Paul, 1956), 74.
11. George Kearsley, *Kearsley's Table of Trades, For the Assistance of Parents and Guardians, and for the Benefit of those Young Men, Who wish to prosper in the World, and become respectable Members of Society* (London: for George Kearsley, 1787), 40.
12. George Rosen, "A Slaughter of Innocents: Aspects of Child Health in the Eighteenth-Century City," *Studies in Eighteenth-Century Culture* 5 (1976): 85.
13. See Joan Lane, *Apprenticeship in England, 1600–1914.* (London: Westview Press, 1996), 39–54 and 87–88.
14. Dorothy George writes about the "worst results of apprenticeship" as large numbers of runaway children turned adrift by the bankruptcy of their masters. See *London Life in the XVIIIth Century* (New York: Alfred A. Knopf, 1926), 265.
15. Jan Fergus, "Provincial Servants' Reading in the Late Eighteenth Century," in ed. James Raven, *The Practice and Representation of Reading in England* (Cambridge: Cambridge University Press, 1996), 202–225.
16. Defoe, *Family Instructor, passim.*

17. Andrew O'Malley, *The Making of the Modern Child: Children's Literature and Childhood in the Late Eighteenth Century* (New York: Routledge, 2003), 40–41.

18. William Fleetwood, *The Relative Duties of Parents and Children, Husbands and Wives, Masters and Servants.* (London: Charles Harper, 1705; New York and London: Garland, 1985), 384–385.

19. Eliza Haywood, *A Present for a Servant-Maid. Or, the Sure means of gaining Love and Esteem* (Dublin: George Falkner, 1743), 32.

20. Jonas Hanway, *Advice from Farmer Trueman to his Daughter, Mary, upon Her Going to Service* (London: B. Boothroyd, 1805), 134.

21. Hecht, *The Domestic Servant*, 74.

22. Haywood, *Present for a Servant Maid*, 32.

23. *The Servants' Guide and Family Manual*, 2nd edition (London: John Limbird, 1831), 24.

24. For example, see Sarah Trimmer, *The Servant's Friend, An Exemplary Tale: Designed to Enforce the Religious Instructions Given at Sunday and Other Charity Schools* (London: F. C. and J. Rivington, 1814), 106.

25. Trimmer, *Servant's Friend*, 64.

26. Defoe, *Family Instructor*, 238.

27. Defoe, *Family Instructor*, passim.

28. *Present for Servants* (1787), v–vi. See also Hanway, Farmer Trueman, 18 and f.

29. Defoe, *Family Instructor*, 238.

30. O'Malley, *The Making of the Modern Child*, 44.

31. Mitzi Myers, "'Servants as They Are Now Educated': Women Writers and Georgian Pedagogy," *Essays in Literature* 16.1 (1989): 57.

32. Jonathan Swift, *Directions to Servants in General* (London: R. Dodsley, 1745), 7.

33. William Seaton, *A Present for Servants* (1787), iv.

34. Daniel Defoe, *Everybody's Business is Nobody's Business; or Private Abuses, Public Grievances: Exemplified in the Pride, Insolence, and Exorbitant Wages of Our Women Servants, Footmen, &c.* (London: W. Meadows, 1725), 10.

35. Kearsley, *Table of Trades*, 95–96.

36. Hannah Wooley writes against this tendency, instructing the maid to view her service as preparation for marriage rather than a job to be taken and left at will: "Be not subject to a change, For a *rouling-stone gathers no Moss;* and as you will gain but little money, so if you ramble up and down you will lose your credit." See *The Gentlewomans Companion; or, A Guide to the Female Sex: Containing Directions of Behaviour, in All Places, Companies, Relations, and Conditions ... Whereunto is added a guide for Cook-Maids, Dairy-Maids* (London: A. Maxwell for D. Newman, 1673), 214. See also Ann Haly's edition of Samuel and Sarah Adams's *The Complete Servant* (1825), 24.

37. Sarah Trimmer, writing at the end of the century, is one of the most brilliant interpolators of the servant's economic agency into a social vision in which all, masters and servants, are the economic winners. See *The Servant's*

Friend, An Exemplary Tale: Designed to Enforce the Religious Instructions Given at Sunday and Other Charity School. (London: F. C. and J. Rivington, 1814).

38. Swift, *Directions*, 6.
39. Swift, *Directions*, 36.
40. Swift, *Directions*, 83.
41. Defoe, *Everybody's Business*, p. 8.
42. Robert Dodsley, *The Footman's Friendly Advice to his Brethren of the Livery; And to all Servants in General* (London: T. Worral, n.d.), 12.
43. O'Malley, *The Making of the Modern Child*, 44.
44. *The Laws Relating to Masters and Servants* (London: H. Lintot, 1755), iii.
45. Hanway, *Advice from Farmer Trueman*, 16.
46. Thomas Broughton, *Serious Advice and Warning to Servants, More Especially Those of the Nobility and Gentry*, 8th edition (London: F.C. and J. Rivington, 1815), 10.
47. Kearsley, *Table of Trades*, 95.
48. Hanway, *Advice from Farmer Trueman*, 142.
49. John Waugh, *The Duty of Apprentices and Other Servants. A Sermon Preach'd at the Parish Church of St. Bridget, alias Bride, August 24th, 1713. Being the Festival of St. Barholomew; At a Meeting of about 1400 Persons of both Sexes. Being part of those who had been Educated, and afterwards put out to Trades and other Services, by the Trustees of the Charity-Schools, in and about the Cities of London and Westminster* (London: G. Strahan, 1713), 23.
50. Waugh, *The Duty of Apprentices*, 24.
51. Sarah Trimmer, *The Oeconomy of Charity; or An Address to Ladies Concerning Sunday Schools* (London: T. Bensley for T. Longman, 1787), 26.
52. Trimmer, *Oeconomy of Charity*, 122–123.
53. *A General Plan of Parochial and Provincial Police* (1787), 6. The problem of children without even "wicked parents" is remarked upon as well. John Bennett writes in *The Advantages of Sunday Schools* (London: C. Wheeler, 1785), p. 12, that "through many parts of the kingdom (but, particularly, the commercial and populous ones) groups of little heathens are seen wandering about without any sense or knowledge of their duty." Many of these "little heathens" were destined to become pauper apprentices, *de facto* domestic servants.
54. *The Servants' Guide and Family Manual*, 253–254.
55. Hanway, *Farmer Trueman's Advice*, 153–154.
56. Samuel Richardson, *The Apprentice's Vade Mecum: or, Young Man's Pocket-Companion* (London: J. Roberts, 1734); reissued by Augustan Reprint Society, Publication Numbers 169–170 (Los Angeles: William Andrews Clark Memorial Library, 1975), 12–13.
57. See Peter Linebaugh, *The London Hanged: Crime and Civil Society in the Eighteenth Century* (Cambridge: Cambridge University Press, 1992) and Lincoln Faller, *Turned to Account: The Forms and Functions of Criminal Biography in Late Seventeenth and Early Eighteenth-Century England* (New York and Cambridge: Cambridge University Press, 1987).
58. Richardson, *The Apprentice's Vade Mecum*, 16.

59. This story culminates in David Garrick's abolition of the "footman's gal-
    lery," a prerogative accorded London footmen since the late seventeenth
    century. Another part of my work on London servants deals with servants'
    use of this public space to claim another form of social agency which was,
    eventually, suppressed.
60. Trimmer, *The Servant's Friend*, 61.
61. Trimmer, *The Servant's Friend*, 51.
62. *The Servant's Magazine; or Female Domestics' Instructor*, xix (1855), passim.

8

CURIOSITY, SCIENCE, AND EXPERIENTIAL LEARNING IN THE EIGHTEENTH CENTURY

Reading the *Spectacle de la nature*

CYNTHIA J. KOEPP

Imagine a nine-volume set of small encyclopedias, intended as a compendium of general knowledge, where an amazing array of topics is presented not alphabetically, but in dialogues—between a count, countess, their young visitor, and an extremely knowledgeable local abbot. Imagine further that these little books are exquisitely illustrated with numerous plates by some of the foremost artists and engravers of Paris. Note as well the author's expressed commitment to innovative pedagogy and his desire to captivate and hold his readers' attention by beginning with the most fascinating information he could find (on strange animals, say, or odd geological formations), and then leading them to more serious and abstract kinds of knowledge such as algebra, physics, and law. When I first came across the Abbé Pluche's *Spectacle de la nature* (1732–1751),[1] I sensed that I had found a wonderfully rich set of texts with much to say about life, learning, and attitudes in the eighteenth century. It reminded me of Rousseau's *Émile* and Diderot's great *Encyclopédie*—books that would appear only two decades later.[2] Yet, when I searched for the relevant scholarship, I discovered that most twentieth-century historians typically dismissed Pluche in one sentence: as a mediocre popularizer of science, as a reductionist blinded by his own teleological faith in Divine Providence, as an apologist for the nobility, or as a purveyor of mere "picture books" for children. In any case, scholars early on had determined that Pluche was not an author who deserved serious attention.

Further research confirmed my instincts that he was worth at least another look.[3] For one thing, Pluche's *Spectacle de la nature* was a phenomenal best-seller throughout Europe. In his classic article on the contents of Parisian private libraries (1750–1780), Daniel Mornet found that the *Spectacle de la nature* was the fourth most common book on the shelves.[4] Before 1800 it had already appeared in at least fifty-seven editions in French, twenty-two editions in English, and numerous other versions in Dutch, German, Italian, and Spanish. In 1770 when the famous publishing house at Neuchâtel (that Robert Darnton has studied so thoroughly) needed a quick bit of cash, a book dealer wrote them saying, "Hey, do a pirated version of Pluche— that's one of the surest ways to make money."[5] This is not an insignificant comment, considering that by 1770 the text was already forty years old and existed in dozens of editions. Even if Pluche were a second-rate thinker (and I don't think he was), one might make the case that if we want to know about popular reading habits, the transmission of knowledge and ideas, and the place of the child in the eighteenth century, the *Spectacle de la nature* would be a good place to start.

And that is what I am going to do. In this chapter, I will offer a series of closely-related arguments to make the case that Pluche matters: he should not be dismissed as an inconsequential children's author or a crackpot vulgarizer. First, I will argue that Pluche is significant for compiling a very informative eight-volume encyclopedia that both advocates some of the best pedagogy of his day and incorporates it throughout the text—a pedagogy informed by curiosity, experiential learning, and the importance of useful, practical knowledge. Second, far from being an apologist for the nobility, Pluche undermines traditional noble values that eschewed trade and manual labor through his championing of artisans, technology, and worldwide commerce. If anything, the Abbé is offering his readers a social critique: a view of the world that would encourage the development of "bourgeois" attitudes, not those of a traditional nobility. Along the same lines, I will suggest that Pluche cannot be dismissed simply as a blind teleologist, but should be acknowledged as an author who contributed to enlightenment thinking. Despite his strong religious faith and belief in Divine Providence (or maybe because of it), Pluche has written a text that promotes the exercise of reason, encourages the reevaluation of utility, and instills belief in progress. Finally, I will conclude by discussing briefly the significance of Pluche's publishing success and suggest reasons why the *Spectacle de la nature* has been ignored.

Curiosity as the Key

In the preface to volume one, Pluche spells out in great detail his philosophy of education and simultaneously offers an implicit critique of the status quo: bad pedagogy, boring lessons, too many abstractions, harsh punishments, little fun, and a failure to recognize the uniqueness of each child. He saw all these tendencies as stultifying and counterproductive to the processes of learning. Pluche is not a pioneer in this respect, because Erasmus, Montaigne, John Locke, and Pluche's own mentor Claude Rollin—to mention only a few—had already argued for more interesting and engaging tutors, more useful and practical lessons, more child-friendly teaching strategies, and a gentler hand of discipline. In the *Spectacle de la nature,* however, Pluche brings the many strands of these progressive theories together, articulates them clearly for the lay reader, and then demonstrates how they could work in practice. His originality and effectiveness as an educator lies in the way he combines approach with content. He both imparts knowledge to his readers as well as guides them as they try to transmit that knowledge to others in interesting and engaging ways.

From the very first sentence of the "Preface," Pluche begins to make the case for his methods. He notes that

> There is no better way to encourage children to think and reason than by building on their curiosity. The desire to know is as natural to us as reason. It exerts itself with force and liveliness through every stage of life, but never with more eagerness than in youth, when the mind, unfurnished

with knowledge, avidly seizes on every object presented to it, gives in willingly to the charms of novelty, and easily contracts the habit of reflection and attentiveness (1:iii).

This is the first of many occasions in the text in which Pluche will make it clear that engaging a child's "curiosity" is the crucial step. That engagement needs to happen before one can start to move toward the ultimate goal: to teach children to think and reason. Here Pluche's reference to "the unfurnished mind" resonates with John Locke's notion of the "blank slate." And, like Locke, Pluche hopes that through his method children will develop or "contract" good habits early on that will enable them to become educated, productive, and moral adults.

Nature as the Best Book

Since, for Pluche, "nature is the best and most complete book," he will first pique his readers' curiosity by going outdoors, in the seemingly familiar world of the backyard garden (1:v). And thanks to new scientific knowledge and inventions—such as the microscope—he can show his readers the amazing characteristics and properties of things when they are observed close at hand. By exposing them to the surprises in nature, Pluche is convinced that young people will be "hooked," their desire to know will be awakened, and real learning will become possible. By beginning with the garden, Pluche also reveals another of his cardinal rules, taken directly from Francis Bacon: never to commence with general axioms and universal ideas, but always to start instead with the particular, concrete, and immediate, "to imitate the order of nature herself, and begin with the first objects that we perceive around us and which are always there" (1:viii).

In this case, then, what exactly is close at hand? At the beginning of volume one, it is the smallest thing of all: the insect. And true to his principle of curiosity, Pluche will devote his first dialogues to things that almost anyone would find fascinating: wasp nests, silk worms, spiderwebs, and butterflies—with exact references to some of the best and latest scientific information on insects cited in the margins (see Figure 8.1). We should not overlook the great service

Tome I.Page 64.

Les Papillons de jour.
Se reconnoissent aux Antennes qui forment vers leur extremite une houpe, ou une espece de massue.

Fig. 8.1 "Les Papillons de jour," Pluche, *Le spectacle de la nature*, Paris: Veuve Estienne et fils, 1749, volume 1, plate facing p. 64. Reproduced by permission of Princeton University Library.

Pluche performed by translating, synthesizing, and making accessible the ideas of many famous scientists and naturalists of his day, whose works were typically published in Latin and available only in expensive folio editions. His sources include articles published in the *Transactions* of the Royal Society of London, the *Mémoires* of the Académie Royale des Sciences in France, and books by many famous authors, such as Anton van Leeuwenhoek, R. de Réaumur, René Descartes, and Isaac Newton. Indeed he was the writer who first explained to a large public readership that the caterpillar, chrysallis, and butterfly were just different forms of the same animal; who described the formation of shells and coral; who discussed the communal activities of ants and bees; and who included engravings that showed what one could see looking through a microscope.

Evidence suggests that readers were captivated by what they found in his books. Charles Bonnet, the great French entomologist, credited Pluche for initiating his fascination with insects. At age sixteen, he read Pluche's riveting description of the "lion pismer" in battle with an ant, and felt an entirely new sensation: "I did not read the book, I devoured it. It felt as if [the Abbé Pluche] had awakened in me a new sense or new faculties; and I would have willingly said that I was only beginning to live."[6] Louis-François Jauffret (known primarily for his interest in the wild boy of Aveyron) first encountered the *Spectacle de la nature* at age fifteen and seems to have experienced a similar epiphany. Early on, he took Pluche's goals and pedagogy to heart, imitated his tone and style, and by age twenty-five found success publishing children's books of his own.[7]

Many others were clearly seduced as well. For example, the English newspaper, *The Bee, or Universal Weekly,* published excerpts from the *Spectacle de la nature* before the English translations appeared in book form, with notes from the editors claiming that readers wanted more of these "remarkable and entertaining conversations."[8] Some readers vehemently defended the *Spectacle de la nature* by writing letters to journals and newspapers to complain about those critics who had given Pluche unfavorable reviews.[9] Both Pluche's contemporaries and later scholars credited this book with sparking the immense interest in natural history that lasted throughout the eighteenth century. He helped create a public receptive to the works of Buffon and Réaumur, as well as for Diderot's great *Encyclopédie.*[10]

The success of the *Spectacle de la nature* with readers, especially young readers such as Bonnet and Jauffret, suggests that Pluche knew what he was doing with his "curiosities." Aware of the importance of introducing children to certain kinds of knowledge at the appropriate moments, Pluche structured the *Spectacle de la nature* to move from the simple and familiar to more complex and abstract knowledge, but only after he has snagged his readers' interest. True to his larger pedagogical goals, the Abbé promised his audience that he would not let things get too difficult too soon: "We will change our path if it proves too rugged" and strike out on the "most agreeable and amusing track—so long as it will lead us eventually to the same place" (1:vii).

Talking in Dialogues

One way to avoid that "too rugged" path, Pluche contends, is to employ the dialogue. He remarks:

> Instead of a methodological discourse or dissertation that often seems boring and disagreeable, we have chosen the style of the dialogue as the most natural and likely to engage all readers. ... Our intention is to entertain the minds of young people with a free conversation, suited to their abilities without perplexing them. We want to go for the most natural: a scene in the country, with people of different conditions. Some will furnish our conversation with their knowledge and others will animate the discussion with their curiosity (1:viii).

The Abbé decided that it would be more effective to introduce knowledge and information through casual discourse, as if topics were coming up by chance in a conversation rather than laid out step-by-step in advance. He asks rhetorically: "What can we gain from this format?" For one thing the ideas will not be so hard to understand, because readers can follow the thoughts of the characters as they converse and get "vivid impressions" of what strikes them as interesting. He hopes that readers will be able to see themselves engaging in these kinds of conversations: the children imagining themselves as participants, the parents and tutors imitating them at home (1:xiii–xiv).

The *Spectacle de la nature* as a "How-to" Book

Although the *Spectacle de la nature* played a major role in increasing an interest in natural history, I want to argue that it is also a "how-to" book on effective teaching and parenting—perhaps one of the keys to its success. Throughout the volumes we can find instructions, demonstrations, and guidance as to how parents might embrace the Abbé's gentler, entertaining approaches to learning and what might be gained if they did.

In a dialogue on spiders, for example, the countess digresses from the main subject for a moment to offer testimony on the efficacy of these methods, as she acknowledges her debt to the prior who educated her son and now has a new boy under his wing. She begins her reminiscences by explaining in her own words the theory behind the principle of "curiosity":

> When you used to take a walk with my son, you gave him a taste of the crafts and sciences in a manner that charmed him. Your method, as it

appears to me, was not so much to make him understand specific things immediately but awaken in him a desire to understand them. Your intention was to make him curious, because curiosity is an active passion that is never indolent. And when this goal is once achieved, all the rest comes without tears or complaints. I have frequently noticed that your discourses and diversions, even your very games, only tended to sharpen the youth's curiosity (1:93).

Here the countess reiterates Pluche's principle that what matters most during the early stages of education is not conveying knowledge, but helping a child become receptive to learning by engaging his curiosity.

Next the countess describes in detail what might be called the prior's modus operandi—the activities he devised for tutor and pupil to do together that she enjoyed watching so much, activities that other adults could easily duplicate with their own children:

It was very pleasant, for instance, to see the curate and his little parishioner discussing, sometimes by the water's edge, which stones were the flattest. And then to observe each of them make his pile and then skip them across the surface of the water. And when they were weary of that activity, to sit down and make observations on the descent of bodies, the level of the water, the lines of incidence and reflection, as I think they called them, the pressure of the air, and many other things that I have now forgotten (1:93–94).

But the countess does not end her story there, for when that discussion was concluded, the prior and student continued walking farther along the beach where they found the inspiration for a new project:

Then they went to work with their sticks on the first smooth bed of sand they saw; there they traced out a map of the Holy Land, or Italy or France and even proceeded to the Indies and Canada. [On another day and another walk] if they lacked sand, they made use of stones, leaves, and apples, with which they sketched out provinces, mountains, and cities. Every day produced some new invention (1:94).

What the countess has shown is that a gifted and sympathetic teacher can turn a walk along the beach into a delightful occasion where skipping stones offers a way to introduce valuable lessons in physics and geography. Even more impressive, the countess explains, is that this method of teaching proves more effective than traditional approaches. Whereas abstract knowledge "just bores or annoys and is quickly forgotten," Pluche's diversions seem to enhance learning and the retention of knowledge. As the countess relates:

> It is impossible to describe the air and delight, with which my son repeated these performances in my presence; everything was so vivid in his imagination and so well organized in his mind, that whatever he learned through this kind of playing was repeated to me in a very exact order, and the prior, without knowing it, gave instructions to two people instead of one (1:94).

Pluche proposes to make learning easier for the pupil by conveying ideas through creative play involving found objects such as stones, sand, and sticks that offer a material and familiar connection to ideas which otherwise would have seemed abstract or remote.

Finally, the prior responds to the countess's praises with his own testimony and compliments:

> I could not have used my time better than devoting some of it to [your son's] improvement. … One cannot be too careful in protecting a young mind from every disagreeable impression. And I can assure your Ladyship, I have employed no part of my time with so much advantage as those hours I have passed away in little amusements with this amiable youth (1:95–96).

This extended exchange offers much advice to readers. First, Pluche is suggesting that engaging a child's curiosity and teaching through entertaining methods will lead to real and lasting knowledge. Through the countess's testimony, he points out that anything, even a simple walk, can provide an opportunity for learning. He also reinforces his conviction that the teacher cannot take too much care to avoid subjecting children to the boring and tedious—that they must be protected at all costs from harsh discipline or constraints that might extinguish their natural desire to know. In short, good lessons should not be painful.

Most significant of all, is how Pluche makes the case in this dialogue that children themselves are important by reassuring adults that spending time amusing and educating young people can be very rewarding—that what looks like play is neither a waste of time for the children nor for the grownups around them.[11] Here and (as we shall see below) in myriad other places in the text, he offers models of family life that encourage sociability and affectionate, playful educational activities. He is, moreover, suggesting to parents in 1732 why children should be encouraged to be seen and heard rather than silenced.

The countess concludes this section by noting that not many people know how to use amusements to teach this way: few can "invent games with a purpose" as successfully as the prior. But perhaps more people will be able to adopt Pluche's methods once they realize that the *Spectacle de la nature* and its various dialogues and entries can show them the way.[12]

Mothers and Young Children

In volume six, Pluche addresses the issue of pedagogy and parenting more directly in over 150 pages of advice to mothers and fathers about their involvement in bringing up their children. Here Pluche reasserts the key ideas that childhood has stages and that each child is unique. He stresses the importance of knowing the right moment to introduce certain kinds of knowledge, that the capacity to learn must be encouraged gently in ways appropriate to the individual child's personality, temperament, and interests. In the discourse entitled "The Exercises of Children," he looks closely at the crucial role the mother can play in the early years of development.

Curiosity is again the operative term. He recommends that the mother be very attentive to her children from their earliest moments. She should introduce only activities and information that "would naturally engage their attention." Never pushing too hard, she should instead "regulate the amount of instruction she gives her children by their actual capacity." She should "silently observe the different dispositions of her children in the smallest matters" (by watching them when they are not paying attention to her), so that she might better determine what strategies and games might prove most effective for each (6:61–62).

Drawing a profile of the ideal mother/teacher, Pluche advises: "Instead of frequently repeating tiresome lectures which do but glance upon the mind, or having recourse to threats, which never succeed, our tender mother successively contrives a thousand new and pleasing methods to influence her children." She must find congenial and effective approaches because while her children are young, she is responsible for teaching them morality and "strengthening their weak reason." The solicitous mother should be creative and imaginative, ready to offer "explanations of everything that arises; little surprises, novelties, lots of interesting illustrations; appropriate music; or walks chosen on purpose to introduce new questions"—activities like that walk along the beach. In short, according to Pluche, the mother should create an environment where everything is employed to encourage her children's curiosity and to fill up the "vacuities of their intelligence which only wants more ideas" (6:62–63). And of course, thanks to the wealth of useful and fascinating information these eight volumes contained, adults actually could find answers to many of the questions that those inquiring young minds would be sure to raise once their curiosity was engaged and they began to look more closely at the world around them: Why does the moon wax and wane? Why do bees live in hives? How could one measure the circumference of the earth without leaving home? How does one spin flax into cloth? How does a telescope work? Readers could easily retrieve the answers woven through those leisurely conversations by consulting the indexes in every volume.

Fathers and Daughters

In the next section, we find another testimonial, so to speak, entitled "Letter from a Father of a Family, on the First Culture of the Mind." Again Pluche steps back, this time turning over the podium to a fictional father who claims to have had some success in raising his own sons and daughters. This father begins by drawing a damning picture of the education a girl typically received, showing it to be frivolous and harmful with its emphasis on the art of pleasing, etiquette, and mindless pastimes. He notes that many parents of a daughter think she is a tender creature and mistakenly "avoid filling her head with anything that requires the least application or constraint." Girls who endure this type of education, he argues, will end up shallow, void of ideas, lacking discernment except in matters of pleasure and dress, and conversant only in the most superficial aspects of life (6:76–77).

Because he believes that daughters also deserve the chance to develop their reason and acquire a share of useful knowledge, he advocates another approach consistent with Pluche's principles in its avoidance of traditional methods and harsh discipline:

> If you begin by loading young minds with morals, maxims, rules, and what is worse, abstractions and disputes, they will only feel the weight of the words and will be always wishing for the end of an exercise that pains them (6:83).

Here (and many other places throughout the volumes), the father insists that one must avoid overwhelming the child. Strict rules of grammar are especially suspect and he instead embraces a sort of "whole language method," when he proposes a number of alternative activities that might appeal to a girl's imagination. His ultimate goal is to help children find their own voices in natural, conversational prose. For example, he talks about various ways a father might help teach a daughter of ten or eleven years to write—first by encouraging her to pen imaginary letters to cousins, merchants, or even a great prince. To discourage girls from adopting artificial styles or affectations, he urges that they should be taught to think of the letter as a conversation—and warns parents that these epistles need not be perfect to be effective exercises:

> If you let daughters record things with the most common conversational phrases, they will become emboldened to write. They will learn that daily writing is not a punishment. Nor should you reproach them for their mistakes. You may point out a few spelling errors, but express no harsh criticism or injurious words (6:84).

And when your daughter gets tired of letters, he suggests: "Encourage her to write stories, and she will make a game of writing." He also recommends letting her take on small writing tasks for others in the household who have not yet learned to write. Or, better yet:

have father himself put her to work, as his first secretary. It takes no more effort that simply sharing his thoughts with her. And tell me, if you please, if it will be the father or the daughter who is more delighted by this arrangement? It is hard to say, but I lean toward the father (6:85–86).

In these passages (and many others) he proves himself to be psychologically astute when he intimates the subtle ways the success of a child's education is dependent on cultivating her sense of self. Here we observe the value of giving children some small responsibilities and the chance to be useful to others—even if they are just beginners. By drawing a connection between a child's self-esteem and education, he is offering further evidence of how harsh discipline or criticism (insofar as it damages a child's confidence) can interfere with learning. Here he also asserts the immense power of fathers to increase their daughters' sense of worth, if they join their girls in certain kinds of useful play. By creating a special relationship—by letting them assume the role of "secretary"—fathers could also help enhance their daughters' motivation to learn. In addition, those kinds of pleasurable moments spent "working" together would further strengthen sentimental bonds and relationships within the family.

Pluche's fictional father also discusses social studies, and recommends taking an historical approach to geography as an interesting way to avoid rote memorization of lists of names and dates. He warns: "Don't make your daughters memorize isolated bare matters of fact; that is not the way to give them a taste for knowledge." Instead, he urges that they be free to write poems and perform plays about interesting moments in history, or have them imagine dialogues speculating about the motivations of various historical personages. Once girls are sufficiently familiar with Holy Scripture, let them learn about the Greek and Norse gods through their symbols, from pictures, and from dramatic readings that they invent. This kind of learning should be really enjoyable as it incorporates visuals, theatrics, and physical activity. Like Pluche, the father urges that parents find ways to waken their curiosity, "for if your children have developed their curiosity, it will never remain idle and will always be ready to turn in the best direction" (6: 63–64, 110).

Liberty and Learning

Near the end of this letter, the fictional father expresses his distress
about how wrongheaded teaching methods for very young boys frequently destroy their love of the classics and literature forever: "The
mistakes committed [at the rudimentary level] are of such a nature that
our most ingenious professors and our best books are often so many
treasures lost, even to those of our children most able to benefit from
them." Frustration with the typical ineffectiveness (and worse) of early
language instruction leads him to reflect on the "pleasures of childhood." Here he offers a more philosophical discussion about the nature
of children, in hopes that these insights might serve as the foundation
for new approaches to teaching. He asserts that young children are
most passionate about two things: amusing objects they can see and
physical play. Hence, he argues, effective instruction should incorporate sights to attract the eye and opportunities to move about.

Accompanying these recommendations, however, is a more important and fundamental message: to learn, children need liberty because
their feelings of pleasure are based partly on the perception of having
the freedom to follow their curiosity, freedom to move their bodies, and
freedom to play at will. Thus, when designing amusing play to facilitate
learning, he advises adults to conceal their aims, while neither confin-
ing nor subjecting the children to regular classroom discipline: "When
children are to be diverted in this way, they must perceive nothing but
their own pleasure and liberty" (6:141). Following his own advice, he
suggests using lots of pictures and engravings to delight the eye. To give
them that sense of freedom of movement, he suggests particular kinds
of toys, especially those with many moving parts or many pieces
designed to be assembled in different ways. What children need are

> objects that belong to them, and instruments which they may dispose of
> as their own property. Give them an old-fashioned clock, a small
> timber-framed house put together with removable pegs, a jack, a small
> crane, rammers, and all the engines for driving piles into the ground to
> be taken apart, with each piece numbered in order to put the whole
> thing together again ... add a box of blocks shaped like bricks as
> well. Soon you will see them practicing masonry of all kinds, and raising

complete edifices. You will see industry and prudence shining through every operation (6:141–142).

Here Pluche reveals his great trust in children's ability to learn through the initiation of free play—entertaining themselves with toys like these will help them gain practical and useful knowledge, prudence, industry, and judgment. And note too that these toys would also introduce basic skills necessary for carpentry or masonry, artisanal work that Pluche prefers to trifling diversions or metaphysical speculations.

Hands-on Science

Thus far, I have tried to stress the ways that the *Spectacle de la nature* explains and justifies its pedagogy's fundamental principles, while simultaneously demonstrating how it can be implemented in the classroom with carefully designed diversions to enhance many aspects of teaching. The sections on science and crafts offer Pluche's readers yet another kind of activity intended to engage children's curiosity, those we now characterize as opportunities for hands-on learning.

Like Mr. Wizard of 1950s television, the Abbé is very good at describing how to carry out experiments that demonstrate various scientific principles that on the printed page may be rather more difficult to grasp. In volume one, for example, he described an experiment that requires a trip to the butcher. In order to disprove the concept of spontaneous generation, Pluche recommends comparing the outcomes of two pieces of fresh raw meat allowed to go rotten in different circumstances. His plan: place one piece of meat in a jar with a lid tightly closed and the other in an open pan, and see which generates maggots (1:26–27). In a section on rivers and oceans, he suggests making various tests on pans of water under different conditions to demonstrate the processes of evaporation (3:137–138). In the entry on microscopes, Pluche offers extensive comparisons of different types, and then describes how to put together the simplest makeshift microscope at home:

> You may procure a microscope by piercing a very small piece of lead with a pin, and by filling the aperture with a very little drop of water, that you put over the orifice with the beak of a clean pen. If that drop remains round

like a bubble over the pinhole, it becomes a lens ... that will prodigiously magnify any small object you shall present to it. And the loss of that excellent microscope may be repaired at a very small expense, by one that is equivalent, or perhaps superior to it in goodness (4:316).

On the next page, in case a reader needs ideas or encouragement, he describes all kinds of things one could look at under a microscope: the scales of various fish, types of wood pulp, fibers, a variety of plants and seeds, pollen, bird feathers, and the flesh of animals (4:317). (See Figure 8.2.)

Perhaps the most comprehensive and interesting of all activities in the *Spectacle* are those he devised to teach about light. For example, he sets up countless trials with prisms to show the breakdown of rays of sunlight into colors (4:170–71). When Pluche discusses the structure of the eye in order to explain how we see, he includes a number of experiments and models that demonstrated the various ways rays of light operate on this organ (see Figure 8.3). Some of the projects are quite simple, requiring only common things such as a piece of straw. For example, having shown readers how to make an object look bigger than it really is, he makes the following suggestion:

Have you got a mind to produce quite the contrary effect on your eye? Take a wheat straw, the smallest part especially, ... put the end of it through a piece of paper, and look at the sun through the tiny pipe of straw. The rays that come through this narrow channel do by no means fill the whole compass of your eye and this shall render the image of the sun, or of any other object, much smaller (4:138).

In his instructions to readers, Pluche adopts an informal tone, speaking as naturally as possible so his readers can follow him each step of the way, just as he promised to do in the *Spectacle*'s preface. In the directions for building an elaborate artificial eye out of cardboard tubes, a glass lens, and other paraphernalia, he even suggests where to place the apparatus at the window for best effect so that the reader will be sure to see that the image received by the eye arrives inverted. But he also anticipates that some readers might be skeptical, so he offers yet another experiment whose materials were probably easier to acquire in the 1730s than now:

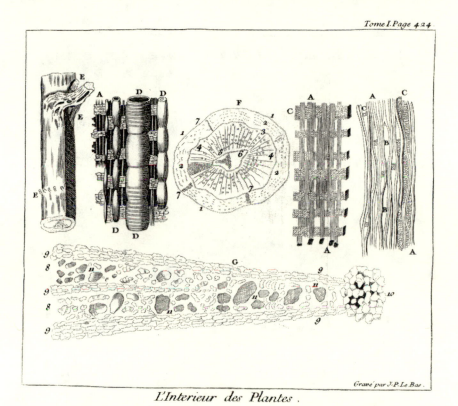

Tome I. Page 424.

Gravé par J. P. Le Bas.

L'Interieur des Plantes.

Fig. 8.2 "L'Interieur des Plantes," Pluche, *Le spectacle de la nature*, Paris: Veuve Estienne et fils, 1749, volume 1, plate facing p. 424. Reproduced by permission of Princeton University Library.

If after the experiment of the glass and tubes, of which I have just shown you the use, you should still doubt that the image of the eye is inverted, you might convince yourself of it by placing—at the hole of a window shutter which looks toward a public place—the eye of a sheep or ox freshly killed. After having cut off its thick outer covering and getting down to the final membrane that contains the liquid, you need to hold some parchment paper behind it ... then you will see everything (the houses, people, and so on) represented clearly on the paper in a wonderful foreshortening. All the images will be inverted" (4:140).

These hands-on activities scattered through the *Spectacle de la nature* give it yet another dimension: it also serves as a toy box or little laboratory chock full of interesting things to do.

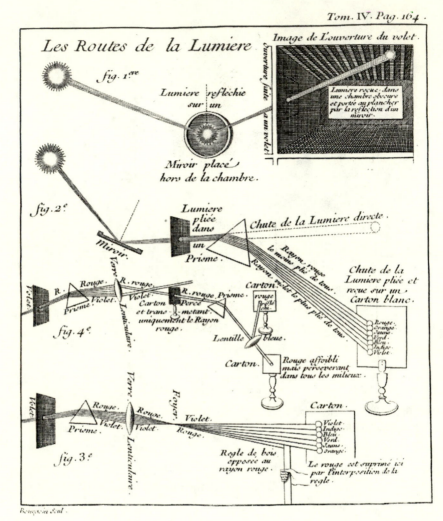

Fig. 8.3 "Les Routes de la Lumiere," Pluche, *Le spectacle de la nature,* Paris: Veuve Estienne et fils, 1749, volume 4, plate facing p. 164. Reproduced by permission of Princeton University Library.

Experiential Learning and Work

Throughout the *Spectacle de la nature,* then, Pluche offers his readers a wealth of entertaining activities that describe new pedagogies and incorporate those teaching methods as they explain the workings of nature. However, Pluche's emphasis on experiential "hands-on" learning is symptomatic of a much larger project that carries with it a social critique. Here Pluche's desire to reform education is in part an attempt to reform attitudes, in particular the traditional denigration of labor and the mechanical arts. Implicit in Pluche's championing of "hands-on" activities is a validation of those who actually work with their hands: the artisans, peasants, and day laborers. As I will argue later, for Pluche, children may be the ideal audience to actualize this change. He reckoned that educating children about the virtues and contributions of those who labor at the bottom of society might be the most effective way to for him to undermine traditional aristocratic values, and thereby encourage the development of a new, enlightened world view that would celebrate utility, reason, commerce, and practical knowledge.

Thus, from the very first pages of volume one, the Abbé Pluche vigorously challenges the attitudes underlying the traditional social hierarchy where mechanical labor stands at the bottom, by showing that acquiring an understanding of manufacturing processes can be quite compelling. Dialogue Three, for example, lays out the life cycle of silkworms, but also includes the countess's descriptions of how to raise silk worms (another activity one could do at home) with more details on silk weaving to come in volume seven. In the dialogue discussing the apple tree's particular characteristics, conversation eventually touches upon the maintainance of orchards, and offers plates of the cider mill and wine press, the text's first technical illustrations (2:365, 385).[13] In Dialogue Four, a scientific exposition on the spider takes an unexpected turn when it describes how the student and the prior, visit a local weaver, learn all the parts of the loom, and try their hands at the machine (both student and prior break many threads in their efforts to understand the process of weaving). The young man responds to this "hands-on experience" at the weaver's with the comment: "Nothing ever amused me better, and I am very desirous of seeing all of the implements of each Artisan one after another. I cannot understand why they should be concealed from us" (1:90). Here Pluche's student voices a protest against the traditional attitudes that keep him aloof from the artisan and discourage upper-class men from witnessing his skills and techniques firsthand. Eventually, the prior will take his charge (and Pluche's readers) to workshop after workshop in Paris, "not in a superficial manner, but by making it his serious endeavor to get a competent idea of the real object and most valuable methods of each particular trade" (1:90). As Pluche will admonish his readers, the only way to understand the craft well is to visit the workshop, talk to the artisan, and try to practice the craft under helpful eyes of skilled practitioners. Parents could initiate similar visits to workshops themselves.

While the Abbé blames noble prejudice for disdainful attitudes toward mechanical skills, he also faults traditional education, with its emphasis on abstract speculation. Pluche deplores that students

> never hear one word of the perfection and usefulness of the arts, or the industry of people whose work supports our lives. ... Everyone of us has seen the sails of a windmill and the wheel of a watermill in action. ... But we know nothing of the structure of them, and can hardly avoid confusing a carpenter with a wood cutter. We all carry watches in our pockets. But do we understand the mechanism? ... It is the same with most common trades: We know the names of them, and no more (1:91).

Throughout this section, Pluche continues to lament students' ignorance. In his opinion, no one would be worse off for

> not knowing about Leibnitz's monads ... But there is also no one who would not be better off were he to acquire a true knowledge of the arts and trades where the common people are occupied. This kind of philosophy is a thousand times more to be esteemed, than those systems whose uselessness is their least fault (7:64, 72).

It is only the search for applied knowledge through an experimental process of trial and error, Pluche contends, that will lead to necessary new knowledge which in turn will allow men to make discoveries in the sciences and in the arts and crafts beneficial to society as a whole. He frequently points to the serious consequences of the harmful divides between theory and practice, the high and the low. For example, to improve agriculture, he writes, we really need serious study of soils, "but our great naturalists are not willing to get down on their knees and crawl on the earth" (1:279). Elsewhere he complains that "There's not yet a decent book on animal husbandry in French, because none of our bright minds will deign to study in the barnyard" (6:280).[14] In these discourses Pluche emerges not as a traditional apologist but an enlightenment reformer, determined to highlight the many ways that the prejudices against manual or mechanical work cost society. He fears that without cooperation between philosophy and the crafts, between theory and practice, between the learned and workers, much valuable knowledge will be lost or left undiscovered. Just imagine, Pluche muses:

> If merely having common minds groping their way has been sufficient to procure for us so many convenient instruments and sure ways of doing things, think of the benefits if attentive and penetrating minds were to employ themselves with the common wants of society. They might be able to draw even more from these experiments, even better methods or finer inventions (7:44–45).

Perhaps his readers—young and mature—could begin to bridge that gap.

In addition to calling for greater collaboration between workers and theorists, Pluche also challenged the prevailing prejudice against the artisan by explicitly comparing the relative value to society of the various "esteemed" professions as opposed to those of the artisanal classes. He writes:

> It is customary for all such as are under no necessity of laboring with their hands, to place themselves at an infinite distance above the working tradesman; they affix an idea of the meanness of his condition, and their contempt of it is universal. The lawyer or accountant would think himself disgraced by marrying his daughter to a shoemaker or a tailor (6:397).

But even a very good lawyer or accountant, Pluche continues, "does not deserve the admiration which is owed to the industrious man who makes us a handsome carriage, or an excellent pump. Those things are truly useful" (6:398). Pluche's forceful emphasis on utility and practical knowledge challenges the traditional social order in important ways: although he knows that many in high places have little interest in the arts and technology, he hopes that his young readers will eventually begin to make different choices.

Indeed, near the beginning of volume seven, he suggests a remedy for that "painful" feeling of uselessness afflicting certain privileged members of society:

> Any gentleman who wants to be useful to society, any country curate whose curiosity and taste hasn't been deadened by the lack of company, if they are motivated to go alone to see the works of nature, or to get laborers to talk about husbandry and cultivation, ought to put in writing all the new things that they observe and learn. They will procure for themselves an agreeable occupation, and thanks to their efforts, they can enrich the public with their discoveries by sending them to the Academy of Sciences, which is like a public depository for discoveries, or the archive of all useful knowledge (7:22–23).

With this bit of advice for elites with time on their hands, we find what could very well be an explanation of how the Abbé Pluche gave meaning to his own life: he found "an agreeable profession" as an author who synthesized information about nature and society into eight rich little books that he hoped could make a difference.

Dialogues and Debates

In my attempt to rehabilitate Pluche, I also want to argue that his pedagogy, especially his extensive footnotes and use of dialogue, makes the *Spectacle de la nature* a much less dogmatic or teleologically blind work than its critics have suggested—indeed, I would say that its very format alone could encourage reason and reflection. In the *Spectacle*'s later volumes, we can find debates over whether a mother should breast feed or not, competing arguments about the causes of poverty, beggary, and unemployment, or diverse opinions about the mechanics of Newton and Descartes. Pluche is very careful to present every argument faithfully—even those with which he disagrees. Moreover, one could always go back to his original sources and compare, because he provides exact citations. We always know what his sources were and hence can determine for ourselves how often he got it right.

Openness and developing a reliance on one's own reason, however, seem even more served by the dialogic format itself.[15] Whatever his intent, Pluche's dialogues give time to competing voices: to opinions that occasionally challenge and undercut each other. At certain moments, the dialogues bring to the surface many of the deep tensions in the society; they have the capacity to make the reader (at least some readers at some moments) acutely aware of social realities and inequities.

In a discussion of ornamental gardens, for example, we see the young chevalier asking the hard questions when he is embarrassed by taking his leisure in front of the hardworking peasants (2:266). At another point, he wonders why hunting is solely a right of the nobility (2:470). And in what looks to be an innocuous discussion of sugar cane and sugar production soon leads to conversations about the plantation and slavery. Our young student ends that dialogue with the following words: "I think the Europeans involved in transporting the poor slaves to the Caribbean are as guilty as the plantation owners" (1:395). This statement from 1732 is decades before any serious abolition movement. I know at least one young reader in the eighteenth century, a fifteen-year-old from Louvain, who noticed that line because he copied it into his notebook.[16]

Finally, I would like to briefly mention gender. As we saw earlier, in volume six, the section on education for girls urged some improvements, such as adding history and geography to the standard curriculum or encouraging them to write in order to develop their imagination and strengthen her reason. However, the dialogues themselves in the *Spectacle de la nature* implicitly underscore an even stronger message: they show us an active and knowledgeable woman participating in the conversations, a countess who can hold forth on many topics. Interestingly, at one moment during a discussion about the attributes of various birds, she actually changes the topic, lamenting her lack of a formal education and expressing her sadness about never having received the same opportunities as her brother, husband, and sons (1:299–302). Whether readers noticed these little eruptions I am still trying to sort out.

A Forgotten and Influential Best-Seller

I would argue that the publishing success alone indicates that the *Spectacle de la nature* clearly touched a nerve, filled a need—and I think it had a great deal to do with new thinking about children and their education that coincided with a burgeoning excitement about discoveries in natural history. New knowledge about bees, wasps, spiders, and silkworms, about science, technology, and the crafts would be presented in ways that would help make a child receptive to looking at work, the social order, and the acquisition of knowledge in a different light—with the help of their parents, tutors, and the Abbé Pluche. The Abbé must have been offering many readers something they wanted or were at least willing to take the trouble to consider.

What is equally important, I think, is Pluche's confidence in the innate abilities of children. He believed that their curiosity could guide them without the threat of harsh discipline; he argued that they could learn to reason if given engaging activities, familiar tools, and the liberty to explore from the very beginning; he trusted their capacity to consider increasingly difficult matters as their abilities to reflect matured; and he hoped many could reevaluate the efficacy of a social system that favored noble leisure while denigrating the work of artisans, peasants, servants, and slaves that made that leisure possible.

For decades now, most scholars have denied Pluche any respect, dismissing the *Spectacle de la nature* as little more than a joke. Indeed, taking their cues from Diderot and d'Alembert themselves, historians have long viewed the *Encyclopédie* as the pioneering work in its championing of the arts, crafts, and technology, claiming that it was the first major work to argue for the dignity and skills of artisans. In the "Prospectus" and "Preliminary Discourse," Diderot and d'Alembert congratulate themselves as the first to actually have gone into the workshops of craftsmen themselves to insure the accuracy of the huge number of magnificent plates illustrating mechanical processes, machines, and tools. Some scholars have traced earlier, less comprehensive predecessors of the *Encyclopédie,* such as Ephraim Chambers's *Cyclopaedia* and John Harris's Lexicon *Technicum.* But almost no one has noticed its striking resemblance to the *Spectacle de la nature.*[17]

Yet twenty years before Diderot, Pluche visited and talked to artisans, keeping careful notes of their techniques. In the *Spectacle de la nature* he argued, even more forcefully than would Diderot, for the dignity of artisans and workers.[18] Before Diderot, he insisted on the values of utility, reason, experimentation, and progress. Before Diderot, he took Bacon's notion that the mechanical arts should be considered an integral aspect of natural history. His *Spectacle de la nature* included more than 200 beautifully produced engravings (with more than 100 devoted to machines and technology). As a runaway bestseller, countless more readers owned the *Spectacle de la nature* than ever even held a volume of the *Encyclopédie* in their hands.[19]

Conclusion

To conclude, I want to briefly suggest reasons that Pluche has been ignored. One might speak of a sort of tyranny of past readings and past readers that continues to dictate what and how we read to this day. Robert Darnton has encouraged us to look at the less visible "forbidden books," suggesting that those were the really influential texts.[20] He and many historians of the Enlightenment have found much to admire in philosophes who attacked dogma, superstition, and blind prejudice—organized religion was a favorite target. But few historians have looked at the many enlightened authors who were also devout ecclesiastics—especially not if their writings fell under the rubric "juvenile literature." Pluche is particularly interesting in this regard: as a Jansenist in a nation of Jesuits, he suffered the loss of prestigious teaching and religious posts. In fact, unemployment led this accomplished man to take up tutoring children and then writing for them in the first place. Yet despite his strong religious faith and belief in Divine Providence (or maybe because of it), Pluche was deeply committed to enlightened tenets of reason, utility, and progress.

Until now, we have often unquestionably accepted Diderot's own proclamations and self-congratulatory praises; we have quoted repeatedly Voltaire's quips about a panglossian Pluche without ever putting them to the test.[21] For an author like the Abbé Pluche—labeled early on as a "populariser" and a "Christian apologist"—this has meant that almost no scholar has looked at the *Spectacle de la nature* seriously in more than a century. I am convinced that over the years historians have simply read some absurd passage from Pluche (yes, they do exist) and repeated it, without ever going back to the texts themselves. For to hold the *Spectacle de la nature* in one's hands, to read the volumes one after the other, is to know what a pioneering book it actually is: in natural history, in pedagogy and experiential learning, in science, technology, the manual arts and crafts, and in the encyclopedic tradition itself. It is time that we take another look at certain vastly influential works such as the *Spectacle de la nature*. It is time that more readers have a chance to experience its wonders, and see what for more than a century so captivated readers all over Europe.

Notes

I am grateful to the Society for Eighteenth-Century Studies, the Lewis Walpole Library, the Friends of the Princeton Library, and the Bibliographical Society of America for providing funds for this research. I wish to thank Dennis Trinkle for his kindness in sharing with me the Pluche materials that he had collected. I also want to thank Michael Witmore and Andrea Immel for organizing the stimulating conference "Seen and Heard: The Place of the Child in Early Modern Europe," for editing this volume, and for their immense patience.

1. Noël-Antoine Pluche, *Le Spectacle de la nature, ou Entretiens sur les particularités de l'histoire naturelle, qui ont paru les plus propres á rendre les Jeunes-Gens curieux, & à leur former l'esprit,* eight volumes in nine books (Paris: Les Frères Estienne, 1732–51). Henceforth all references to the *Spectacle* will appear in the text.

2. Recently I learned that Jean-Jacques Rousseau used Pluche's *Spectacle de la nature* when he was the tutor for Mably's nephews, which confirmed for me that there might be a relationship here. I hope eventually to write an essay exploring the sources of Rousseau's pedagogy, especially the possible role of the Abbé Pluche. For more on the connections between Pluche's text and Diderot's *Encyclopédie,* see below.

3. In a recent article, Dennis Trinkle points out there have been no books and almost no articles devoted to the Abbé Pluche published in either French or English, and argues that Pluche and the *Spectacle de la nature* definitely deserve further study. See Trinkle, "Noël-Antoine Pluche's *Spectacle de la nature*: an encyclopaedic best-seller," in *Studies on Voltaire and the Eighteenth Century* 358 (1997): 93–114. The only full length work is an unpublished thesis by Caroline V. Doane, "Un success littéraire du XVIIIe siècle: *Le Spectacle de la nature* de l'abbé Pluche," (thèse dactylographiée, Paris: Sorbonne, 1957).

4. Daniel Mornet, "Les enseignements des bibliothèques privées (1750–80)," *Revue d'historie littéraire de la France* 17 (1910): 460–477.

5. Quoted in Robert Darnton, *Edition et sedition: L'univers de la littérature clandestine au xviiie siécle* (Paris: Gallimard, 1991), 52. My translation.

6. Charles Bonnet, *Mémoires autobiographiques,* ed. Raymond Savioz (Paris: J. Vrin, 1948), 46.

7. See Robert-Marie Reboul, *Louis-François Jauffret: Sa vie et ses oeuvres* (Paris, 1869), 23. Like Pluche, Jauffret wanted learning to be fun and wanted to celebrate the wonders of the natural world. So, just as the

Spectacle de la nature begins with a promenade in the garden, Jauffret first conducted a series of actual promenades and staged festivals in the woods where children could celebrate the likes of Pluche and other famous writers in natural history. Then he published accounts of these events, as well as many other books and magazines. Later Jauffret also became an expert on deaf mute children. As the founder of the *Société des observateurs de l'homme* (the first scholarly organization to practice anthropology), Jauffret became extremely interested in the scientific study of children, their socialization, and the connections between childhood and adult identity.

8. *The Bee, or Universal Weekly Pamphlet,* containing something to hit every man's taste and principles 6 (March-July, 1733): 247–250, 342, 1020.

9. See the *Mercure de France,* January 1733, 530, where a young writer offers an ardent defense of the *Spectacle de la nature,* refuting last month's review point by point. See also L'Abbé Desfontaines, *Les Observations sur les écrits modernes* 2 (Paris, 1736), 225–238.

10. See Frédéric Godefroy, *Histoire de la litérature française,* 2nd ed (Paris, 1877), 232. See also Jacques Proust, *Encyclopédie* (Paris: Armand Colin, 1965), 12–14.

11. The message—that children are worth the time—is underscored by the *Spectacle de la nature* as a whole, since the first four volumes depict three adults spending a lot of time conversing with a fifteen-year-old on all sorts of topics. The dialogues drop out after the fourth volume; conversational discourses continue until the end.

12. Many other authors noticed Pluche's success and seemed to follow his lead. Writers such as Jauffret, the Abbé Nollet, Oliver Goldsmith, Priscilla Wakefield, and the editors of the *Universal Magazine* of London—to name only a few—found inspiration in its pages, borrowed its tone, imitated its format, or excerpted its articles (sometimes under their own names) and had best-selling careers too. See Koepp, "Pirating and Publishing Best-Sellers in the 18th Century: The Abbé Pluche and his Imitators," forthcoming.

13. Volumes five, six, and seven of the *Spectacle de la nature* are primarily devoted to the arts and crafts, with countless plates illustrating workshops and work techniques.

14. True to his goals, in another dialogue about which is the most useful animal, Pluche chooses the ass whom he compares to a peasant—a category he also sees as grossly undervalued and yet absolutely essential to society. See *Spectacle,* 1:352–356.

15. See Mikhail Bahktin, *Dostoevsky's Poetics* (Ann Arbor: Ardis, 1974), 3–37, for a discussion of the "side-glancing" polyphonic voices in dialogues that can challenge and undercut a dominant perspective.

16. Bibliothéque Nationale, Fonds Français, MS, 15326. Prince d'Elbeuf, "Analyse du *Spectacle de la nature* de M. Pluche."

17. See, for example, Frank A. Kafker, ed., *Notable Encyclopedias of the Seventeenth and Eighteenth Centuries: Nine Predecessors of the Encyclopédie,* 194 (Oxford: The Voltaire Foundation, 1981). Dennis Trinkle is one who

also notes the resemblance and this oversight. See Trinkle, "Encyclopaedic Best-seller," 116.

18. André Viala, "Les idées de l'abbé Pluche sur la société," La Régence, ed. Henri Coulet (Paris: Armand Colin, 1970)

19. Records indicate that Diderot purchased at least three copies of the *Spectacle de la nature* in the months just before he wrote the "Prospectus" to the *Encyclopédie*. I investigate more fully the connections between these two texts in an essay entitled "Anticipating the *Encyclopédie:* Artisans and Mechanical Arts in the *Spectacle de la nature*," in *Perceptions of Labour in Late Medieval and Early Modern Europe*, Josef Ehmer and Catharine Lis, eds. (Aldershot: Ashgate, forthcoming 2006).

20. See Robert Darnton, *The Forbidden Books of Pre-Revolutionary France* (New York: W.W. Norton, 1996).

21. See Eric Palmer, "Pangloss Identified," in *French Studies Bulletin* 84, where the author argues that in his novel, *Candide*, Voltaire actually modeled his character Pangloss after Pluche, not Leibnitz.

9

"GOVERNESSES TO THEIR CHILDREN"

Royal and Aristocratic Mothers Educating
Daughters in the Reign of George III

JILL SHEFRIN

By the end of the eighteenth century, the image of the aristocratic mother teaching her own children was becoming part of the iconography of sentiment, as well as of rational or enlightened domesticity.[1] But half a century earlier, a group of aristocratic Englishwomen were being praised by their contemporaries for their active role in the education and nurturing of their children. It is clear from the tone of the remarks that they were somewhat unusual, but the evidence of their activity provides a counter to the historical perception that active child-centered parenting[2] by aristocratic mothers largely followed a philosophical and practical shift which had originated with the gentry and middle classes.[3] Throughout the second half of the century, an increasing number of books offered both theoretical and practical advice to mothers on the nurture and education of their children—including how to engage in educational play with young children.[4] The audience for this advocacy was middling and elite, as only mothers who could afford servants and tutors could be enjoined to a greater participation in the daily activities and education of their children, and only children of a certain socioeconomic level could be provided with the sort of education and educational play endorsed by the theorists.

Women from all levels of society whose children received any education had, traditionally, almost invariably been responsible for much of the care and education of their daughters and their young sons. Only women from wealthy high-status families were in a position to abdicate involvement with their children.[5] But the problem existed, and was presumably exacerbated by increasing wealth in the eighteenth century. Locke warned against leaving children to the care of servants, and women such as Lady Ellenor Fenn were responding to a perceived need when they offered instruction to mothers in how to play with as well as teach their children. What this chapter demonstrates is that a prominent and influential group of aristocratic women in the middle decades of the century, besides themselves taking advantage of the opportunity to be more public in displaying their own education, were concerned to provide their daughters with an education that reflected their own Enlightenment values and principles.[6] One important influence on their practices was the work of a particular educational theorist and practitioner: a middle-class French governess with numerous connections to an influential circle of educated elite women—Jeanne Marie Le Prince de Beaumont.[7]

The women discussed in this paper raised their children in the 1740s, 1750s, and 1760s. They had access to, and were influenced by, Enlightenment thinkers. They wanted their daughters' education to include scientific study and they placed a high value on reason.[8] They subscribed to the sentiments voiced by the *Critical Review,* in its review of de Beaumont's *Magasin des enfans* in 1757:

> … how much the happiness of society, and the good of mankind, depends upon the education of its individuals, … [and on the teaching of] a just way of thinking, speaking and acting to young people, according to their different stations of life [and] … to enlighten the understanding, [and] … form the heart to goodness.[9]

Their daughters were taught to make reasoned judgments based on virtue, piety, rationality, and learning. These girls studied not only religion and reason, but French, geography, history, natural science, physics, and philosophy. This program is articulated in many of the writings of de Beaumont, who also served as governess to a number of their daughters.

Before addressing the case of Mme. de Beaumont,[10] it is necessary to survey the current state of research into the history of girls' education in the eighteenth century. The bulk of the recent work on the education of aristocratic girls has come from historians of education or women's writing, and the focus has been on content rather than method.[11] Recent work by scholars such as Harriet Guest, Sylvia Harcstark Myers, and Deirdre Raftery examines what women in seventeenth- and eighteenth-century England could or did learn, but, with the exception of Kenneth Charlton in his recent *Women, Religion and Education in Early Modern England* (1999), does not address how or what they learned as children.[12]

Important work also has been done on the role of the mother in children's literature of the period, which also saw a blossoming of books by and for women about the education of children. Lady Ellenor Fenn, in the introduction to her *Art of Teaching in Sport* (1785), suggested that young mothers might require instruction on how to teach and play with young children: "a youthful mother may be glad of a hint how to improve her child in sporting with it."[13] Educational pastimes increasingly bore titles such as *Pronunciation Taught as an Amusement by means of Cuts by an Indulgent Grandmother* (Darton and Harvey, 1804). The fiction of the period is filled with stories of girls whose mothers (or governesses in the role of mothers) are role models of rational domesticity. They teach virtue and reason, providing examples from their own gentle wisdom. Mitzi Myers's examination of Mary Wollstonecraft's *Original Stories* (1788; 2nd ed. 1791),[14] for example, offers a detailed analysis of the figure of Mrs. Mason, an ultra-rationalist governess, and discusses how, through the mother-governess figures of their fictions, Wollstonecraft and other female writers for children offer "a new mode of female heroism—in rationality, self-command, and autonomy."[15] Wollstonecraft's message—grounded in her feminism—is perhaps more overt than that of many of her contemporaries, but the mother (or mother-substitute) character who teaches girls to think rationally can be found in publications for children from the *Magasin des enfans* (1756) through the first decades of the nineteenth century.[16]

General histories of formal schooling give short shrift to girls' education,[17] and studies of aristocratic education in the eighteenth century—such as that included in John Cannon's *Aristocratic Century: the Peerage of Eighteenth-Century England* or George Brauer's *The Education of a Gentleman: Theories of Gentlemanly Education in England, 1660–1775*—focus almost exclusively on the education of sons.[18] But Cannon's statement that "Locke's concept of … a tabula rasa necessarily gave decisive significance to the role of the teacher and, if anything, eighteenth-century thinkers tended to exaggerate the importance of education,"[19] applies equally to the education of daughters. As Mary Hilton and Pamela Hirsch point out in their recent work, *Practical Visionaries: Women, Education and Social Progress, 1790–1930*:

> to examine the established history of education is still to find a master narrative which consistently foregrounds the ideas and activities of men. … [While] women are not completely absent. … They appear … as wives, sisters, followers, assistants and believers; rarely as leaders, ideologues, founders or policy makers. The central work of philosophy, experimentation, political and institutional leadership is firmly ascribed to men.[20]

It is a narrative that excludes not only female educationists but also, to a great extent, female pupils.

The story of de Beaumont, who lived in England between 1748 and 1762, and that of her pupils, fills something of this gap. Changes in educational theory and practice occur over extended periods, and can be examined from many perspectives; to isolate a particular figure or set of events can be misleading. However, I believe that Jeanne-Marie Le Prince de Beaumont was an important influence on the development of progressive educational practice in England in the mid-eighteenth century, particularly the evolving role of aristocratic mothers in the education and general upbringing of their daughters, a role that, increasingly, came to encompass intellectual and moral, as well as religious and domestic, teaching. De Beaumont's publications are a valuable historical source. Their content details her highly developed theories of education; surviving multiple editions indicate the popularity of her ideas; subscription lists detail her personal connections to court circles; and if we accept, even with reservations, her insistence that the series of *Magasin* are heavily based on her real teaching practices and experiences, her works provide a detailed record of the teaching of one group of aristocratic girls in the 1750s.

Although the bulk of theoretical work on the role of the mother in education dates from the last quarter of the century, a careful reading of the correspondence of educated elite women throughout the second half of the century reveals a number of references to active mothering, both affectionate and educative. For example, in 1750, Catherine Talbot wrote to Elizabeth Carter: "There is … a little rising generation that I contemplate with pleasure, as I know three or four excellent mothers of future Dukes and Earls, that take the most serious care of their large little families. I spent yesterday evening with two young Countesses, and was delighted to hear them comparing the tempers and capacities of their children, and how they read their book, and said their catechisms."[21] The implication here is that even if the mother has not taught her children to read or say their catechism, she is hearing their lessons, and that this interest is the subject of the writer's approval.

On a visit to England in the same year, the French writer Marie Anne Fiquet du Boccage was much struck with the "maternal tenderness" of "English ladies of all ranks," citing the Duchess of Richmond who "is remarkable for taking particular care of her family. She herself prepares her daughters for inoculation, and during the operation shuts herself up with them at an apothecary's, for fear her children in the cradle, brought up under her inspection, should have the small-pox before the proper age. Few of our women of fashion have so much maternal tenderness as to deprive themselves of pleasure during six weeks for the good of their families."[22]

Surviving correspondence of aristocratic women at this time (and, even more, of their children) reveals affectionate maternal indulgence together with a real awareness of the limitations in the abilities and attention spans of young children.[23] And although many eighteenth-century upper-class women still received only a basic education (reading, writing and arithmetic, domestic skills, social accomplishments), it is not difficult to find examples of much more intellectually sophisticated female education, and both ends of the spectrum can be found throughout the century. The differences in the formal education of Lady Mary Wortley Montagu, her daughter, the Countess of Bute, and her granddaughter, Lady Mary Stuart, provide some idea of the range of experience of aristocratic girls up to the 1760s. Wortley

Montagu's childhood education fits what has traditionally been perceived as the more common model. Complaining of her poor education at the beginning of the century, she wrote: "My own [education]
was one of the worst in the world, being exactly the same as Clarissa
Harlow's, her pious Mrs. Norton so perfectly resembling my governess
(who had been nurse to my mother). ... I could almost fancy the author
was acquainted with her. She took so much pains from my infancy to
fill my head with superstitious tales and false notions, it was none of
her fault I am not at this day afraid of witches and hobgoblins, or turn'd
Methodist. Almost all girls are bred after this manner."[24] She was
thus largely self-educated. For her granddaughter, Wortley Montagu
recommended a serious and comprehensive education including history, geography, philosophy, arithmetic, Latin, Greek, and modern
languages. The languages, both ancient and modern, would enable the
girl to "read books in their originals, that are often corrupted and all-
waies injur'd by translations."[25] In a lengthy and detailed letter to Lady
Bute, she argues,

> Learning (if she has a real taste for it) will not only make her contented
> but happy ... No entertainment is so cheap as reading, nor any pleasures
> so lasting. She will not want new fashions nor regret the loss of expen-
> sive diversions or variety of company if she can be amus'd with an author
> in her closet. To render this amusement extensive, she should be permit-
> ted to learn the languages. ... as you say her memory is good, she will be
> very agreeably employ'd this way.[26]

The puzzling anomaly in Lady Mary's advice is that, although she
recommends it for her granddaughter, clearly would have preferred
such an education for herself, and associated with other intellectually-
minded women, she did not provide her daughter with such an extensive education. Her rationale appears to have been that her daughter
was expected to make a great marriage, while her granddaughter was
not. Indeed, her complaint that "Allmost all girls of quality are educated as if they were to be great ladys, which is often as little to be
expected as an immoderate heat of the sun in the north of Scotland,"[27]
suggests that the proper education of a great lady was contradictory to
that she practiced for herself and endorsed for her granddaughter.

This serves in part as a reminder that Lady Mary spoke for an earlier generation; when proposing the diverse curriculum for her daughter, she also wanted Lady Bute to instruct her "to conceal whatever learning she attains, with as much solicitude as she would hide crookedness or lameness."[28] By the date of Wortley Montagu's letter, however, educated women were more openly displaying their intelligence and learning in elite circles—some members of that world, others there under the auspices of patronesses.[29]

Lady Mary Wortley Montagu's life is well documented, and her opinions and experience of education are frequently cited. A much less well-known contemporary was the Countess of Pomfret, a woman whose story illustrates some of the problems in defining and retrieving details of female education in this period.[30] A friend of Lady Mary Wortley Montagu and a Lady of the Bedchamber to Queen Caroline, the Countess of Pomfret was an enthusiastic patron of educated and talented women, including the young Elizabeth Carter. Her diary of her journey to France and Italy in 1739–1741 records meeting both Signora Laura Bassi, who taught at the University of Bologna (having received her doctorate there in 1732), and the Venetian portrait artist, Rosalba Carriera. Her patronage of Mme. de Beaumont also reflects this interest. Lady Pomfret's diaries and many of her letters survive. Although these sources indicate an enthusiastic rather than an especially talented woman, she does appear to have been generous and devout, with a modicum of intelligence and a taste for culture, and to have raised her daughters according to the same principles.[31]

Her relevance to this story is her role as Mme. de Beaumont's employer and patron. When Lady Pomfret's eldest daughter, Lady Sophia Carteret, died shortly after the birth of her daughter in 1745, Lady Pomfret assumed the care of the infant, also Lady Sophia.[32] Arriving in England, Mme. de Beaumont met the Countess of Pomfret, and was hired by her as governess to Lady Sophia, the youngest daughter of Lord Granville, a position de Beaumont occupied until at least 1754.[33] Granville later praised his adolescent daughter for achieving "all [the] real improvements of education." Sophia Carteret's correspondence with her father before her marriage, and her diaries after she became Lady Shelburne, indicate a serious-minded young woman with a taste for mild scholarship.

Although probably employed by Lady Pomfret from 1748 or 1749, de Beaumont was advertising for other pupils in 1751, and later in the decade prepared a prospectus for a school in London. It is unclear from the existing evidence, but the school seems to have been in operation in the late 1750s under the day-to-day supervision of a young Huguenot teacher, Mlle. de Vins, rather than Mme. de Beaumont herself. There is no concrete information on the circumstances under which Mme. de Beaumont taught other girls during the time she was responsible for the education of Lady Sophia, but, like the children in her *Magasin des enfans* (London, 1756; translated into English as the *Young Misses Magazine* in 1757),[34] they may have "spent three afternoons a week together with" Lady Sophia, being instructed "by way of amusement."[35]

We are fortunate in the range and extent of the sources relating to Mme. de Beaumont's educational philosophy and practice that have survived. These include the letters and diaries of at least two of her pupils and of some of their mothers (in one case grandmother), some of her own correspondence, advertisements for her school and for pupils, and her published works, both theoretical and fictional.[36] The subscription list to the *Magasin des enfans* is also revealing, including as it does a lengthy list of peers and their wives and daughters.[37] As well as Lady Sophia Carteret, daughters of the second Earl of Egremont, Lord North, and Lord Hillsborough were among de Beaumont's pupils. The sequel to the *Magasin des enfans, Magasin des adolescentes* (1759?), is dedicated to Lady Sophia and refers to her appearance in the books as Lady Sensible, while the third work in the series, *Instructions pour les jeunes dames* (1764) is dedicated to the Countess of Egremont and Mrs. Grenville, described by Mme. de Beaumont as "mothers who were governesses to their children." They will, she writes, "be admired for brightness of genius, excellence of disposition, and goodness of heart. ... As [your children] are cultivated by able and careful hands," she declares,

> you will ... reap the fruit of your labour a hundred fold. Your daughters will tread in your steps, and in time, will value themselves on the glorious appellation of governesses of their children, which you so justly deserve. Your sons, who contrary to custom, have also employed your cares, will

tread in the paths of their fathers, and like them, fill with applause the principal posts of the state.[38]

De Beaumont claimed that the characters in the *Magasin des enfans* and its sequels were drawn from life. In the introduction to the *Des adolescentes,* referring to the incorporation of new characters, she explained:

> I copy from nature; my young people furnish me with all sorts of originals, and this abridges my work very considerably … In a dozen characters that I have chosen, I point out the general methods to be followed by those who undertake the instruction of youth. There are none of their scholars but what may be reduced to one or other of the characters presented here to the public. The shades which make the difference are almost imperceptible, and cannot be observed without the greatest attention.[39]

Although de Beaumont maintained that her pupils in real life were "neither so good nor so bad" as the characters in her stories, the grounds for treating her series of fictional school stories as historically accurate records of her teaching experiences are, I believe, solid.[40] Although the known historical figures of Mme. de Beaumont's pupils represent only a small sample of aristocratic daughters in the third quarter of the century, the pattern of their education has a broader application. There were only about 400 families of rank in Britain at this time, the majority of whom had members with positions in the government, the opposition, or at court.[41] Those girls whom I have definitely established as pupils of Mme. de Beaumont were the daughters of politically prominent peers, and she was clearly aware of the importance of teaching her pupils the responsibilities accompanying their rank. Mrs. Affable tells the girls:

> There is a respect due to order and distinction of ranks, which is, if well considered, a respect due to society and the whole of the commonwealth, to prevent disorder and confusion. But the respect due to sovereigns, or those in whom the supreme authority is vested, is of a still superior order, and is, in reality, a respect due to God, whom they represent on earth … God is honoured in the submission paid to his representatives, who have their power from him; and this honour is part of our duty to God. …

Remember this, children. You are all young ladies, all well born; but this
implies an obligation to be more virtuous than others; if you are not, you
will not appear more, in the estimate of thinking persons, than a daughter
of Noah lost in the croud, ... [who,] had [she] received the same education [as] you ... would, perhaps, have been more virtuous than you are.[42]

De Beaumont was a formative influence on these girls and their
circle, including their mothers. As the young women themselves went
on to marry prominent peers and politicians, de Beaumont's potential
influence spread. Her educational treatises were widely read, and her
status as an author patronized by various aristocratic hostesses ensured
her a wide reception amongst the elite. She developed close relationships with her pupils, who remained extremely attached to her. Some
corresponded regularly for many years, and, after she returned to
France, half a dozen of them traveled together to visit her there on the
occasion of her sixtieth birthday.[43] De Beaumont's talents as a teacher
are evident in her declaration of the abilities of her pupils:

I have merely writ down the conversations that have passed between me
and my scholars; ... experience has taught me that those instructions are
not above their reach. Among my young people there are children of
twelve years of age that will not let a sophism be passed upon them for a
syllogism, they will tell you very gravely about a book they are reading:
*The author has taken leave of his subject; he says very weak things. His prin-
ciple is false; his inferences must be so.* What is more ... [they] will prove it.
We don't form a true judgment of the capacity of children; nothing is
out of their reach, if they are taught by little and little to form an argument, or rather to discourse on a subject. Now-a-days ladies read all sorts
of books, history, politicks, philosophy, and even such as concern religion. They should therefore be in a condition to judge solidly of what
they read, and able to discern truth from falsehood ... I tried two years
successively what young ladies were capable of, and after repeated trials,
was fully convinced, that we are all born geomatricians; ... it is no such
hard task to ... display the connate geometrical ideas of children twelve
years old. To give still farther satisfaction to the reader, nothing shall
appear in this work, that was not well understood by eight young ladies
of that age. Their objections shall be repeated as they made them; if they

are found too much above their years, the blame must not fall upon me, but the young ladies, who have too much wit for their age. But as I write chiefly for their benefit, I cannot be dispensed from writing what I know is agreeable to them, and no ways above their reach.[44]

Mme. de Beaumont first expressed her educational principles in print in an essay entitled "Avis aux parens & aux maîtres, sur l'education des enfans" in her *Lettres diverses et critique* (written after she came to England, but published in Nancy). She argued passionately for the importance of trained and knowledgeable teachers, and for parental (particularly maternal) involvement in education and childrearing, irrespective of rank.[45] Because of the interest in her and her work, *Lettres* sold out in London within fifteen days of its publication in 1750. Arriving in England with advantageous connections, she had been adopted by the ton as a fashionable author and invited to the homes of aristocratic patronesses. Mme. du Boccage, encountering her at the home of Elizabeth Montagu, described her as "Mrs. Prince, of our city of Rouen, who composes excellent treatises concerning the education of young persons, and is very successful in reducing them to practice."[46] Her first publication in England was in 1750: the *Nouveau magasin français* was a monthly periodical, published in 1750 and 1751, and then sporadically until at least 1755.[47] It consisted of essays, plays, short serialized works of fiction, and correspondence on various subjects (including natural and moral philosophy and the education of women) and was primarily addressed to adolescent girls and young women of the middle and upper classes. It was, in some ways, imitative of the *Spectator*—at this time frequently recommended as suitable reading for girls.

The *Magasin des enfans*, together with its sequels, the *Magasin des adolescentes* (1759?; translated as *The Young Ladies Magazine* in 1760), and the *Instructions pour les jeunes dames qui entrent das le monde, se marient, leurs devoirs dans cet état, & envers leurs enfans* (1764), is not only a collection of instructive stories for children, it is an explicit exposition of Mme. de Beaumont's educational philosophy. The prospectus for a school she established in London in the late 1750s advised parents to examine the conversations and stories in the *Magasin des enfans* to understand her teaching methods. The study of philosophy included an exposition of will, understanding and reason which appears to be taken from Descartes,[48] and the text of the lessons in geography implies the use of dissected maps (jigsaw puzzles). Teaching toys were consistent with de Beaumont's philosophy, and we know her school made use of them.[49] The story that provides the framework for these lessons is that of Lady Sensible (aged twelve in the first book), her governess Mrs. Affable, and a number of other young ladies under Mrs. Affable's tuition, aged between five and eighteen years.[50] *Des enfans* is about six girls; eleven more appear as new characters in *Des adolescents*. The girls in the first book—Lady Witty, aged twelve; Lady Mary, aged five; Lady Charlotte, aged seven; Lady Trifle, aged ten; and Lady Tempest, aged thirteen, meet at Lady Sensible's house several afternoons a week, where they engage in instructive conversation in French in a relaxed environment (see Figure 9.1.) They retell stories from the Bible in their own words (presumably demonstrating both familiarity with—and comprehension of—the text as well as their skill in French); they listen to Mrs. Affable's moral fairy tales. The stories and tales launch discussions of complex moral problems, requiring the girls to think about and understand what they read. Throughout de Beaumont's work, rational, educated ladies are held up as models, and the educated rationalist invariably triumphs.

Specialists in early children's books know Mme. de Beaumont's *Magasin des enfans* as an early work of fiction for girls, which included the story of Beauty and the Beast. (Her retelling of that tale has become the classic one.)[51] French critics have granted her a larger role in the history of their children's literature, but not necessarily in the history of education, and there have been relatively few critical or historical studies of her in either language.[52] The author of over seventy works, she was a skillful writer for both children and adults whose lessons—at least in her earlier books—were mostly offered with a light touch.[53]

Apart from her contribution to the literary fairy tale, Mme. de Beaumont is often dismissed as a pietistic and didactic writer of conduct literature. One recent critic sees her as a pious governess whose moral fairy tales, fables, and selected Bible stories offer "the worried tone of a well-meaning teacher raising her pupils to face their future obediently and decorously, to ... obey their fathers and that inside the brute of a husband who might be their appointed lot, the heart of a

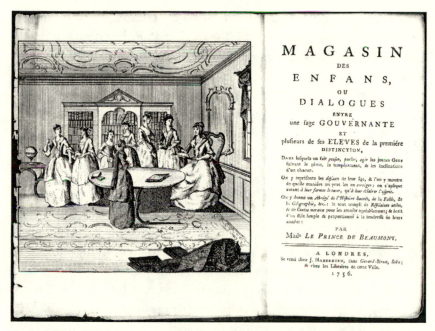

Fig. 9.1 Mrs. Affable is shown conversing with her aristocratic pupils in the frontispiece to Le Prince de Beaumont, *Magasin des enfans, ou dialogues entre une sage gouvernante et plusiers de ses eleves de la premiere distinction* (London: J. Haberkorn, 1756). Reproduced by permission of the E. W. & Faith King Collection of Juvenile Literature, Miami University Libraries, Oxford, Ohio.

good man might beat, given a bit of encouragement."[54] But this is to impose an ahistorical perspective. It is true that all her writings are strongly didactic, but she believed both in teaching girls to think analytically, and in offering them a broad and balanced curriculum. Her patrons were readers with artistic and cultural interests. For them, faith was both personal belief and public code. When these eighteenth-century aristocrats praised the education—or educational abilities—of a particular woman, teacher or pupil, they were praising a complex combination of values, skills, knowledge, and faith. The centrality of virtue and piety in the lives and educations of these women hinders an analysis of this complex blend, and sometimes obscures for modern readers the real extent of their intelligence and education, or the quality of their published work.[55]

A woman who joined the Enlightenment discourse on education, Mme. de Beaumont's ideas were grounded in Locke's theories of individual will and the innate potential for rational thought which had been developed by David Hartley into "associationism."[56] She believed that early impressions affected the moral and rational values of the future adult. Her writings illustrate the complex relationship between reason and faith in the work of Enlightenment thinkers who continued to be devout Christians.[57] She taught children to use reason and judgment to interpret knowledge within a Christian framework, and she was a strong advocate of what came to be called rational domesticity.[58] She stressed virtue, but she also demanded rational thought.[59] The subtitle of the *Magasin* declares it to be "dialogues between a governess and several young ladies of quality her scholars: in which each lady is made to speak according to her particular genius, temper and inclination; their several faults are pointed out, and the easy way to mend them, as well as to think, and speak, and act properly; no less care being taken to form their hearts to goodness, than to enlighten their understandings with useful knowledge."[60]

A close reading of Mme. de Beaumont's text (at least in the two *Magasins*) reveals a woman for whom piety was only one element in the character of the moral and rational educated woman, one who accepted her responsibilities intelligently—and intelligently assessed any new circumstances encountered, including proposals of marriage.[61] Key to Mme. de Beaumont's philosophy is a statement in the dedication of the *Instructions pour les jeunes dames* to Lady Egremont and Mrs. Grenville: "You are truly mothers to ... [your] children, whom you have brought into the world; and amidst the indispensable avocations arising from your rank, you find means of attending to the culture of their mind and the formation of their heart."[62]

Through Lady Pomfret, Mme. de Beaumont's influence extended to the royal family. Lady Charlotte Finch, the second of Lady Pomfret's six daughters, became Royal Governess on the birth of the Prince of Wales in August of 1762, with eventual responsibility for all fifteen children of George III. Conforming to Mme. de Beaumont's dicta, Lady Charlotte was herself a hands-on parent and governess. She educated her own daughters (and her son until he went to Eton), and herself taught the Princess Royal and the other older royal children to read. Her own eldest daughter, also Charlotte, appears to have been a sometime pupil of Mme. de Beaumont's.[63]

Lady Charlotte's letters show her to have been warmhearted and affectionately indulgent with her own five children. She wrote to her mother of her return home in 1759: "with the greatest joy imaginable, I was receiv'd by all these dear little souls [her children], who have not been one moment from my elbow ever since I came, & I have attended them all to bed."[64] Contemporaries consistently describe her as kind, affectionate, generous, of great moral probity, and, very simply, good.[65] On her appointment, Elizabeth Montagu wrote to Elizabeth Vesey, referring back to Lady Pomfret:

> I agree with you in all you say of Lady Charlotte Finch. I have often wish[e]d, for the sake of the world, that Lady Pomfret had had as many daughters as the woman shewn at Mrs. Salmon's Waxwork. Lady Charlotte added to her great virtues has very fine talents, and its strange as true, and true as strange, that there is not a house in England, where her virtues cou[l]d be so well placed ... as at Buckingham House. No other Court w[oul]d have pleased her, nor w[oul]d she have pleased any other Court.[66]

Many years later, on the death of one of Lady Charlotte's nieces, a Mrs. Baker, Elizabeth Carter wrote: "This amiable young woman has left her friends all the consolation that can be derived from a reflection on the consequences of her virtues. During the short time in which she had an opportunity of acting for herself she plainly appeared to be pursuing the same plan of duty and usefulness in society for which the excellent family to which she belongs is so remarkably distinguished."[67] Sarah Trimmer, a prominent educationist of the same generation as Lady Ellenor Fenn, dedicated her *Easy Introduction to the Knowledge of Nature* (1780) to Lady Charlotte, declaring that she had "had the happiness to obtain the sanction of your Ladyship's approbation ... as the great success with which you have educated the Royal Family, so evidently proves, ... your Ladyship is perfectly acquainted with the most happy arts of winning the attention of children, and the most proper method of conveying religious and moral instruction to their tender minds."[68]

Although the queen did entrust her children to a governess, it is clear she retained as active an involvement in their upbringing as her duties permitted, and Lady Charlotte's position was no sinecure.[69] Between them, the two women created a climate in which moral instruction and piety were blended with a liberal curriculum using progressive pedagogical practices. The extensive collection of works on education in the queen's library (over one hundred titles by the time of her death) is only one indication of her interest in the subject.[70]

According to the prospectus for her school, Mme. de Beaumont's pupils were always under the eye of herself or another instructor: "repas, travail, prière, récréation, tout se doit passer sous ses yeux. Cet article est de la plus grande conséquence."[71] Mothers, too, should exercise constant supervision: Queen Charlotte regularly sat in on her daughters' lessons.[72] The princesses read widely, but only approved books: Princess Elizabeth was twenty-five before she read a book that had not been vetted by her mother. The princesses also studied a broad range of subjects. Queen Charlotte had a particular interest in botany, but took an intelligent interest in all the sciences, and she suggested to her brother Charles for his daughters a "plan d'instruction" which she had followed with her own, which included "un petit cours de l'electriciti & de pneumatique," which would, she hoped, give them "quelques petites idées de physique."[73]

By the late 1760s, the English court offered its own portrait of royal domesticity and piety, as George III and Queen Charlotte produced a steady stream of children and presented themselves to public view as a family. These public appearances included the gardens at Kew, where contemporaries described seeing the children at play. The princesses played cricket, hockey, and other strenuous games with their brothers.[74] They were lively and active children, and, given their numbers, it is not entirely surprising that one nursery assistant was dismissed for banging Prince William's head against a wall.[75] Mrs. Affable's pupils are also encouraged to get exercise and to get rid of excess energy:

> *Mrs. Affable.* As it is not above three o'clock, you may stay in the garden till four, and jump and run about as much as you will, provided you do not go in the sun; I that am old and cannot walk, chuse to stay here with lady Sensible, who is a little indisposed.[76]

In the education of the royal children, as determined by Lady Charlotte and the queen, we can see a notable example of the application of many of Mme. de Beaumont's practices. Like Mme. de Beaumont's pupils, they benefited from some of the most creative concepts and techniques of the time.[77] Experimentation and novelty included both elegant conversation as a structure for lessons and the use of creative play. Again, like Mme. de Beaumont's pupils, they played with dissected maps—this last confirmed by the survival of the set of sixteen cartographical jigsaw puzzles from the royal nursery, the property of Lady Charlotte Finch Lady Ellenor Fenn in 1784 sent copies of her published children's books to Lady Charlotte for the royal children. The gift quite possibly included her elaborate *Set of Toys,* a pastime intended to teach grammar, spelling, and arithmetic. Frederika Planta (one of the sub-governesses to the royal children) designed cards "which contain[ed] the History of England, ore [sic] more properly an idea of it, & ... reduced the chronology of England to a game, by means of which the Princesses are better chronologists, than I was 3 years ago."[78] In a letter of 1774, Planta wrote of her work with the royal children: "I have gained their affection by making their learning as much play as possible." Also recalling Mme. de Beaumont's methods, she records choosing "some striking facts" from history and retelling them "in words adapted to her [the five-year-old Princess Augusta's] capacity & ... [telling] them as diverting stories. This method has taken, & she [the princess] tells them again in words of her own, with as much pleasure as she would a fairy tale." Miss Planta concludes, "It is amazing how much the little creature knows of the history of England, down as low as James I."[79]

In Mrs. Affable's fairy tales, in conversational anecdote, and in history, rational behavior is the sought-after resolution. Her stories reinforce the message in the praise for rational pious women by educated men, and it is mirrored in the life of at least one of her pupils. The letters of Lord Granville to his youngest daughter, Lady Sophia Carteret, make clear his preference for educated women. He praises her studiousness and skills: "You have almost got yr mothers way of writing, who wrote better both in French & English, better than any body I ever knew, & all this by following yr Grand Mamma's instructions in aid of her uncommon genius."[80] And, a week later, "You improve yr selfe in every letter you write there is such an ease, & spirit in yr expressions, & without the least affectation, that yt [I] am realy delighted to hear from you."[81]

Mme. de Beaumont's stories reflect the advanced ideas of a woman passionately committed to education, particularly to the education of women as rational creatures. Her writings make clear that she saw herself as a woman with a mission, as demonstrated in her praise of the Countess of Egremont and Mrs. Grenville for adding weight to her "efforts for engaging parents to take on themselves [the] ... duty" of educating their children.[82] Her work consistently reflects the ideas first broached in her *Lettres diverses et critique*.

In the course of research into the history of the set of Lady Charlotte's dissected maps, I not only discovered that Mme. de Beaumont's story was linked to Lady Charlotte's, but that it was Mme. de Beaumont (not John Spilsbury or, as was recorded in the provenance for the puzzles, Lady Charlotte herself) who was responsible for this educational pastime and who was selling dissected maps in London before 1760.[83] Lady Charlotte would have been familiar with Mme. de Beaumont and her dissected maps through the latter's connection to Lady Pomfret, Lady Sophia Carteret, and her own daughter, Charlotte, also a pupil of de Beaumont's. Surviving references in the correspondence of both Lady Caroline Fox and Mary Delany also link de Beaumont to dissected maps, as well as confirming her high profile in society.

These dissected maps thus offered a specific and practical illustration of the progression and popularizing of a new educational concept, enabling me to trace their use from an individual middle-class French governess, through the family of her aristocratic patron and employer, to the royal nursery. The links also reveal the extent of Mme. de Beaumont's influence, as the practices of this creative schoolmistress can be seen to have directly affected the education of a number of both royal and aristocratic daughters. Her popularity indicates the extent of the interest in progressive educational theory and practice among serious-minded aristocratic women—including both Lady Charlotte Finch and the Queen, as well as at least two of the daughters of the Duchess of Richmond: Lady Caroline Fox and Emily, Duchess of Leinster, both of whom also eagerly embraced the theories of Rousseau. More specifically, the correspondence between these last two includes a reference to the "Beaumont wooden maps."[84] Mme. de Beaumont's dicta fell on sympathetic ears, her position reinforcing the care already taken by mothers like the Duchess of Richmond and the Countess of Pomfret.

Of course, the majority of intellectually-minded aristocratic and gentlewomen were not scholars, but their patronage of women artists, writers and thinkers reflects the value they placed on the education of their daughters. This circle of women, in a clear meeting of minds, welcomed Mme. de Beaumont as a writer and continued to provide her with patronage and employment throughout her years in England. And the repeated praise for Lady Charlotte Finch, particularly by her educated female contemporaries, identifies her as an outstandingly successful example of rational domesticity, firmly placing this model of female education in the royal court.

Notes

This chapter could not have been written without the knowledge gained from my research for the Cotsen Family Foundation on Lady Charlotte Finch, Royal Governess to the children of George III, and her dissected maps. The chapter also was presented, in a revised form, at the *Joint Study Day* of the Children's Books History Society and the Textbook Colloquium, British Schools Museum, Hitchin, Bedfordshire, June 21, 2003. I would also like to thank Carol Percy for her suggestions on revising the paper and Trinity College at the University of Toronto for their ongoing support.

1. Most famously, the portrait of *Georgiana, Duchess of Devonshire, with her Daughter*, by Sir Joshua Reynolds (*c.*1784–86); but also, for example, *Lady Cockburn with her Three Eldest Sons*, by Reynolds (1773). Both are portraits of aristocratic mothers playing with their young children.

2. There does not appear to be a consistent term in use by historians of education for education that is structured around the needs and abilities of the child.

3. See Philippe Ariès, *L'Enfant et la vie familiale sous l'Ancien Régime* (Paris: Librarie Plon, 1960); Lawrence Stone, in *The Family, Sex and Marriage in England, 1500–1800* (Harmondsworth: Penguin, 1979), cites examples of parental overindulgence among the elite, but sees broad social changes toward the nurture and education of children as originating with "professional people, wealthy merchants and the squirearchy" (285). This is also one of the premises behind Leonore Davidoff and Catherine Hall's *Family Fortunes: Men and Women of the English Middle Class, 1780–1850* (Chicago: University of Chicago Press, 1991). Certainly there is evidence of a contemporary perception that elite women were unsuited to educate their children, even the very youngest, being of limited abilities and what Mitzi Myers describes as "culturally disposed toward puerility" (Mitzi Myers, "Impeccable Governesses, Rational Dames, and Moral Mothers,"

Children's Literature 14 [1986]:44.). But it is also true that prominent Enlightenment thinkers, most notably Locke, had already argued that women were not innately subordinate, and should receive a similar education to men. Thus, by the eighteenth century some "women were allowed to enjoy ... intellectual pursuit[s] at a time when their formal education was minimal and their intellectual prowess barely acknowledged" (Deirdre Raftery, *Women and Learning in English Writing, 1600–1900*. Dublin: Four Courts Press, 1997, 44–5) by the mainstream. This is an oversimplification of both positions and leaves unaddressed the large issue of the popular merging of many of Locke's ideas with those of Rousseau after the publication in Britain of *Émile* in 1762. It is true, however, that there was increasing support by theorists for what we would today call child-centered education and for the substantial involvement of elite mothers in such education.

4. This increase was partly a reflection of the enormous overall increase in publishing in the last quarter of the century.

5. Kenneth Charlton, Amanda Vickery, Linda Pollock, and others cite less elevated elite women who cared for and educated their children with minimal domestic help, but the evidence of the interest taken by the mothers of de Beaumont's pupils offers a corrective to Stone's argument that at "the highest level of society, among the court aristocrats and among some of the wealthy squires, there were many families in the eighteenth century in which both husband and wife were too immersed in politics and the social whirl of London and the court to bother themselves with their children, who for the first six to eight years were left in the hands of wet-nurses, nurses, governesses, and tutors. ... These were not harsh or cruel parents, merely indifferent ones who had little interest in their children and saw little of them" (Stone, 286).

6. This concern was partly demonstrated in their own active nurturing and teaching roles. See also Clarissa Campbell Orr's unpublished paper, "Rational Religion and Aristocratic Feminism, c.1700–1800: Some Themes and Contexts" as delivered at the Clark Library Seminar, "Genealogies of Feminism," 2001, especially her discussion of protofeminism. It appears that this sort of abdication of responsibility was never as common in Britain as in France. See Margaret H. Darrow, "French Noblewomen and the New Domesticity, 1750–1850," *Feminist Studies* 5 (Spring 1979): 41–65 for a discussion of French elite women and mothering; also Fiquet du Boccage's comments later.

7. Born in 1711 into a middle-class Rouen family, Jeanne Marie Le Prince spent several years at the convent at Ernemont where she trained as a charity school teacher. In 1735 she left, moving to Lunéville, where she became a Reader to Elisabeth Thérèse, daughter of the Dowager Duchess (and Regent) of Lorraine, to whom she also taught dancing and singing and acted as a companion. Following the death of Elisabeth Thérèse in 1742, the Regent presented Jeanne Marie with forty-five thousand livres. In 1743 she married a debt-ridden alcoholic young French aristocrat, the godson of her first patron, Lisebonne du Montier. Antoine Grimard de Beaumont was a personal and financial embarrassment to his bride, who

managed to get the marriage annulled. He died in a duel in 1745. She paid his debts, put her daughter in a convent school, and in 1748 went to England, where she remained for fifteen years, a successful writer and teacher.

8. See, among others, Raftery's discussion of women and scientific education (Raftery, Chap. 2, *passim*).

9. *Critical Review*, August 1757, p. 177.

10. I have followed eighteenth-century usage, which refers to Mme. de Beaumont or Mme. Beaumont, not Mme. Le Prince de Beaumont.

11. The education of girls certainly differed from that of their brothers, whose studies were still largely bounded by a classical curriculum (although this did include geography, mathematics, and other subjects on which classical authors had written). Only a small number of women read Greek and Latin, but many more read the classics in translation, and a sizable number read French or Italian. A few also studied Hebrew. French was still the lingua franca of the British and European upper classes, male and female. Scientific studies were often more available to women than classical languages and literature—as new disciplines they sometimes lacked the clear association with male learning.

12. See Deirdre Raftery, *Women and Learning in English Writing, 1600–1900*, 1997; Kenneth Charlton, *Women, Religion and Education in Early Modern England*, 1999; Charlton, "'Not publike onely but also private and domesticall': Mothers and familial education in pre-industrial England," *History of Education*, 1988, 17, no. 1, 1–20; Charlton, "Mothers as educative agents in pre-industrial England," *History of Education*, 1994, 23, no. 2, 129–156; Sylvia Harcstark Myers, *The Bluestocking Circle: Women, Friendship, and the Life of the Mind in Eighteenth-Century England*, (Oxford: Clarendon, 1990); Harriet Guest, *Small Change: Women, Learning, Patriotism, 1750–1810*, 2001; Alan Richardson, *Literature, Education, and Romanticism: Reading as Social Practice, 1780–1832*, 1994; Kathryn Sutherland, "Writings on Education and Conduct: Arguments for Female Improvement' in Vivien Jones, ed. *Women and Literature in Britain, 1700–1800*, 2000; Jane McDermid's "Conservative feminism and female education in the eighteenth century," (*History of Education*, 1989, 18, (4): 309–322) also discusses this issue, although her arguments focus on the last quarter of the century. See also Susan Skedd, "Women Teachers and the Expansion of Girls' Schooling in England, c. 1760–1820" in Hannah Barker and Elaine Chalus, eds. *Gender in Eighteenth-Century, England. Roles, Representations, and Responsibilities*, 1997: 101–121; Clarissa Campbell Orr's work on Queen Charlotte; and my own *"Such Constant Affectionate Care": Lady Charlotte Finch, Royal Governess to the Children of George III*, 2003, as well as John Brewer's discussion of Anna Larpent in *Pleasures of the Imagination: English Culture in the Eighteenth Century*, 1997. Cohen's summary in *Fashioning Masculinity* (1996) of the historical evolution of the role of educated women in France and England in defining a gentleman also provides valuable insights for this discussion.

13. Lady Ellenor Fenn, *The Art of Teaching in Sport* (J. Marshall, c. 1790), 37.

14. Mitzi Myers, "Impeccable Governesses, Rational Dames, and Moral Mothers," *Children's Literature* 14 (1986): 31–59.

15. Ibid., 34.

16. This is not the place to enter into a discussion of the dichotomy that an ahistorical feminist analysis may perceive in the fundamental acceptance of these women with the role of the female as nurturer (virtually universal in the genre at this time). These eighteenth-century women authors created mother figures who were role models, female characters who were intelligent, educated, rational, and pious. Although many of these authors were not feminists in the sense that Wollstonecraft was, they were striving to create a place in their society for the truly adult woman. Mitzi Myers also points to the shift that allowed women to be seen as authorities on the education of children, both as authors and as the dominant character in juvenile fiction. ("Impeccable Governesses," 32–33). Sarah Fielding's *The Governess; or, Little Female Academy* (London: A. Millar, 1749) is also the story of a governess and her charges, but Mrs. Teachum instructs "those committed to her care in reading, writing, working, and in all proper forms of behaviour" (Fielding, 1), *not* in the application of reason or in the broader and deeper curriculum of de Beaumont's Mrs. Affable.

17. Valuable work has been done; see Gillian Avery, *The Best Type of Girl: A History of Girls' Independent Schools*, 1991; Dorothy Gardiner, *English Girlhood at School*, 1929; Josephine Kamm, *Hope Deferred: Girls' Education in English History*, 1965; Susan Skedd, "Women Teachers and the Expansion of Girls' Schooling in England, ca. 1760–1820," and so on.

18. John Cannon, *Aristocratic Century: the Peerage of Eighteenth-century England* (Cambridge: Cambridge University Press, 1984); George Brauer, *The Education of a Gentleman: Theories of Gentlemanly Education in England, 1660–1775* (New York: Bookman Associates, 1959).

19. Cannon, 36–37.

20. Mary Hilton and Pamela Hirsch, *Practical Visionaries: Women, Education and Social Progress, 1790–1930* (Harlow: Longman, 2000), 1. Kenneth Charlton makes a similar point in the introduction to his *Women, Religion and Education in Early Modern England* (London & New York: Routledge, 1999), 4, when he acknowledges his "increasingly immediate awareness" in the course of research into the education of women, of "the continuing influence of a male-oriented cultural biography."

21. Catherine Talbot to Elizabeth Carter, December 17, 1750, *A Series of Letters Between Mrs. Elizabeth Carter and Miss Catherine Talbot; from the Year 1741 to 1770.* ed. Rev. Montagu Pennington (London: F.C. & J. R. Rivington, 1809), 1: 369.

22. Marie Anne Fiquet du Boccage. *Letters Concerning England, Holland and Italy* (London, C. Dilley, 1770), 29–30.

23. And indulgent fathers, too: on April 3, 1755, William Finch wrote to his wife, Lady Charlotte, of their son, George, aged three years, "The pretty boy is as well & charming as it is possible to be. He was cook in his kitchen this morning and drest a dinner for me, & when I had dined, I said, I thank you Master Cook. He thought I had said Nasty Cook & I assure you it was a good while before I could make it up."

William Finch to Lady Charlotte Finch, 3 April 1755. Records Office of Leicester, Leicestershire and Rutland, Finch family papers, DG7/Box 4953/Bundle 30.

24. Lady Mary Wortley Montagu to Lady Bute 6 March 1753. *The Complete Letters of Lady Mary Wortley Montagu,* ed. Robert Halsband (Oxford: Clarendon Press, 1966), 3: 26. In fact, Lawrence Stone cites Lady Louisa Stuart (a granddaughter of Lady Mary Wortley Montagu and possibly influenced by her grandmother's reminiscences), who wrote that "the education of women had then [in the first decades of the eighteenth century] reached its lowest ebb" (Stone, 230). Stone's argument is that as "male education had been shifting from the intensely scholarly classical education of the late sixteenth century to the shallower and more aesthetic training in the seventeenth century of the 'virtuoso,' ... Similarly, the standard female education among the aristocratic elite had also become more purely ornamental" (Stone, 229). Thus, aristocratic girls were no longer taught the same degree of housewifery, but not until later was this replaced with a broader curriculum. Stone's argument is flawed however, as there are a number of documented examples of seventeenth- and early eighteenth-century girls being taught history, geography, the sciences, and so on.

25. Lady Mary Wortley Montagu to Lady Bute, Jan. 28, 1753, Halsband, 3: 20–24.

26. Ibid.

27. "You will tell me, I did not make it a part of your education. Your prospect was very different from hers, as you had no defect either in mind or person to hinder, and much in your circumstances to attract, the highest offers. It seem'd your business to learn how to live in the world as it hers to know how to be easy out of it. It is the common error of builders and parents to follow some plan they think beautifull (and perhaps is so) without considering that nothing is beautifull that is misplac'd. ... Thus every woman endeavors to breed her daughter a fine lady, qualifying her for a station in which she will never appear, and at the same time incapacitating her for that retirement to which she is destin'd." Lady Mary Wortley Montagu to Lady Bute, Jan. 28, 1753, Halsband, 3: 20–24.

28. Mary Astell's *Serious Proposal to the Ladies for the Advancement of Their True and Great Interest* (1694–97), for example, suggested a college for learned women, but this spoke to the place of intellectual women rather than to the education of girls. And it must be remembered that Lady Mary was somewhat quarrelsome, considered an eccentric, and lived abroad for many years. She thus perhaps spoke from an extreme of personal experience when she wrote of books as companions. Also, Lady Mary was discussing the education of individual girls—her daughter and granddaughter—rather than making any kind of general statement.

29. This is not to suggest there was not still considerable prejudice among elite men. Horace Walpole's criticisms of Lady Mary Wortley Montagu and Lady Pomfret are two examples (see footnote 30), and Lord Chesterfield was known for his low opinion of the intellectual abilities of women.

30. Lady Pomfret has suffered historically from Walpole's vituperative dismissal of her. He described her as a sort of Mrs. Malaprop, with a "paltry air of significant learning." See Walpole to Sir Horace Mann, November 23, 1741, *Horace Walpole's Correspondence*. W.S. Lewis, ed. (New Haven: Yale University Press, 1937–1983), 17: 210. She was, he said "half witted, half learned, half ill-natured, half proud, half vulgar" ("Anecdotes of Lady Mary Wortley Montagu and Lady Pomfret," *Walpole Corres.* 14: ii, 247, Appendix 5.) When, in 1755, she donated part of the Arundel marbles, purchased by her father-in-law, to the University of Oxford, he dismissed this as an attempt to buy her way into intellectual credibility. In consequence of this gift, she is buried in St. Mary's Church, Oxford. Modern accounts have depended largely on Walpole's character sketch, making it difficult objectively to assess the extent of Lady Pomfret's intelligence or education. See also Finch MSS. Records Office for Leicestershire, Leicester & Rutland for Lady Pomfret's diaries and correspondence. DG7; *Correspondence between Frances, Countess of Hartford (afterwards Duchess of Somerset) and Henrietta Louisa, Countess of Pomfret, 1738–1741,* ed. W. Bingley. (London: Richard Phillips, 1805); and George Paston, *Little Memoirs of the Eighteenth Century* (London: Grant Richards, 1901).

31. For example, in 1732, four of her children performed in the children's production of Dryden's *Indian Emperor,* portrayed by Hogarth and produced to celebrate the tenth birthday of Lady Caroline Lennox. See Jill Shefrin *"Such Constant Affectionate Care": Lady Charlotte Finch, Royal Governess, and the Children of George III* (Los Angeles: Cotsen Occasional Press, 2003), Appendix 2.

32. Sophia Carteret was the daughter of Lady Pomfret's eldest daughter, Lady Sophia Fermor, who married John, Baron Carteret (later Lord Granville) in 1744 and died shortly after the baby's birth in 1745.

33. De Beaumont was introduced to the Countess by James Edward Oglethorpe, the military commander and philanthropist. General Oglethorpe was a committed Hanoverian and a Protestant, but his mother and sisters were Jacobites, and his sisters had been brought up at the French Court. He was also the founder of the colony of Georgia. See P. K. Hill. *The Oglethorpe Ladies and the Jacobite Conspiracies* (Atlanta: Cherokee Publishing Company, 1977).

34. The *Magasin des enfans* was published in London by John Haberkorn in 1756; published in English by Long & Pridden in 1757 and by John Nourse in 1760. Nourse had published a third English-language edition by 1776. As well, it had appeared in five editions in Lyon by 1768.

35. Jeanne-Marie Le Prince de Beaumont, *The Young Misses Magazine* (London: J. Nourse, 1776), 8.

36. References are admittedly scanty except in case of Lady Frances Allen, whose correspondence with Mme. de Beaumont after the latter's return to France is held in the library in Vire, Normandy.

37. Subscription list from the first edition of the *Magasin des enfans* (London: John Haberkorn, 1756). The typesetter's English leaves something to be desired: "Liste des souscrivans: Sa M[ajestie]. l'Imp[eriale] de toutes les Russies; Sa A.I. le Grand Duc de Russie; S.A. I. la Grande Duchesse de

Russie; S.A.I. le Duc Paul Petrowitz; La Duchesse de Beaufort; Mlle. Trembler; Milady Vicomtesse d'Allen; Mlle. Allen; Lady Brook; Milord Guilford; Milord Hillsborough; Lady Mary Hills[borough]; Madame Cavendish; Mr. Spencer; Madame Spencer; Milord Carlisle; Milady Carlisle; Madame la Marquise de Gray; Milady Comtesse de Pomfret; Lady Sophia Carteret; Mlle. Fox; Milady [Charlotte?] Finch; Mlle. Match; Lady Catherine Perceval; Mlle. Cluterburgh; Mad. la Baronne de Munchousen; Madame de St Jean; Madame Felem; Madlle. Preston; Milady Comtesse de Northumberland; Milord Carisford; Milady Carisford; Madame [Elizabeth?] Montagu; Milady Blessenthon; Milady Sandwich; Milady Cardigan; Milord Scarbrough; Milady Grinville; Milady Croniel [Conyers]; Milady Penne; Milady Anne Dawsor [Dawson]; Madame Carters [Elizabeth Carter]; Madlle. St Albans l'âinée; Madlle. St Albans cadette; Madame Pitt; Mr Cooper; La Comtesse de Coneusgeby; Milord Warsmouth; Mr. Howard; Madame Howard; Madlle Howard; Mr. Howard, fils; Milady Kildair; Mr. Seguin; Mr. le Chevalier Schawb; Mr. le Prince Galitein; Mr. le Comte de Rantzau; Milady Françoise William; Milady Fitz-William; Milord Chesterfield; Madlle. Sutton; Mr. le Colonel Sandford; Mr. Hubert, Esqr.; Milady Mascarcene; Mrs. Hills; Milady Arabella Denis; Mrs. Fisdal; Mrs. Clinton; Mrs. Yorick; Madame la Duchesse de Roxbury; Le Comte d'Esterasy Amb de Vienne; Le Baron de Pos, Ministre de Suède; Mr. de Fonk, Ministre de Saxe; Mr. le Comte de Bosomoski Aitman de l'Ucraine, Président de l'Académie des Sciences; Mr. le Chambellan Juan Juanowitz de Chevalloff, Curateur de l'Université Impériale de Moscou; Mr. le Chambellan, C. de Cheremetoff; Mad. la Comtesse, née Prsse de Sreaski; Mr. le Vice-Chancellor, C. de Varamo; Messrs. les deux Chamb. de Varamo; Mr. le Baron, Chamb. de Strogonoff; Mr. Fermor, Général en Chef; Mr. le Chambellan, Prince Galit[s?]in; Mr. le Chambellan, Baron de Sieven; Mr. le Prince Chachouskoi, Commissaire de Guerre; Mr. le Prince Mentsicoff; Mr. le Prince Couratlin; Mr. de Nareskin, Maréchal de la Cour; Le Comte Juan de Chernichoff; Mr. Condoidi, Premier Medicin de Corps; Mr. le Conseill Léoploff; M. le Conseiller Lapcoff; Mr. Sousadieo, Premier Chirurgien du Corps; Messrs. Vainac & Compagnie; Mr. Frederick Wilhelm Poiquenpoth; Mr. de Serigny; Mr. Martin; Mr. Guemgros; Mr. Dunoyers; Mr. Bertir."

38. Le Prince de Beaumont, Dedication "Pour servir de suite au Magasin des adolescentes"to *Instructions pours les jeunes dames*. Translated as *Instructions for Young Ladies on their Entering into Life, their Duties in the Married-State, and Towards their Children* (London: J. Nourse, 1764), 4–6.

39. Jeanne-Marie Le Prince de Beaumont, *The Young Ladies Magazine, or Dialogues Between a Discreet Governess and Several Young Ladies of the First Rank under her Education* (London, J. Nourse, 1760), Introduction, xvii.

40. We know some of Mme. de Beaumont's other pupils, but not by which characters they are represented in the stories. (It is tempting to match known given names, ages, circumstances and temperaments, but I have not so far succeeded in achieving dependable matches. For example, at least three of Mme. de Beaumont's pupils came from families with estates

in Ireland, and one of those was called Mary. One of these, Lady Mary Hillsborough, was also approximately the right age for the character of Lady Mary (whose mentions a visit to her home in Ireland) in the stories, but historical record of her character suggests that she was more likely to have been portrayed as either Lady Violent or Lady Tempest. The first two volumes were published in 1756 and 1760. The character of Lady Mary is five years old in the first and eight in the second, but the latter volume begins with one of the girls complaining that Mrs. Affable has been away for almost two years, so this is not a dependable chronology either.

41. To take Lady Charlotte Finch as an example, two of her husband's sisters were married to, respectively, the Duke of Somerset and the Earl of Mansfield and his brother was the Earl of Winchelsea and Nottingham, a title inherited by Lady Charlotte's son when his uncle died without male issue. One of her sisters married a son of William Penn. Her brother was the second Earl of Pomfret and her oldest sister had married John Carteret, Earl Granville. Granville and Mansfield were both prominent Ministers of the Crown, and Lady Charlotte's husband was Vice-Chamberlain. Her niece, Lord Granville's daughter, married the Earl of Shelburne, also a prominent politician.

42. *Young Misses Magazine*, 1: 152–153.

43. The letters of Frances Allen, later Lady Frances Mayne, are in the Bibliothèque de Vire in Normandy.

44. Le Prince de Beaumont, *The Young Ladies Magazine*, 1: xx–xxi. The progressive beliefs of Lady Ellenor Fenn and Mrs. Barbauld are reflected in the extreme simplicity of their writings for very young children; de Beaumont's pupils were older and her high expectations of their abilities were equally novel. Lady Fenn's lessons included the use of games and simple cuts.

45. One English contemporary who also argued for the critical importance of parental responsibility in the education of children was Mrs. Thomas Slack. In the introduction to her *Pleasing Instructor*, also published in 1756, she declared (writing only of sons): "In all the systems of education I have seen, the duty of the scholar seems to be defined with the most scrupulous exactness. But in none do I find any hint given of the duty of parents; an object, in my opinion, of infinitely more concern and magnitude. An instance of filial ingratitude may cause a pang of exquisite anguish in a single breast; but the neglect of one's boy's education may sow the seeds of whole races of depravity, and perpetuate darkness, error, and vice to a long posterity. There are few duties in the life of man equally important with that of the care and education of his children, and few so generally mistaken and neglected." (London: G.G.J. & J. Robinson, 1785), viii.

46. Du Boccage, 38. Her ambiguous reference to "Lady Montagu" could refer to any of Lady Mary Wortley Montagu, the Duchess of Montagu, or Mrs. Elizabeth Montagu. Lady Mary was not in England in 1750, but the duchess was a friend of Lady Pomfret's. Elizabeth Montagu was, of course, also a literary patron.

47. Apparently as late as 1758: see Patricia Clancy: "A French Writer and Educator in England: Mme Le Prince de Beaumont," *Studies in Voltaire and the Eighteenth Century*, 201 (1982): 195–208 n. 21.

48. The range of scientific subjects includes explanations of why some things float and others sink, the progress of caterpillar to chrysalis and, finally, butterfly, and the nature of the atom.

49. See Shefrin (88–123) for a discussion of Mme. de Beaumont's dissected maps.

50. These are Lady Witty (age twelve), Lady Mary (five), Lady Charlotte (seven), Lady Tempest (thirteen), Miss Molly, Lady Fanny (five), Lady Violent (eight), Lady Trifle (ten), Lady Bella (eleven), Lady Sophia (twelve), Lady Rural (fourteen), Lady Louisa (seventeen), Lady Sincere (seventeen), Lady Lucy (eighteen), Lady Frivolous (eighteen), and Lady Zinna (eighteen). I have given the age for those characters appearing in the *Magasin des enfans* as they appear at the beginning of that work, they are therefore assumed to be several years older in the second and third books.

51. See Clarissa Campbell Orr, "Rational Religion and Aristocratic Feminism c. 1700–1800: Some Themes and Contexts." Unpublished paper given at the William Clark Andrews Memorial Library, UCLA conference, "Genealogies of Feminism," October 19–20, 2001:

> On returning home with gold, Beauty begs her father to use it for her sisters' dowries and insists on returning to the Beast's castle. She is given an apartment in the castle: and what does it contain? This is the significant thing, and a clue that there is something redeemable about the Beast: she finds her set of rooms includes "a large library, a harpsichord, and several music books." Here is cultural permission for the young ladies to whom these books were addressed to get into the library their father's owned and to *read*. These are the cultural tools for negotiating the unruly aggression of male sexuality, and perhaps too for looking beyond its magnetic allure to qualities of mind and heart.

52. Geneviève Artigas-Menant, "La vulgarisation scientifique dans *Le Nouveau magasin français* de Mme Leprince de Beaumont," *Revue d'histoire des sciences* 44, 3/4 (July–December 1991): 343–357; Alix Deguise, "Madame Leprince de Beaumont conteuse ou moraliste?" in Bonnel, Roland and Catherine Rubinger, eds. *Femmes Savantes et Femmes d'Esprit: Women Intellectuals of the French Enlightenment*, 1994; Adrian Kempton, "Education and the Child in Eighteenth-Century French Fiction," *Studies on Voltaire and the Eighteenth Century* 124, (1974): 299–362. Also two articles by French literature scholar Patricia Clancy: "A French Writer and Educator in England: Mme Le Prince de Beaumont"; and "Madame Le Prince de Beaumont: Founder of Children's Literature in France," *Australian Journal of French Studies* 16, nos. 1–2 (1979): 281–287; and general works on eighteenth-century French children's literature such as Isabelle Havelange and Ségolène Le Men. *Le magasin des enfants: la littérature pour la jeunesse, 1750–1830* (Bibliothèque Robert-Desnon, 1988: Catalogue of an exhibition, December 1988-Jan 1989). There also have been two biographies of her: Marie Antoinette Reynaud, *Madame Le Prince de Beaumont, Vie et oeuvre d'une éducatrice*. (Unpublished thesis, Lyon, 1971); and Jean Marie Robain. *Madame Leprince de Beaumont*

intime. Avec ses principaux contes et ses documents inédits (Paris: La Page et
la Plume, 1996); and one work on the history of "Beauty and the Beast,"
Betsy Hearne's *Beauty and the Beast: Visions and Revisions of an Old Tale,*
(Chicago & London: University of Chicago Press, 1989).

53. Admittedly with lapses into conventional pietistic and moralistic platitudes.
54. Marina Warner, *From the Beast to the Blonde* (London: Chatto & Windus,
    1994), 293. Warner's account of the details of Mme. de Beaumont's life
    contains a number of frequently repeated inaccuracies. It is, however, true
    that the last of the three *Magasins* marks a change in the tone of her argu-
    ments, but whether this is attributable to the increasing age of the pupils
    (by that time of marriageable age), to her own possibly jaundiced view of
    men after she left Thomas Pichon, her highly unsatisfactory common-law
    husband in London, or to her increased piety is unclear.
55. This is particularly ironic in the case of the bluestockings, who established
    intellectual credibility with male contemporaries partly though a public
    association of virtue with learning, as they attempted to protect themselves
    from the traditional association of learned women with loose living. See
    Sylvia Harcstark Myers, *The Bluestocking Circle, passim* for a discussion of
    this question. My thanks to Clarissa Campbell Orr for several fascinating
    and helpful discussions on the fugitive solution to the problem of how these
    women themselves defined "education," "wisdom" and similar attributes
    and values.
56. See the Introduction to Hilton and Hirsch for an excellent summary of
    this development:

    ... the ideas of the Enlightenment, a new belief that reason
    should guide the affairs of mankind rather than superstition, faith or
    revelation, stimulated several progressive women to join the writers
    who were transforming the conduct book into a public discourse of
    educational principles. In this they drew on the educational works
    of John Locke and David Hartley (1705–1757). Locke's conviction
    that neither man nor woman was born weighed down by original
    sin, but instead each child's mind was a *tabula rasa* with an innate
    potential for reason, gave rise to a vision of the citizen as a self-
    determining individual whose obligation to the state came from his
    or her own voluntary action. Subsequently Hartley developed a scien-
    tific basis for the belief that infants could be moved from early sense
    impressions to moral attitudes. He argued that, through associating
    pleasant sensations with moral values in their early years, children
    would develop strong and good principles for life. This "association-
    ism" as it was called, in early education was seen as a science which
    offered a new authority to middle-class women educationists. (3)
57. Clarissa Campbell Orr has recently provided an excellent analysis of the
    court of George III and Queen Charlotte as a center of the Christian
    Enlightenment in "Queen Charlotte as Patron: Some Intellectual and
    Social Contexts," *The Court Historian* 6 (2001): 183–212.
58. Interestingly, her Roman Catholicism does not seem to have been an
    issue either for her or for her employers, all members of the Church of
    England.

59. William Gilpin, headmaster of the progressive boys' school of Cheam (Surrey) from 1752 to 1777, subscribed to a similar philosophy. He wrote to one parent: "It is my endeavour, rather to reign in the imagination of boys, and to spur their reason. It is my wish to improve their sense, and if possible their judgement." Like Mme. de Beaumont, Gilpin wanted to form character and teach children to think: facts could be picked up at any time by anyone with a properly trained mind and well-developed character. Gilpin's intent was to educate boys to be honorable and rational. Gilpin also approved the use of educational pastimes: a surviving letter written from one pupil to his parents indicates that dissected puzzles were used at Cheam in teaching cartography and geography.

60. The format of the work is reminiscent of Fielding's *Governess* (1749), which also was the story of a group of girls under the care of a strict but affectionate governess. Fielding's work also used moral tales to teach behaviour and judgement, but, despite the fact that the author herself learned Greek, the school's curriculum is apparently restricted to "reading, writing, working, and ... all proper forms of behaviour," although they also learn some botany and visit a stately home. See Jill Grey's introduction to the Oxford University Press facsimile edition of 1968 for a further discussion of the school represented in *The Governess*.

61. A similar position is attributed to Elizabeth Carter in Harriet Guest's recent *Small Change*, and the argument also exists in the some seventeenth-century discussions of women's education.

62. *Instructions for Young Ladies on their Entering into Life, Their Duties in the Married-State, and Towards their Children*, 1: 5.

63. Of a visit Lady Charlotte and her daughter, Cha, were to make to Lady Pomfret, she wrote that she would "discard Made. Beaumont for two or three lessons, to leave her [Cha] at liberty." See the correspondence of Lady Charlotte to Lady Pomfret, early in 1754. Records Office of Leicester, Leistershire and Rutland, DG7/Box 4953/Bundle 30.

64. Lady Charlotte to Lady Pomfret, 21 September 1759. Records Office of Leicester, Leistershire and Rutland, DG7/Box 4953/Bundle 30.

65. Lady Charlotte conformed in other ways to Mme. de Beaumont's model. The Royal Governess was praised for her affection and kindheartedness. Mrs. Affable is physically demonstrative, uses endearments, and encourages the girls with positive reinforcement.

66. Elizabeth Montagu to Elizabeth Vesey, 1772, Reginald Blunt, *Mrs. Montagu, "Queen of the Blues": Her Letters and Friendships from 1762 to 1800* (London: Constable, 1923), 261.

67. E. Carter to E. Vesey, April 28, 1772. Pennington, 4:60. Another example of how the family was perceived can be found in Mme. de Beaumont's dedication of *The Young Ladies Magazine* (1760) to the fifteen-year-old Lady Sophia Carteret. She refers to "the daily examples you have from those that are dearest to you." Le Prince de Beaumont, 1: v.

68. Sarah Trimmer, *An Easy Introduction to the Knowledge of Nature, and Reading Holy Scriptures*. London: J. Dodsley, 1783 (3rd ed.), dedication. Thanks to Matthew Grenby of the University of Newcastle for this reference.

69. There is a contradiction in the application of this argument to the lives of Queen Charlotte and other prominent women of the period. Some mothers taught, others supervised, and the latter was still acceptable to Mme. de Beaumont if the governess had been carefully chosen and was supervised. She never expects the mothers of her pupils to function as exclusive teachers. The Countess of Egremont is praised by Mme. de Beaumont for bringing up her daughters herself, but those daughters were also pupils of Mme. de Beaumont. Even Mme. de Beaumont herself left her daughter in a convent school in France from 1748 until shortly before her own return to that country in 1762. It is impossible to determine whether she did this pragmatically, having a career to pursue elsewhere, or whether she had sufficient faith in the educational system at the French convent school to be content leaving her daughter in their hands for many years.

70. Christie's *A Catalogue of the Genuine Library, Prints, and Books of Prints, of an Illustrious Personage [Queen Charlotte], Lately Deceased.* "Which will be sold by auction, on Wednesday 9th of June, 1819, and the following days, by Mr. Christie, at his rooms in Pall-Mall, where catalogues may be had, and at Messrs. Nichol's, Booksellers to His Majesty, Pall Mall."

71. "… eating, working, praying, playing, everything under the eye of [Mme. de Beaumont]. This is of the greatest importance."

72. Lady Fenn suggests a mother should see herself as "mistress of the revels among her little people" *The Art of Teaching in Sport*, 6).

73. Queen Charlotte to Grand Duke Charles of Mecklenburg-Strelitz, July 9, 1782; ibid., 125–126.

74. Morris Marples, *Six Royal Sisters, Daughters of George III* (London: Michael Joseph, 1969) 13.

75. "About this time a great fracas happen'd in the royal nursery. Lady Charlotte Finch had gone on business to her sons [*sic*] house in Rutlandshire. Upon some petty provocation from Prince William [Mrs. Abbott] had not only the presumption to strike him, but knock'd his head against the wall. Upon which she was desired by the Queen to discontinue her attendance on the Princes till Lady Charlotte's return that she might decide whch was proper to be done on such an occasion. When Ldy. Charlotte came to examine into all the consequences of this extraordinary affair, she pass'd a sentence of expulsion on the offender: prohibiting her ever setting foot again in the royal nursery & desiring all the attendants of the Princes to cease any future intercourse with her. It was said, however, that she was allotted her sallary by way of pension but her occupation was gone forever." *The Diaries of a Duchess. Extracts from the Diaries of the First Duchess of Northumberland (1716–1776).* ed. James Greig (London: Hodder and Stoughton, 1926), 145.

76. *Young Misses Magazine*, 1: 69.

77. Historically, royal children often receive a broader education than many of their contemporaries (although for girls this is more likely to be true if they are themselves going to inherit the throne). Well-educated princesses include George IV's daughter, Princess Charlotte of Wales; and Henry VIII's daughters Mary I and Elizabeth I.

78. Recalling the pastimes of Jane Johnson, Planta creatively designed her own schoolroom pastimes. We know the queen approved the use of the cards, for she offered to translate them into German. Frederika Planta was one of two sisters who served the royal children. Their brother was the Keeper of Manuscripts and Medals at the British Museum.

79. Mrs. Mary Campbell to her daughter, Mrs. Rebecca Phraser, at Philadelphia, quoting Miss Planta, dated only 1774. RA. Queen Victoria's papers Y.171.81.

80. John Carteret, Lord Granville to Lady Sophia Carteret, October 6, 1759. Carteret MSS. Bodleian, Lyell Manuscripts Empt. 37.

81. Ibid., 38, October 14, 1759.

82. "Dedication," *Instructions pour les jeunes dames 'pour servir de suite au Magasin des adolescentes,'* 4–6.

83. Until my discovery of the connection between Mme. de Beaumont and dissected maps, their invention had been attributed to the mapseller John Spilsbury, who completed his apprenticeship in 1760. See Shefrin, *"Such Constant Affectionate Care"* and Linda Hannas, *The English Jigsaw Puzzle, 1760–1890* (London: Wayland, 1972).

84. Caroline Fox, Lady Holland to Emily, Marchioness of Kildaire, 28 September 1762, Fitzgerald, Brian, ed. *Correspondence of Emily, Duchess of Leinster, 1731–1814* (Dublin: Stationery Office, 1937), 1:343.

10

Spectral Literacy

The Case of *Goody Two-Shoes*

PATRICIA CRAIN

> A shoemaker when he has finished one pair of shoes does not sit down
> and contemplate his work in idle satisfaction. ... The shoemaker who so
> indulged himself would be without wages half his time. It is the same
> with a professional writer of books. ... I had now quite accustomed
> myself to begin a second pair as soon as the first was out of my hands.
>
> —Anthony Trollope, *Autobiography*

According to its title page, *The History of Little Goody Two-Shoes*,
published by John Newbery in London in 1765 and one of the earliest
novels for children, recounts "The Means by which [Goody] acquired
her Learning and Wisdom, and in consequence thereof her Estate."[1]
To readers who know of the novel beyond its residue in the catchphrase,[2] *Goody* is largely remembered as a tale of educational and
social advancement, a baby *bildungsroman* promoting Enlightenment
virtues and values—rationality, self-sufficiency, literacy—which are
rewarded in the end with the requisite "coach & six" (see Figure 10.1).
Printed anonymously, like most early children's books, but variously
attributed to Oliver Goldsmith or John Newbery among others,
Goody became a staple of Anglo-American children's publishing for
150 years in its original and in later redactions, and survives on the
pantomime stage as well as in the schoolyard slur. *Goody Two-Shoes*
features centrally in every history of children's literature and children's

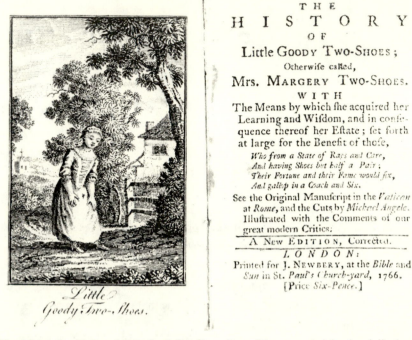

THE
HISTORY
OF
Little GOODY TWO-SHOES;
Otherwife called,
Mrs. MARGERY TWO-SHOES.
WITH
The Means by which fhe acquired her
Learning and Wifdom, and in confe-
quence thereof her Eftate; fet forth
at large for the Benefit of thofe,

Who from a State of Rags and Care,
And having Shoes but half a Pair;
Their Fortune and their Fame would fix,
And gallop in a Coach and Six.

See the Original Manufcript in the *Vatican*
at *Rome*, and the Cuts by *Michael Angelo*.
Illuftrated with the Comments of our
great modern Critics.

A New EDITION, Corrected.

LONDON:
Printed for J. NEWBERY, at the *Bible* and
Sun in St. *Paul's Church-yard*, 1766.
[Price *Six-Pence*.]

Little
Goody Two-Shoes.

Fig. 10.1 *The History of Little Goody Two-Shoes.* New edition, corrected. London: J. Newbery, 1766, frontispiece and title page. Reproduced by permission of Princeton University Library.

publishing; beyond this, the historian Isaac Kramnick has positioned *Goody* as an example of Anglo-American "radical bourgeois ideology," and literary scholars have offered nuanced readings in the context of eighteenth-century aesthetics, publishing history, legal history, and the history of childhood.[3] In this chapter, I'm reading *Goody* with an eye toward what it can tell us about the prehistory of the cultural key concept identified as "literacy."[4]

We have come to think routinely of literacy as among the funda-mental forms of cultural capital, and, a little less routinely, education has been called starkly "a process of human capital formation."[5] Liter-acy is thus often to be found in the general neighborhood of capital if never exactly nestled next to it in the vault. The literacy that comes to be represented to, through, in, and by children in the eighteenth cen-tury establishes a discursive relationship between, broadly speaking, literacy and property, when concepts of property were notably fluid, and long before the term "literacy" had come to represent, as it did only in the late nineteenth century, a fully consolidated object of "acquisition," as in the pat phrase "literacy acquisition." It is of course anachronistic to speak of "literacy" in the eighteenth century; in *Goody* what we might call "literacy" is identified as "learning" and manifests as the mechanics of alphabetization.[6] The literacy that *Goody* promotes and practices is largely reading and not writing. The eighteenth-century curriculum offers reading instruction before and in isolation from writing; few of *Goody's* students, then, would appear in the historian's archive of early modern literates, an archive dependent on signatures (on marriage registers, for example).[7]

The novel's plot takes up a rural orphan girl, who is motivated to learn her letters and to spread this knowledge through teaching; like many another novel heroine, near the end of her story, the orphan marries well, and she lives to see those who reduced her to poverty reduced in their turn. *Goody* borrows the common property of the Cinderella/Dick Whittington formula and returns it with interest for circulation as a commodity in the eighteenth-century public sphere.[8] Like other children's books of the time, *Goody* cannibalizes genres: satire, mock epic, ghost story, fairy tale, primer, courtesy or conduct book, picaresque, fable, adventure. *Goody* shares with other "adult" eighteenth-century novels the riches-(or at least competency)-to-rags-to-riches trajectory, and an episodic, digressive narrative, and even contains a mini-novel (a twelve-page *Vicar-of-Wakefield*-like tale), as though advertising the genre to the next generation of consumers.

Goody on the Commons, Goody in the Public Sphere

> The first idea which must be given him is therefore less that of liberty than that of property.
>
> —J.-J. Rousseau, *Emile*

The half-title that appears over the first page of text reads: "The Renowned History of Little Goody Two-Shoes; Commonly called, Old Goody Two-Shoes," a naming that the novel's first words comically retract: "All the world must allow, that *Two Shoes* was not her real Name" (4). With this gesture, the narrative satirically both establishes and calls into question the identity of the heroine and begins with a genealogical, or an ontological, question mark. While the fairy tale's "once upon a time" opens onto the space-time of fantasy, an eternal elsewhere, "All the world allows" marks the here and now of life lived out in the public sphere, with a nod toward a social contract; a knowing and worldly voice articulates and asserts the world's interest in the identity and the fate of a little girl.

Like so many novels, this one opens with a crisis of property, laid out in a self-consciously political "editor's" introduction. The space of the novel is mapped as a farming village, tyrannized by the local lord and his lackey, who between them hold all the legal offices in the parish of Mouldwell: overseer, church warden, surveyor of highways, and justice of the peace. Farmer Meanwell has for a long time leased his land from Sir Timothy Gripe; Farmer Graspall gathers up the leases on all of Sir Timothy's farms; Meanwell gets embroiled in lawsuits to try to maintain his own lease and ends up in penury. "As soon as Mr. Meanwell had called together his Creditors, Sir Timothy seized for a Year's Rent, and turned the Farmer, his Wife, little Margery, and her Brother out of Doors, without any of the Necessaries of Life to support them" (9). Although this catastrophe is attributed in part to "the wicked Persecutions" of the two villains, it is also a result of "the Misfortunes which [Meanwell] met with in Business" (5) placing some of the responsibility on Farmer Meanwell himself and on a world in which business can have special, even fatal, dangers. As legal historian Robert Gordon has put it, "To be in business at all [in the eighteenth century] ... was to surrender a large discretionary authority over one's person and property."[9] The opening frame ends with a lament, or a jeremiad, about the consolidation of farmland: "These reflections, Sir, have been rendered necessary, by the unaccountable and diabolical scheme which many Gentlemen now give into, of laying a number of farms into one, and very often a whole Parish into one Farm; which in the end must reduce the common People to a state of vassalage ... and will in Time depopulate the kingdom" (11–12). The introduction often has been read as evidence of authorship (echoes of "The Deserted Village" and *The Vicar of Wakefield* make Oliver Goldsmith a prime suspect) and as evidence of the mixed motives of and mixed audiences for early children's literature.[10] In later editions, it is often dropped, sometimes explicitly, as being too radical, and its details get condensed to a sentence or two of text.[11] But the local anxieties of the editor's polemic motivate the narrative's investment in elaborating an alternative to the shackles of land and leases and their inevitable losses on the shifting economic ground of the eighteenth century.

By Chapter 1, the parents die apace leaving Margery and her sibling Tommy reduced to a Hogarthian—or Hobbesian—existence of begging in the street. The orphaned child is perhaps the most vulnerable victim of the practices decried in the introduction;[12] pushed to the spatial and social margins, Margery and Tommy must live on hedgeberries and charity from the poor, who had once been the objects of their father's charity. If the center is inhabited by economic practices that the editor abhors, including, along with the land-grabbing, the ascension "by Marriage and by Death" (5) of Sir Timothy to his estate, Margery and Tommy's loss of family and exile to the margin promises a critique, perhaps a renovation, of the center.

Central among the deprivations of the orphan is the loss of private life, with its affection and protection, but also with its expectations, responsibilities, and duties; lacking these, Goody to some extent accesses the role and voice of the mythic orphan. As we shall see, Goody draws to herself the power of those whom she implicitly and explicitly supplants in the course of her history, or, of those whom she repossesses or forecloses on: the aristocrat, the witch, the spirit, the romance hero, Cinderella *and* her fairy godmother, the landlord, to name some of these. At the same time, as an entity by definition inhabiting the commons—she belongs to no one and everyone— Goody emerges as a product of print and of the eighteenth-century public sphere.

Shoes

> I would also advise ... to have his Shoes so thin, that they might leak and let in Water. ...

> —John Locke, *Some Thoughts Concerning Education*

How poor was Margery? She was so poor that she owned only one shoe. An unnamed gentleman brings the children to the attention of the clergyman Mr. Smith and offers to set Tommy up to make a living at sea, first by outfitting him in a new "Jacket and Trowsers"; the benefactor gives Mr. Smith money to buy Margery some clothes and orders for her "a new Pair of Shoes" (17). If the first function of Tommy's clothes is a published display ("Pray look at him," the narrator instructs, offering up an illustration), the second is an intimate gesture: when he and Margery part as he heads for London, he makes use of his new clothes by wiping Margery's tears with "the End of his Jacket" (19). With Tommy gone, Margery is inconsolable: "she ran all round the Village, crying for her Brother" (20). Enter, the shoemaker, bearing new shoes: "Nothing could have supported Little *Margery* under the Affliction she was in for the Loss of her Brother, but the Pleasure she took in her *two Shoes*. She ran out to Mrs. *Smith* as soon as they were put on, and stroking down her ragged Apron thus, cried out, *Two Shoes, Mame, see two Shoes*" (20–21).[13] From this moment, she becomes "little Goody Two-Shoes."[14]

For Goody as for Tommy, the gift of clothing functions as an investiture. In their discussion of Renaissance clothing, Peter Stallybrass and Ann Jones note that "it was investiture, the putting on of clothes, that ... constituted a person as a monarch or a freeman of a guild or a household servant. Investiture was ... the means by which a person was given a form, a shape, a social function, a 'depth.'" Just as Tommy's proudly displayed new look dresses him for the sea of masculinity he is about to set sail on, Goody's shoes invest her with some to-be-specified new powers, along with her very name. Clothing, Stallybrass and Jones remind us, "reminds."[15] But if Tommy's new clothes make sense, what do Goody's shoes "remind" us of?

Powerful symbols, shoes, "[t]otems of mobility and promise," as the theater critic John Lahr has called them.[16] Expensive necessities in the north, shoes define boundaries between genders and races and classes. Shoes, more vividly than any other garment, enact the melding of the sexual fetish with the commodity fetish. For us, if not quite yet for the eighteenth-century shopper, shoes actually *signify* "fetish": In a recent American Express ad, the image of one shod and one unshod female foot tempts in multiple registers ("Two is better than one" reads the slug), representing the pleasures of getting and spending, the enjoyment of shopping for and wearing impossible shoes, the attractions of a mesh-stockinged foot as well as of a lethally pointy red Blahnik-style phallic/vaginal shoe. These erotics at the level of the state seem to have motivated Imelda Marcos, and Marie Antoinette before her, who is said to have owned five hundred pairs.[17] While their husbands provided boots for armies, these wives performed a glamorous, witchy burlesque of state power. Shoes, as these two shoppers must have known, are traditionally thought to bring good luck; hence their use in marriage rites and the phenomenon of "chimney shoes," embedded in houses presumably to ward off evil spirits.[18]

Magical shoes in fairy tales compress distances (seven-league boots) and enable revelation and elevation in the case of Cinderella. The Stith Thompson *Motif Index of Folk Literature* notes 196 references to shoes;[19] one of these is a tale in which a task requires a hero to "come neither barefoot nor shod," a riddle that he solves by coming with one shoe on and one off. The single shoe, then, might sometimes signal shrewdness. In her work on fairy tales, Marina Warner notes several fabulous (in every sense) shoes, including a cult of the virgin's foot in Naples, where "Mary's own slipper" is rumored to reside.[20] Even the shoemaker has special status, not only for his role in fairy tales but also, as tradition has it, as one of the most literate of working people in the seventeenth and eighteenth centuries.[21]

Shoes resonate as both cultural icons and material artifacts, infused with powers to traverse real and symbolic distances, to attract, reveal, master, protect, and fascinate; a bare necessity, they are symbols as well of excess and accumulation. Goody Two-Shoes, then, is named for the shoes that have been given to her; more precisely, though, her name is echoed back to her from her oral repetition of delight in the shoes: "And so she behaved to all the People she met, and by that Means obtained the Name" (21). In the old-fashioned sense, she "published" her emotional investment in them, like a town crier. Biographically unhinged from genealogy, her name poetically or tropically shifts from the satiric allegory and metaphor of "Meanwell" to the synecdoche and metonymy of shoes. Her patronymic is overwritten by the metonym that her public gives her by acclamation. Goody as diva, perhaps. But also, in the repudiation of inheritance

her re-christening represents, Goody stands as a new kind of child—
the child as a kind of commons, not only resourceful in herself, but a
general resource as well. Goody's identity is established, or rather
denominated, not by the Lockean fantasy of property in herself, but
rather by acceding to the common property in herself held by others.[22] And although the shoes set Goody on her peripatetic way, they
also suggest a certain fixity and stability; the shoes render her the
opposite of footloose or vagrant.

Goody's "Two Shoes, Mame" is the last passage in the text and the
only really vivid one, in which, for the modern reader, Margery
Meanwell resembles the kind of child we've grown used to encountering in literature. But the shoes, grounding and indispensable, function
to transform that child, riven with emotion, into an adult-like agent.
As the tautological "Two-Shoes" overwrites her surname, the generic
"Goody" for "good wife" supplants her Christian name. This humble
status marker, not normally given to children, makes her into a mini-
woman overnight. Propelled from a world of virtues and vices (Mean-
wells and Graspalls) to a world of things, "Goody" bridges the two
realms, embedding in the person of the child both goodness and
goods. If metonymy is the trope of realism, as Jakobson suggests,
Goody's name also might shift her from one genre toward another, as
the subsequent names in the novel are all nonallegorical.[23] Moreover,
because shoes of course normally *come* in pairs, "Two-Shoes" names a
tautology, which, by emphasizing Goody's new normative and whole-
some status, calls attention to the disruption of poverty.

For her great losses (home, farm, parents, sibling) Goody's two
shoes offer as a fully sufficient substitute an intimate commodity,
which transforms her grief into an energizing delight associated with
her new things. The sequence of actors in the biography of these
shoes—her protectors, the Smiths; the mysterious philanthropist; the
shoemaker—gives the impression that, made to measure and by hand,
and purchased in benevolence, the shoes emerge from a preindustrial
economy, imbued with practices of auratic artisanry and of a communal
circle of gift, charity, deference, and obligation.[24] And yet, of course,
they are commodities as well as gifts.[25]

Once the shoes are sutured to the child, they circulate her, not only
through the episodes of her "history," but also across the pages of her

book, and, not least, onto the bookshelves of shops and into the hands of consumers—probably, rather frequently, as gifts.[26] Like the shoes, the book circulates and disseminates Goody. As two models of the commodity, shoe and book, each perhaps aspires to be like the other; the shoe might like the prestige and the distribution networks belonging to the book, while the book would like to be a necessity with built-in obsolescence, and a channel into the fashion system. Both commodities get their wish, over time. And the book is the model for the kind of commodity that shoes begin to turn into by the end of the eighteenth century: mass produced, branded, and distributed, rather than local and made to measure.[27]

Not long after getting back on her newly shod feet, Goody is made homeless once more. Graspall and Gripe reappear, threatening to ruin the kindly Smiths if they keep harboring Goody. The Smiths, becoming risk-averse at the thought that "the People who had ruined her Father could at any Time have ruined them" (23), throw Goody out. Immediately following this moment, the narrative recounts that "Little Margery saw *how good,* and how wise Mr. Smith was, and concluded, that this was owing to his great Learning" (24; my emphasis). Although Mr. Smith's goodness seems, to say the least, a cloistered, even a merely "bookish" virtue, since he casts an orphan girl back onto the wide world, this observation motivates Goody to learn to read.

One might attribute this abrupt narrative illogic to the slapdash nature of hackwork. Whatever its source, the solecism lends an element of the dream or fantasy, which have this same paratactic quality: I was in my room, I was on the street. The narrative drops whatever anxiety it had about Goody's homelessness, as though the shoes now magically provide home-like protection; they don't ward off evil, but they do ward off the effects associated with it. It may not be paradoxical to say that the shoes provide an aura of hominess while at the same time they seem to rob Goody of affect; although she sobbed with grief when her brother went to sea and was delighted to the same degree by her shoes, she doesn't even seem to register that she's cast out again. With this leap in narrative and emotional logic the homeless orphan girl propels herself into literacy, and in a way propels *Goody* into literary history.

The Alphabetic Fantastic

Goody's method for teaching herself aligns her with what will become a tradition of slave autodidacticism that Frederick Douglass records in his narrative eighty years later;[28] in Goody's version, "she used to meet the little Boys and Girls as they came from School, borrow their Books, and sit down and read till they returned" (25). Before long, she is teaching the alphabet to her playmates. Along with her shoes, then, Goody is associated with another interesting set of objects: the alphabet letters. Following Locke's prescription in *Some Thoughts Concerning Education* to make learning to read playful,[29] she calls her spelling lessons "the Game" (26) and carries around what the text calls her "rattletrap"[30] letters that she has cut from wood: ten sets of lowercase and six sets of uppercase letters (25–26) (see Figure 10.2). The reader isn't likely to pause over this, but if she does, she will note that Goody is carrying around in her little basket 416 pieces of wood. Suddenly she's in the realm of the mythic, like the blues singer who says a matchbox holds his clothes. And though 416 pieces of wood are too many for a girl to carry, those sixteen sets of letters make for scarcity, once you begin to compose (as any printer would tell you). The narrative is silent on these contradictions, and, like the miracle of the loaves and fishes, the letters endlessly offer themselves, just as many as required, as the children make syllables with them (ba, be, bi, bo, bu [33]) and words (Bread, Apple-pye, Turnip [35]) and sentences ("*The Lord have Mercy upon me, and grant that I may honour my Father and Mother, and love my Brothers and Sisters, Relations and Friends, and all my Playmates, and every Body, and endeavour to make them happy*" [38]).

Goody's materializing of the letters, bringing them into the world of bread and turnips and apple pies, requires the tale to glide noiselessly across into the fantastic or the marvelous. The most interesting analysts of the novel have noted the force of the irrational in the text, finding that the narrative offers up to the reader the sensations associated with "rawhead and bloody bones" while, following Locke, rationally debunking the content of the same superstitions. But the tendency is to assume that the alphabet is on the side of the rational, while the alphabet in fact initiates the fantastic in this novel.[31]

28 *The* Renowned Hiſtory *of*

I once went her Rounds with her, and was highly diverted, as you may be, if you pleaſe to look into the next Chapter.

C H A P. V.

How Little Two-Shoes *became a trotting* Tutoreſs, *and how ſhe taught her young Pupils.*

IT was about ſeven o'Clock in the Morning when we ſet out on this important

GOODY TWO-SHOES. 29

important Buſineſs, and the firſt Houſe we came to was Farmer *Wilſon's.* See here it is.

Here *Margery* ſtopped, and ran up to the Door, *Tap, tap, tap.* Who's there? Only little goody *Two Shoes,* anſwered *Margery,* come to teach *Billy.* Oh Little *Goody,* ſays Mrs. *Wilſon,* with Pleaſure in her Face, I am glad to ſee you, *Billy* wants you

Fig. 10.2 Goody the trotting tutoress with her basket full of letters for teaching reading and spelling. *The Renowned History of Little Goody Two-Shoes.* New edition, corrected. London: J. Newbery, 1766, pp. 28–29. Reproduced by permission of Princeton University Library.

Of course, in a novel you can have as many things in a basket as you want to. And the printing of all the words and sentences that the letters-in-the-basket are said to produce supports the fiction, or the lie, that Goody's letters are sufficient, a fiction further abetted by the often food-associated words that Goody has her charges spell: beef, turnip, plumb pudding. Indeed, in the illustrations of the original, she looks like Little Red Riding Hood, but instead of the dutiful, if dallying, daughter, carrying mother's food to grandmother, she's a little Cadmus, carrying letters instead, which can merely represent food. Yet this is not seen as their lack, but as their bounty. Goody supplants and, in a way, repossesses the stock role of storyteller or old wife.[32] But instead of producing ephemeral talk, she manufactures treen letters. In her role as type-founder instructing the children in composing, she seems less like a dame-school teacher than like a stand-in for the printer and bookseller John Newbery.

Goody's Economic Bildung

> Send a treasure token token
>
> Write it on a pound note pound note
>
> —Adam Ant, *"Goody Two-Shoes"*

In *Idler* 19 (1758), Samuel Johnson satirized Newbery as "Jack Whirler": "that great philosopher ... whose business keeps him in perpetual motion, and whose motion always eludes his business; who is always to do what he never does, who cannot stand still because he is wanted in another place, and who is wanted in many places because he stays in none" and concludes that Jack Whirler "lives in perpetual fatigue ... because he does not consider ... that whoever is engaged in multiplicity of business must transact much by substitution, and leave something to hazard; and that he who attempts to do all will waste his life in doing little." Whirler's perpetual motion and breathless pursuit of commerce render him a phantom, "equally invisible to his friends and his customers," an emanation of a commercial economy devoted to the movement of commodities and of dematerialized property.[33]

Goody comes to embody the literacy that accompanies this new commercial figure, mirroring his ephemerality while supplying for him a kind of ballast. As she labors to materialize and distribute the letters, what she produces—the homemade letters, not intended for exchange, given freely—might be classed as what the anthropologist Annette Weiner has called "inalienable possessions," things that their creators "keep-while-giving." Like the cloth that circulates in Maori exchange, one of the subjects of classic anthropology that Weiner revises, the letters as conceived in *Goody* are the product of female labor. Such "inalienable possessions are the representation of how social identities are reconstituted through time. ... These possessions then are the most potent force in the effort to subvert change, while at the same time they stand as the corpus of change."[34] As such, Goody's letters constitute a mainstay in the midst of dangerous speculative paper, a substitution for such previously inalienable possessions as land, for those who have lost, or could never have attained an estate.

If, within the novel, Goody's letters are a hybrid kind of property, the novel of *Goody* is merrily self-conscious about its own status as a print commodity and as an engine of commerce. The novel shares with other Newbery productions the aroma of the bookshop and the apothecary (like many booksellers, Newbery also traded in patent medicines[35]), not only in the waggishness of the narrative voice, but in its marketing of the advantages of being "lettered" and of the sensual attractions of print. The illustrations engage the reader interactively, and the narrator demands a physical engagement with the text: "Pray look at him" (17); "as you see in the Print" (27); "see here it is" (29); and "Now, pray little Reader, take this Bodkin, and see if you can point out the Letters" (31), and so on. Such gestures insist on the fact that the story comes into being solely and unabashedly for the print marketplace; not just learning to read, but an entire world of commerce becomes an interactive component in the book. In the most famous example of this print-commodity effect,[36] after the editor's introduction, as Chapter 1 opens, Goody's father was "seized with a violent fever in a Place where Dr. *James's* Powder was not to be had, and where he died miserably" (13). What is Dr. James's Powder? The back leaves of the Newbery editions advertise all manner of things found in Mr. Newbery's shop, including "Dr. James's Powders for Fevers, the Small-Pox, Measles, Colds, etc. 2 shillings 6."[37] Her father dies for lack of a commodity available at Newbery's shop; it's a condensed and displaced version of why he really does die: for lack of property. He dies, in fact, because he existed in a world in which subsistence and sustenance depended on real property, on expanses of land. Goody, it would seem, survives and thrives by establishing her identity in portable goods—shoes for example—and, materialized as her quasi-magical "rattletrap alphabets," the inalienable property of literacy.

Thanks to her shoes and her rattletrap alphabets, her teaching becomes her livelihood, as she becomes a "trotting tutoress" (28) "instructing those who were more ignorant than herself" (25). Goody soon becomes Mrs. Margery Two-Shoes, President of ABC College (65–6). Much of the narrative is then given over to her pedagogy, which employs, among other things, a lamb, a lark and a dog; a raven named Ralph, who can speak, read, and spell (70) and a pigeon named Tom who can only spell and read. Except for two, who were, notably, gifts, the animals were all abused or menaced, and Goody purchases them from their abusers, removing them from what appears to be a dangerous commons, full of nasty little boys, and bringing them under the protective sign of the alphabet. The animals serve Goody and her students, in their turn, and are mentors in their own right: Tippy the lark teaches early rising, Ralph supervises the capital letters, Tom Pidgeon carries important messages and "took Care of the small" letters (72), Will the Ba-Lamb rewards good children by carrying their books (78), and Jumper the dog is "the porter of the College" (77) and goes so far as to save the lives of Goody and all of her students when the schoolroom collapses (98).[38] The salvation of (and then by) the animals underscores the ethic that learning one's letters is meant to encourage (as in the somewhat shaky logic of Mr. Smith's goodness). Goody doesn't plead or beg for the animals or proceed legally to save them; she merely, without fanfare, lays out cash for them. It's one of few such transactions in the novel (the purchase of shoes and clothing, and the expenditures noted in Goody's will at the end are others), but suggests a renovated purpose for money. Through this exchange, the animals are removed from circulation and brought into a space of safety, identified with literacy, converting the old regime's landed estate into a virtual and portable protectorate, in which animals, like small children, will be safe-guarded. (This even though for much of the narrative, Goody's own material existence continues to be abject; like an impoverished aristo-crat starving on his inalienable land, she continues to sleep in barns until at least Chapter 5 [39]).[39]

Along with the safety of animals and children, the novel actively promotes the economic security of women. Toward the end of Goody's story, when Sir Charles Jones proposes, "She would not consent to be made a Lady, till he had effectually provided for his Daughter" (130). Not only does the daughter receive a settlement, but, in a surprise move, so does Goody: "[J]ust as the Clergyman had opened his Book" at the wedding ceremony, "a gentleman richly dressed ran into the church, and cry'd, Stop! stop!" (132). The alarming stranger is "Tom Two-Shoes," who insists on seeing "that a proper settlement was made on her" (133). The careful details of property settled for the safety of women answers the economics of the opening, with its lesson of the recklessness of relying on the suspect promises of heritability. The novel's economic *bildung* goes one step further. Sir Charles dies (like Mr. Meanwell, of a "violent fever" (134), though no mention is made of Dr. James's Powder). "Lady Margery" purchases "the whole Manour of *Mouldwell*" and "threw it into different farms" (136–137); in her will, she set aside a certain portion of land to be planted with potatoes for the use of the poor, "but if any took them to sell they were deprived of that Privilege ever after" (139). The poor are prohibited from commodifying their potatoes;[40] if they break the taboo in order to rise up out of Mouldwell, they'd better keep walking. Cash is a worrisome matter in *Goody*. Though it purchased Goody's shoes, and Goody redeemed her animals with it, she has a King Midas nightmare after she acquires her wealth: after "seeing her Husband receive a very large Sum, her heart went pit pat, pit pat, all the Evening, and she began to think that guineas were pretty things" (141–142). Associated with excitation and mobility, cash destabilizes, whereas Goody's transactions function as social balms and sedatives.

The final episode in the genealogy of Goody's marriage settlement, in a section of the "Appendix," recounts the adventures of Goody's long-lost brother,[41] who, as if acknowledging a new matriarchal regime, returns with Goody's surname. In this mini Robinsoniade, Tom Two-Shoes became a castaway "on that Part of the Coast of *Africa* inhabited by the *Hottentots*" (145). In the company of a lion, he explores "*Prester John*'s country," and in "Utopia" he comes upon a statue inscribed by an Arabian philosopher with a riddle ("On May-Day ... I shall have a Head of Gold" [147]). Solving the puzzle, Tommy digs at the spot where the shadow of the statue's head falls on May 1, and uncovers a treasure chest, engraved "As thou hast got the GOLDEN HEAD, / Observe the *Gold Mean,/* Be *good* and be happy" (150). It is this money that Tom settles on Goody. Her money, then, comes from the dead, like inherited wealth, but it's positioned in colonialist terms as emerging from a kind of commonwealth, a world-historical past, here figured as Africa and the "East," and as a boon marked as a legacy to the quick-witted, rather than to the high-born.

Spectral Literacy

Can write my name in heaven in invisible ink.

—Elvis Costello, *"Little Goody Two-Shoes"*

The sleight-of-hand that brings Goody her marriage portion under-
lies the economics of literacy throughout the text. Although the novel
devotes many of its pages to the mechanics of alphabetic literacy, the
representation of reading is perhaps not what we have since come to
expect. Goody doesn't help tenants read their leases or their almanacs.
It's not only that this is not the instrumental literacy that we might
imagine for mercantilism; no one is reading the Bible, either. After
the early scene of borrowing books, Goody is portrayed only once
as reading anything herself. Her own literacy mainly serves to gain
her employment only to reproduce her own literacy. The economy of
literacy Goody inhabits resembles nothing so much as a speculative
bubble as her faith in literacy leads her to circulate her facility in literacy, which leads to more tutoring in literacy. The benefits that accrue
to others are largely philanthropic and therapeutic, oblique consequences of the presence of the good and kind Goody. This enclosed
system requires a faith in the association between literacy and respectability, virtue, wealth, safety. In other words, an association between
literacy and the traditional attributes of inherited wealth in land.

The easy illogic of Goody's economy hints at magic, just as the
episodes describing Goody's motives and Goody's basket opened
fissures into the fantastic or the marvelous. But beginning in Chapter
6 (about a third of the way into the novel), *Goody* the book situates
Goody the girl more explicitly in relation to occult forces. The village
attends the funeral of Lady Ducklington—"Who does not know
Lady *Ducklington,*" begins this chapter (45), echoing the opening's
"All the world must allow"—about which the narrator (sounding very
Newbery-like) moralizes that "the Money they squandered away,
would have been better laid out in *little Books for Children,* or in Meat,
Drink, and Cloaths for the Poor" (46; my emphasis). After the funeral,
"about Four O'Clock in the Morning, the Bells were heard to jingle in
the Steeple, which frightened the People prodigiously, who all thought
it was Lady *Ducklington*'s Ghost dancing among the Bell-ropes" (48).

After much fearful hesitation the villagers unlock the church door and "what Sort of a Ghost do ye think appeared? Why Little *Two-Shoes*, who ... had fallen asleep in one of the Pews ... and was shut in all night" (49). Goody recounts being accosted by a mysterious presence which had "laid, as I thought, its Hands over my Shoulders" (52) and touched her neck with "something ... as cold as Marble, ay, as cold as Ice" (52–53), a presence that is revealed to be Neighbour Saunderson's dog. Thus does the poor, diligent, homeless, ABC-toting little girl, envoy of a new form of property relations, disperse and displace the ghost of Lady Ducklington, emblem of the useless, spendthrift, aristocratic order.

If Goody here stands in the ghost position, assuming the prestige of both ghosts and ghost-busters, later in the narrative she supplants the hero of old romances. Goody invents something she calls a Considering Cap, a three-sided hat, each side of which bears a motto: "I may be wrong," "It is fifty to one but you are," and "I'll consider of it," while "The other parts on the out-side, were filled with odd Characters, as unintelligible as the Writings of the old Egyptians" (115). The cap functions as a "Charm for the Passions," a Dr. James's Powder for the temperament. But here, along with the rational messages, are illegible characters, supplementing the rational with the force of the ancient and the occult. The narrative notes that the Wishing Cap of the medieval romance of Fortunatus is "said to have conveyed People instantly from one Place to another" and lauds a Cap that instead transforms the "Temper and disposition" (119). In the original romance of Fortunatus, the Wishing Cap and a bottomless purse, with which Goody's bountiful basket echoes, descended to the hero's sons who lost the first and burned the second.[42] *Fortunatus* is, in effect, a monitory tale of inheritance. Goody's cap inverts the expected roles of inherited and acquired or created property. The hero's Wishing Cap induced mobility but led to exhaustion in the next generation; Goody's Considering Cap functions, by contrast, to stabilize and fix in place, to tranquilize, and to render productive. An invention of a self-made girl rather than a questionable legacy, Goody's Cap circumscribes the kind of mobility that her literacy promotes.

Among the novel's most appealing traits are Goody's animal familiars. In a famous episode, suspicious aspects of her husbandry and her role as a local weatherwoman, using a barometer to help the farmers figure out when to bring in the hay, lead to an accusation of witchcraft. The narrator characteristically moralizes that "it is impossible for a Woman to pass for a Witch, unless she is very poor, very old, and lives in the Neighbourhood where the People are void of common sense" (127). Acquitted at the witch trial, Goody's rationality manages to charm Sir Charles Jones there, and she soon becomes his wife. For all the debunking of witchcraft, the original illustrator and all subsequent ones relish Goody's bewitching qualities, posing her with her creatures perched on her shoulders and arms.[43]

When Goody dies "a Monument, but without Inscription, was erected to her Memory in the Churchyard, over which the Poor as they pass weep continually, so that the Stone is ever bathed in Tears" (140). For all of Goody's good works, the poor are still poor. And though this passage echoes Gray's "Elegy" of 1751, even the "Elegy" permits the poor more than Goody is allotted: "frail memorial," for example, "uncouth rhymes," and "Their name, their years, spelt by th' unletter'd Muse." (Even a dormouse, earlier in Goody's narrative, receives an epitaph [114].) Why is Goody's monument uninscribed? Did the villagers in fact never learn how to read? Or did no local engraver learn how to write? Or is this the final melding of Goody the girl with Goody the commodity: She's an artifact like Jack Whirler, who exists only in circulation? I'll return to the question of Goody's lack of inscription.

In his essay on Gray's "Elegy" (1751) and Anna Letitia Barbauld's "Warrington Academy" (1773), John Guillory begins with the paradox that the vernacular canon "is at once conceived to be ... 'common' property, while ... literacy itself is by no means a universal possession." He notes the complex negotiation required to assign "the cultural value of a symbolic commodity such as vernacular literacy" and finds that "the distinction between classical and vernacular literacy corresponds roughly to the difference between two relations to property, to wit, entitlement and acquisition." In Anna Letitia Barbauld's poem about the Dissenting Academy at Warrington, an institution designed to educate a new class, the poet "insists upon the equation of knowledge with the form of property. Such property is acquired; it is not passed on like noble blood." Of the locodescriptive genre, the poem of place, to which the "Elegy" and "Warrington

Academy" belong, Guillory notes that "it is uniquely situated between the [classical] commonplace book and the vernacular anthology" and provided "the new class of literate professionals" a site to "stand together in a common place, a place which was, at the same time, private property."[44]

More so than Gray and Barbauld, *Goody*, for all her country ways, inhabits and speaks from Grub Street, but the politics of literacy the novel promotes resonate with those that Guillory lays out. Directly addressing the new child of vernacular pedagogy and satirizing classical learning, *Goody* represents the alphabet as universally available, even to the most abject; nature itself, in the person of Goody's mascots, seems to want to distribute the alphabet freely. But, in its explicit framing of the narrative in terms of property, *Goody* at the same time expresses ambivalence over what kind of property literacy constitutes.

Property, as a concept, as a form of capital, and as a set practices, is easily as layered and problematic in the eighteenth century as the practices of literacy. Many scholars have recounted the transition to new forms of property in an increasingly market-driven culture in both England and America across the eighteenth century. "In the late eighteenth century, property in contracts, property in hopes and expectations," writes Robert Gordon, noting a key aspect of this transformation, "was becoming the prevalent form of commercial property: paper money, shares of the public debt, certificates of stock in land or insurance companies, mortgages on land or inventory, bills of exchange, promissory notes, accounts receivable."[45] For the formation of both persons and publics, shifts in the meaning of property have profound consequences, since property in land grounds both the Lockean concept of identity and the republican formula for virtue. J.G.A. Pocock writes that "Land and inheritance remained essential to virtue, and virtue to the ego's reality in its own sight," but "the ideal of personality-sustaining property was no sooner formulated than it was seen to be threatened" (463); and further that "the rise of forms of property seeming to rest on fantasy and false consciousness" made "the foundations of personality themselves appear imaginary" (464).[46]

The mode of literacy that Goody, the girl and the novel, promotes and circulates is a kind of homeopathic remedy to the problems posed by property in the late eighteenth century. For the self haunted by forms of property passing away and frightened by the spectral nature of paper property and by the phantasmagoric nature of the commodity, Goody's therapy substitutes a literacy that incorporates and renovates these forms. She treats the dematerialization of property with the fantastic materiality of letters. In *Goody,* literacy is meant to be an inalienable property that can be absorbed into the person, supplementing the Lockean formulation that a person has "property in himself," and extending this entitlement to the smallest orphan girl. Unlike an estate or an heirloom, literacy lacks substance; it has nothing to offer but the paper it's written on, a promise of unspecified bounty. It's true no one can take it away from you, but chances are you can't trade it in for anything either.[47] And what does it amount to once you have it? It's hard to say; certainly it's famously hard to quantify.[48]

If part of the work of *Goody* is to acclimate the reader to new forms of property, the problem it faces is to establish a site for alphabetization that will supply a mimetic form of propertyinternalized, spacious, timeless. Such mimetic property offers a purchase for subjectivity, especially for those for whom other forms of property, perhaps even especially property in the self, are problematic—the dispossessed, women, children, the poor, slaves. Goody's monument lacks inscription perhaps in order to return Goody to an undated and unnamed common property, to a world that maintains itself by talk and memory, and doesn't make the kind of distinctions implied by Gray's "Elegy" between simple and complicated, unlettered and lettered lives. Pierre Bourdieu writes of cultural capital, especially in its "embodied" state (that is, in the person, rather than in its "objectified" state in books and works of art), that

> It cannot be accumulated beyond the appropriating capacities of an individual agent; it declines and dies with its bearer. ... [I]t defies the old, deep-rooted distinction the Greek jurists made between inherited properties (*ta patroa*) and acquired properties (*epikteta*), i.e., those which an individual adds to his heritage. It thus manages to combine the prestige of innate property with the merits of acquisition.[49]

In the case of Goody, the gift of the two shoes, which sets Goody's "history" properly in motion, might now be seen as an act of sympathetic magic by which the commodity confers on the recipient the accumulation of cultural capital. The literacy that is the legacy of this capital is constructed as a haunted piece of property, and Goody is the new old-wife whose spells only seemed to have transformed entirely into spelling.

Notes

I wish to acknowledge the McKnight Land-Grant Professorship at the University of Minnesota, which provided me with research time and resources to write this essay. Librarians at the American Antiquarian Society (especially Laura Wasowicz), the Pierpont Morgan Library, and Princeton's Cotsen Children's Library (especially Andrea Immel) were invaluable. In addition I would like to thank those who invited me to present this work and the students and other colleagues who helped me to understand Goody at the University of Minnesota, Princeton's Cotsen Conference, Johns Hopkins's ELH Colloquium, the University of Delaware, the University of Iowa Center for the Book, the Rutgers History of the Book Seminar, and the Society for the History of Authorship, Reading, and Publishing Conference. Thanks to Carol McGuirk and Lisa Gitelman for emergency readings and good advice.

1. Unless otherwise noted, I will be referring to *Goody Two-Shoes: A Facsimile Reproduction of the Edition of 1766*. Intro. Charles Welsh. (Detroit: Singing Tree Press, 1970). Subsequent references will appear parenthetically in the text.

2. The history of the catchphrase has been difficult to trace. *Brewer's Dictionary* naturally attributes it to the novel, but it seems unlikely that the expression had currency before the mid- to late nineteenth century, and probably evolved from pantomimes and sentimental versions of the novel. Adam Ant and Elvis Costello have built lyrics around "Goody Two-Shoes," which remains an oddly vital element of popular speech.

3. Isaac Kramnick, *Republicanism and Bourgeois Radicalism: Political Ideology in Late Eighteenth-Century England and America* (Ithaca: Cornell University Press, 1990). Ronald Paulson reads the novel in a chapter on children's literature in *The Beautiful, Novel, and Strange*, which sees the child as "an intriguing but strange … subject matter for writers … with the built-in poignance of victimization and the nostalgia for a freedom from 'custom, or borrowed opinions' of the Lockean child in pursuit of the word"; his reading is especially alert to the narrative effects of alphabetization. *The Beautiful, Novel, and Strange: Aesthetics and Heterodoxy*. (Baltimore: Johns Hopkins University Press, 1966), 197. Jan Fergus's interest in *Goody* emerges from her analysis of "the bookselling records of the Clays of Daventry, Rugby, Lutterworth, and Warwick," in which she finds that *Goody* is a big seller to the boys at Rugby and speculates interestingly about the model of subjectivity the novel presents. See chapter 11 in this volume. Martin Kayman reads Goody as "an agent for Lockean culture" (24) who reclaims imaginative and legal rights of possession; "Lawful Possession: Violence, The Polite Imagination and

Goody Two-Shoes," in *Violência e Possessão: Estudos Ingeles Contemporâ-
neos*. Ed. David Callahan et al. (Aveiro: Universidade de Aveiro, 1998),
21–28. Seniel Lucien offers a detailed psychoanalytic reading; see *"Little
Goody Two-Shoes:* An Early Model of Child Development," *International
Journal of Women's Studies (*6:2 March/April 1983), 148–161; see also
Lucien's three-part article "'Goody Two-Shoes' Variations on a Theme:
From Cinderella through Horatio Alger and Beyond," *Folklore* (Calcutta,
India) (23:8 Aug 1982), 163–174; (23:9 Sep 1982), 194–98; (23:10, Oct
1982), 215–220. Gillian Brown notes *Goody* as an example of "stories of
children who made their lives into moral and economic success." *Consent
of the Governed: The Lockean Legacy in Early American Culture* (Cambridge,
MA: Harvard University Press, 2001), 36. Many references to the novel
seem to refer rather to Victorian redactions, as in Maria Tatar's mention
of *Goody* among works that "presented idealized and sentimentalized
versions of reality" (*Off With Their Heads! Fairytales and the Culture of
Childhood* [Princeton, NJ: Princeton University Press, 1992], 72).

4. In treating literacy as a keyword I am drawing on both Raymond
   Williams's *Keywords* (*Keywords: A Vocabulary of Culture and Society,* [New
   York: Oxford University Press, 1976]) and Reinhart Koselleck's *Futures
   Past: the Semantics of Historical Time* (Tr. Keith Tribe [Cambridge, MA:
   MIT Press, 1990]). Williams's keywords are "record[s] of an inquiry into
   a *vocabulary:* a shared body of words and meanings in our most general
   discussions, in English, of the practices and institutions which we group
   as *culture* and *society*" and the meaning of each tends to be "inextricably
   bound up with the problems it was being used to discuss" (13). He
   discusses "literacy" under "Literature," a keyword that "corresponded
   mainly to the modern meanings of literacy, which, probably because the
   older meaning had then gone, was a new word from lC19. It meant both
   an ability to read and a condition of being well-read" (151). As a historian,
   Koselleck pursues key concepts which chart how "experiences come to
   terms with the past; how expectations, hopes, or prognoses projected into
   the future are articulated into language" (xxiii) in order to "seek out the
   linguistic organization of temporal experience wherever this surfaces in
   past reality" (xxv). His work is part of a larger collaborative project on key
   historical concepts in the lexicon *Geschichtliche Grundbegriffe.*

5. The quotation is from R. S. Schofield, "Dimensions of literacy,
   1750–1850," *Explorations in Economic History*, 10:4 (1973): 437. Pierre
   Bourdieu describes the three "guises" in which "capital can present itself":
   "as *economic capital,* which is immediately and directly convertible into
   money and may be institutionalized in the form of property rights; as *cultural capital,* which is convertible, on certain conditions, into economic
   capital and may be institutionalized in the form of educational qualifications; and as *social capital,* made up of social obligations ('connections'),
   which is convertible, in certain conditions, into economic capital and may
   be institutionalized in the form of a title of nobility" (243). Bourdieu is
   writing partly in response to what he sees as the inadequacy of economists'
   quantifying of education in simplistically monetary terms (243–4). Pierre
   Bourdieu, "Forms of Capital," in John Richardson, ed. *Handbook of theory*

and research for the sociology of education (Westport, CT: Greenwood Press 1986), 241–258. John Guillory theorizes cultural capital specifically for the literary field in *Cultural Capital: The Problem of Literary Canon Formation* (Chicago: University of Chicago Press, 1993).

6. This "literacy," according to the OED, is an American coinage of c. 1883 and a back-formation from "illiteracy" (*Oxford English Dictionary,* s.v. "literacy"). Social energies seem to coalesce around the term in the late nineteenth century; as Jenny Cook-Gumperz describes the general trajectory of literacy: "it can be argued that the shift from the eighteenth century onwards has not been from total illiteracy to literacy, but from a hard-to-estimate multiplicity of literacies, a *pluralistic* idea about literacy as a composite of different skills related to reading and writing for many different purposes and sections of a society's population, to a twentieth-century notion of a single, standardised *schooled literacy.*" (Jenny Cook-Gumperz, *The Social Construction of Literacy,* ([Cambridge: Cambridge University Press, 1986], 22).

7. See, for one of many examples of the literacy-as-signing method and its discontents, Lawrence Stone's classic "Literacy and Education in England, 1640–1900": "Throughout this chapter, the word 'literacy' should be understood to mean the capacity to sign one's name, which for periods before the nineteenth century is nearly all we now know or indeed are ever likely to know in the future. We do not know now, and may never know, the precise relationship between the capacity to sign one's name—alphabetism' might be a better word for it—and true literacy, that is the ability to use the written word as a means of communication." (*Past & Present,* 42, 1969), 98.

8. Dick Whittington comes into print as a ballad in 1605. James Raven, *Judging New Wealth: Popular Publishing and Responses to Commerce in England, 1750–1800.* (Oxford: Clarendon Press, 1992), 8; Cinderella comes into English in the 1729 translation of Perrault's *Histories, or Tales of Past Times.* For a discussion of the meeting between the traditional fairy tale and the print marketplace, of the appropriation of fairy-tale motifs by "didactic" writers of the eighteenth century, and the Romantic valorization–and misreading–of the fairy tale, see Alan Richardson, *Literature, Education, and Romanticism: Reading as Social Practice, 1780–1832* (Cambridge: Cambridge University Press, 1994), 112–127.

9. Robert Gordon, "Paradoxical Property," in John Brewer and Susan Staves, eds. *Early Modern Conceptions of Property* (New York: Routledge, 1996, 95–110), 99.

10. In addition to Oliver Goldsmith, who was a member of the Newbery stable, the printer Newbery is himself a likely candidate, as is Giles Jones, another Newbery regular. See Sylvia Patterson Iskander, "*Goody Two-Shoes* and *The Vicar of Wakefield,*" *Children's Literature Association Quarterly* (13:4 Winter 1988), 165–68; S. Roscoe, *John Newbery and His Successors 1740–1814* (Wormley, Hertfordshire: Five Owls P, 1973); John Rowe Townsend, ed., *John Newbery and His Books: Trade and Plumb-Cake for Ever, Huzza!* (Metuchen, NJ: Scarecrow, 1994); Wilbur Macey Stone, "The History of Little Goody Two-Shoes," *Proceedings of the American*

Antiquarian Society, [Oct. 1939] 333–370, and Charles Welsh, Introduction to *Goody Two-Shoes: A Facsimile Reprint of the Edition of 1766* (Detroit: Singing Tree Press, 1970) iii-xxiv.

11. In the rewrite by Mary Jane Godwin (William's second wife) in 1804 (*The history of Goody Two-Shoes and The adventures of Tommy Two-Shoes,*[London: Tabart, 1804]), for example, "everybody knows, that, in this happy country, the poor are to the full as much protected by our excellent laws, as are the highest and the richest nobles in the land; and the humblest cottager enjoys an equal share of the blessings of English liberty with the sons of kings themselves" (3) and Farmer Meanwell is "too noble-minded to retain a property which now could not justly be called his" (4). Some American editions of the 1790s add a patriotic motto: "*Such is the state of things in Britain.* AMERICANS, prize your liberty, guard over your rights, and be happy" (*The History of little Goody Two-Shoes,* [Philadelphia: W. Young, [1793]), 13; see also *The History of Little Goody Two-Shoes* (Wilmington, DE: Peter Brynberg, 1796).

12. Eighteenth-century Poor Laws allowed parishes to apprentice out their wards, and pre-industrial poor children were subject to the same kinds of miserable labor conditions as they were in later, more visible industrial scandals. See Ivy Pinchbeck and Margaret Hewitt, *Children in English Society, Volume I: From Tudor Times to the Eighteenth Century,* (London: Routledge; Toronto: University of Toronto Press, 1969), 308–312. Children on their own were easily exploited; their own crimes could subject them to capital punishment from the age of seven, and crimes against children were not normally punished severely in a culture that routinely employed children as chimneysweeps and prostitutes. Pinchbeck and Hewitt, *Children in English Society, Volume II: From the Eighteenth Century to the Children Act of 1948,* (London: Routledge; Toronto: University of Toronto Press, 1973), 251–252, 355–361.

13. Seniel Lucien reads this as the substitution for Goody's brother, as well as for her sexual lack in contrast to Tommy who, the narrative points out, had two shoes all along. Lucien sees this as part of the maturation process represented by the text. The incest that hovers around Goody and Tommy in this reading is emphasized in Victorian sentimentalized versions of the text. (And Goody becomes progressively more deprived, ending up barefoot in some re-tellings.)

14. Although she here acquires the name that makes her name, Goody is called by many variations on her name; Jan Fergus has noted a total of seventeen names that she goes by.

15. Peter Stallybrass and Ann Jones, *Renaissance Clothing and the Materials of Memory* (Cambridge: Cambridge University Press, 2000), 2, 3.

16. *The New Yorker,* February 17 and 24, 2003, 191. For the most thorough and shrewd reading of shoes as "powerful symbols of mobility and icons of and for desire," see Paula Rabinowitz's *Black & White & Noir: America's Pop Modernism* (New York: Columbia University Press, 2002), 172, 171–192.

17. Shari Benstock and Suzanne Ferriss, eds. *Footnotes: On Shoes,* (New Brunswick, NJ: Rutgers University Press, 2001), 1.

18. Lucy Pratt and Linda Woolley, *Shoes* (London: V&A Publications, 1999), 25.

19. A few of the Folk Motif Index "Shoe" entries are to horseshoes (Stith Thompson, *Motif-Index of folk literature: a classification of narrative elements in folk tales, ballads, myths, fables, mediaeval romances,* CD-ROM ed. [Bloomington, Ind.: Indiana University Press, 1993]). Film has inherited the focus on shoes as a marker, particularly for women. Rabinowitz identifies a closetful of examples in American noir films. In addition, in Agnes Varda's *Vagabond* (1986), the heroine's fatal downward skid seems inevitable once the zipper on her boot breaks; she's literally hobbled from there on, until her death. In "High Angles on Shoes," Maureen Turin notices the visual trope of women with one shoe on and one shoe off, in Fellini's *Nights of Cabiria* (1957) and Visconti's *Ossessione* (1942) (in Benstock and Ferriss, 58–90, 77).

20. Marina Warner, *From the Beast to the Blonde: On Fairy Tales and Their Tellers* (London: Chatto & Windus, 1994), 203.

21. John Campbell, "Occupation and Literacy in Bristol and Gloucestershire, 1755–1870," *Studies in the History of Literacy: England and North America,* ed. W. B. Stephens, Educational Administration and History Monograph, no. 13. (Leeds: Museum of the History of Education, University of Leeds, 1983, 20–36) 20, 27. Shoemakers, like the more radical weavers, as village or town rather than country folk, had more access to and uses for reading and writing than farmers and laborers. The shoemaker persistently figures in philosophy; in his introduction to Jacques Rancière's *The Philosopher and His Poor,* Andrew Parker notes the philosophical position of the shoemaker, both in his own right and as a ubiquitous exemplum. For Rancière, workers' archives revealed that "the most militant trades were those, like the shoemakers, … whose work allowed them to imagine doing something else than that to which they seemingly were fated, while for philosophers from Plato on, the shoemaker is a figure against whom philosophy constitutes itself. Andrew Parker, "Editor's Introduction: Mimesis and the Division of Labor" in Jacques Rancière, *The Philosopher and His Poor* (Durham, NC: Duke University Press, 2003), xi.

22. Although children were not technically property, the "right to" them belongs to the father and before 1814 "child-stealing" was treated like a crime against property, and was usually punishable only if the perpetrator was stealing the child's clothes (Pinchbeck, *Children,* 2: 360, 362). See also Mary Ann Mason, *From Father's Property to Children's Rights: A History of Child Custody in the United States* (New York: Columbia University Press, 1994), 6–10, for the comparable situation in the American colonies.

23. Roman Jakobson, "Two Aspects of Language and Two Types of Aphasic Disturbance," in Jakobson and Morris Halle, *Fundamentals of Language,* ('S-Gravenhage: Mouton, 1956, 55–82), 76–82. The exception to the shift from the allegorical is Mr. Lovewell, the hero of the novel-within-the-novel that Goody tells (82–94). Other Newbery books' heroic names are metonyms with metaphoric tendencies: Giles Gingerbread (who "lives on learning"), Tommy Telescope, Tommy Thumb.

24. Aside from the classic work of Marcel Mauss on the gift (*The Gift: The Form and Reason for Exchange in Archaic Societies*, tr. W. D. Halls [New York: Norton, 1990]), I am relying on the following for thinking about the economic, social, and affective lives of things: James Carrier, *Gifts and Commodities: Exchange and Western Capitalism since 1700* (New York: Routledge, 1995); John Frow, "Gift and Commodity," in *Time and Commodity Culture: Essays in Cultural Theory and Postmodernity* (Oxford: Clarendon Press, 1997), 102–217; Annette Weiner, *Inalienable Possessions: The Paradox of Keeping-While-Giving* (Berkeley: University of California Press, 1992).

25. Arjun Appadurai offers a biographical definition of the commodity: "the commodity situation in the social life of any 'thing' [is] defined as the situation in which its exchangeability (past, present, or future) for some other thing is its socially relevant feature" ("Introduction: commodities and the politics of value," *The Social Life of Things: Commodities in Cultural Perspective*. Ed. Arjun Appadurai [Cambridge: Cambridge University Press, 1986, 3–63]), 17. See also Igor Kopytoff, "The Cultural Biography of Things: Commodization as Process," in The Social Life of Things, 64–94. It's also worth contrasting Goody's shoes with later literary children's shoes. The shoes in Edgeworth's much-reprinted "The Purple Jar," for example, which Rosamond rejects in favor of what turns out to be a perfect image of the enchanting commodity: a jar whose pretty color turns out to be only the water it contains (in *The Parent's Assistant* [Dublin: Chalmers, 1798]). And of course Dorothy's shoes, the spoils of her violent descent into Oz, currency-silver in Baum's original, they become glittering technicolor red for the film and are finally auctioned in 1970 for $15,000 (Salman Rushdie, *The Wizard of Oz* [London: British Film Institute, 1992] 46); see also Turin. In Rushdie's fantasy of the auction "Orphans arrive, hoping that the ruby slippers might transport them back through time as well as space, and reunite them with their deceased parents" (60).

26. See Stephen Nissenbaum on the tradition of giving books as presents (*The Battle for Christmas*, [New York: Knopf, 1996], 140–150). My impression from looking at archives of children's books is that a high percentage of them are inscribed as gifts by relatives and teachers, the sentimental value added perhaps making them most likely to survive. In the advertisements at the back of *Goody* Newbery lists gift books specially titled for Christmas, New Year's, Easter, Whitsuntide, Twelfth-Day, Valentine's Day, and one all-purpose Fairing. Jan Fergus has discovered that Goody was a best-seller to the boys at Rugby, some of whose purchases may have been as gifts as well, (see chapter 11 in this volume).

27. See Carrier on "Changing Circulation Relations" in the eighteenth century, 61–83.

28. "The plan which I adopted, and the one by which I was most successful, was that of making friends of all the little white boys whom I met in the street. As many of these as I could, I converted into teachers. With their kindly aid, obtained at different times and in different places, I finally succeeded in learning to read." Douglass similarly purloins his writing skills at the shipyard where he works by noting that timber is marked

with letters signifying what part of the ship each is meant for and making lessons for himself by reading the lettered city around him. *Narrative of the Life of Frederick Douglass, an American Slave* (New York: Penguin, 1986), 82, 86–7.

29. *Some Thoughts Concerning Education,* in *The Educational Writings of John Locke,* ed. James Axtell (Cambridge: Cambridge University Press, 1968, 110–325), 255–257.

30. The first citation in the OED is to *Goody,* and defines it as "Nick-nacks, trifles, odds and ends, curiosities, small or worthless articles." In the nineteenth century the word becomes slang for "mouth" (OED, *sv* "rattletrap").

31. In Ronald Paulson's reading, for example, "The order Two-Shoes gives to experience, alphabetizing it and using reading as a child's defense against hardship, is followed by ... the supernatural explanation and the prudential one, invoking, respectively, witchcraft and wisdom ... that ask for a sense of both/and instead of either/or, a kind of randomness that includes the irrational and is far outside the order of Two-Shoes's alphabet," 197.

32. By the beginning of the nineteenth century, Goody Two-Shoes circulates in the culture as precisely this kind of figure. In the 1809 *Alphabet of Goody Two Shoes* (Philadelphia: Johnson and Warner), a standard image-and-rhyme alphabet book, which uses Goody's brand prestige but little else from the novel, the figure of Goody is already melded with Mother Goose, Old Mother Jumper, and other stock "old wives," in an image of an old woman accompanied by this rhyme: "V was a Village,/ Where liv'd near the brook,/The renown'd Goody Two-Shoes/Who sends you this book." In this example, Goody embodies the now literate "old wife," but it would seem that she sometimes travels simply as a traditional story-teller. Matthew ("Monk") Lewis records in his Jamaican journal the "Nancy" stories of the local "Goody Two-Shoes" "called by the negroes, 'Goosee Shoo-shoo'": "A glass of rum, or a roll of *backy,* is sure to unpack Goosee Shoo-shoo's budget" (*Journal of a West India Proprietor, 1815–1817,* ed. Mona Wilson [London: Routledge, 1929]), 212. In this figure, Goody's alphabet basket loops back into an oral *copia.* See also Needham's interesting account of the story Lewis takes from Goosee, which shares some of the central concerns of the original *Goody* (though Needham treats the novel as a generic "nursery tale"), including the substitution for a lack (in Goosee's story, the hero wonderfully is missing his head) and proper rules for marriage. Lawrence Needham, "Goody Two-Shoes" / "Goosee Shoo-shoo": Translated Tales of Resistance in Matthew Lewis's *Journal of a West India Proprietor,* in *Between Languages and Cultures: Translation and Cross-Cultural Texts,* eds. Anuradha Dingwaney and Carol Maier (Pittsburgh: University of Pittsburgh Press, 1995), 103–118.

33. Samuel Johnson, *The Idler* and *The Adventurer,* ed. W. J. Bate, John M. Bullitt, L. F. Powell, *The Yale Edition of the Works of Samuel Johnson,* vol. 2 (New Haven, CT: Yale University Press, 1963), 60, 62, 60. According to Johnson's editors, Newbery may have been the publisher of the *Universal Chronicle* that ran the *Idler* essays and may have even suggested the idea of

the series to Johnson; Newbery published the first collected *Idler* in 1767, xv–xix.

34. Weiner, *Inalienable Possessions*, 44–65, 11.
35. "Booksellers had been associated with the sale of patent medicines since the mid-17th cent. [*sic*], as described in John Alden, 'Pills and Publishing: Some Notes on the English Book Trade, 1660–1715,' *Library*, 5th ser., 7/1 (Mar. 1952), 21–37," James Raven, 51n29.
36. Throughout, the narrative uses as a device this production-transparency of the kind we're now accustomed to on TV and in blogs. For example, the final text before the advertisements at the back of the book, "*A* Letter *from the* Printer, *which he desires may be inserted*," adds a few anecdotes about the "sagacity" of dogs and begins: "Sir, I Have done with your Copy, if you please; and pray tell Mr. Angelo to brush up the cuts, that, in the next Edition, they may give us a good Impression" (155). The "Mr. Angelo" reference completes the joke on the title page, probably by the same compositor-wit: "See the original Manuscript in the *Vatican* at *Rome*, and the cuts by Michael Angelo."
37. A pricey formula, equivalent to today's prescription drugs (about £10), costing a couple of days' wages for a laborer, while the book itself is only sixpence. Even this, according to S. Roscoe, was "a fairly stiff price in an age when the wages of a skilled workman were seldom more than 7s 6d a week and often as low as 5s," 13. According to James Raven, in "1760 two shillings could buy a stone of beef or a pair of shoes," 57. Newbery was at least as famous for his patent medicines as for his books. According to Townsend, Dr. James's Powder was a widely used (by, among others, King George III) if toxic remedy, which is thought to have been responsible for the death of Goldsmith; it seems to have consisted of "phosphate of lime and oxide of antimony," and continued to be produced by Newbery heirs until 1941, 21, 22, 159.
38. This event echoes the story that appears in Cicero's *De oratore* of the poet Simonides, who was called away from a banquet hall just before its roof fell in; his ability to clearly remember where everyone was sitting and hence identify the dead is said to be the foundation of the rhetorical memory art. See Frances Yates, *The Art of Memory* (Chicago: University of Chicago Press, 1966), 1–2. Is Goody's version renewing the story for alphabetic and vernacular pedagogy?
39. Thomas Laqueur suggests that eighteenth-century charity school teachers received in the range of £ 6 to £10 a year, although Goody for much of the narrative is freelance and so even poorer. "In Bilton, New Ainstey, a parish with 123 families and no endowed or charity school, we learn of 'two poor, honest, sober and well-meaning persons who teach children to read, and instruct them in ye Church catechism'; in Bainton, Harthill, there was no school but there were '[t]wo poor women [who] teach a few children to read.'" "The cultural origins of popular literacy in England, 1500–1800," *Oxford Review of Education*, 2:3 (1976), 257–258.
40. They are also prevented from becoming, themselves, intermediaries— pedlars, in effect—a suspicious class for a moral economist like Goody. See Carrier *Gifts and Commodities*, 66ff on the regulation of market

transactions to privilege the local, direct sale in the seventeenth and eighteenth century.

41. Tommy's adventures become a more visible feature of nineteenth-century redactions, whose illustrators especially take up the image of the Africans, as such images circulated as part of the colonial and racialized discourse of children's primers, geographies, and natural histories. Mary Belson Elliott publishes an entire book devoted to Tommy's adventures, sending him to Jamaica instead of Africa, and embroiling him in a slave uprising there; Tommy's skill, seemingly gender-appropriate, is writing rather than reading, though he has the same affinity with animals as Goody (London: Tabart, 1809). An 1837 Baltimore verse edition (Bayly & Burns) illustrates Tommy with American Indians.

42. According to an English translation of *The history of the birth, travels, strange adventures, and death of Fortunatus* (London 1682), although at least one children's redaction, in *The Child's New Play-Thing* (Boston, 1750), compresses the tale into one generation. David Blamires notes that Fortunatus appears in print in German in 1509 and remains a popular children's chapbook and tale into the nineteenth century. Newbery, as usual, is both plugging and cannibalizing one of his own products, the *Pretty Book for Children* (1761), which contained a version of the story. *Fortunatus in His Many English Guises,* (Lewiston: Mellen Press, 1996), 1–9.

43. Victorian editions, reluctant to imagine—or encourage—a contemporary, poor, female autodidact, gothicize the tale, situating it in a medieval or renaissance setting, and stage the witch trial à la Joan of Arc; Goody's witchery becomes a kind of monumental saintliness. See for example, *Story of Goody-Two Shoes* (New York: McLoughlin Bros, [1869?]). Similarly, in a verse rendition by Lydia Very from the 1860s, die-cut to Goody's outline, Goody is part Joan, part Minerva, part Virgin Mary (*Goody Two Shoes.* ([Boston]: L. Prang & Co. [between 1863 and 1868?]).

44. John Guillory, "Literary Capital. Gray's 'Elegy,' Anna Laetitia Barbauld, and the Vernacular Canon," in John Brewer and Susan Staves, eds., *Early Modern Conceptions of Property* (New York: Routledge, 1996., 389–410), 389, 402, 407.

45. Gordon, "Paradoxical Property", 99. See also Gregory S. Alexander's analysis of early American property debates: "So transformed [that is, into commodity], property might become a solvent that dissolves the political bonds of the community." (*Commodity and Propriety: Competing Visions of Property in American Legal Thought 1776–1970,* (Chicago: University of Chicago Press, 1997), 35. James Raven notes that during "the second half of the eighteenth century, new manufacturers guided industrial expansion, extending the depth and diversity of the domestic market. At the same time, short-term credit crises provoked urgent discussion both of the causes and results of economic instability and of the definition of legitimate risk-taking. ... In another commercial sector, the fundamental question posed by writers of didactic, imaginative literature was whether value in society was to be measured by wealth, station, or behaviour. In reality, late eighteenth-century society was dominated by monetary considerations." Raven, *Judging New Wealth,* 252.

46. J.G.A. Pocock, *The Machiavellian Moment: Florentine Political Thought and the Atlantic Republican Tradition* (Princeton, NJ: Princeton University Press, 1975), 463, 464.

47. Other forms of nonmaterial property in the eighteenth century with which this construction of literacy is affiliated are "skill" and "liberty." On the former, see John Rule, "The Property of Skill in the period of manufacture," in Patrick Joyce, ed. *The Historical Meanings of Work*, (Cambridge: Cambridge University Press 1987); on the latter, see John Phillip Reid, *Constitutional History of the American Revolution: The Authority of Rights* (Madison: University of Wisconsin Press, 1986), 31–33. Both skill and liberty began to have some protection under law; literacy too, under the general rubric of "education," emerged in the early American republic as an equivalent to property, and a potential substitute for it. See especially Robert Coram, *Political Inquiries: to Which Is Added a Plan for the Establishment of Schools Throughout the United States.* (Wilmington, DE: 1791).

48. Historians of literacy have attested to a disconnect between economic development and literacy acquisition in the seventeenth to nineteenth centuries. See, for example, Kenneth Lockridge, *Literacy in Colonial New England: An Enquiry into the Social Context of Literacy in the Early Modern West* (New York: Norton, 1974). "Literacy did not march forward with commercialization and social development," according to Harvey Graff, "Literacy and Social Development in North America: on Ideology and History," in Stephens, 82–97, 88. Indeed some historians of literacy chart a descent in literacy rates that accompanies increased population density and industrialization.

49. Bourdieu, "Forms of Captial," 245.

11

SOLACE IN BOOKS

Reading Trifling Adventures at Rugby School

JAN FERGUS

When Samuel Johnson criticized Hester Thrale for "putting Newbery's books into children's hands as too trifling to engage their attention," she urged in rebuttal "the numerous editions and quick sale of Tommy Prudent or Goody Two-Shoes: 'Remember always (said he) that the parents *buy* the books, and that the children never read them.'"[2] Johnson's reply voices a conviction about children's reading that has been current since the introduction of children's books, but that this study of eighteenth-century child readers at Rugby School challenges. The bookselling records of the Clays of Daventry, Rugby, Lutterworth, and Warwick, which extend from 1744–1784,[3] show that when Rugby schoolboys—generally from professional or gentry and occasionally plebeian backgrounds—were empowered to purchase books on their own, they frequently chose *Goody Two-Shoes* as well as other Newbery books that combined adventure with moral instruction.

I argue here first that the schoolboys' choices explode a number of tired but still received ideas about eighteenth-century reading: that the "new" children's books played an insidious and invidious role in the Enlightenment educational program; that we can easily distinguish between elite and plebeian audiences and tastes (or between readers of classics and chapbooks); as well as that (as Johnson assumes) children won't pick what adults think is good for them to read if given the opportunity to choose. Second, I attempt in this study to construct reader response through purchase patterns and other information present in the bookselling records even though interpretation of such necessarily limited data is problematic. Despite such problems, this essay tries to imagine why a text that children no longer read might have been vital to contemporary audiences. This exercise in historical imagination concludes—again contrary to Johnson—that a book like *Goody Two-Shoes* is far from "trifling." The adventures and lessons that Margery Two-Shoes and other Newbery as well as chapbook heroes and heroines undergo within their inimical fictional worlds perform some of the dilemmas and anxieties that boys faced in schools such as Rugby, where hundreds of children were left by a few adults to supervise themselves. In the state of licensed war that often ensued, I will argue that schoolboys could find solace and support in the safer spaces offered by reading stories of endurance and survival like *Goody Two-Shoes*.

This exercise in historical imagination is made possible because bookselling ledgers for Rugby School have fortunately survived almost in entirety for 1744–1784: they include accounts for 85 percent of the 670 boys admitted to the school between 1742 and 1784, and for another thirty-nine boys not listed in the extant school registers.[4] John Clay and later his sons Thomas and Samuel made obtaining books very convenient for Rugbeans. They offered credit to every schoolboy and took orders at least once a week from 1744 through July 1781, during weekly visits to their shop in Rugby; afterward, the shop was open every day. The ledgers are consequently full of very small transactions— a few pence here and there for paper, pens, ink, and over fourteen hundred children's books and chapbooks as well as for the Latin and Greek textbooks that they all bought. During this period, no other bookshop operated in Rugby; the only other local source for reading matter was a stall that sometimes sold used books in the market square. Because the boys were not allowed to leave the School without special permission, the Clays thus enjoyed a virtual monopoly as booksellers to these generally elite boys aged from about six or eight to eighteen, the sons of professional men, gentlemen, even the occasional aristocrat, although a few children of local residents also attended.

The Clays' ledger accounts were eventually sent to the boys' housemasters, to be settled by their parents perhaps twice a year. That is, these accounts had to stand official scrutiny. For the few years that records of daily transactions also exist, we can see that schoolboys sometimes paid in cash to borrow certain novels, evidently because they did not want their reading to be scrutinized in this way. But I have not encountered any such censorship for purchases of children's books; perhaps they were felt to be more approved reading matter. In general, the boys' choices emphasize points that some historians of children's books may overlook. Children make choices about what they read; we can agree with Samuel Johnson here. They have individual tastes as adults do, they don't always prefer what others may expect of them, and they sometimes read material that does not seem to suit their chronological age—that is, they may read what seems above or below their comprehension. In other words, they have agency.

The twenty most popular children's books and chapbooks bought by Rugby boys are listed below; Sydney Roscoe's dates for the Newbery books and his identification numbers are given in parenthesis.[4]

Copies   Titles

Copies	Titles
61	Newbery's *Robinson Crusoe* (1768?; J93; two may not be Newbery's) plus nine chapbook versions, 6*d* and 8*d*
50	Newbery's *Gil Blas*, 1*s* (1774?; J213)
49	Newbery's *Food for the Mind, Riddle Book*, 6*d* (1757; J190b).
48	Newbery's *Gulliver's Travels*, 6*d* (1773; J5)
42	Newbery's *History of the World in Miniature*, 2 vols., 1*s*6*d* (1763; J77)
38	Newbery's *Tommy Trip's History of Birds and Beasts*, 6*d* (1752; J308)
38	Newbery's *Tom Jones*, 1*s* (1768; J132)
35	Newbery's *Mother Goose's Tales*, 9*d* (1768?; J279)
35	*English Hermit*, 1*s* (abridgement of novel imitating *Crusoe*) plus ten versions at 6*d*
34	Newbery's *Museum*, 1*s* (1753; J253)
34	Newbery's *Fairing, or Golden Toy*, 6*d* (1764; J110)
31	Newbery's *Lilliputian Magazine*, 1*s* (1751; J219)
30	*Unfortunate Englishman*, 1*s*
30	*History Book*, 8*d* (chapbook)
27	Newbery's *Joseph Andrews*, 1*s* (1769; J131)
26	Newbery's *Goody Two-Shoes*, 6*d* (1765; J167)[5]
25	*History of Guy, Earl of Warwick*, 8*d* (chapbook)
24	Newbery's *Be Merry and Wise*, 6*d* (riddles and jests) (1753; J358)
22	Newbery's *Tom Thumb's Exhibition*, 2*d* (1774; J355)
20	Newbery's *Pilgrim's Progress*, vol. 1, 9*d* (1787?; J47)

These titles may at first seem unsurprising: abridged classic novels and other adventure stories and miscellanies predominate. But in contradiction to Samuel Johnson's dictum, *Goody Two-Shoes*, even if not the most popular book among the boys, was a solid seller, in seventeenth place (among 193 titles of children's books and chapbooks—thus over 170 sold less well) thanks to twenty-six purchases between 1766 and 1784.

These results would astonish not just Johnson but modern scholars like Geoffrey Summerfield who have labeled this work didactic, thinking it likely to be bought only by parents and imposed on reluctant children.[6] Those familiar with the story may also be surprised at its appeal to Rugby boys: after all, it has no hero but, rather, a heroine. *Goody Two-Shoes* charts the struggles of a very young girl to survive after evil landlords have twice left her destitute, first by dispossessing her parents (who shortly die) and then by threatening the adults who shelter her. Despite such powerful adult enemies, Margery Meanwell triumphs. Boy readers of *Goody Two-Shoes*, then, must to some extent identify themselves with this girl's subject position.

To consider what might make this indentification possible among privileged boys, we must look at how their lives were scripted in public schools like Rugby in the eighteenth and (since these were very conservative institutions) through the early twentieth century as well in some respects. Essentially, boys ruled themselves, which meant that the older and stronger boys were in charge; masters imposed discipline only in classes and enforced a few rules about not leaving the grounds. Although at Rugby in the eighteenth century, prefects or "praeposters" did not have flogging powers as they later did, they had special privileges and, like all older boys, they ruled over fags who acted as their servants. As Edward C. Mack concludes,

> The eighteenth-century prefect-fagging system was the political manifestation of control of the schools by the student bodies: it was a government of boys functioning in almost complete independence of supervision by the masters. The older and stronger boys, supported by the sanction of custom, ruled the schools like feudal oligarchs under the titles, at different institutions, of prefect, monitor, or praepostor.[7]

The notion that English manliness and independence could best develop under this sort of oligarchic tyranny was angrily rejected by Sidney Smith in an 1810 review. Asserting that "every boy is alternately a tyrant or slave," Smith concluded, "Boys, therefore, are left to their own crude conceptions, and ill-formed propensities; and this neglect is called a spirited and manly education."[8] But his attack was unusual. The system was upheld even by those like Edward Gibbon who escaped it and "secretly rejoiced in those infirmities, which delivered me from the exercises of the school [Westminster], and the society of my equals."[9]

Obviously, to enjoy this "society of equals," boys had to be wrenched from families and virtually isolated at school. Evidences of the harshness of this exile at Rugby are offered by some surviving letters of a mother to her sons who entered at midsummer 1788, unfortunately too late to be included as customers in the Clays' bookselling records, which extend for Rugby through 1784. These were John Plomer Clarke (nearly twelve) and his brother Richard (ten). Mary Clarke writes to hope that her sons are "reconciled" to Rugby (17 Oct. 1788)[10] and to refuse to let them come home or even to receive a visit from their father, himself a former Rugbean:

> we *must not* break our resolution of considering ourselves *fifty* or a *hundred* miles apart, only with this pleasing reflection (which I have mentioned in a former letter) that we can frequently hear of each other; & in case of illness, be with you, in little more than an hour. (Aug. 5, 1788).[11]

Mary Clarke is pleased that her son John has "got so good a Master to Fag for, as the Eldest Spooner, as we have heard him very highly spoken of indeed." Abraham Spooner was one of five brothers who so despised the "wickedness" at Rugby (probably drinking) that they later would not send any of their own sons to the school.[12] Spooner himself, aged seventeen or eighteen, evidently advised John to fight back. Mary Clarke admonishes John,

> We could wish to hear of your going out a little more among the Boys, & that you would associate with those of your own age, & *fight* your way through the little world you are in, as Dick *does* we don't mean or wish

you to be quarrelsome (which we know is not *your* disposition, any more than Richards) but be advised by Spooner, & dont *take* a blow. (Aug. 5, 1788).

A few months later, his mother congratulates John on having *"fought a battle"* (Oct. 25, 1788).

The school was, then, as Mary Clarke put it, a "little world," a microcosm of society in which a boy tested and discovered himself by, as John Chandos puts it, "making his way, unaided by privilege, in a society of his equals and superiors."[13] Character was supposed to be formed by boys struggling, even fighting, among themselves, not by emulation of or exhortation by masters—the model usually associated with Thomas Arnold at Rugby a century later. Crossover between elite and popular culture is evident in these customs too: Jürgen Schlumbohm's article in this volume cites the importance for boys of "fighting between more or less tightly knit groups" within German village life.

The system of education amounted to a kind of licensed war, then, but a war in which victory was assured to any boy who could endure and survive. Simply by getting older, a boy triumphed. As Chandos argues, boys would "go home as fags and return as masters," and as a result, "the quality of their lives was changed beyond imagination" (Chandos 99). In his view, having experienced "honourable trial by ordeal, creditably endured," they became the "giants" in George Lyttleton's 1832 description of how older boys seemed to younger ones:

> to a little boy, the whole world of school seems large; there are giants of 5ft 9ins and super men of 6ft; his feeling of awe and admiration is increased by receiving an occasional blow from these huge animals, as he creeps about among the few of his own diminutiveness, mightily impressed with the words and mightiness of the race of giants towering above him (Quoted by Chandos, 99–100).

Lyttleton's description is decidedly Gulliverian, and I imagine that, like the adult Lyttleton, Rugby boys too interpreted their school experience in terms of their favorite children's books and chapbooks, Newbery's abridgment of *Gulliver's Travels* being one, and, I will argue, *Goody Two-Shoes* being another.

Who were the boy readers of *Two-Shoes?* Its sales history, like that of most of the Newbery books, peaked in 1781 when Samuel Clay inherited the Rugby business. He or his assistant took almost daily orders at the school, and he seems to have obtained some books in quantity to offer to the boys. For example, it is likely that the six copies of Francis Newbery's edition of a one-shilling *Gil Blas* sold on September 1, 1781, were impulse buys prompted by Clay's or his assistant's having brought copies to the school with him. Samuel Clay possibly did the same with *Goody Two-Shoes* on October 20, 1781, when he sold the book to three boys one after another—a sizable proportion of the eleven copies he sold between 1781 and 1784. Yet it had appealed to Rugby students before his possibly more vigorous marketing: between 1766 and July 1781, fourteen copies of *Goody Two-Shoes* were taken by boys whose ages ranged from at least eight to fourteen or fifteen.[14] Overall, the average age of buyers was a bit more than nine, based on the thirteen whose birth years I have found. Although it is possible that some bought the work for their sisters or brothers at home, the dates of purchase occurred after holidays at midsummer and Christmas rather than before them, when obtaining presents would be likeliest. The youngest purchaser, Charles Stuart-Menteth, was the son of a clergyman in Lincolnshire and had entered Rugby at seven in 1776, about a year before he bought *Goody Two-Shoes;* he was created a baronet in 1838. The oldest, William Bird, had lost his father three years before he entered Rugby in 1761, at about ten, so he was fourteen or fifteen when he acquired *Goody Two-Shoes* on February 15, 1766, not long after it was first issued in 1765; Bird became a lieutenant-colonel of the Middlesex Militia and a justice of the peace for Middlesex. Many of the boys, like these two, were born or rose to the privileged status enjoyed by little Margery, the heroine, when at the end of her tale she becomes Lady Jones. What then appealed to these boys in this tale? That is, how did elite boys at Rugby from eight to fourteen read *Goody Two-Shoes,* and why did they?

These questions would be difficult enough to answer if we were investigating contemporary children's reading, for how we read within culture is a vexed question now. The questions are incomparably more vexed if we wish to examine historical reading. Although some Marxist and postmodern explorations of ideology imply that readers are helplessly indoctrinated by cultural texts, many theorists of reading practices suggest possibilities of resistance and of active dialogue.[15] Prominent among them is Michel de Certeau, who sees the reader as "poaching" actively from texts, not as passively manipulated or controlled by them.[16] Roger Chartier, following de Certeau, speaks of readerly "appropriation" of texts, an activity through which readers construct a text's meaning for themselves, refashioning what they consume.[17] Reading practices characterized by appropriation are skeptical and can be subversive, can even give rise to cultural practices that Dick Hebdige, borrowing Umberto Eco's phrase to analyze punk style, calls "semiotic guerilla warfare."[18] Possibilities for resistance exist, too, in the pluralities of texts themselves. Looking at how French philosophic texts or *libelles* were put together before the revolution, Chartier notes their

> overlapping genres, criss-crossing motifs, and ... blending of levels of discourse such as political denunciation, pornographic description, and philosophical reflection. This very plurality, inscribed in the texts themselves, makes it impossible to conclude that they were read in an identical manner by all their readers or that their interpretation could be reduced to any one simple ideological statement.[19]

Many eighteenth-century fictional texts, not just *Goody Two-Shoes*, are plural in this way, and readers can adopt different subject positions as they read them, crossing generational and gender lines, for instance. In discussing literature for children, Mitzi Myers proposed that "cross-writing"—or the "dialogic mix of older and younger voices ... in texts too often read as univocal"—produces texts that invite such readings.[20] These include adult fictions abridged for children, romance tales abridged for adults (usually in chapbooks) and appropriated by children, fictions written for children with an eye to adult readers. All were bought by Rugby boys. John Newbery's children's books in particular proclaim cross-writing even in titles such as *A Collection of Pretty Poems for the Amusement of Children Six Foot High* (1757; J74). Such texts allowed boys to create an alternate home, a child's space, where they could be children in a different way than a hostile, exacting school culture permitted. They could imagine a more attractive community,

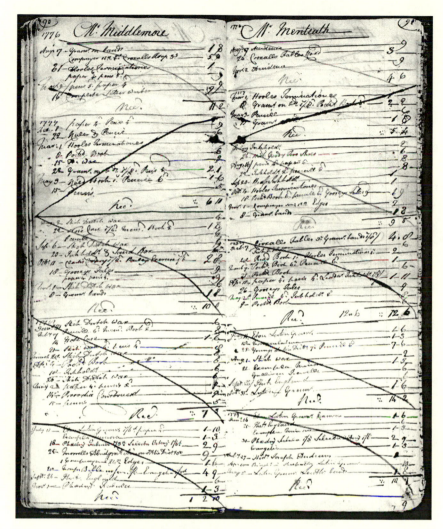

Fig. 11.1 Detail from the ledger showing the book purchases of the Rugby School pupil Charles Stuart-Menteth for 1777, which included a copy of *Goody Two-Shoes*. From John Clay ledgers, Daventry D2932 p. 91. Reproduced by permission of the Northamptonshire Record Office.

peopled by empowered children and adults perhaps more benevolent than those at school.

I will argue for at least two ways for Rugby boys in their world of licensed war to read their cross-written, cross-genre, plural texts, using *Goody Two-Shoes* as my case study. First, stories of survival and endurance can console, inspire, beguile. Second, the mixtures of elements in riddle books, fairy tales, and other fictions can be appropriated by children in various ways, as they construct how different parts work against each other and as they adopt multiple subject positions. Although the texts may provide conventional maxims and moral saws at the surface, children can easily read them against the grain. My approach in offering some suggestions on how boys may have read these texts is to ask what subject positions, what scripts, and what narrative pleasures they offer, or what coping mechanisms and strategies for survival, rather than to look solely at their overt moralizing, their ideological content.

Perhaps the best strategy, then, for approaching Rugby boys' reading of *Goody Two-Shoes* is to look first at two opposed modern readings of the work. Isaac Kramnick has read it as "designed to serve ideological objectives," like other eighteenth-century children's books; "this literature self-consciously expressed the values of [the] middle class and served as an important vehicle for the socialization of children to these values."[21] *Goody Two-Shoes,* according to Kramnick, indoctrinates children with bourgeois ideology: "success comes to the self-reliant, hardworking, independent individual" (Kramnick 217). In response, Ronald Paulson has argued that the work operates in a far more complex way, like Oliver Goldsmith's *The Vicar of Wakefield* and other literary and satirical texts of the 1740s through 1760s.[22] It "blurs the lines between the worlds of adult and child" (1078), as *The Vicar* does, and it thus offers child readers multiple subject positions:

> The structure of the book *Goody Two-Shoes* is itself jumbled, additive, and reassembled like the alphabet games. … The parts are collected randomly (including inserted epistles and verses) and an "adult" part is added (at the beginning and end) to the children's; the book fragments into exemplary episodes, songs, and stories which have to be reassembled by the reader after the model of Two-Shoes' teaching method and to serve roughly the same purpose for the child with his "wandering" mind (1084).

Accepting part of Paulson's reading, Patricia Crain's essay in this volume argues compellingly that *Goody Two-Shoes* elaborates the connection between literary acquisition and property that will by the end of the nineteenth century permit literacy to supplant property as a source of not only virtue but subjectivity. Crain offers as well a summary of the important incidents in this fragmented, multifarious text, whose readers can adopt multiple subject positions not merely within this text, but in many other eighteenth-century children's books as well as novels. Constructing the text as simply didactic and bourgeois, as Kramnick does, ignores its discontinuities and complexities, best thought of as bricolage. The child heroine is permitted to grow up and die (as seldom happens in modern children's literature), and the tale is full of general satire on human behavior as well as specific satire against legal chicanery and land enclosure, ironic references to other texts (the final offer to publish Margery's will surely glances at Richardson's *Clarissa*), and religious and prudential teaching, not to mention fables and vignettes that underscore human perversity, recommendations to improve parish government, animal rights arguments, precepts and examples on how to be charitable to the poor. Paulson is certainly right to speak of an "additive" structure (1084), a connection with "the tradition of satiric fiction for adults" (1080), and "a genuine fairy tale quality" (1086). He is also right in emphasizing the way that linguistic structures compensate for "affliction in adversity" (1083) and in seeing Margery Two-Shoes as a heroine of subversion, a "prophet of how to overcome or order a hard life" (1088). For him, her story "recapitulates the *Robinson Crusoe* plot of a man isolated in a precarious situation who builds up a world of his own as a substitute for the world he has lost" (1082).

The comparison to Crusoe is apt. Margery's story is one of endurance and survival, ingenuity and adaptability, like his. Paulson points out that her nature is as multiple as her name, though he gives just three versions of it (Paulson 1088). In fact, she has at least seventeen names, from the Little Goody Two-Shoes of the title and Old Goody Two-Shoes of the half title[23] to Margery Meanwell, Little Margery (or Margery), Goody Two Shoes, Little Two Shoes, Little Goody, Two Shoes, Madge, Mrs. Goody Two Shoes, and Little Madge; once she is given charge of the A. B. C. College, Mrs. Margery, Mrs. Margery Two Shoes, and Mrs. Two Shoes; and after she marries, Lady Jones or Lady Margery. The play here with "identity" seems outrageous and points not just to the protean nature of status and identity (and of the narrative) in this work but to the various strategies that Margery employs to survive and then flourish—among them, student, teacher, advisor, ghostbuster, informer, storyteller, talker to animals, scientist, nurse, parish patroness. Like her alter ego the suspected witch Goody Giles (or Jane or Joan or Madam Giles), she is a witch turned bene- factor. She is almost an icon of female power and possibility.

How would eminently literate boys from eight to fourteen at Rugby School construe this multifarious story? Again, we cannot know. But as a Crusoe-like or Job-like tale of adversity, in which surviving until you grow older results in triumph, it reflected the schoolboys' own condition: dispossessed of their homes, orphaned in effect, exiled to a harsh world with incomprehensible and arbitrary laws that afforded no protection to the weak, and subject to the tyranny of the strong and powerful. As Chandos argues, however, in public schools endur- ance eventually leads to power. The subservient inspiringly become the privileged, as Goody Two-Shoes herself does. For John Chandos, boys who endure at Rugby and other institutions become "aware of having entered into possession of the School. The very air they breathed was charged with the scent of inheritance" (Chandos 99). But while first disinherited, such boys might, as Patricia Crain argues in this volume, take the literacy that Goody offers as a kind of therapy for propertylessness as well as powerlessness.

But I would make one other argument. I suggest that the boys enjoyed in *Two Shoes* and in other children's books the pleasures of adopting fluid identities. At a liminal period of their own lives, before taking on the "mastery" that their class and educational privileges afford them, they might especially enjoy the fluidity of Margery's names and subject positions. And this fluidity might assist them to adopting more resistant readings not simply of texts but of their lives as well. Here I would suggest that the *female* heroine of *Goody Two-Shoes* may have made the story all the more compelling to some boys. She was of course a good teacher—better than the ones they had—and they may have wished to have one like her. In fact, she may well have reminded boys of their mothers' teaching; Mary Clarke of Welton had taught her sons Latin before they entered Rugby (C [W] X5347 Aug. 27, 1788). But, more important, and more surprising, gender lines do not seem as policed among boys in the eighteenth century as they are now. And possibly boys at school saw themselves as disempowered and thus to some extent feminized. Evidence for this implication is present in a short-lived periodical published in 1792 at Westminster School, titled *The Flagellant,* and conducted by Robert Southey and three friends.[24] The nine numbers contain—apart from some very conventional material (as in the *Spectator* or *Rambler*) that explains the title, invites correspondents, and satirizes fashionable male and female follies—Southey's vigorous denunciation of flogging in the fifth number (for which he was finally expelled) and a surprising vignette that focuses on disempowered women. The fourth number reflects, "It has often given me pain to see an advertisement from an elderly lady for some young woman of genteel appearance and good connections ... fair victim to ill-humour," who will "undergo—a lower place at the table, a silent voice in conversations, and an unconsulted inclination" (*Flagellant* 56). The writer continues, "how very irksome to the meanest, most insensible, and most indolent mind, dependence is" (*Flagellant* 57), as if he is reading his own disempowered situation into the advertisement.

In any case, boys' willingness to cross gender lines at Rugby, at least, is suggested by purchases of *Ladies Pocket Books* (17 copies) or *Ladies Memorandum Books* (6 copies) at a shilling, even a *Ladies Diary* (one at 6*d,* another at 9*d*); such works might contain recipes and addresses to ladies as well as less gendered contents.[25] The Newbery version of Mother Goose tales—often associated with girls—was one of the ten most popular children's books at the school. Four Rugby boys bought Newbery's *The Little Female Orators* (J222) and at least two tutors at the Daventry Dissenting Academy bought Sarah Fielding's *The Governess, or the Little Female Academy* (Noel Hill and Thomas Belsham, ML 692, p. Jan. 18, 1765; D2930, Jan. 7, 1771). Thomas Gibbs of Barbadoes, who entered Rugby in 1742, subscribed to Eliza Haywood's serialized *Female Spectator,* and much later, at least three boys purchased copies of the *Lady's Magazine* (one of them the same Abraham Spooner who advised young John Plomer Clarke to fight). Thomas and Samuel Hunt, who entered in 1778, bought the first two issues of the *Ladies Poetical Magazine* on February 10, 1781 (D3400). Finally, women wrote at least twenty-one of the seventy novels that Rugby boys bought and borrowed overall, and in fact the novel that was *borrowed* by the most boys in the shortest time was Frances Burney's five-volume *Cecilia.*

Overall, the boys' eagerness to import the female perspectives and experiences afforded by such works as *Goody Two-Shoes* and *Cecilia* into their all-male enclave is remarkable, though (as the list of the most popular children's books at Rugby also suggests) they certainly enjoyed male adventures also. *Goody Two-Shoes* values cooperation, mutual help, and community in an inimical world—values promoted by literacy, by reading. In this volume, Patricia Crain reads Goody's story as promulgating "faith in an association between literacy and respectability, virtue, wealth, safety," and Jürgen Schlumbohm cites Friedrich Paulsen, born a peasant's son, who evoked "a hidden place, inside or outside of the house" where he went "with a book in my hand," trying to read, also safe from interruption. Like Paulsen, Margery creates her own safe space in the parish, but unlike him as a worker, a teacher. And just as she extends that safe space to her community, so child readers might, despite oppression, create safe spaces, individually or communally, turn some tasks into play, and take various pleasures in the multiple offerings of this complex text. I would argue, then, that the power and long-term promise of endurance and survival as well as community, along with the temporary pleasures of fluid identity within miscellaneous plots that the boys could enjoy in *Goody-Two Shoes*, made reading it (and works like it) an alternative safe space within their inimical world that may have been more consoling to children than was anything else in their schools.

Notes

1. Hester Lynch Piozzi, *Anecdotes of the late Samuel Johnson, LL.D., during the last twenty years of his Life*, ed. S. C. Roberts (Cambridge: Cambridge University Press, 1925), p. 14.
2. Ruth Portner and I have described the Clays's shops and their business records in detail in our essay, "Provincial bookselling in eighteenth-century England: the case of John Clay reconsidered," *Studies in Bibliography* 40 (1987): 147–63. These records are on deposit in the Northamptonshire Record Office, hereafter NRO. I am grateful to her for the invaluable help given me in researching and thinking about this essay and also to two brilliant eighteenth-century scholars who are no longer with us: Janice Farrar Thaddeus and Mitzi Myers. I also am extremely grateful to Andrea Immel for indispensable advice, expertise, and encouragement. This essay forms part of a larger work, *Provincial Readers in Eighteenth-Century England*, to be published by Oxford University Press, two chapters of which will be devoted to schoolboy reading.

3. The 1933 edition of the Rugby School Register lists 421 boys' entrances to Rugby School from 1744 through 1780, not including re-entrances; see *Rugby School Register, Volume 1, From April 1765 to October 1857,* rev. and annot. Godfrey A. Solly (Rugby: George Over, 1933), hereafter cited as Register 1933. The 461 Clay ledger accounts must be reduced by 39 (because 39 boys' accounts do not appear in Register 1933) and increased by 150 (because the Clays lumped brothers' accounts together; 150 younger brothers' purchases are thus represented), yielding 572 boys of the total 670, or 85 percent.

4. Sydney Roscoe, *John Newbery and His Successors 1740–1814, a Bibliography* (Wormley: Hertfordshire: Five Owls Press Ltd, 1973). For the Newbery books, dates of publications and item numbers have been supplied from Roscoe. The Clays also sold 106 copies of Newbery's *History of England* (J258) at sixpence, but 87 of these copies were purchased in the first 18 months of Thomas James's headmastership, July 1778 through December 1779—far more than any other non-schoolbook in the 41 years that the records cover. No other little book shows a similar pattern of extremely concentrated and widespread sale. The advent in 1778 of Dr. James as headmaster is almost certainly responsible for what appears to be the use of this children's book in the school, perhaps for translation into Latin.

5. *Goody Two-Shoes* is seventeenth in popularity among Rugby boys if Newbery's *History of England* is included, sixteenth if not.

6. Geoffrey Summerfield, *Fantasy and Reason: Children's Literature in the Eighteenth Century* (Athens, GA: University of Georgia Press, 1984), p. 248. Summerfield is one of the more insistent among scholars who criticize didacticism in the Newbery tales.

7. Edward C. Mack, *Public Schools and British Opinion 1780 to 1860: An Examination of the Relationship between Contemporary Ideas and the Evolution of an English Institution* (London: Methuen and Co., 1936), p. xiii.

8. [Sidney Smith], rev. of *Remarks on the System of Education in Public Schools, Edinburgh Review* 16 (1810), pp. 327, 322. Another well-known attack on public school education was made by William Cowper in his poem *Tirocinium* (1784); less well known is Henry Layng's earlier poetic satire on flogging, *The Rod* (Oxford: Jackson, 1754).

9. Edward Gibbon, *Memoirs of My Life and Writings … illustrated from his letters, with occasional notes and narrative, by the Right Honourable John, Lord Sheffield,* Bicentenary Edition, ed. A.O.J. Cockshut and Stephen Constantine (Hartnolls, Bodmin, England: Ryburn Publishing, Keele University Press, 1994), p. 71.

10. These letters are loosely packed in a box, NRO C(W) X5437. All further references in the text to Clarke of Welton letters will be to this source and will cite only dates. Cited by permission of the Northamptonshire Record Office.

11. The boys evidently did not return home till November, though they lived just 8 or 10 miles from Rugby. Richard had behaved so ill that only Mary's pleading with their father allowed him to come home: "In consequence of Rich:^ds gaining *Merit Money,* & your promising that *he,* as well

as *yourself*, will observe our orders, in keeping yourselves, *clean*, and *decent* in your *persons*, & *apparel* [Richard's clothing had been shabby and torn earlier], I have at *last* gained permission for him to come home with you" (Nov. 11, 1788). Evidently Mary was not entirely in accord with her husband's desire to isolate their sons at Rugby: in the same letter of August 5 reinscribing the notion that Rugby is to be thought of as fifty or a hundred miles away, she writes, "I shall just mention (entre nous) your father *chid me* the other day for proposing to him, to take a ride to *Rugby:* he said he knew *that* would soon be the case, & with *all Mothers* whose Boys were within eight, or ten miles of them so I promis'd to behave better in future, & not disgrace myself, by such proposals." She goes on to defend her writing so often to her sons: "it is not necessary to treat *you* as *children*, who (in *your situation*) shou'd rather be taught to forget home than have their feelings too frequently awaken'd by often writing, but as I think the case is *very different* with you, & y^r. Brother, I shal be an advocate for, our correspondence by [Samuel] Clay continueing every week, regularly." Clearly, the threat that hangs over her is having her sons sent farther off; she goes on, "One more remark I must add, that as long as you can be happy at *Rugby*, we shall not think of, either *Uppingham* or Winchester the tho^t. of either would *almost destroy* me. to have my Boys so far off that I could only hear of them by letter, & *that* very seldom, would imbitter all my moments of absence from you, & I am inclin'd to believe, would render yours, no less unhappy." Clay's neighborly carrying of letters back and forth between Mary Clarke and her sons was a common enough practice.

12. Sidney Selfe, *Chapters from the History of Rugby School* (Rugby: A. J. Lawrence, 1910), p. 17.

13. John Chandos, *Boys Together: English Public Schools 1800–1864* (New Haven, CT: Yale University Press, 1984), p. 74. Subsequent references will appear in the text.

14. See Register 1933 for birth dates and other information about entrants. Whenever possible, I calculate a boy's age based upon this source. Again, unless otherwise indicated, all boys whose age and purchasing I specify attended school alone; no older or younger brother's acquisitions complicate the account.

15. Henry Jenkins's *Textual Poachers: Television Fans and Participatory Culture* (New York: Routledge, 1992) explores fans' resistant responses to rewritings of series such as *Star Trek*.

16. Michel de Certeau, *The Practice of Everyday Life*, tr. Steven F. Rendall (Berkeley, CA: University of California Press, 1984), p. 174.

17. This concept appears through most of Chartier's work; see the "Introduction" to *The Cultural Uses of Print in Early Modern France*, transl. Lydia G. Cochrane (Princeton, NJ: Princeton University Press, 1987), pp. 6–7 for a concise discussion.

18. Dick Hebdige, *Subculture: The Meaning of Style* (London: Methuen, 1979), p. 105.

19. Roger Chartier, The *Cultural Origins of the French Revolution*, transl. Lydia G. Cochrane (Durham, NC, and London: Duke University Press, 1991), p. 87.

20. Myers's first use of the valuable term "cross-writing" occurred in a paper delivered at the Modern Language Association Convention, 1993, "Canonical 'Orphans' and Critical *Ennui:* Rereading Edgeworth's Cross-Writing," published under the same title in U. C. Knoepflmacher and Mitzi Myers, eds., *Children's Literature* (1997), 25:116–36. The quotation is taken from the editors' introduction, "'Cross-Writing' and the Reconceptualizing of Children's Literary Studies" (25:vii).

21. Isaac Kramnick, "Children's Literature and Bourgeois Ideology: Observations on Culture and Industrial Capitalism in the Later Eighteenth Century," ed. Perez Zagorin, *Culture and Politics From Puritanism to the Enlightenment* (Berkeley, CA: University of California Press, 1980), 213–40; pp. 204, 211. Kramnick is at a great disadvantage interpreting *Goody Two-Shoes,* however, because he does not consult the original edition. He cites a London, 1965, edition in his notes; I have not been able to find any such edition in the British Library, in the New York Public Library, or in any electronic list. The edition Kramnick used could not have been a facsimile or reprint of the original, for he refers to "John Newberry" (p. 216). Too, in his plot summary, Margery marries not Sir Charles Jones but "Mr. Jones," and she confesses "to her young readers that after she had married she had in fact been tempted to live a life of idle luxury with all her riches" (p. 219)—not in the original.

22. Ronald Paulson, *The History of Little Goody Two-Shoes* as a Children's Book, *Literary Theory and Criticism: Festschrift Presented to René Wellek in Honor of his Eightieth Birthday. Part II: Criticism,* ed. Joseph P. Strelka (Bern: Peter Lang, 1985), pp. 1075–1092; 1075. Subsequent references will appear in the text. See also Paulson's later version of this essay, "The Strange, Trivial, and Infantile: Books for Children," *The Beautiful, Novel, and Strange: Aesthetics and Heterdoxy* (Baltimore and London: Johns Hopkins University Press, 1996), pp. 176–197.

23. I am grateful to Patricia Crain for this information about the half-title.

24. *The Flagellant* (London: Printed for the Author and Sold by T. & J. Egerton, near Whitehall, 1792). I consulted the copy at the Houghton Library, *46–2066. Subsequent references will appear in the text.

25. Before his death in 1767, John Newbery published a *Ladies Complete Pocket Book* for 1768, price one shilling. It contained recipes, a "Serious Address" to the ladies of Great Britain, notes on a good country wife, a "Character" of "Samandra, a Town Lady," as well as a table to calculate wages and a marketing table; a copy that belonged to Frances Sneyd is deposited in the WCRO, CR 136/A [555].

12

PERFORMANCE, PEDAGOGY, AND POLITICS

Mrs. Thrale, Mrs. Barbauld, Monsieur Itard

WILLIAM McCARTHY

This chapter considers relations among intended pupil performance, pedagogy, and politics in the work of three teachers between 1766 and 1806. The first, Hester Thrale, is an upper-middle-class wife and mother teaching her children at home and recording their progress in an album. The second, Anna Letitia Barbauld, is a celebrated poet who has taken up schoolteaching as a profession and who then writes innovative and very well received elementary teaching books. The third, Jean-Marc-Gaspard Itard, is a young doctor in Napoleonic France who is presented with a rare scientific opportunity, the challenge of educating a feral child, and whose reports to a government ministry document his efforts.

These and other documents, to be mentioned as I go, show a range of Enlightenment-era teaching practices and performance expectations from the standpoint of the teachers themselves. I will describe those practices and expectations with a view to getting a sense of what the teachers were trying to do, to what degree they succeeded, and whether their aims and methods align with any political preferences. Conventional accounts of Enlightenment pedagogy that I know of, from F. J. Harvey Darton in 1932 to Alan Richardson in 1994, seem wedded to the story that Enlightenment education was a regime dedicated in one way or another to the oppression of the child. (Its oppressiveness has traditionally been thought to be epitomized, in fact, by the books of Mrs. Barbauld.)[1] One problem with that story is its presumption that the *effects* of Enlightenment teaching on pupils are in fact known. But the effects of Enlightenment teaching, it seems to me, are among the very things we need to investigate, if we can; and I shall notice or suggest a few specific effects occasionally as I go. Another problem with the conventional story is the very fact that it does regard Enlightenment teaching as a single-minded enterprise. But the records of these three teachers suggest, instead, three teachers with different aims trying different things. The records do suggest overlaps and analogies, but they also suggest oppositions between the aims and methods of the teachers, who on some questions would have agreed but on others would have disagreed, sharply. Finally, the records suggest that analogies might be drawn between issues in teaching *then* and in teaching *now:* analogies that would imply that we today have not entirely left the Enlightenment and its debates behind us, and that possibly we should revise the story about the politics of Enlightenment teaching. So, be warned: we have much ground to cover, and a winding road ahead. As this is meant to be an empirical inquiry, let us marshall the texts and see where they lead.

On September 17, 1766, Hester Thrale, wife of a well-to-do London brewer, began a record of the "Corporeal & Mental Powers" of her daughter, Hester Maria, in an album she called "The Children's Book." At age two, Hester Maria Thrale could clearly repeat the Pater Noster, the three Christian virtues, and the signs of the Zodiac from Isaac Watts's verses. She knew all her letters and could spell little words; she knew the numerals one to nine and could count to twenty; she knew all the heathen deities and their attributes. She could not yet read.[2] (see Figure 12.1).

At age two and a half, Hester Maria knew the compass points and the solar system, the comets and constellations. She could describe all the nations on the globe and list the islands, seas, gulfs, straits, and principal cities. She knew the cardinal virtues in Latin, page one of Lily's *Grammar,* the days of the week and months of the year, the twos of the multiplication table, the Nicene Creed, the Ten Commandments,

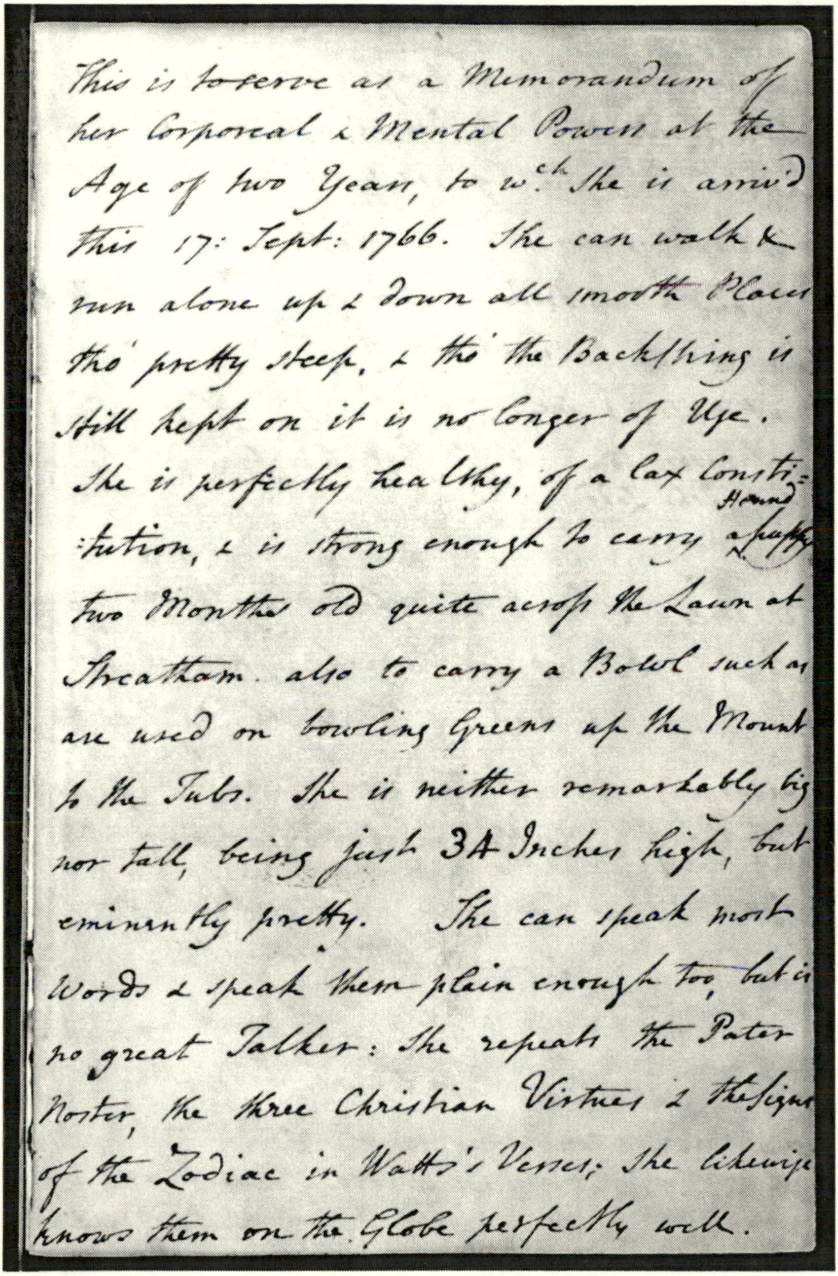

This is to serve as a Memorandum of
her Corporeal & Mental Powers at the
Age of two Years, to w.ch She is arriv'd
this 17: Sept: 1766. She can walk &
run alone up & down all smooth Places
tho' pretty steep, & tho' the Back/String is
still kept on it is no longer of Use.
She is perfectly healthy, of a lax Consti-
:tution, & is strong enough to carry a puppy
two Months old quite across the Lawn at
Streatham. also to carry a Bowl such as
are used on bowling Greens up the Mount
to the Tubs. She is neither remarkably big
nor tall, being just 34 Inches high, but
eminently pretty. She can speak most
Words & speak them plain enough too, but is
no great Talker: She repeats the Pater
Noster, the three Christian Virtues & the Signs
of the Zodiac in Watts's Verses; She likewise
knows them on the Globe perfectly well.

Fig. 12.1 Hester Maria Thrale at two years. Detail from Mrs. Thrale, *Children's Book,* entry for September 17, 1766 (MS Hyde 35 (3)). By permission of the Houghton Library, Harvard University.

the catechism, and the names of the richest, wisest, and meekest men in the Bible (pp. 24–25) (see Figure 12.2).

By age four and a quarter, she had added to her repertoire the Latin grammar through the five declensions, a fable in Phaedrus, and an epigram in Martial. By then she could also read "tolerably" (p. 29). Hester Maria went on to be a "prodigy," at least of memory. At six and a half she was examined by the headmaster of Abingdon Grammar School, who, after hearing her parse lines from Dryden's *Virgil*, explain the difficult words and their derivations, give an account of every hero mentioned in Pope's *Temple of Fame*, name the situation, latitude, and longitude of every place her questioner could think of, and list the old Runic and Gothic gods, declared that, had the exam been conducted in Latin, Hester Maria would have qualified for an Oxford degree (p. 43). She grew up to be a cool and proper lady who married an admiral.

Hester Thrale had a son, Harry, of whose performances she was also proud. At age three he could repeat the catechism and a Latin-Greek grammar through the distinction between singular and plural. He could name the Muses and the heathen gods, their attributes and offices; he could also name the three Fates, three Furies, four infernal rivers, four elements, the days of the week, and the months of the year (p. 36). At four he could read the Psalms "smartly," and could repeat the Latin grammar through the genders, making adjectives and nouns agree (p. 44). At five he knew all the Latin declensions so well that he could not be tricked into saying them wrong (p. 49); at six he was set to regular formal study of Latin at school (p. 59). What Harry would have gone on to do in later life can't be known. He died at age nine.

The Thrales had a second son, Ralph, who did not thrive. One day in 1775 a surgeon took a look at Ralph and exclaimed, "This boy is in a State of Fatuity. ... you may see he labours under some nervous complaint that has affected his Intellects." Hester was horrified; she rejected the boy as "a thing to hide & be ashamed of whilst we live" (p. 115). The Thrale servants and Ralph's siblings tried to console Hester by calling attention to Ralph's achievements, however limited: he noticed this, he admired that (p. 117). But she couldn't bear his being an "ideot," and took his condition as a punishment for her pride in her other children. Like Harry, Ralph did not survive childhood.

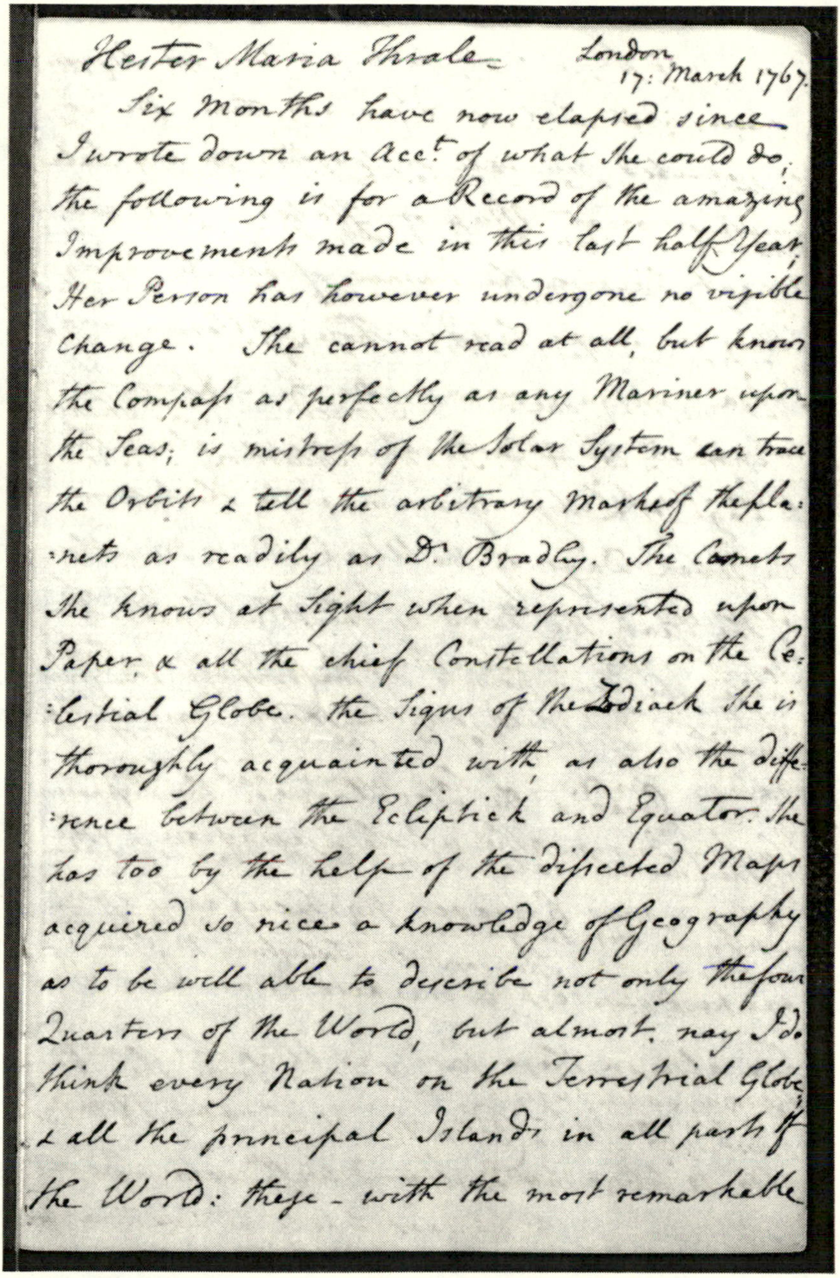

> Hester Maria Thrale   London
> 17: March 1767
>
> Six Months have now elapsed since
> I wrote down an Acc.t of what She could do.
> the following is for a Record of the amazing
> Improvements made in this last half Year.
> Her Person has however undergone no visible
> Change. She cannot read at all, but knows
> the Compass as perfectly as any Mariner upon
> the Seas; is mistress of the Solar System can trace
> the Orbits & tell the arbitrary Marks of the pla:
> :nets as readily as D.r Bradley. The Comets
> She knows at Sight when represented upon
> Paper, & all the chief Constellations on the Ce:
> :lestial Globe. the Signs of the Zodiack She is
> thoroughly acquainted with, as also the diff:
> :rence between the Ecliptick and Equator. She
> has too by the help of the dissected Maps
> acquired so nice a knowledge of Geography
> as to be well able to describe not only the four
> Quarters of the World, but almost; nay I do
> think every Nation on the Terrestrial Globe
> & all the principal Islands in all parts of
> the World: these — with the most remarkable

Fig. 12.2   Hester Maria Thrale at two years and eight months. Detail from Mrs. Thrale, *Children's Book*, entry for March 17, 1767 (MS Hyde 35 (3)). By permission of the Houghton Library, Harvard University.

About Thrale's pedagogy we know little. She refers to a few specific books like Lily's *Grammar,* and to "dissected Maps" (that is, jigsaw puzzles; p. 24), and to having compiled "a little red Book" for her daughter, who "went thro' it" on examination days (p. 29). Probably it contained information items of the sort she lists as her daughter's repertoire. Clearly Hester Thrale placed a high value on remembering information, and the information she thought important was of the type urged on us some years ago by E. D. Hirsch as indispensable to "cultural literacy."[3] Much of it, such as Latin and Classical mythology, Thrale regarded as socially indispensable: "*Indispensable* to a Gentleman's appearance in proper Company," she assured her nephew many years later.[4] Thrale was socially and politically conservative, in later life militantly anti-French Revolution and antireform at home. Musing over conservative politics then and conservative politics now, one could ask whether Thrale's idea of the socially indispensable and E. D. Hirsch's of the culturally indispensable overlap, in principle if not in content. But Thrale was not antifeminist. She was proud of her own Latin and ready to impart Latin to her daughter as well as her son (if not to the same degree), and obviously she was proud of her daughter's mental achievements. The aim of Thrale's teaching, however, seems only to have been to get the child to recite existing repertories of knowledge. And that, probably, is why her pedagogy seems invisible. She would have employed, without much reflection, whatever pedagogy came ready-made to hand, for she was not aiming at anything new.

In July 1774 the celebrated poet Anna Letitia Barbauld and her husband opened a school at Palgrave in Suffolk. During the next eleven years they taught the classics, English composition and literature, French, math, history, geography, and rudiments of the sciences to boys "intended for any of the Professions, or Trade" (I quote their advert).[5] Their pupils—who numbered, I estimate, about 130—ranged in age from three to eighteen; Barbauld herself taught the youngest of them Reading and Religion. The best records of the pupils' performance were the letters Barbauld wrote periodically to their parents. Almost none of those letters survive today. One that does was written to her brother about his son George. At age eight, George Aikin was not a stellar pupil. He liked zoology and enjoyed comparing birds killed in hunting with the descriptions of birds in zoology books by Thomas Pennant and Oliver Goldsmith. In everything else his improvement was slow. He didn't quite know the four first rules of arithmetic. He could read fables and children's books in French; he could speak French distinctly, and he recited an assigned piece "very prettily" at the end-of-term exam although he won no prize, being too much above the beginners but not as advanced as others. His spelling was careless, so much so that Barbauld made him write something every day to improve it. He lacked, she believed, "that taste & genius necessary to relish a literary life," and he seemed to have no "curiosity, or vivid feelings of any kind." But he was sociable and practical-minded, and she thought he would do well in trade. Also, he had gotten over telling lies (p. 330). George Aikin did go into trade, but failed. Eventually he lived up to his zoological interests by becoming an agricultural estate agent. He reported for *The Monthly Magazine* on the annual sheep-shearing at the Duke of Bedford's estate, and his one surviving letter concerns a cure for sheep rot.

From her report even on the unpromising George, ideas of Barbauld's teaching may be gathered. She concerned herself much less than Hester Thrale with the state of a pupil's information; her interest was the state of his skills. She addressed her teaching to the pupil's performance. George's performance in spelling was weak, so she assigned him a daily writing task. She evidently did not believe in memory drills: George is not set to write the same word fifty times over but, rather, to write some kind of composition. She offered rewards for performance (prizes, evidently awarded by performance categories) rather, it would seem, than punishment for non-performance. She attended to a pupil's general character and individual interests, seeing him as a whole person. She valued curiosity and vivid feelings in a pupil.

Other evidence of Barbauld's teaching comes from a Palgrave old boy, William Taylor, reviewer, critic, philologist, and one of the first English admirers of German literature. In an 1823 memoir of a fellow-pupil at Palgrave, the writer Frank Sayers, Taylor recalls how Barbauld taught composition:

[S]he read a fable, a short story, or a moral essay, to them aloud, and then sent them back into the schoolroom to write it out on the slates in

their own words. Each exercise was separately overlooked by her; the
faults of grammar were obliterated, the vulgarisms were ... [stylistically
purified], the idle epithets were cancelled, and a distinct reason was
always assigned for every correction; so that the arts of enditing and of
criticising were in some degree learnt together (p. 307).

The description will sound familiar enough to teachers of writing
today. But the very fact that Taylor describes her method suggests
that in 1823, almost fifty years on, it must still have seemed novel.
Notice that it did not include punishment for committing solecisms;
instead it appealed to the pupil's intelligence by giving reasons. It thus
enacted a favorite ideal of the Enlightenment, the replacement of
bodily force by rationality. Barbauld can be numbered among those
Enlightenment schoolteachers, such as William Gilpin and David
Williams, whom modern school historians have characterized as
"progressive" for rejecting bodily punishment in favor of ethical or
rational appeals.[6]

The effects of Barbauld's writing pedagogy can perhaps be esti-
mated by comparing the later careers of Palgrave boys with those of
boys from two other schools, Eton and Westminster. Nine of the 130
or so Palgrave boys went on to be authors in any capacity in later life;
that's just under seven percent of the student body.[7] During the years
when the Barbaulds were teaching at Palgrave, 355 boys attended
Eton and 306 Westminster; of that total of 661 boys, twenty-two, or
3.3 percent, went on to be authors. Palgrave's nine boys is double the
percentage from Eton and Westminster. It would seem that something was being done at Palgrave that was not being done at Eton and
Westminster. But it would not have been only Barbauld's formal
writing pedagogy that produced these results. She made sure that the
school was awash in writing, herself producing a weekly newspaper
for it which probably incorporated contributions by the pupils. There
were also end-of-term recitation galas and annual theatrical evenings.

Barbauld never proposed a theory of pedagogy; on the contrary, her
1798 essay "On Education" argues the futility of pedagogy theory. Nevertheless, her greatest teaching tool, the reading primer *Lessons for Children,* enacts a theory, and certainly not by accident. The theory enacted
by *Lessons* can be described, in terms current today, as "whole-language"

reading instruction. Indeed, it is possible that Barbauld invented that mode of instruction; at least, she seems to have been the first to publish it. *Lessons* stands in sharp contrast to previous reading primers, which typically open with the alphabet, proceed to inventories of consonant-vowel combinations (Phonics, in today's terminology), and close with moral maxims or Bible stories. *Lessons* assumes that the child is starting to read between two and three years old (the age at which Hester Maria Thrale could not yet read) and has already learned the alphabet, but is not ready to make the conceptual leap to moral maxims and Bible stories. Instead, *Lessons* plunges directly into simple but real sentences using a small vocabulary drawn from experiences a child would be likely to have if, like Barbauld, he was middle-class and lived in rural England. The sentences are structured as daily-life transactions between Mother and her son, Charles.

By describing Barbauld's reading pedagogy as "whole-language" and previous pedagogy as "Phonics," I have of course invoked a political hot potato of today. A few years ago, Nicholas Lemann reported in *The Atlantic Monthly* on a battle in California between partisans of Phonics and proponents of whole-language teaching. Whole-language reading pedagogy assumes that learning to read is like learning to speak in the first place, "a natural, unconscious process best fostered by unstructured immersion." In Phonics, on the other hand, children must "learn the letters and letter combinations that convey the English language's forty-four sounds; then they can read whole words by decoding them from their component phonemes."[8] "[P]honics," Lemann noted, is "a longstanding cause of the political right," while "whole-language is generally a cause of the left."

Were they so aligned in 1778, when *Lessons* was published? Not on the surface. The innovations of *Lessons* were recognized and appreciated even by social conservatives like Sarah Trimmer, who declared its method of "*familiar conversation* ... much better suited to the capacities of young children than any that preceded it."[9] Yet aspects of today's dispute may be latent in the difference between the old primers and Barbauld's. Certainly lists of phonemes, whether in early primers or in modern phonics, would have to be learned by memory, for the isolated sounds that they encode are not part of a child's normal verbal experience. And Barbauld, as I've noticed, compared with conservative

Hester Thrale, was less interested in what pupils could memorize than in what they could do. It would have been possible, moreover, in 1778 to criticize Phonics on the ground that merely learning to sound out words is not necessarily the same thing as understanding them. This distinction between performing and understanding was clear to early critics of the apparent success of the Abbé de l'Épée in France, who in the 1770s and 1780s taught the deaf to take dictation from sign language and demonstrated to his pupils by having them transcribe complex texts from his signs. His pupils could translate signs into writing and writing into signs, but they could neither follow written instructions nor originate sentences of their own.[10] They had learned not language but a routine.

Because Barbauld did not articulate the theory embodied in *Lessons for Children*, I do not know whether she would have criticized Phonics in these terms. The book itself, however, is manifestly designed on the principle of securing the child's understanding at each step in an incremental process. I argued this case in detail at my previous Cotsen appearance, and will just briefly summarize it here. The principle of *Lessons*, as formulated by another Palgrave old boy in an 1801 essay on *The Order and Method of Instructing Children*, is that "a child [ought never] to spell and pronounce what has not been previously presented to his understanding."[11] *Lessons* proceeds analytically and incrementally, laying the groundwork for complex concepts by first producing the simpler concepts that compose them. As an example, take stories. Barbauld considered "a connected story" to be "above [the] capacity" of a child from two to three, so before she tells a story she introduces the child to elements of narrativity: the concept of past-present-future, the idea of sequentiality (things that follow in an order, like the days of the week). Barbauld addresses the child's understanding through his prior experience.

The aim of Palgrave School, I have proposed elsewhere, was to produce what Barbauld's friend, the radical thinker Joseph Priestley, called "intelligent citizens": citizens who could manage and criticize public affairs. The Barbaulds belonged to a political out-group, Protestant Dissent, many of whose members in the 1770s through 1790s advocated reform of government. They were political opposites of Hester Thrale. A number of Palgrave boys did go on to adopt reformist politics; in some quarters the school acquired the reputation of being a hotbed of radicalism. The most influential Palgrave boy was Thomas Denman, who became Lord Chief Justice of England and in that capacity drafted the Reform Bill of 1832. If intelligent citizens are people who understand what they read, who may write more often than average, who are curious about the world, and who are accustomed to having their mistakes explained to them rather than being beaten for making mistakes, Barbauld's teaching would seem to have been well suited to the aim of her school.

My third text is the story of Victor, the "Wild Boy of Aveyron," as told by Harlan Lane twenty-five years ago in his absorbing book of that title.[12] Victor, aged around twelve, emerged from a forest in south-central France in 1800. He had been living a solitary, animal life for nobody knows how long; when captured he was mute, and, although he possessed considerable survival skills (such as speed and agility, especially in climbing trees), he responded to very few social cues other than those relating to food—and his response to food cues was survivalist rather than social. He presented, obviously, an altogether different pedagogic problem from Hester Maria Thrale or the boys at Palgrave School. With Victor the question was whether he could be brought to any kind of social performance, by any method.

Most observers were sure that he could not. One of them was Philippe Pinel, a hero in the conventional history of psychiatry because he reformed the regimen at La Bicetre, freeing the mental patients from chains. His lengthy report on Victor, nevertheless, dismisses the boy as an "idiot" and therefore uneducable; exactly like Hester Thrale with her son Ralph, Pinel refuses to see in Victor's behaviors—as he does in the behaviors of all "idiots"—any potential for improvement. Whatever skills idiots appear to possess, Pinel asserts again and again, are merely tics, "automatic imitation." Nothing can be done for them.

Nevertheless a Pinel pupil, Jean-Marc-Gaspard Itard, undertook Victor's education. His motives do not seem to have been politically idealistic: he was a young doctor looking for interesting experimental work, and a patron appointed him to the post that put him in charge of Victor and gave him his chance. What Itard found was that he had to reconstruct Victor into a social being. To do this, Harlan Lane explains, Itard "merely had to teach the boy the distinctions, categories,

needs, language, and mental processes that were normally the unpro-
grammed result of socialization" (pp. 73–74)—all the things a social-
ized child learns unconsciously day by day in its family. Itard began by
training Victor's senses, developing his ability to discriminate among
sense impressions and to focus attention on them. He induced Victor
to develop needs that could only be satisfied socially. He laid several
layers of groundwork for language acquisition: auditory training, vocal-
isation training, shape recognition prior to attempting the alphabet.
Itard's reports on his efforts document his ingenuity, resourcefulness,
and patience in attempting what was, at the time, an unprecedented
project. Once Itard committed himself to teach Victor, he necessarily
committed himself to accept as his starting point the needs, interests,
and deficiencies his pupil actually had. He had to tailor his teaching to
his pupil and regard his pupil as a whole being, however defective.

To compare Itard's situation vis-à-vis Victor with Barbauld's vis-à-
vis George Aikin is certainly to compare great things with small, but
the analogy is nevertheless observable, and it prompts reflections.
Barbauld, too, tailored her teaching to her pupil's needs, addressing
herself to George's defective spelling. On this issue, then, we might
set Barbauld and Itard together on one side, teachers who put the
needs of the pupil ahead of the imperatives of subject-matters. On the
other side, I set Pinel and Hester Thrale, who agree so utterly that no
teaching can help an idiot. That seems to imply their being committed to a notion of learning (of what counts as learning) that overrules
the particularity of any pupil and, by extension, even dictates who
shall be considered teachable. If learning is defined as a repertory of
academic information, then clearly the Victors and Ralph Thrales are
unable to learn; they become unteachables. Defining the category of
the teachable, we begin to see, is one of the contested issues raised by
these texts. On the other hand, Hester Thrale, as a feminist, counted
her daughter in the category of those who may learn Latin, a social
decision not all of Thrale's own friends would have made. And just to
further complicate the story, although Barbauld aligns with Itard on
addressing the pupil's needs, she might well have aligned with Pinel
and Thrale in presuming the unteachability of idiots.[13]

Another analogy can be drawn between Itard's pedagogy with
Victor and Barbauld's pedagogy. Like Barbauld's, Itard's pedagogy

was analytical. He approached each task by breaking it into components, and his experience in training Victor often compelled him to break what seemed irreducible components into even smaller units. One example of Itard's method can be described briefly. Victor has learned to use assemblages of metal letters and printed cards in a simple, Wittgensteinian sort of language Itard has taught him. The vocabulary of this language, like that of Barbauld's *Lessons for Children,* was chiefly household names (p. 146). Now, for easier communication, Itard wants to teach Victor to write the words. But it turns out that the act of writing even a single word, and a word Victor already knows, is far too complex for Victor to learn straight off. Victor needs preparation, and Itard provides it as follows:

> I proceeded ... by giving Victor practice in imitating large-scale movements, such as lifting his arms, putting his foot forward, sitting down and getting up the same time as I did; then opening his hand, closing it, and repeating many finger movements—first simple, then combined—that I performed in front of him. I next put a long pointed rod in his hand and another in my own, and made him hold it as if it were a quill for writing, with the double intention of giving more strength and poise to his fingers ... and of making visible, and consequently capable of imitation, even the slightest movement of the rod (pp. 148–149).

Victor is now ready to face the blackboard, chalk in hand, and make his first marks. This incremental preparation is analogous to Barbauld's method in *Lessons for Children,* as in her treatment of "story."

Harlan Lane credits Itard with "creat[ing] a whole new approach to education, centered on the pupil, closely adapted to his developing needs and abilities ... an approach we have accepted so thoroughly as our ideal that we scarcely imagine any other or credit anyone with its discovery" (p. 5). At the same time, Lane traces Itard's approach to various antecedents: the philosophy of Condillac, and methods of teaching the deaf developed by the Abbé de l'Épée and the Abbé Sicard. By making analogies between Itard and Barbauld I do not mean to promote her pedagogy as a "source" of his. That would not have been necessary in a culture whose prevailing idea of psychology derived from John Locke. When a person's mental furniture is widely regarded as a construct built up from simpler bits, a pedagogy that

proceeds from simple to complex by gradations ought to be predict-
able. Different practitioners explore its possibilities independently of
one another.

Victor's education did not end happily. It was broken off partly
by the onset of puberty, which seems to have thrown Itard badly off
stride, and partly by cessation of government funding. Victor had made
great progress, and Lane believes he could have made much more, but
he ended up "warehoused," half-socialized and fearful, till his death in
1828.

It is no discredit to Itard's resourcefulness and inventiveness to say
that the greatest importance of his project was that he undertook it at
all. Doing so was, I would say, intrinsically a political act, as not doing
so would also have been. A commentator at the time criticized those
who declared Victor an idiot and therefore unable ever to acquire "the
use of reason. This severe sentence," the commentator protested, would
have "deprived [Victor] forever of the great endowment of our species"
(p. 128). The best gloss on this remark is probably another remark,
years later, by a disciple of Itard, Edouard Séguin, who undertook to
teach a class of people hitherto held unteachable, namely idiots:

> I did not have to look about me very long to find a class of unfortunates …
> a class without standing, a category apart and yet one that has until lately
> been mixed in with convicts, and remains today confused with the insane
> and the epileptic; I mean the idiots (p. 263).

"A class without standing" is a class deprived of "the great endowment
of our species": it is excluded from the definition of "the human." The
politics in play in both of these remarks is a politics of inclusion; the
teacher adopts the role of advocate for the wrongfully dispossessed and
downtrodden, seeing them as deprived of a human right.[14]

Séguin was a socialist, and his phrase "a class without standing"
sounds like early Karl Marx on the proletariat. Should we imagine,
then, a "left–right" divide between those who would include and those
who would dismiss idiots and wild children—and, by extension, any
other contested category of creature in human shape? A divide over the
definition of "the human" and therefore over who is entitled to human
rights and human care? It is tempting to do that. It is tempting to read
the move from Thrale and Pinel to Itard and Séguin as a progress

narrative. To the degree that we do, we participate in the Enlighten-ment's faith in progress and the improvability of the human species, and its desire to extend the reach of our good will. Enlarging the cate-gory of the teachable was one of Enlightenment's heroic stories.

It is tempting also to align the difference between Barbauld and Thrale along a left–right axis, Barbauld seeking to form intelligent citizens (and apparently succeeding!), and Thrale filling future ladies and gentlemen with culturally certified information. That difference is so similar to controversies about the proper aims of schooling in the United States today that it is all too easy to assimilate Barbauld to readers of *The Nation* and Thrale to partisans of *The National Review*. And, mutatis mutandis, perhaps we should so assimilate them. To do so would be to acknowledge the Thrales and the Barbaulds as our intellectual and ethical forebears, and to recognize the origins in The Enlightenment of debates that are still carrying on in our darker days.

Notes

I should like to dedicate this chapter, were it worthy of her, to the memory of Mitzi Myers, from whom, and from whose work, I learned most of what I know about literature for children. I should like also to thank Andrea Immel for continuing support and good counsel.

1. F. J. Harvey Darton, *Children's Books in England: Five Centuries of Social Life* (Cambridge, 1932), and Alan Richardson, *Literature, Education, and Romanticism: Reading as Social Practice, 1780–1832* (Cambridge, 1994). I discuss this bias in more detail in "Mother of All Discourses: Anna Barbauld's *Lessons for Children Princeton University Library Chronicle*, 60 (Winter, 1999):196–219.

2. Mary Hyde, *The Thrales of Streatham Park* (Cambridge, MA: Harvard University Press, 1977), p. 21. "The Children's Book" is printed in full by Hyde. Subsequent page references in text.

3. E. D. Hirsch Jr., *Cultural Literacy* (New York, 1987).

4. Quoted in William McCarthy, *Hester Thrale Piozzi: Portrait of a Literary Woman* (Chapel Hill: University of North Carolina Press, 1985), p. 257.

5. All information relative to Palgrave School and Barbauld's pedagogy there (apart from *Lessons for Children)* comes from William McCarthy, "The Celebrated Academy at Palgrave: A Documentary History of Anna Letitia Barbauld's School," *The Age of Johnson*, 8 (1997):279–392. Page references appear in text.

6. See, for example, W.A.C. Stewart, *Progressives and Radicals in English Education, 1750–1970* (Clifton, N.J.: Augustus M. Kelley, 1972).

7. This figure results from reconsideration of the numbers I originally esti-mated in "Celebrated Academy," p. 368.

8. Nicholas Lemann, "The Reading Wars," *The Atlantic Monthly*, November 1997, pp. 128–134. References are to pages 129 and 130.

9. Quoted in McCarthy, "Mother of All Discourses," p. 201.

10. See Harlan Lane (cited in note 12), p. 86.

11. Quoted in McCarthy, "Mother of All Discourses," p. 206.

12. Harlan Lane, *The Wild Boy of Aveyron* (Cambridge, MA: Harvard University Press, 1976). All quotations from French sources are from Lane, in his translations, and are cited in my text.

13. Thrale records with disgust that Charles Burney resented his daughter's learning Latin: "a narrow Souled Goose-Cap the Man must be at last" (*Thraliana,* ed. Katharine C. Balderston, 2nd ed. [Oxford: Clarendon Press, 1951], p. 502). Barbauld regarded skeptically the efforts of the Abbé d'Hauy to teach the blind to read (Barbauld, *Works,* ed. Lucy Aikin [London: Longman et al., 1825], 2:105).

14. That, at least, is a benign reading of the remarks. No doubt Foucault's reading would see them as further, sinister efforts to internalize in the patient the chains of social control, as in his reading of Pinel's reform (*Madness and Civilization,* tr. Richard Howard [New York: Vintage Books 1973], pp. 259–269).

13

OTTO'S WATCH

Enlightenment, Virtue, and Time in the Eighteenth Century

ARIANNE BAGGERMAN
RUDOLF DEKKER

On January 26, 1793, Otto van Eck, twelve years old at the time, was shocked to discover that his watch was no longer in his pocket. "Straightaway I looked in all the places where it could and should have been, but I couldn't find it anywhere. Now I'm afraid, it will only be found after a long time, but I won't give up all hope and at first light tomorrow I will have another good look to see if I can find it. Papa has been kind enough to say nothing about it, but now that I have lost my watch, Oh!. ..." (see Figure 13.1).

Otto recorded the loss in his diary that he had then been keeping for two years. Two days later he wrote that he had still not found his watch. And on January 30, he complained, "I have not got my watch back and I think I will never find it again. I regret this, especially because my great-grandfather Mouchon always had it in his pocket, so it was a memento of the good man, which aunt Paulus gave me as a present. I hardly dare tell her that I have lost it." But on Sunday February 3, Otto's luck changed, "Today the weather was rainy and windy, but I walked out when the sun appeared for half an hour and I had finished my lessons, and then I found my watch. It was hanging from a pear tree in the orchard and I remember now, how last Saturday, the day I lost it,

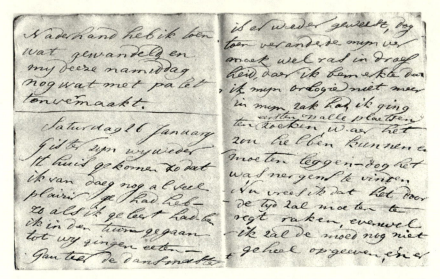

Fig. 13.1 Otto van Eck's entry for Saturday January 26, 1793 where he describes the loss of his watch. By permission of the Gelders Archief, Arnhem (The Netherlands), Family Van Eck 0545, inv. Nr. 82 (entry 1793–01–16).

I climbed a tree for fun and the chain must have caught on a branch and pulled it from my pocket without my feeling it as I was climbing. The steel chain was a bit rusty, but when I wound the watch it went very well, in spite of hanging in wind, rain, hail and snow for nine days. Oh, I am so happy."

These diary entries, in which childish grief and happiness alternate, contain unusual information on the daily life of a young boy from the Dutch elite. Otto had a watch, an heirloom moreover, but he did climb trees wearing it near the country house where he lived. It also becomes clear how important time was for Otto, or rather, how important time had to be for him, according to his parents. This was also true for the diary that Otto kept at their behest. Writing daily reports on his doings was meant to teach their son a better awareness of time, among other things. The first quotation that Otto took from a book he had read, runs, "Le temps perdu ne se retrouve plus" (June 22, 1791). Time wasting, that was exactly what Otto's parents repeatedly warned him against.

Could things be worse? Otto's panic at the loss of an object so charged with symbolism—heirloom from the past, beacon in time, signpost to the future—was not exaggerated. The importance of this object appears, among other things, from the care often spent maintaining watches, by inscriptions of former owners as the instrument was handed down from generation to generation. Numerous notes in family archives with explanations and accounts of costly repairs to worn-out timepieces, bear eloquent witness to their importance. When Pieter Blussé, a publisher in Dordrecht, a contemporary of Otto van Eck, gave Sophia Vermeer, his beloved fiancée-to-be, a present as a token of their relationship, he deliberately chose a watch and encouraged her to wear the object as ostentatiously as possible: "Wear your watch in plain view, and you will honour and please me." The gift was also supposed to put pressure on the uncooperative guardians of the girl, whose procrastination was intended to prevent the marriage from taking place.[1] No less deliberate was the action of a clockmaker's son from Geneva a couple of decades earlier, when he threw away his watch in a devil-may-care gesture. Losing your watch may well have been reprehensible, but discarding it came close to a criminal offense. Jean-Jacques Rousseau protested against inexorable developments such as the triumph of the technocratic world over a society that had formerly followed the rhythms of nature.[2]

Enlightened Theories of Education

Otto was raised with the aid of books written by educationists influenced by Rousseau, advocates of concepts such as learn-as-you-play and learning by example. The strain of cultural pessimism in his thought, however, was from another source. Just like the philanthropine pedagogues J. B. Basedow and C. G. Salzmann, household words in Otto's home, the young boy's parents held an overwhelming belief in a future utopia, based on scientific achievement. In their view, then, a watch was the summit of technical contrivance and a programme at the same time: modern life was to be regulated by the hands of the clock. Time and again Otto was exhorted by them not to waste time, but to spend it usefully. Already as a ten-year-old—maybe even earlier, but no diaries have come down to us from this period—Otto's life was regulated by a daily timetable dictating the moment he rose, his lessons for school, his reading of books, his partaking of meals, hour by hour. Even his "leisure time," those few hours that, although fraught with danger, he loved to spend outside in the garden, was kept within strictly scheduled bounds, its limits set by a large clock which could be clearly heard everywhere as it rang out the inevitable signal that it was time to come in.[3]

It was precisely during the period that Otto grew up when the division between work and leisure time grew more distinct. A part of the dictionary published by Noël Chomel in 1793, the year in which Otto lost his watch, included an entry "relaxations" (*Uitspanningen*): all those things "which man, after performing work of any kind, takes up in order to replenish energies lost through the work of body or mind, and to revive them." This was followed, moreover, by a long warning against "wild merriment," which could only lead to "painful remorse".[4] That was a view Otto's parents held, because they tried to guide Otto in the use of his "free" time as well: "This morning I rose so early that after I had read about Moses' wonderful education, I still had time to go for a walk, with father's permission" (June 7, 1791). Otto was well aware of the importance of the division between schoolwork and leisure. On May 6, 1791, he wrote that he would obediently do the homework assignments he had been set "without thinking of any relaxations, before they have been entirely completed."

The insistence on the useful employment of spare time may have been connected to another development in enlightened circles. That after death there would be an eternal afterlife had been taken for granted for ages. Now people had begun to question the truth of this, though sometimes not seriously. That this doubt had been the subject of a discussion between Otto and his parents, appears from one of his entries. On Sunday December 20, 1794, he wrote, "Had a useful conversation with papa about man, which proved, that if there were no eternity, people would still be happier on earth when they fulfilled the will of God." The words "if there were no eternity" prove that this point was debatable within the van Eck family. Entertaining such a doubt had serious implications for the way in which the time people spent on earth was valued: the idea that time was a scarce commodity took on a new weight.

Otto's parents belonged to the progressive part of the Dutch upper classes. His father, Lambert van Eck, whose family came from Tiel, was a judge in The Hague, his mother was a regent's daughter from Delft. In national politics too, they favored innovation. Lambert van

Eck had acquired his progressive ideas during his student days in Leiden, and in the 1780s he sided with the Patriots. In 1795 he was to play a prominent role in the Batavian Revolution and he was elected to the National Assembly. Otto's uncle Paulus was the first chairman of this body, and his wife, the aunt Paulus previously mentioned, had presented Otto with his watch.

Otto van Eck kept his diary between 1791 and 1797, between the ages of ten and sixteen. Almost every day he wrote down what he did, which books he read, what lessons he took, whom he played with, whether he had pestered his little sister, played with his goat, or had been looking at the birds on the market in Delft. Otto's life and education can be followed from day to day. His parents tried, especially by a strict control of his reading, to force Otto's education into an enlightened and politically correct mold. He was to be forged into a model citizen of the imminent nineteenth century. They regarded Otto as the new man in a new society that would emerge as the result of the reforms to be implemented throughout Europe after the success of the French Revolution.

Among the rational values that children were to be taught as iterated in the enlightened pedagogical writings of the period, the treatment of time played a central role. In his 1781 alphabet book, the Patriot professor J. H. Swildens instructed his young readers on the word "hour," as follows: "The hours fly, each in its turn. Remember this, and learn to spend them well: for none of them will ever return." The verse was illustrated with an engraving showing a father teaching his son to tell the time (see Figure 13.2). When Otto started writing his diary, he was long past the stage of learning to read, which explains the lack of a direct reference to Swildens. The passage about "le temps perdu" previously quoted reflects the same message. In books that we know Otto read, he encountered this theme time and again. On September 25 1791, he noted, "I have also read that spending your time well is the best way of getting through this world. We have an example of this in Kluge." (Kluge was the protagonist in a story by the German pedagogue and writer, Salzmann, that appeared a year earlier.[5] Salzmann tells of a poor farmer attaining prosperity through frugality and useful employment of his time. This story marks the origin of the idea that "Time is money." On October 21, 1791, Otto wrote the following

Fig. 13.2 Headpiece by N. van der Meer for J. H. Swildens, *Vaderlandsch A-B Boek voor Nederlandsche Jeugd,* Amsterdam: W. Holtrop, 1781, p. 25. Reproduced by permission of Princeton University Library.

passage: "[I read] in madame La Fite about a young man, who, in the absence of his parents, did nothing but waste his time, in spite of the fact that his younger sister admonished him not to be idle, but because he did not follow her advice, he did not enjoy his parents' homecoming, for they didn't even want to hug him, since they had heard that he had made so little."[6]

A similar caution against idleness also appears in one of the children's verses by Hiëronymus van Alphen, which are not mentioned in the diary but were so immensely popular that it is highly likely that Otto was familar with them.[7]

> Never must I be idle
> But do all things with a will and industry
> Pray, learn, write, read,
> Play, and work, all in good time.
> Dear mother cannot stand it

When time is wasted.
Laziness, she says, is stealing time,
And life is so short!

Thinking about Time and the Future

The exhortations by philosophers to spend time usefully was nothing
new in itself: the same advice can be read in moralist tracts from the
sixteenth and seventeenth centuries. This message took on another
dimension indicative of a different awareness of time between 1750
and 1850, the period in which historical awareness changed fundamentally, according to the German historian R. Koselleck, and that
he called the Sattelzeit.[8] Around 1800, the static world view based on
the Bible retreated, at least in the enlightened elite circles to which
Otto's parents belonged, and was replaced by a dynamic model based
on natural science with a strong developmental perspective. In other
words, the concepts of an open future and malleable social institutions that man could actively shape had been born.[9] Indeed, the word
toekomst (future) in the meaning of time to come, only entered the
Dutch language around 1800, probably under the influence of the
German *Zukunft*.[10]

The change in time awareness is often also represented as a shift
from a cyclical to a linear conception of time. Traditional, preindustrial societies related time to the rising and the setting of the sun, the
tides of the sea, the changing seasons, or the comings and goings of
migrating birds. The example of birds was used by John Locke, who
was conscious of the fact that changes in the awareness of time had
been developing for over a century in his own era. The new, linear
awareness of time was evolving during the period when better
mechanical measuring tools were being developed. This mathematical concept of time entailed a perception of a future that was not simply a repetition of actions, but a series of unique events. In its wake,
the meaning of the term "revolution" also changed from a transfer of
power within the elite, to the sense of a more fundamental, political
restructuring or a new beginning. It was no coincidence that during
the French Revolution a new calendar was introduced. The Batavian
revolutionaries called 1795 "the first year of our freedom."

The changeover from a cyclical to a linear concept of time must not be regarded as an abrupt transformation, because the two coexisted to a certain extent. While the linear sense of time is associated with technological progress and future development, it is also connected with the notions of finiteness, death and destruction as well.[11] Thus the new conception of time had pessimistic overtones in the eighteenth century because the progress of time could also be characterized as decline. Cyclical time awareness, on the other hand, is associated primarily with balance and recurrence, but can also be linked to such technological innovations as the turning hands of the clock.[12]

The intrinsic properties of time were subject to intensive debate during the eighteenth century. The entry on time in Diderot's famous *Encyclopédie* runs to twenty-seven pages.[13] The central issue was the question that Newton's disciple Samuel Clark posed in vain to the universal scholar G. W. Leibniz: why did God not create the world six thousand years sooner or later? For centuries, scholars believed that time had been created by God six millennia ago following the Bible. In the enlightened physicotheology of the eighteenth century, some thinkers reduced God to the force that had set the cosmic clockwork in motion, the Great Watchmaker. The metaphor is a telling one. In this modern view, God did not actively intervene in people's lives, but He was only present on earth in the passage of time. The calculations that situated creation six thousand years ago based on passages from the Bible came under fire. The world was older, as fossil evidence showed, so that the only question became, how much older? In other words, the widely accepted concept of the "great chain of being," God-created nature in which all things had their own place, was now put in a time perspective. The earth man inhabited had not been created in six days, but was the result of an ongoing process of change and, according to the optimists, progress.[14] The Frenchman G. L. Leclerc de Buffon (1707–1788), whose work was also on Otto's reading program, designed a new history of the world divided into a number of stages, with the motto 'Le grand ouvrier de la nature est le temps.'

In science, time came to be increasingly regarded as a serious problem.[15] On the one hand, orientation was toward objective time in the tradition of Aristotle, on the other, toward subjective time, following

St. Augustine. In early modern times, scientists such as Descartes were especially occupied with the question of how time was to be measured. This was done with the aid of repetitive movements; time was regarded as a mathematical variable of movement, like that of the earth around the sun, or of the moon around the earth. The repeating movement of a clock was used as a more precise unit of measurement.

A fundamentally different approach was proposed by Isaac Newton. His point of departure was "absolute time": time has its own properties and is therefore independent of the created world, and thus "real time," not a human construct. In Newton's view, time flowed steadily, irreversibly, as a sequence of indivisible moments. A movement can slow down or accelerate, but time flows on, always at the same speed. John Locke, in *An Essay Concerning Human Understanding*, added a new dimension to the discussion. He wondered about man's awareness of time. Locke regarded time as a stream of ideas in the brain in which sequence and duration could be distinguished. That is why, so he thought, people have no perception of time when they are asleep.[16] Locke thus focused on subjective time.

These two conceptions dominated the discussion in the eighteenth century. Could both exist at the same time, or was only one type of time possible? The latter view was taken by Leibniz, among others. According to him, two sorts of time could not exist simultaneously, for why would God have created two? When forced to choose, he discarded Newton's idea of time. Later, Immanuel Kant in his *Kritik der Reinen Vernunft* attempted to take a step forward by reconciling the two conceptions. Kant's view was explained by Paulus van Hemert in his *Beginzels der Kantiaansche Wijsgeerte* (Principles of Kantian Philosophy), which appeared in 1796. A reviewer in *Vaderlandsche Letteroefeningen* summarised the matter for an even wider audience.[17] In the nineteenth century, the problem was to take an ever more prominent place in philosophical and scientific debate, in which time was no longer regarded as "flowing" but, rather, as an elusive division between the future and the past. Several Dutch scientists wrote on the subject in the eighteenth century, among them P. van Musschenbroek, a pupil of Newton, and W. J. Gravensande. De Chalmot's popular dictionary, the modest Dutch version of the *Encyclopédie*, featured a succinct account of the discussion, including the opposition between "independent time" and "relative time," in terms accessible to a broad readership.[18]

Technology and Punctuality

The technical improvements to clockwork were synchronous to the changing conception of time. To the end of the seventeenth century, a watch's decorative function was more important than its actual utility. They were generally executed in elaborately decorated precious metal. Thanks to technological improvements such as the application of coiled springs and the addition of minute hands, watches became more precise and thus more reliable.[19] Prior to these improvements, watches had served mainly to confirm an estimation of the time already made; during the eighteenth century they were first regularly consulted to tell the time.[20] This development, in which the clock regulated time, marked a fundamental change in the way people treated their timepieces. Punctuality grew into a much appreciated virtue in the eighteenth century. In *De man van bedrijf* (*The Man of Business*), a handbook or conduct book translated from the English intended especially for entrepreneurs and businessmen, this was stressed repeatedly: "A well-regulated allocation of time is one of the main occupations of a man of business."[21] At the same time, others already saw the looming danger of this punctuality degenerating into terror: *De man naar de klok* (*The Man by the Clock*) was the title of a comedy from 1780.[22] The main character was continually counting hours, minutes, and seconds against a backdrop showing several timepieces. Betje Wolff and Aagje Deken, in the novel *Willem Leevend*, drew a critical picture of a female character who swore by strict order: "everything according to the clock."[23]

This was also the origin of the eighteenth-century preoccupation with limiting the duration of a night's rest, as sleep was increasingly regarded as time lost. The idea is reflected, for instance, in the item "sleep" in De Chalmot's dictionary, in which the author recounts how, as a young man, he tried to make do with five hours of sleep, but after three months he had grown very thin and listless, and almost fell asleep on his feet. He regretted this and concluded that people only spent about one-third of their lives in useful occupation. Children

slept so much because of their "weaker brains." The author recommended tea as an "antidote." The growing popularity of stimulants
such as tea and coffee in the eighteenth century also can be regarded
in this light. In the same dictionary there is an entry on coffee which
states that it is a useful beverage that keeps sleep at bay and is effective
when wakefulness is required, or if one wants to stay up at night. This
was an entirely new use of the beverage, which before then had been
recommended for entirely different medicinal purposes, such as a
remedy for earache and dropsy.[24] Children should also sleep less.
Pieter 't Hoen sang the praises of the dawn for children in his *Fabelen
en kleine gedichten* (*Fables and little poems*), in the lines:

> By untiring diligence you must
> Turn away your lust for sleep
> Morningtide is the right time
> For learning quick and much.[25]

That the development and dissemination of timepieces were factors in
the changing perception of time is clear. On the degree to which the
technical factor was decisive, and the whole question of cause and effect
has excited a lively controversy among historians. According to Lewis
Mumford, it is not the steam engine but the clock that should be
regarded as "the key machine of the modern industrial age."[26] The mechanization of the world view was mainly to be attributed to this invention.
Carlo Cipolla has pointed out that the development of mechanical clocks
was a typically European phenomenon that did not arise from a need for
exact measurement of time but, rather, from an interest in technical ingenuity.[27] For centuries these machines had been less precise than sundials
that, moreover, remained in use as points of reference for setting clocks
and watches. When the sun had risen to its zenith, the clock was set for
twelve noon. Because the course of the sun differs depending upon the
geographical location, there was a system of "local time" all over Holland,
just as in the rest of the world. In Holland, there was only a maximum of
fifteen minutes' difference between local clocks. But even that small
difference was a big nuisance when railway timetables appeared. Only in
1909 was uniform time introduced into the Netherlands. It goes without
saying that this was the time of the capital city, Amsterdam.

Many historians take the view that the rise of the mechanical clock is closely connected to the rise of the bourgeois striving for rationality. There is indeed a number of phenomena supporting this view, but it needs some qualification.[28] The first public clocks appeared in cities, not in the countryside. Urban market hours, for instance, were regulated by the ringing of the town bells. The great interest in timepieces in the highly urbanized Republic also could point to the connection between the rise of timepieces and the rise of bourgeois society. Both the spiral spring and the pendulum clock had indeed been invented by a Dutchman, Christiaan Huygens. After Huygens had published his *Horlogium oscillatorium* in 1673, Salomon Coster, clockmaker from The Hague, was granted the privilege to make clocks according to this principle. Such clocks appeared in an increasing number of interiors, and usually occupied a central place in people's houses. In contrast to public tower clocks, they had a permanent regulatory presence in daily life. Abroad, the Republic was to become known as the country where the tow barges sailed on time. Historians' observations about the opposition between city life regulated by the clock and life in the country regulated by nature are supported by contemporary anecdotes. In a seventeenth-century joke by the writer Aernout van Overbeke from The Hague, a city dweller asked a farmer the time of day. The farmer replied that it was the time at which the animals were watered, which prompted the city dweller to ask, "Why are you standing here, then?" The contrast between traditional country life and more modern time perception was the source of fun here.[29]

At the same time, it should be noted, however, that the demand for mechanical clocks was initially greater from clerics than from laymen. Monks had to be able to tell in the dark at what time they were to sing early mass.[30] Moreover, in despite of Van Overbeke's anecdote, in seventeenth-century Holland house clocks were required by farmers who wanted to rise before dawn to milk their cows, as a regional study from Limburg makes clear.[31] In the course of the seventeenth century, house clocks became more common, especially on farms, where there were no town clocks to go by. The simple Limburg upright model was especially popular, produced in great numbers in the country which the study of household inventories confirms.[32] Around 1730, in the small town of Weesp, clocks were to be found in a quarter of all households, while in the surrounding countryside almost 80 percent of the farmers had one. By Otto's times almost every farm had a clock, whereas in houses in towns this was still far from being the case. In short, the technological development of the timepiece did take place in urban surroundings, but it was stimulated by the growing demand for mechanical time measurement in the countryside.

Unequivocal, Yet Ambiguous

That an entirely unequivocal instrument such as a timepiece can be the locus of an ambiguity is also supported by the multiform symbolism of clocks and watches in texts and illustrations. Sometimes the meaning is consistent with the traditional story of the mechanization of the world view. This is true, for instance, of the watch depicted in the portrait of the Delft postmaster Lambert Twent, which he commissioned in 1695. He is accompanied by his four sons, all of whom are busily occupied with letters and seals. The central focus, however, is on the watch that is on the table in front of them, which seems to be saying: We are men of the clock, with us the post is in capable hands.[33]

More numerous are the paintings from which entirely different meanings can be distilled than a one-dimensional mechanization of the world view. Dutch burghers liked to be depicted with a watch in their hands as a sign of wealth and good taste. A watch worn as a piece of jewelry is shown in the portrait of Helena Leonora de Booys-de Sieveri, which Cornelis Jonson van Ceulen painted in 1650. The case was embellished with a painted Biblical scene of Judith and Holofernes. By contrast, the watch in such paintings would be a symbol for the temporality of life on earth, and had thus come to replace hourglasses, which were often found in still lifes but very seldom in household inventories of the time. An early instance of a watch with such a meaning is to be found in the painting by Gerard ter Borch of the husband and wife De Liederkercke and their seventeen-year-old son Samuel, painted in Delft or Leiden. The mother is handing the watch to her son. The watch, which is central in the painting, could be a reference to the transfer of life from one generation to the next. But it is also quite possible that it was painted shortly after the early death of Samuel in 1655 and that the clock functions chiefly as a memento mori.[34]

In Jan Luiken's book *Het leerzaam huisraad* (Homely wisdom), a book of emblems that was reprinted many times, the clock is laden with meaning.[35] In this case, the moral is a purely religious one. The clock is kept alive by its burden, according to Luiken, if you do not raise the weight, the clock will live no longer. In other words, religion is of more importance than earthly matters. In the days that Otto grew up, the connection among enlightenment, virtue, and time had become so hackneyed that this inseparable threesome became the subject of a humorous discussion by Arent Fokke in 1799.[36]

Hours, Days, Months, Years

It has already been shown that by 1800 a young boy of twelve with a watch in his pocket was not an exceptional phenomenon. Delft inventories show that watches had become widely used in the elite circles of the town. Men often possessed several watches.[37] Possession was not limited to the elite, however. Among members of the middle classes these objects also became more common during the course of the eighteenth century. Of even greater interest in the analysis of Otto's perception of time is the connection that the historian Stuart Sherman has noted between the simultaneous rise of clockwork and of diary keeping in seventeenth-century England.[38] Writing a diary was not a pastime, but functioned much like a clock as a means of coming to grips with time. Perhaps it is no coincidence that the entire family of Christiaan Huygens should have been diligent keepers of diaries. The *pater familias,* the poet and statesman Constantijn Huygens, was the great example, who not only kept a diary, but praised clockwork in some of his poems.[39] None of Christiaan's diaries have survived, but there is one by his brother Constantijn Jr., which tells us among other things that he had an upright clock and had a pocket watch repaired.[40] The terms themselves of "diary" or "journal" (the latter used by Otto), confirms the primacy of the temporal element in this form of writing. Numerous passages from Otto's diary suggest that his parents constantly repeated to him the message that time was a scarce commodity that had to be employed wisely. Thus, May 1793 concluded with a resolution that certainly did not originate solely with Otto: "Oh, how quickly time flies, and so it will keep on flying until the hour of our death. May I always be as well aware as I am now that I must spend it well, so that on my deathbed I need not regret the way I used it." That he did not always live up to this pious wish, appears, for instance, from an entry on the last day of the year 1795. Otto wrote that he had spent the day "pleasantly": "I did not attempt to pass the time in idleness as much as I did yesterday." On July 18, 1791, it is very easy for the researcher to identify the message's source: "One should be frugal of the time given to other people, says papa, for it is soon lost in that fashion." Otto's parents would have found ample support for such sentiments from the authors of the books that Otto read. Thus, Otto could glean from a children's book by Madame de la Fite that amusement was allowed, as long as such time was usefully employed (October 15, 1791). The distinction between time and free time is a recurring theme in the diary. Otto must learn to be averse to "idleness" (October 29, 1792). Although he was aware of the danger of an "empty mind" (October 29, 1792), his parents regularly faulted him for not having done anything useful (June 14, 1794). Now and then Otto—so his parents—was satisfied. On October 22, 1792, he noted that for once he need not reproach himself for spending his time uselessly and idly. On another day he wrote, "I certainly knew what to do with my time" (January 12, 1793). Sights seem to have been set very high, as appears from an entry on May 20, 1794. Otto had risen particularly early on that day, but his father reproached him for not having employed that time usefully, saying he could just as well have remained asleep. Occasionally, Otto had to learn the value of punctuality by trial and error. On February 3, 1794, he was five minutes late for the coach that was to take him home from Delft, so that he was forced to make the journey on foot.

Not only does the subject of time management occupy a central place in Otto's diary, but the duty of keeping a diary was itself regulatory. When Otto described the course of his day, he did so chronologically as a rule, often stating the exact time at which activities took place. That Otto was not the master of his own time is clear from the aforementioned entries. But one of his first diary entries, on May 8, 1791, shows that Otto did not always give up without a fight:

> Today I did not go to church and got up so late but I could not finish my
> tasks before dinner, but part of them could only be started at six, and not
> before Mama had called me to do so, even though I had all afternoon. In
> addition I did not keep my word to be silent while I could not fall asleep,
> so she is sending me to bed at eight.

In another connection, historians have described the relation between
power and control over time by the way in which entrepreneurs
imposed a new time discipline on their workers beginning during the
Industrial Revolution. In the course of a few generations the traditional
working hours disappeared, as factories were increasingly regulated by
the clock.[41] Recent research has worked out the relation between time
and power in more detail. The lower a person's position in the social
hierarchy, the less freedom he has to dispose of his own time, with
slaves or prisoners having the least control of all.[42] If power can be
wielded through the ability to regulate someone else's time, then con-
versely, ignoring a time discipline can be an act of subversion. The
aspect of exercising power through regulation of time is apparent
throughout in Otto's diary. By means of his watch, the clock, and the
outside bell, Otto's parents controlled his behavior and the rhythm of
his life. And instead of meting out corporal punishment, they sent their
son to bed early when they wished to discipline him. Reciprocally, Otto
occasionally retaliated by staying in bed or coming home late. Keeping
the diary was part of this strategy. Otto had to write in it daily, by order
of his parents, who would review it at fixed times. There are several
passages where he writes in so many words that this daily task sometimes palled. He sometimes tried to convey other messages to his parents through the diary, for instance his desire for a beautiful humming
top that he had seen in a toy shop. But as far as convincing them to
relax the discipline of making regular entries in the diary, his efforts
were not very successful, for his parents kept hammering on this recurring obligation.

The precision with which Otto noted events in his diary, as urged
by his parents, does, on the other hand, make it easy to imagine his
life's rhythms and to sympathise with him. Thus, the unfolding of the
seasons reveals itself in his observations on budding trees in spring,
and which "grow by the hour, in a manner of speaking." That the

same process was taking place in himself, appears from his observations on November 5, 1792. Otto had been ill in bed, and for the first time in weeks put on his clothes. He did not succeed without a struggle, so that it was clear that he had "grown remarkably." His awareness that he was growing to adulthood, not just physically but also spiritually, is illustrated by an observation on the subject of his first horse, a small cob. His great joy on June 12, 1793, over this present, a milestone comparable to getting a modern-day driver's licence, elicited the following insight: "How a person is for ever longing for something else. First I was very happy with the goat, but that doesn't count for much now since I much prefer riding a cob, and who knows how quickly that will bore me, and I shall want to ride a full-size horse."

Otto's diary has a rhythm of its own, with its careful entries of the times the events of his life took place. As his daily schedule hardly changed over the years, the diary has a somewhat monotonous cadence. Otto usually rose at seven. We know this because he recorded now and then that he had risen earlier than usual around six, or that he had overslept until eight or nine o'clock, sometimes even later (May 25, 1793). Evidently, no one woke him up, so he had to keep track of time himself. When Otto rose early, he did so to take care of his birds and rabbits. In 1794 he wrote that a visit to the cowshed was part of his fixed morning routine (March 11, 1794). In any case, he had to be up and about at around seven. Then, if he had time, he would read for a bit, usually an edifying text, followed by morning prayers. Breakfast was taken with the other members of the family, and the meal was usually combined with collective reading. In 1791, when he started keeping the diary, Otto went to school in The Hague, which started at nine o'clock. Just like a modern commuter, he would travel there by tow barge from Delft, or ride along with his father, who went to the courts of law in The Hague. School lasted till noon. Back home in De Ruit the main meal of the day would be served, concluding with dessert, at which reading aloud would take place.

In 1792 Otto was ill for a considerable time. When he recovered, he did not go back to school. From then on he was taught by tutors at home, had private lessons in Delft, or worked under his parents' supervision. At home, the same hours he was used to at school were maintained. From nine to twelve he would work on his lessons.

This was followed by a lunch break after which lessons would resume until about five. Otto speaks of "morning business" and "afternoon business." That was not the end of his day, however. Between five and seven he had time to spend however he liked. When he played outside, he was called in by the ringing of a bell. Then there would be "evening business," which mainly consisted of reading instructive books with his parents. In winter, evening business could commence only after the candles had been lit. He thoroughly enjoyed the twilight hour (May 21, 1794). He would have a cup of chocolate or tea, later a glass of wine (August 12, 1795), punch (November 5, 1796), or coffee (April 24, 1797). The sequence of drinks in itself reflects the fact Otto was growing up, for coffee was without a doubt the most adult beverage in the list. Around eight there would be supper, a light meal. When he was ten, Otto probably went to bed at nine o'clock, for when he was sent to bed early as a punishment, it was at eight (May 8, 1791). Two years later, the same punishment was inflicted at half past nine, when he was clearly allowed to stay up later, at least until ten o'clock (July 20, 1793). There was one daily activity that Otto was never allowed to skip: writing in his diary. Otto lived by the clock: he had his own pocket watch, there was a large standing clock in the hall of De Ruit, and there was an outside bell that rang when he had to come home. When Otto did not himself remember the time, he was reminded by his parents. They would continually impose time limits: getting up, meals, homework, lessons, bedtime, all Otto's activities were timed by his parents.

The weeks, months, and years also had their own rhythm. Otto's weekly schedule did not change substantially over the years. Weekdays were dedicated to studying at school or at home. His teachers came on fixed days, although the pattern was disrupted on more than one occasion because of inclement weather, illness, or misunderstandings. Otto took some lessons in Delft, and that also went for catechism every Wednesday from noon until one. There were a few more fixed points in the week. On Thursdays there was a cattle market in Delft. Nearly every week Otto would go there and sometimes bought rabbits or birds. On one occasion he went there because a calf from De Ruit was to be sold.

Saturdays had their own fixed ritual. On that day Otto had to write his weekly letter to his uncle Pieter Paulus (May 24, 1794). The letter had to be finished by ten o'clock in order to be in time for the post, which adhered to a strict timetable. From 1795, Friday nights were spent in attendance at the "Physisch Genootschap" (The Physics Society) in The Hague, whereby Otto and his father hoped to increase their scientific knowledge. But Sundays established the weekly rhythm. In the morning the family would go to church, but not invariably. On more than one occasion illness or the weather would prevent them from going, and the time would be spent reading a sermon at home. The rest of the day was not spent in observance of Sabbath rest. It was a day for receiving visitors, and Otto would play in or around the house. Quite frequently there would still be some "business" for Otto to accomplish, and of course, the diary would have to be written in that night.

Through the rhythm of days, weeks, and months, Otto learned the essence of time. Many passages in his diary bear witness to his growing awareness of it. The beginning or the end of the month often called for a note. On February 2, 1792, he wrote, for instance, "Another month of the year 1792 has passed by like a shadow, and the others will pass in the same way, no doubt. I shall employ my time well, so that I shall have no regrets at the end of the year." And, on October 1, 1792, "Another month has gone by already, how quickly time passes." On March 31, 1794, "It appears to me, that the older I get, the faster time passes." He talked about it with his mother, "It seems to me as if the month of June has passed very quickly. It seems like only a few hours ago that we said goodbye to the month of May. Mama told me about this and I am experiencing it now: the older I get, the faster time passes away before my eyes" (June 30, 1794). Otto learned that perception of time is subjective and connected to age, just as it is today. Otto's remark is the earliest known statement by a child recording this feeling.

As a child grows up, the time span it can comprehend increases. A year is so long that a child of ten years old or younger can hardly conceive of it. But the rhythm of the year is recorded in the diary, although without clear evidence of Otto's conscious awareness. One of his first entries, in May 1791, referred to the fair at The Hague. Traditionally, a fair was one of the important milestones in the year in a town or village. For a boy like Otto, this was even more emphatically the case. Schools were closed for the week. Each year he visited the fairs at Delft or The Hague, sometimes both. Often he was taken by his grandmother Mouchon. On one such visit with his father, Otto saw tightrope dancers, which evidently made quite an impression on him. For ordinary people the annual fair was central to their time perception. From judicial archives it appears that in the lower levels of society people still calculated in days or weeks before or after the local fair. Cultured people such as the van Ecks did take part in the entertainment, and the popular feast had not yet lost its meaning as a mark in time.

Descriptions of the Christian holidays in the diary are not particularly vivid. One of Otto's typical entries for Thursday, June 2, 1791, runs, "As it is Ascension day, I did not go to school, but talked about it with Papa this morning. I spent the rest of the day playing without giving it another thought, which did not make Mama very happy." At Christmas 1794, Otto wrote that a suitable reading took place in the morning, but the rest of the day was spent pleasantly enough. On several occasions Otto mentions the annual days of prayer, ordained by the Estates General, during which prayers drawn up by the authorities would be read in all reformed churches. This low-key attention to Christian feast days was a matter of conscious choice, as became clear to Otto after reading Zollikofer's sermons on "the useful employment of Christian feast days."[43] They served "1. To remind us of God's great good deeds to humanity, 2. To engender a holy joy in us, 3. To unite us with our brethren and finally to offer up our entire lives to God."

Beginnings and endings of school holidays were noted often by Otto, which makes him a modern child. During his education at home, these holidays also were kept. It is remarkable that in spite of this he was always supposed to do something about his "business." His father, to Otto's joy, also had fixed holidays (August 2, 1792). In this respect, he was a modern civil servant. There was one annual holiday the family preferred not to honour: the birthday of the hereditary prince of Orange. Lambert van Eck sided with the political opponents of the stadholder. Schools were on holiday on this day, but Otto had to attend to his "business." To make merry in honor of the Prince of Orange was frowned on for political reasons, as was already made clear to Otto when he was eleven (August 23, 1791).

The changing of the seasons marked the course of the year most clearly for Otto. In spring he noted when the shrubs and trees were budding, when sowing and planting took place, when the fruit trees were trimmed and the hay was made. He recorded when grass-butter was served for the first time in the season (March 31, 1794), and when they had the first sun-ripened mange-tout (May 20, 1794). He himself went in search of plovers' eggs, a traditional amusement in early spring (April 2, 1794). In the autumn, Otto wanted to see how a cow or a pig from their own stock was slaughtered, which would provide the family with meat. As this event took place but once a year, he was granted permission by his parents (November 20, 1792). He also recorded the beginning and ending of the ban on fishing, which he had to respect in spring. On June 1, 1795, he noted with relief that he could take up his favorite pastime again.

The changing of the seasons sometimes elicited more contemplative remarks from Otto, as on November 26, 1792: "Today I really felt that winter has arrived. When I'd done my lessons this morning, and went for a walk, it was as cold as it was in February and the water in the pond was quite frozen. The tops of all the trees that have to be replanted are being cut, and this gives a wintry aspect to the wood. The hooded crows add to the general picture. Oh, how quickly has lovely summer passed, just as our lives will. That we may spend the time the good God gave us in such a way that, when our everlasting spring begins, we can sufficiently account for it." Three days later, father van Eck had the first fires laid in the house.

And of course there were the family's annual holidays, especially birthdays. On their birthdays, he would, of course, have to congratulate his parents or sisters. For his father or mother he was supposed to compose a poem. Celebrations, in general, were not very elaborate. There is a typical entry on February 19, 1793, when he, along with the entire family, had forgotten his mother's birthday. He remembered the day after, congratulated her and asked for her forgiveness. He wrote, "[I] assured her that my wishes were no less sincere, even though they were a few hours late." A year later, on November 12, 1794, Otto, unlike his sisters, forgot to make a birthday poem for his father. He wrote, "[I] hope he realized that my wishes, conveyed by word of mouth, were meant equally sincerely." Otto had learned his lesson now. On his mother's next birthday we can read, "I got up earlier this morning, and the first thing I did was to hand Mama a poem to congratulate her on her birthday, which I had made especially for the occasion" (February 19, 1795).

No elaborate birthday celebrations took place, however. Presents were not even given. Work went on, normal visits took place, no more nor less than usual. It is clear that Otto would have liked more festivities. On occasion he would see to this himself, as appears from his own description on his mother's birthday in 1795, "When it was dark, I surprised Mama by firing my guns and lighting a little firework, which frightened her, however, as she hadn't expected it." Now and then Otto recorded birthdays of other members of the family: Uncle Paulus turned thirty-nine on April 10, 1793, his sister Doortje was eleven on April 26, 1793, grandmother Van der Goes was forty-six on November 18 of the same year, his girlfriend Tietje Philip was sixteen on July 27, 1794. No further details were added. Otto's own birthdays also passed quietly. He never mentioned presents, children's parties, decorations, or visits by friends or family. These trappings were not to arrive until well into the nineteenth century. On the contrary, Otto's birthdays were supposed to be suitable occasions for pious thoughts, expressing gratitude that God had spared him thus far, and hoping that he would remain in His good graces. When Otto turned fifteen, he recorded the visit of his Uncle Vockestaert and two distant cousins, but although Otto calls this "quite a company," it was not especially festive. His main entertainment, so he wrote, was a walk in the moonlight (July 5, 1794). Maybe Uncle Paulus's gift of a couple of weeks earlier had an ulterior motive. It was a toy printing set, the only gift recorded by Otto in all the years that he kept his diary. The year before Otto had also received his cob in the middle of June, and two years earlier he had been surprised with a goat in the same month. There seems to be a pattern to this; the actual birthdays were avoided. This picture is confirmed in other sources, including diaries.[44] There was no cult around birthdays, and as marks in time they were of inferior importance.

Neither was New Year's Eve, an important marking of time in the present era, a major holiday. Staying up till midnight, now such an important event in the child's life, was never mentioned by Otto. He did stay with his uncle Paulus on two occasions over the new year, and on New Year's Day would accompany his uncle in the carriage, "taking around cards." These were visiting cards, expressing the intention to pay a visit, the precursors of the modern season's greeting cards. Sometimes the new year would make Otto contemplative as in 1795: "Behold, (in a few hours, which will also pass very quickly) this year will be gone, for ever and ever. The main question each one must now ask himself is this one: 'How much good have we received from God this year and in what ways, by our actions, have we shown our gratitude.' Truly a weighty question, which we can neither consider nor answer without shame …"

The beginning of the new year marked both the cyclical and linear perception of time. This is also true of Otto's diary as a whole. The awareness of time that his parents wanted to give to him was modern and enlightened. Living by the clock, with the emphasis on useful employment of time, the sharp limitation of leisure time, all this breathes the spirit of modernism. But, by contrast, traditional time markings remained of importance, like the annual fairs and the changing of the seasons. New Year's Eve, the boundary between the new and the old, was a recurring moment of looking back and looking forward.

In spite of Otto's pious resolutions, prospects were bleak for the van Eck family in 1797. Lambert van Eck had made good progress in his career two years after the Batavian Revolution, but his rise was suddenly interrupted. Together with a number of other members of the National Assembly, he was imprisoned after a radical coup in 1798. That same year Otto caught a drawn-out cold which was eventually diagnosed as tuberculosis. As Otto's end drew near, Lambert van Eck was allowed to leave the prison under a military escort to be present at his son's deathbed. Otto's father left the report of his son's final days. The doctor had given up all hope. "Otto understood, or rather perceived this sentence with much resignation, prayed God for support as he was so unprepared to undertake the journey into eternity without his worldly guide (meaning me), but he trusted to His power that could still save him, and declared naively that this would please him infinitely better, if God would but wish it." But all hope was in vain.

On March 30, 1798, Otto died. Three days later he was buried in Scheveningen, at the cemetery called Ter Navolging [For Emulation].

The name of the cemetery seems cynical, but in fact it expressed the Enlightenment idea to place cemeteries outside built-up areas for hygienic reasons. Lambert van Eck was an early advocate of this manner of interment, and had been instrumental in the establishment of this burial ground in the dunes just a few years before. But he could not have foreseen that Otto was to be one of the first to lie there. His imprisonment, and the illness and death of his son had made Lambert van Eck lose all faith in progress, which had still sounded so proudly in the name of the cemetery. From prison he wrote to his wife that he had lost "all philosophy."[45] A few years later, he too exchanged this world for the eternal one.

Notes

This text is an adapted and translated version of an article published under the title of "Otto's horloge: Verlichting, deugd en tijd in de achttiende eeuw," in *Tijdschrift voor sociale geschiedenis* 25 (2000) 1–24. An earlier German version appeared in K. von Greyerz u.a. ed., *Von der dargestellten Person zum erinnerten Ich. Europäische Selbstzeugnisse als historische Quellen (1500–1800)* (Köln 2001), 113–135. These publications are part of our studies into the world of Otto van Eck, based on his diaries, also published by us, *Dagboek 1791–1797* (Hilversum: Verloren, 1998) and *Kind van de toekomst: De wondere wereld van Otto van Eck (1780–1789)* (Amsterdam: Wereldbibliotheek, 2005).Other related publications are: Arianne Baggerman, "Lezen tot de laatste snik: Otto van Eck en zijn dagelijkse literatuur (1780–1798)," in *Jaarboek voor Nederlandse boekgeschiedenis* 1 (1994) 57–89; Idem, "The cultural universe of a Dutch child: Otto van Eck and his literature," *Eighteenth Century Studies* 31 (1997) 129–134; Idem, "Otto en de anderen. Sporen van jonge lezers in schriftelijke bronnen," in: B. Dongelmans i.a. ed., *Tot volle waschdom. Nieuwe hoofdstukken voor de geschiedenis van de kinder- en jeugdliteratuur* (Zutphen: Biblion, 2000), 211–225; R. Dekker, *Uit de schaduw in 't grote licht. Kinderen in egodocumenten van de gouden eeuw tot de romantiek* (Amsterdam: Wereldbibliotheek, 1995). This paper was written thanks to a stay at the Institute for Advanced Study, Hebrew University Jerusalem and our contributions to the conference held there, "The History of Emotions" (June 1998). The title of this text refers to [A. Fokke], *Het onscheidbaar drietal redewezens verlichting, deugd en tijd, op eene zonderlinge zinspelende wijze geschetst* (Haarlem 1799) [*The Inseparable Trio of Concepts Enlightenment, Virtue and Time, Sketched in a Special Allusive Way*].

1. Arianne Baggerman, *Een lot uit de loterij: Uitgeverij A. Blussé en zoon 1744–1823* (The Hague: SDU, 2000).

2. G. J. Whitrow, *Time in History: The Evolution of our General Awareness of Time and Temporal Perspective* (Oxford:Oxford University Press, 1988) 148. Cf. Georges Poulet, Studies in Human Time (Baltimore: Johns Hopkins University Press, 1974) 158–184, on Rousseau: Mark J. Temmer, *Time in Rousseau and Kant: An Essay on French Pre-Romanticism* (Geneva: Droz, 1958). Cf. Rudolf Wendorff, *Zeit und Kultur: Geschichte des Zeitbewusstseins in Europa* (Opladen: Westdeutscher Verlag, 1980).

3. K.P.C. de Leeuw, M.F.A. Linders-Rooijendijk, and P.J.M. Martens eds., *Van ontspanning en inspanning: Aspecten van de geschiedenis van de vrije tijd* (Tilburg: Gianotten, 1995), especially the contributions by Linders-Rooijendijk and De Leeuw.

4. N. Chomel, *Vervolg op [...] algemeen huishoudelijk [...] woordenboek VI* (Campen/Amsterdam: J. A. De Chalmot, 1793), 6339–6344.

5. C.G. Salzmann, *Sebastian Kluge: Ein Volksbuch* (Leipzig: Crusius, 1790).

6. M.E. Bouée, dame de la Fite, *Entetriens, drames et contes moraux* (The Hague, 1788).

7. H. van Alphen, *Kleine gedigten voor kinderen*, P.J. Buijnsters ed. (Amsterdam: Delta, 1998), 39.

8. R. Koselleck, *Vergangene Zukunft: Zur Semantik geschichtlicher Zeiten* (Frankfurt: Suhrkamp, 1979), 63.

9. A survey of the subject, focusing on the situation in the Netherlands: R. H. Kielman, "'Geloof mij, het einde nadert." Tijdsbesef en toekomstperspectief rond 1800,' *Leidschrift* 14 (1999), 123–151.

10. *Woordenboek der Nederlandsche Taal* XVII, 1 (The Hague/Leiden: Nijhoff, 1960), 503–508.

11. H. Arthur, *The Idea of Decline in Western History* (New York: Free Press, 1997).

12. M. O'Malley, *Keeping Watch: A History of American Time* (New York: Viking, 1990).

13. *Encyclopédie ou dictionnaire raisonné des sciences, des arts et des métiers* XVI (Neufchate: Société typographique, 1765), 93–120.

14. G.J. Whitrow, *Time in History: The Evolution of Our General Awareness of Time and Temporal Perspective* (Oxford: Oxford University Press, 1988), 146.

15. Ph. Turetzky, *Time* (London: Routledge, 1998).

16. J. Locke, *An Essay Concerning Human Understanding* (orig. 1687) ed. by A. D. Woozley (London/Glasgow: Fontana/Collins, 1964), 144–153, esp. 145.

17. P. van Hemert, *Beginzels der Kantiaansche Wijsgeerte* (Amsterdam: Wed. J. Doll, 1796), review in *Vaderlandsche Letteroefeningen* (1796), 121.

18. 'Tijd,' in: N. Chomel and A. de Chalmot, *Algemeen huishoudelijk [...] woordenboek* (Leiden/Leeuwarden: J. A. De Chalmot, 1778) 3735–3736. A. Baggerman, 'Het boek dat andere boeken overbodig zou maken: De mislukte lancering van een achttiende-eeuwse Nederlandse encyclopedie,' *Jaarboek voor Nederlandse boekgeschiedenis* 6 (1999), 139–165, especially 149–152.

19. The second hand only found general application in the 19th century, see M. Elias, *Het horloge in den loop der eeuwen* (Zutphen: Thieme, 1935), 116.

On Dutch clocks, see J. Zeeman, *De Nederlandse staande klok* (Zwolle: Waanders, 1996).

20. O'Malley, *Keeping watch*, 8.
21. Review in *Vaderlandsche Letteroefeningen* (1793), II: 341.
22. Th. G. Hippel, *De man naar de klok* (Amsterdam: Pieter Meijer, 1780), translated from the German; reprinted Alkmaar 1792.
23. B. Wolff and A. Deeken, *Historie van den Heer Willem Leevend* 8 vols. (The Hagu: Isaac van Cleef, 1784–1785), III: 138.
24. Chomel and De Chalmot, *Woordenboek* I 399–403, here 401; P. Reinders and Th. Wijsenbeek, *Koffie in Nederland: Vier eeuwen cultuurgeschiedenis* (Zutphen: Walburg Pers, 1994), 107–108; J.J. Voskuil, 'De verspreiding van koffie in thee in Nederland,' *Volkskundig Bulletin* 14 (1988), 68–93.
25. P. 't Hoen, *Fabelen en kleine gedichten voor kinderen* (Amsterdam: De Ruijter, 1803), 33, "De morgenstond."
26. L. Mumford, *Technics and Civilization* (London: Routledge, 1934), 14.
27. C. Cipolla, *Clocks and Culture, 1300–1700* (New York: Collins, 1977). Cf. D. Landes, *Revolution in Time: Clocks and the Making of the Modern World* (Cambridge MA: Belknap Press., 1983).
28. G. Dohrn-van Rossum, *History of the Hour: Clocks and Modern Temporal Orders* (Chicago: University of Chicago, 1996).
29. A. van Overbeke, *Anecdota sive historiae jocosae. Een zeventiende-eeuwse verzameling moppen en anekdotes* ed. R. Dekker, H. Roodenburg and H.J. van Rees (Amsterdam: P. J. Meertens Instituut, 1991), nr. 1721.
30. J. LeGoff, "Au Moyen Age: temps de l'église et temps du marchand," *Annales ESC* 15 (1960), 417–423.
31. P.Th.R. Mestrom, *Uurwerken en uurwerkmakers in Limburg 1367–1850* (Maastricht/Leeuwarden: Eisma, 1997).
32. H. van Koolbergen, "De materiële cultuur van Weesp en Weesperkarspel in de zeventiende en achttiende eeuw," in: A. Schuurman i.a. ed., *Aards geluk: De Nederlanders en hun spullen van 1550 tot 1850* (Amsterdam: Balans, 1997) 121–161, met voetnoten tevens in *Volkskundig Bulletin* 9 (1983) 3–53.
33. Anonymous portrait, The Dutch Postage Museum, The Hague.
34. E. de Jongh, *Portretten van echt en trouw: Huwelijk en gezin in de Nederlandse kunst van de zeventiende eeuw* (Zwolle: Waanders, 1986), no. 32, 167–169; no. 53, 236–238, cf. a family portrait with an hourglass in a central position: Pieter Danckerts de Ry, "Oude vrouw met jongen," *Idem* p. 24.
35. Jan Luiken, *Het leerzaam huisraad* (Amsterdam: Wed. P. Arentz en K. Vander Sys, 1711), 64. In: Idem, *Spiegel van het menselyk bedryf* (Amsterdam: Weduwe Pieter Arentz, 1694) 65, "de orlosimaaker" was included, with a comparable moral: "… als 't gewicht is afgelaapen, van deese korte leevens tyd, daar is geen ophaal weer te koopen."
36. [A. Fokke], *Het onscheidbaar drietal redewezens verlichting, deugd en tijd, op eene zonderlinge zinspelende wijze geschetst* (Haarlem: Bohn, 1799).
37. Thera Wijsenbeek-Olthuis, *Achter de gevels van Delft: Bezit en bestaan van rijk en arm in een period van actheruitgang (1700—1800)* (Hilversum: Verloren, 1987, p. 462.

38. S. Sherman, *Telling time: Clocks, Diaries and English Diurnal from 1660–1785* (Chicago: University of Chicago Press, 1997).
39. C. Huygens, *Koren-bloemen: Nederlandsche gedichten* (Amsterdam: Johannes van Ravesteyn, 1672), II: 501.
40. C. Huygens den zoon, *Journaal van Constantijn Huygens den zoon* (Utrecht: Kemink, 1876), I: 373, 60.
41. C. Huygens den zoon, *Journaal van Constantijn Huygens den zoon* (Utrecht, 1876), I: 373; 60.
42. H. J. Rutz ed., *The Politics of Time* (American Ethnological Society monograph series no.4, 1992). See also the work by J. Fabian, *Time and the Work of Anthropology: Critical Essays 1971–1991* (Reading: Harwood, 1991).
43. G. J. Zollikofer (1730–1788), *Predigten* 2 vols. (Leipzig: Wedimanns Erben, 1772–1774). Otto probably read the translation *Leerredenen. Naar den tweeden druk in het Nederduitsch overgezet,* 11 vols. (Amsterdam: s.n. 1773–1789).
44. In the diary that the regent's son from Zeeland, Pieter Pous (1777–1851), kept from 1790 little attention is paid to birthdays. RA Zeeland, *Familiearchief Mathias-Pous-Tak van Poortvliet* 330–334.
45. RA Gelderland, FA Van Eck inv. 57, 15–3–1798.

14

THE SCHOOL OF LIFE

Reflections on Socialization in Preindustrial Germany

JÜRGEN SCHLUMBOHM

The history of childhood is sometimes seen as being shaped, in a fundamental way, by the change of communication media. Neil Postman, for example, has argued that the rise of childhood was closely related to the emergence of print media because print created a separate world for adults that children could only access through a long process of learning. From the late fifteenth to the early nineteenth century, the distinction of a special sphere of childhood was established for ever larger parts of Western societies: "The period between 1850 and 1950 represents the high-watermark of childhood." Since then, that special sphere has begun to disappear because electronic media make it impossible to keep the world of adults hidden from children.[1]

In this chapter, I plan to explore the extent to which the world of children was actually isolated from that of adults during the eighteenth and early nineteenth centuries in German-speaking countries, examining the role books and verbal communication played in the socialization of children. In undertaking such an analysis, I am particularly interested in the putative impact of print media and of verbal communication—contextualizing that impact in terms of social class and cultural contexts, probing the relationship between these and other factors that may have been overlooked in the arguments described above. I will not be attempting to provide a comprehensive survey of childhood in eighteenth- and nineteenth-century German-speaking countries, but, rather, will be presenting some observations and reflections that can serve as a starting point for a critical discussion of widely shared general views.

My main focus will be on the socialization process as it happened outside of the schools, a process for which there is not always abundant evidence.[2] Indeed, outside of more or less bureaucratic institutions like schools, there is no well-defined group of sources from which to start such an investigation. It is true that prescriptive texts, like decrees and laws, sometimes include statements (usually in the form of complaints) about common practices. Occasionally we find topographies published by doctors, pastors, or bureaucrats that contain useful observations about the "physical" and "moral" education of children. More often than not, however, such evidence is too general to be completely convincing. In some regards, autobiographical texts are best suited for our purpose. Not only do they frequently describe the author's childhood, they also tend to show, in explicit words or by the structure of the narrative, how early experience shaped a given writer.[3] This advantage is inseparable from the disadvantage that these connections are constructed and selected in retrospect. Here letters, diaries, and family papers can serve as a complement, although in general they are available only for educated and well-to-do families.[4] Such documents were roughly contemporaneous with the events they described. In spite of this fact, even the most intimate diary and the most spontaneous family letter will end up structuring and stylizing the events they depict, this according to the perspective of the author and the anticipated expectations of the addressee.

The School of Life

Let us first consider the world of ordinary peasants' and townspeople's children, that is, the great majority, not the elites. There we find ample evidence suggesting that print media, writing, and verbal communication in general had a rather limited impact, and that the world of children was not clearly separated from that of adults. Friedrich Paulsen was born as a peasant's son in the north of Germany during the first half of the nineteenth century, in the period called the "high-watermark of childhood" by Postman. To give a sense of his life and writing, I quote his memoir at length, where he writes that he was

formed ... not so much by speaking and listening, than by direct participation in the whole range of life and activity, which my parents' house encompassed. ... There, the whole world was present, as a living reality: Nature with all the riches of her forms and products was accessible and familiar to us. ... We knew it, not from a short Sunday afternoon excursion, but from daily and most intimate acquaintance. We have waded through, and fished in, every ditch. ... We have ploughed on every field, and worked in every fen. ... We had the rain rush down upon us, and in the burning sunshine we lay naked in the sand. We have romped on horseback, we have taken many a wild ride without saddle and bridle. ... We have caught fish with nets and snares. Listening to the birds, we have found their nests, we have taken the eggs from the lapwings and partridges. ... In short, the whole of nature was within the reach not only of our eyes, but also of our hands and feet, we lived with it as a part of it. And as nature, so was the whole of human existence within our range, near, palpable, understandable. All the elementary arts of culture had their place in the household; ... we saw ... all [the things] being made, ... the bread and the beer, the shirt and the jacket. Almost nothing came into our orbit of which we did not know from our own experience how it was produced. ... And it was not much different with human conditions, the private and the public ones. ... In the village, everybody knows about each other, not only since yesterday and the day before, but since his parents and grandparents. You see the conditions from which he has emerged, under which he lives, his wife and children, his home and his work, his thriving and his failure. ... And similarly with public affairs. I knew the district officer (*Landvogt*) and the actuary in [the town of] Bredstedt ... I knew the officers of the community and the parish assembly ...; my father had had the office for many years, and I had helped him as a hodman and messenger. I knew about legal transactions, about mortgages and stamped papers, about purchase deeds and leases. From an early age, such documents passed through my hands. Similarly with taxes and duties ... I knew about all these things by my own experience and view, before I first heard the names of 'state' and 'society': in Frisian language, there are no words for them. Social structure was also

simple and transparent to us. The village was a community of life, easy
to overlook. The independent peasant holdings formed the supporting
skeleton. The trades leaned on them. ... A third group was formed by
the pastor, the teacher, the doctor, the officer. ... Similarly, social strati-
fication, class formation was evident in its primitive form. There were
land-rich peasants ... who did not do any physical work themselves; then
a very large layer of middling peasants who regularly participated in agricultural toil, to a greater or smaller degree; then a layer of small owners
who ... earned an additional income as carters, retailers, day labourers or
artisans. Finally, there were the actual day labourers. ... And last, on the
margin, a very small layer of poor people. Most of them had come down
by sickness or misfortune, other families were ruined by their own fault,
by drinking and laziness. They lived on occasional jobs and begging.
Some inmates of the poorhouse, disabled old people, unprovided, usually
illegitimate, children, cripples, idiots were at the tail.[5]

These are only short excerpts from five pages of a panegyric on a
type of children's life that was characterized by inclusion, in which all
the senses were active, words were not dominant, but active participation in the world was crucial.[6] Implicitly, Paulsen constructed a hierarchy of the modes of learning, based in part on a hierarchy of the senses.
Learning by doing, by using one's hands and feet, was best; next came
seeing things and actions; learning by listening and by reading was
much less valued; learning at school appeared as only the last
resort—which may seem surprising coming from a nineteenth-century
German professor of pedagogy. (This is what Paulsen had become.[7])
The counterpart to Paulsen's narrative of his own experience was, of
course, childhood and life in big cities, which he characterized in terms
of print media: "How abstract and superficial and scanty are the
notions of the child in a big city. He sees nature only on paper, the picture book and the school manual give pale representations of field and
forest, of animals and plants. ... Compared to learning by participation, what effect can school lessons have which, if it please God, the
child in a city receives on the 'services done by the Hohenzollern
dynasty to the middle-class and peasants' or about the 'depravity of the
social democratic doctrines'? Or what can such a child learn from
newspapers or talks?" (see figure 14.1). For the son of a peasant, the

balance was easy to strike. Paulsen notes that "an ever increasing portion of our nation" grows up in big cities, leading to a "progressive deprivation of youth," not only to a "deprivation with regard to joy," but also a "deprivation with regard to chances for education."

Fig. 14.1 Picture books taught middle and upper class children about animals which peasants' children knew from daily experience: "Several species of mice," including the domestic mouse (1) and the field-mouse (8). Friedrich Bertuch, *Bilderbuch zum Nutzen und Vergnügen der Jugend*. Prague: Peter Bohmanns Erben, 1822–1827, volume three, "Tiere," plate XLVII. Reproduced by permission of the Cotsen Children's Library, Princeton University Library.

Even if not all contemporaries agreed with this assessment, many other sources confirm that, at least for children in the countryside, non-verbal and nonpedagogical modes of learning prevailed. "The school of life has brought him up," said the professor of public law Sylvester Jordan about his own childhood, as a son of an illiterate shoemaker in a Tyrolean village at the end of the eighteenth century.[8]

What did the "school of life" teach children? Corporal toil came first for many, probably for the majority of children. Friedrich Paulsen underlined the variety of jobs as they changed over the course of a day or the seasons of the year. Some authors describe a sequence of stages according to ages: from the fourth year of his life, a boy accompanies the cowboy; at the age of six, he becomes a gooseherd; aged nine, he advances to the rank of a cowboy; at twelve he is promoted to be a stableboy; at the age of sixteen, he becomes a junior farmhand.[9] Jobs could only be so varied for the sons of peasants who owned substantial holdings; poor households did not require or offer such a broad range of tasks. Especially in the families who were involved in cottage indus-try, work was specialized and monotonous. A well-known example is the production of toys. Here the children of the rural poor contributed greatly to the manufacturing of articles that well-to-do children used for play.[10] Wherever working space and living space were not sepa-rated from each other, work was the main activity of family life, at least in terms of time spent on it. This is true for peasants as well as for most rural and urban artisans.

It is "not for moral reasons" that parents of this kind "exhort their children to ... work ...., but because of the ever-present desire for gain," remarked a clergyman from a rural industrial area.[11] But in most cases, it may have been more a matter of survival than of gain, and of course parents were evenly yoked with heavy workloads. Sylvester Jordan recalled this function of children without sentimentalizing. His parents had "some pieces of land and some meadows, which they cultivated— as they did not own any *draught animals*—with the help of their chil-dren."[12] Severe punishment threatened those who did not complete their quota of work. In the spinning trade, for example, a child would have a thread wound around his or her finger which would then be set alight.[13] As it was for adults, toil was often a heavy burden to children. But the extent and type of the workload varied considerably according to circumstances; so did the perception and recollection of it. Even Paulsen, whose memoirs were so good-tempered, did not gloss over in silence the fact that, as a boy, he "bitterly hated" harrowing: "Hardly anything is more fatiguing than stumbling a whole long day across the furrows of the freshly ploughed field." But there were many other jobs that he liked. The professor's narrative reveals how proud he was of what he had learned as a boy: "I have piled up hundreds of loads of hay and grain, with the pleasure which a skilled hand feels about his achievement. This job is not just so easy as a layman might imagine. A sense of balance and junction is required for making sure that a high cartload does not fall or slide on worn-down and uneven roads." Advancing with age to more demanding and more highly valued tasks gave satisfaction. After young Friedrich had helped his father as a "plough boy ... who governs the horses" for some years, he "later ... handled the plough himself, which he liked much better" than harrowing.[14]

Poor people's children often had to work outside their parents' home for other people from an early age. This was the case of Sylvester Jordan, to whom "no kind of toil remained alien": "It was precisely in his most tender age that he was strained in an almost incredible way by jobs of all sorts, including the most disgusting ones;" he "even had to work by the day as a thresher and flax-braker."[15] Paulsen did remark the difference between his own experience of helping his parents with a whole range of jobs that changed with the seasons, and the fate of poorer boys and girls, who worked in other people's households as servants in a more or less permanent way: "After the tasks of spring, a major break in the work in the fields began about mid-May and lasted until early July. During this time, I had hardly anything to do and went to school again. The number of children at school had usually melted down considerably. The bigger children, starting with age twelve or even earlier, boys and girls, either went into service after Easter for the summer period, or they were employed at home. The poorer ones were usually hired out as herdsboys in far-away villages. ..."[16] In some regions, there were real "children's markets" in which big numbers of boys and girls tried to find a place as herdsmen, nurses, or servants. Such was the case in Upper Swabia where children came from Tyrolea and Western Austria (Vorarlberg).[17]

Some of those who looked back to a childhood full of toil remembered that, from an early age, contributing to their family's survival had been a source of self-confidence. The son of a widow who worked in the cottage industries recalled: "The boy was ... a living member of the family, working and suffering with the others, contributing, if only by the means of his apparently insignificant labours, towards the household's livelihood."[18]

In addition to work, there is still another field in which children learned by doing and actively participating, one that is easily overlooked if we focus too much on childhood in well-to-do and educated families of the middle class. I am talking of children's peer groups, be they loose and fluctuating or tightly knit. In part, this sociability of children was bound up with work: in herding cattle or picking berries or gathering wood for heating, several children went together.[19] By contrast, children met in the gaps between their work tasks, played together, and shared a sphere of freedom. It appears that life in peer groups was more developed for boys, but girls could enjoy it as well.[20] We hear about this part of children's life in towns and cities as well as in the countryside. In its radical form, however, this sphere was not accessible to children of the middle class and the nobility.[21] Many an autobiographer remembered it as the most wonderful aspect of his childhood, whereas pedagogues, doctors, and authorities tended to look at it with anxiety (see Figure 14.2). The basic characteristics of children's peer groups in preindustrial times were: First, they were neither looked after, nor pedagogically guided by adults. A baker's son recalled: "How much have we played as little boys, and none of us had ever seen a book of plays or a picture book! We played everything in the world and imitated it in children's play ...—all that without a teacher. ... Yea, we acted as legislators, without Parliament. ..." To him, "the unsupervised freedom of the street" had been the "happiest freedom" enjoyed during childhood.[22] Second, street life was accessible to children from a very early age. Some observers saw three-year-olds among the street children: "In the countryside, ... parents usually let their children stroll around right after their third year of life, without any supervision, all day long."[23] Others remarked even that children began to "run about in the streets ... without supervision" as soon as they could walk.[24] Finally, the plays and activities had their own rules and laws, made and implemented by the children themselves. "We observed these rules more strictly than written laws," wrote one autobiographer.[25] Some remembered the order of the boys' group as strictly egalitarian: "Boys are born republicans, they have equality amongst themselves, they know only the domination of their own power and are always ready to resist any other authority in their sphere."[26] Others, however, recalled that the difference between the children of poor and those of well-to-do villagers did matter even in street life, although it could be overcome to some extent by physical strength.[27]

For boys, fighting between more or less tightly knit groups was one of the most prominent activities. They defended the territory that they claimed to be theirs, be it a neighborhood in a town or the mark of a village. This dynamic is particularly visible in, but not limited to,

Fig. 14.2 Mischievous boys, playing in the street without adult supervision, were presented as a warning by enlightened educators. Their behavior was as punishable as that of the drunkard who destroyed a window, and at whom the urchins threw dirt, or as that of the thief who stole eggs from the woman's basket, or that of the other thief who stole the former's hat. Detail from the engraving by Daniel Chodowiecki, *Kupfersammlung zu J. B. Basedows Elementarwerke für die Jugend und ihre Freunde.* Berlin and Dessau, 1774, table XXXII. Reproduced by permission of the Cotsen Children's Library, Princeton University Library.

the formal peer groups of adolescents.[28] For adults, such groups of children could be "like an anarchic band of robbers" who took the fruit they wanted from the fields and orchards. Karl Rosenkranz, the Hegelian philosopher, who had grown up in the town of Magdeburg around 1800, even depicted himself and his childhood friends as "little communists."[29] The view that the needs of subsistence should prevail over the property rights of the few was, however, part of the vision of a "moral economy,"[30] and was still widely shared, except for among the middle classes. Insofar as this free life of children was not opposed to the values of the adult world, it can be seen as a way to appropriate those values. "The forest was my home," wrote Georg Weber, who grew up as the son of a poor artisan's widow. "With climbing-irons, which I strapped to my feet with leather ties and whose sharp hooks I pressed into the bark, I was able to swarm up the highest slick trunks like a squirrel in order to cut off dead branches in the tree-tops with a hatchet. This provided for the wood which our home needed. ... The rangers of the forest disliked me very much. Several times I was accused at the town court, and sometimes even arrested for some days in the jail because my mother could not pay the fine. I did not feel that I had committed a punishable deed. The inhabitants of villages near forests have the notion that the forest belongs to the people and that using the wood for household needs is allowed. Shutting the forest to them, where they pick wood and berries, appeared to them as a great wrong. ... In the perception of the people, the forest is common property of everybody, like water and sunlight. It is considered the right of the poor, to use the gifts of nature for their vital needs."[31]

Not My Wds?

"With regard to speech, he was reticent. Even when he did not have has his day of silence—and he had many of them in the course of a year—he did not say many words." This is what Friedrich Paulsen reports of his father, pointing out implicitly how limited the place of verbal communication was in the rural way of life that he had experienced as a child. Paulsen's mother, however, was of a different nature. She had been seized by the religious Awakening, tried to pass on her faith to her son and "therefore liked to tell about how she had found the way of peace—as she was generally more inclined to talk about her inner experience than father was."

During the early modern period, and well into the nineteenth century, the spoken language in rural areas of Germany and even in towns and cities, as far as ordinary people are concerned, was not the language of books, that is, not High German, but a dialect. Young Paulsen thus had to function in three different languages: "The language in my parental home was Frisian. ... In addition, my ear and tongue got used to Low German, from an early age; it was the language of the home in quite a few families. ... I think, I have learnt to *speak* High German only at school; I could understand and read it already earlier. I had hardly acquired a reliable proficiency in it, before, at age eighteen, I was compelled to speak it daily to my class mates at the Gymnasium in Altona." The three languages functioned as media in distinct, though partially overlapping spheres of communication: "High German was the language of the church, the school and the state. ... Low German was the language of the town, the market, and, increasingly, of the family as well. Frisian, the old native language of the population, was but the language of the home and the village."[32]

In spite of all qualifications, Paulsen did not conceal from his readers that for him, and in some regards for his parents, too, books did matter. At age three, he found a primer among his modest Christmas gifts: "I do not know when I began to study the alphabet, tutored by my mother. ... Anyway, when I started school in the fifth year of my life, I could read perfectly." Rather in passing, Paulsen mentions that his parents owned more books than just the Bible and the Prayer book. His mother had collected quite a few books of devotion and of sermons, whereas his father owned "a small selection" of "historical and geographical literature." Every evening, the father read a section from a book of devotion to his family. On Sunday, it was often the son's turn. "On Sunday afternoon, when my fellows played outside, I often had to read aloud a sermon. That is, it was not a strict order, but the unspoken wish [of my mother], which I hated about as much to fulfill as to elude." Most "horrible" to the boy was the fat volume in quarto with the sermons "by the old August Hermann Francke," the head of the Halle Pietists. For when this book was chosen, he was sure "not to be released before an hour. ... The eighteenth century had time and insisted that clergymen did not eat their bread idly." In spite of this fact, some light reading fell into young Friedrich's hands, whereas his parents despised novels, "stories, which are not true." The first book of this type was an edition of *Robinson Crusoe*. Aged seven or eight, he read it with "passion" and since, unlike his father, he had "a strong drive towards communication" each time he had "read a section, he first went into the thrashing floor and told the farmhands how Robinson was getting on." Soon the boy was seized by "a strong desire for reading." It was fed by the teacher's "circulating library." A new world was opened to the boy by the tales in "popular calendars and similar products," later by "juvenile stories, texts concerning natural sciences and history as well as first pieces of German and Nordic literature." This world was increasingly attractive to young Paulsen: "With a book in my hands, I have often looked for a hidden place, inside or outside of the house, in order not to be discovered and called for a work task or an errand."[33]

Other children in the countryside also learnt to read before going to school, or independent of school. This was true of Sylvester Jordan, although both his parents did not know how to read and write. "In his seventh year, he went to the poorly organised village school during winter—there was no school in summer. He could not even learn to read at this school. ... But in the course of summer he made much progress, with the help of his elder brother ... as well as of persons who came to his father's house to bring or fetch shoes to be repaired or to talk politics with his father, for example about the French war. Now he was able to read the Sunday text fluently to his parents from the gospel, which they had bought for him. He learnt how to write in the same way. ... He was encouraged to read and write especially by his paternal uncle, called Franz, a popular folk poet."[34]

Significantly, some children from poor and distressed families remembered later that by reading books "a completely new world" was opened to them. Such was the case of Karl Friedrich Klöden, who grew up as son of a noncommissioned officer and subordinate official, and later became director of a technical school. For him, like for many in the late eighteenth century, Joachim Heinrich Campe's German version of Daniel Defoe's *Robinson Crusoe* was the key to this new world. Not only did his "knowledge of the world, of persons and of things" grow by reading this book: "How wonderful, how pure and noble did the idea of an educational institution appear to me in a family like Campe's: There, pupils were so eager for knowledge and asked such sensible questions; parents and friends taught so willingly and so decently, and all means of instruction were at hand. To me, this juvenile life appeared to be completely different from mine! I had had no idea of such a higher existence, and realized only now how much was missing to me, what a noble form family life and instruction could reach. It was a flash of lightning, falling into a dark night. But it did not blind, it enlightened and has lighted through all my life."[35] On the one hand, reading books like novels from the humble local lending library could make a child, who experienced "a hard youth full of toil and hardship," forget "the difficulties of real life" for some time.[36] On the other hand, for many an autobiographer coming from a poor laboring family, the sphere of reading and writing represented the higher world into which he strove to climb. It was in this way that kin and neighbors perceived a child from the lower classes who was particularly interested in books. When little Friedrich Paulsen, while visiting relatives, was attracted most of all by his deceased grandfather's big bookcase, and "for hours turned over the leaves and read in these treasures," his aunts would say: "He will be a pastor, he is not fit for being a peasant."[37]

Childhood Protected and Controlled

The children of the educated middle class, and to some extent those of well-to-do families as well, were already born into the world in which words and books played a crucial part. Not coincidentally, in this social context the life of children was usually much more insulated from the influences of the adult world. Here children did not have to work and contribute to the economic survival of the household. Because, for many middle-class professions, work increasingly moved into spaces outside the family home, many children did not know their father's work from their own experience, but only by conversations at the family table. Economic and public activities were not visible to the child in the way which Paulsen described with regard to rural society. The reasons are not only the more complex structures of the middle class's economy and public sphere, but also a strong tendency towards seclusion of the family, and a sustained effort to confine children in the sphere of domesticity, especially, but not exclusively, young children and girls.

In the eighteenth century, the isolation of children in the home could sometimes be extreme, like in the case of the later historian Johann Friedrich Böhmer. He grew up, as son of a jurist, in Frankfurt on the river Main—and saw the river first at the age of eleven. This was not on a walk he did by himself—"walking alone" was considered as "indecent for children," but during one of the Sunday "promenades," in which the family showed itself to the public in Sunday clothes and in a regular order (see Figure 14.3). In terms of knowledge, young Johann Friedrich did not actually have to see the river with his own eyes, for it was "known to him already that it flows past the city." In spite of this fact, he kept this early summer day in mind "for ever as one of his sweetest reminiscences." When looking across the river to the wealth of flowers on the hills, he "was suddenly seized by a deep longing for nature, and he began to weep, and came home stirred up in his very heart. This was reason enough for his worrying mother not to allow promenades of this kind for the rest of the year, 'because the air was no good for the boy.' If the boy wanted to go out, he had to content himself with the small garden behind the house. There he planted a small tree, in memory of the promenade on the river Main, and in his notes he reported its growth." For this boy, the "parental home" was "like a locked castle."[38]

The sphere of domesticity was much more spacious for the middle class than for ordinary people. Above all, it was more strictly marked off by walls, fences, and intensive control. This was a vital precondition for bringing up children according to a consistent scheme, as middle-class parents in the eighteenth century increasingly tried to do. Karl Rosenkranz recognized this fact particularly well, as he had grown up under different conditions and had enjoyed street life very much: "For the independence of the families it is to be desired that each had a house of their own. ... Only in such a family home is a consistent upbringing of children possible, because alien influences cannot intrude so easily."[39]

Fig. 14.3 Children of the educated middle class learned about nature on promenades, guided and taught by parents or teachers. Christian Felix Weisse, *Der Kinderfreund: Ein Wochenblatt,* XCIII. Stück bey 12 April 1777, Leipzig: Siegfried Lebrecht Crusius, 1777, plate facing p. 21. Reproduced by permission of the Cotsen Children's Library, Princeton University Library.

Soon, however, parents and pedagogues noticed that too strict an isolation of children in an enclosed domestic sphere could have undes- ired side effects. On the one hand, it was a matter of physical health. Now "physical exercises" (*Leibesübungen*), directed and supervised by an instructor in a special "exercise area," were to reap the benefits of play in the street while avoiding the "dangers."[40] "The advantages of the street" were to be "moved into the courtyard, the garden or even into the room," as one pedagogical writer said.[41] On the other hand, too little contact with other children could lead to "shyness" and "awkwardness in social intercourse," which was the case of Johann Friedrich Böhmer.[42] For these reasons, some middle-class parents began to allow at least their sons to play in the street with other boys, although not at such a young age as children of the laboring poor.[43]

Most of these parents found that the influence of the peer group on their children remained limited because relations within the family were so intensive and because learning at school and in a school-like manner was so important. Many middle class parents tried to shape family life according to pedagogical concerns, and to distinguish con- sciously what to do and discuss in the presence of children, and what in their absence. Family meals exemplify these efforts: the seating order, attitude, rank order in access to food and in conversation—all this was meant to put on stage the family as a hierarchically ordered, as well as an intimate, tightly knit microcosm.[44]

In a case that the author presented like a model family, the father, who was "an absolute autocrat in his house," inspired his children with "awe" mixed, however, with "cordial love." Compared to him, the mother appeared to the son as "a gentle calm character, full of humility and love." As a consequence, the son's affection for both his parents was clearly gradated: "The love of my parents, especially that of my ten- der mother, has made me reciprocate with love." The father endeavored to treat his children consistently according to pedagogical principles. His son reminisced: "Rarely, our father ordered or forbade anything to us, and even less frequently he punished us. But his affectionate grave attitude towards us implied a non-spoken demand for modesty, discipline and obedience, which we found impossible to resist." The mother, too, guided the children less by words than "by the example of her behaviour." "A single glance" from her side could "deeply shame and thoroughly stir" the son. Thus the constellation of father, mother, and son was shaped in a way as to favor the internalization of norms. Originally, the father's "order" had been "external and burdensome" to the son. "But soon it became an interior drive for me, which carried the moving power in itself." Even the "company of other mischievous boys" and later the "company of other ... boyish adolescents" who were full of "pride" and "idle chatter" could not lastingly lead him away from this path.[45]

To be sure, not all fathers were actually present in their families to the extent as the clergyman whose son wrote down this report about his parental home. But the stereotype that fathers were not interested in their children as long as they were small is not generally true either. At least in the late eighteenth and early nineteenth centuries, some middle-class fathers read medical and pedagogical advice books about infants. From the very beginning, they wanted to be involved in the discussion about the upbringing of children, if not in the actual handling of them.[46] Not only mothers but also fathers spent time with their baby children and wrote down notes about their development. The Hamburg jurist Ferdinand Beneke kept a diary about his daughter Emma, and when she was hardly a month old, he proudly noted that he was not only an affectionate but even a useful father: "She seems to have a special instinctive inclination to me. When she cries and nobody can lull her, I only need to take her in my arm and sing a song for her, and she is quiet and even delighted. I almost believe to perceive a sense of music in her."[47]

The way in which mothers and fathers cared for their children was modified from their early days by gendered expectations. It was not by coincidence that Beneke recorded signs of musicality in his daughter. A merchant's widow noted about her seven-year-old daughter "above all the talent to charm and delight those who are with her. Sunny cheerfulness of her nature, grace in every movement, skill in all kinds of tasks, and a musical ear which shows up in singing and reciting." Sons were praised for more active, and to some extent aggressive, modes of behavior. They were expected to be successful at school, as a first step to a professional career.[48] The training in "female" kinds of work for daughters was no less demanding, and usually it was mothers who laid this claim on them. Therefore, some daughters reminisced that "although we loved our mother very much, we almost feared her even more, more than our father, who actually was much sterner."[49] Middle-class parents usually did not expect their sons to participate in housework or in caring for younger siblings. The difference between males and females seems to be more strictly defined in the middle than in the lower classes. With the latter, housework and "real" work was more blurred, and sometimes sons had to look after their younger brothers or sisters.[50] Occasionally the sense for difference was particularly strong on the margins between socio-cultural spheres. The son of an impoverished merchant's widow, who was the daughter of a clergyman, reports how forcefully his mother insisted that her family continued to appear as belonging to the "better sort" (*feinere Klasse*). Clothing, hairstyle, and High German language were important symbols of this. The daughters had to help her mother with knitting stockings for a merchant-manufacturer, although the mother tried to hide this labor from outsiders as much as possible. The son, however, remembered: "I could not earn (*erwerben*) anything. ... Again and again, I heard the reproach that I ate and cost the family money, but did not earn anything. It hurt me, but how should I have earned anything?"[51] This boy's feeling of being incapable is in striking contrast to some sons in the laboring classes who were proud of being able to help their widowed mothers by earning money.[52]

Although the written and printed word was clearly more important for middle-class children[53] than for those in the lower classes, the lived order embodied in the practical and symbolic actions of their everyday world nevertheless had a more fundamental impact, even on the children of the educated middle class. In the middle class this world was, above all, the family, whereas for many other children, peer group and street life could be as important as the family.

It should not be overlooked, however, that there were ruptures, dislocations, and contradictions in middle-class experiences of childhood, as in any other. They could be caused by the death of a parent, the resulting gap, or difficulties with a stepparent. Contradictions may have been felt particularly strongly where the expectation was for parents to act in a consistent and disciplined way and to be a model for their children. A fascinating example is the "psychological novel"

Anton Reiser published 1785–1790 by Karl Philipp Moritz, a text that is strongly autobiographical.[54]

A final point is in order here, as attempting to give a survey of a vast field always runs the risk of oversimplifying. I want to emphasize that there was not only a great deal of variance in every sociocultural group (however defined), but that probably every individual child experienced discontinuities in his or her life (to a greater or lesser extent) and was subject to different claims from various persons and institutions. Every child, moreover, was likely to have sensed ambivalences and contradictions in the behavior of significant persons around him or her. It would have always required an active effort of the child and adolescent to construe a more or less coherent concept of his or her life. When writing memoirs, most authors record the positive result of this endeavor, often in the form of a success story about upward mobility.[55] Whereas an autobiographical text, once written or even published, has a fixed shape, the inner concepts of one's life are changing all the time and can easily be shaken. Therefore, we should perhaps not expect too much consistency between various modes and contexts of learning but, rather, look for traces of heterogeneous elements and contradictions. That, however, is the stuff of another essay.

Notes

1. Neil Postman, *The Disappearance of Childhood,* (New York: Delacorte Press, 1982), p. 67.
2. Introductions into historical studies of socialisation include Andreas Gestrich, *Vergesellschaftungen des Menschen: Einführung in die Historische Sozialisationsforschung,* (Tübingen: edition diskord, 1999); Ulrich Herrmann, "Historische Sozialisationsforschung," in Klaus Hurrelmann and Dieter Ulich, eds., *Handbuch der Sozialisationsforschung,* 5th ed., (Weinheim: Beltz, 1998), pp. 231–250.
3. See, e.g., Jürgen Schlumbohm, "Constructing Individuality: Childhood Memories in Late Eighteenth-century 'Empirical Psychology' and Auto-biography," *German History* 16 (1998): 29–42.
4. German examples: Anne-Charlott Trepp, *Sanfte Männlichkeit und selbstän-dige Weiblichkeit: Frauen und Männer im Hamburger Bürgertum zwischen 1770 und 1840,* (Göttingen: Vandenhoeck, 1996); Rebekka Habermas, *Frauen und Männer des Bürgertums: Eine Familiengeschichte (1750–1850),* (Göttingen: Vandenhoeck, 2000).
5. Friedrich Paulsen, *Aus meinem Leben,* Jena: Diederichs, 1909, pp. 54–59, also for what follows. There is an English translation: Friedrich Paulsen,

An Autobiography, tr. and ed. Theodor Lorenz, (New York: Columbia University Press, 1938). In this chapter, however, references are to the German original, and the translations from Paulsen and other German sources are mine.

6. The classical reference for this point is Philippe Ariès, *Centuries of Childhood: a Social History of Family Life*, New York: Knopf, 1962; French original: Paris 1960; cf. Wilhelm Roessler, *Die Entstehung des modernen Erziehungswesens in Deutschland*, (Stuttgart: Kohlhammer, 1961).

7. On the connection between young Paulsen's experiences and his later pedagogical views, which opposed the exclusive predominance of ancient languages in the Prusso-German *Gymnasium*, see Reinhard Kränsel, *Die Pädagogik Friedrich Paulsens*, (Bredstedt: Nordfriisk Instituut, 1973); cf. Dieter Stüttgen, *Pädagogischer Humanismus und Realismus in der Darstellung Friedrich Paulsens*, (Alsbach/Bergstraße: Leuchtturm-Verl., 1993); Edgar Weiß, *Friedrich Paulsen und seine volksmonarchistisch-organizistische Pädagogik im zeitgenössischen Kontext*, (Frankfurt/Main: Lang, 1999).

8. Article "Sylvester Jordan," in Karl Wilhelm Justi, *Grundlage zu einer hessischen Gelehrten-, Schriftsteller- und Künstlergeschichte vom Jahre 1806 bis zum Jahre 1830*, vol. 19, (Marburg: Garthe, 1831), pp. 290–313, quote 290.

9. "Die Erziehung des Lippischen Landmanns (1789)," in Jürgen Schlumbohm, ed., *Kinderstuben: Wie Kinder zu Bauern, Bürgern, Aristokraten wurden 1700–1850*, (Munich: dtv, 1983), pp. 81–87.

10. Ingeborg Weber-Kellermann, *Die Kindheit: Kleidung und Wohnen, Arbeit und Spiel: Eine Kulturgeschichte*, (Frankfurt am Main: Insel, 1979), pp. 208ff.

11. Johann Jakob Simmler, "Versuch einer Beschreibung der Grafschaft Toggenburg … (1785)," in Schlumbohm, *Kinderstuben*, pp. 88–95, quote 92.

12. Jordan, p. 293. Emphasis added.

13. Eduard Schoneweg, *Das Leinengewerbe in der Grafschaft Ravensberg*, (Bielefeld: Gundlach, 1923), p. 101.

14. Paulsen, pp. 48, 52. The son of a peasant who was active not only in agriculture, but also as a baker and innkeeper and thus ran a particularly versatile economy, reports: "My father had implemented a classification of tasks and activities …, which were distributed among the children. Every year, each child rose to a higher class. … In this way, we were accustomed to a specific task, and the parents did not have to force, threaten or scold us. A hint was often enough to set each child to painstaking work. Moreover, this scheme had the positive effect that we considered the higher class of tasks as a honourable distinction, and looked forward to the subsequent year when we should advance further. At least I remember clearly how much this sort of ambition motivated me." Johann Baptist Schad, *Lebensgeschichte*, vol. 1, 2nd ed. (Altenburg: Hofbuchdruckerei, 1828), p. 9.

15. Jordan, p. 293.

16. Paulsen, p. 49.

17. Otto Uhlig, *Die Schwabenkinder aus Tirol und Vorarlberg*, Innsbruck: Wagner, 1978. On child labor in general see Marjatta Rahikainen,

Centuries of Child Labour: European Experiences from the Seventeenth to the Twentieth Century, (Aldershot: Ashgate, 2004).

18. Heinrich Koenig, *Auch eine Jugend*, (Leipzig: Brockhaus, 1852), p. 61.

19. Paulsen, p. 49; Georg Weber, in Irene Hardach-Pinke and Gerd Hardach, eds., *Kinderalltag: Deutsche Kindheiten in Selbstzeugnissen 1700–1900*, (Reinbek: Rowohlt, 1981), p. 265.

20. Susanne Mutschler, *Ländliche Kindheit in Lebenserinnerungen: Familien- und Kinderleben in einem württembergischen Arbeiterbauerndorf an der Wende vom 19. zum 20. Jahrhundert*, (Tübingen: Tübinger Vereinigung für Volkskunde, 1985), pp. 85 ff., 91 ff.; cf. Schlumbohm, *Kinderstuben*, p. 222.

21. Jürgen Schlumbohm, "'Traditional' Collectivity and 'Modern' Individuality: Some Questions and Suggestions for the Historical Study of Socialization: The Examples of the German Lower and Upper Bourgeoisies around 1800," *Social History* 5 (1980): 71–103; idem, *Kinderstuben*, pp. 9ff., 72ff., 220ff., 312ff.; Jürgen Zinnecker, "Straßensozialisation. Versuch, einen unterschätzten Lernort zu thematisieren," *Zeitschrift für Pädagogik* 25 (1979): 727–746; idem, "Vom Straßenkind zum verhäuslichten Kind. Kindheitsgeschichte im Prozeß der Zivilisation," in Imbke Behnken, ed., *Stadtgesellschaft und Kindheit im Prozeß der Zivilisation: Konfigurationen städtischer Lebensweise zu Beginn des 20. Jahrhunderts*, (Opladen: Leske und Budrich, 1990), pp. 142–162; Imbke Behnken and Agnes Jonker, "Straßenspielkinder in Wiesbaden und Leiden: Historische Ethnographie und interkultureller Vergleich," in ibid., pp. 163–200.

22. Heinrich Hansjakob, *Aus meiner Jugendzeit*, (Stuttgart: Bonz, 1910), pp. 115, 117.

23. Johann Peter Frank, *System einer vollständigen medicinischen Polizey*, (Mannheim: Schwan, 1780), vol. 2, p. 267.

24. A. F. Nolde, *Medicinisch-anthropologische Bemerkungen über Rostock und seine Bewohner*, (Erfurt: Henning, 1807), vol. 1, pp. 108–109.

25. Karl Friedrich von Klöden, *Jugenderinnerungen*, Max Jähns, ed., (Leipzig: Grunow, 1874), quoted from Schlumbohm, *Kinderstuben*, p. 274.

26. Adam Henß, *Wanderungen und Lebensansichten*, (Jena: Frommann, 1845), p. 70.

27. Otto Krille, in Hardach-Pinke and Hardach, p. 211. This refers to the second half of the nineteenth century, however.

28. John R. Gillis, *Youth and History: Tradition and Change in European Age Relations 1770 - Present*, (New York: Academic Press, 1974), pp. 26 ff.; Andreas Gestrich, *Traditionelle Jugendkultur und Industrialisierung: Sozialgeschichte der Jugend in einer ländlichen Arbeitergemeinde Württembergs 1800–1920*, (Göttingen: Vandenhoeck, 1986), pp. 92ff.

29. Karl Rosenkranz, *Von Magdeburg nach Königsberg*, (Berlin: Heimann, 1873), pp. 8–9; cf. August Bebel, in Hardach-Pinke and Hardach, p. 277.

30. Edward P. Thompson, "The Moral Economy of the English Crowd in the Eighteenth Century," (1971), in id., *Customs in Common*, (New York: The New Press, 1993), pp. 185–258; idem, "The Moral Economy Reviewed," in ibid., pp. 259–351.

31. Georg Weber, in Hardach-Pinke and Hardach, p. 265.

32. Paulsen, pp. 11, 15, 25–26.
33. Ibid., p. 19, 28ff., cf. 81ff., 96ff.
34. Jordan, pp. 291–292.
35. In Schlumbohm, *Kinderstuben,* p. 284. See the picture of Campe's ideal family on the front cover of this volume. On Campe's *Robinson Crusoe,* first published in 1779–1780, see Reinhard Stach, *Robinson der Jüngere als pädagogisch-didaktisches Modell des philanthropistischen Erziehungsdenkens,* (Ratingen: Henn, 1970); Hans-Heino Ewers, in Theodor Brüggemann and Hans-Heino Ewers (eds.), *Handbuch der Kinder- und Jugendliteratur. Von 1750 bis 1800,* (Stuttgart: Metzler, 1982), column 215–233; Angelika Reinhard, *Die Karriere des Robinson Crusoe vom literarischen zum pädagogischen Helden: eine literaturwissenschaftliche Untersuchung des Robinson Defoes und der Robinson-Adaptionen von Campe und Forster,* (Frankfurt/Main: Lang, 1994); Silke Köstler-Holste, *Natürliches Sprechen im belehrenden Schreiben: J. H. Campes "Robinson der Jüngere" (1779/80),* (Tübingen: Niemeyer, 2004).
36. Georg Weber, in Hardach-Pinke and Hardach, pp. 264, 266–267; cf. G[eorg] F[riedrich] Schumacher, *Genrebilder aus dem Leben eins siebenzigjährigen Schulmannes, ernsten und humoristischen Inhalts; oder: Beiträge zur Geschichte der Sitten und des Geistes seiner Zeit,* (Schleswig: Taubstummen-Institut, 1841), pp. 38ff. Cf. Jan Fergus's contribution to this volume for the significance that other children's books had for the boys in an English elite boarding school.
37. Paulsen, p. 65.
38. Johannes Janssen, *Johann Friedrich Böhmer's Leben 1795–1863* (Johann Friedrich Böhmer, *Leben, Briefe und kleinere Schriften,* J. Janssen, ed., vol. 1), (Freiburg i.Br.: Herder, 1868), pp. 8–9. On the middle-class ritual of Sunday promenades see Gunilla-Friederike Budde, *Auf dem Weg ins Bürgerleben: Kindheit und Erziehung in deutschen und englischen Bürgerfamilien 1840–1914,* (Göttingen: Vandenhoeck, 1994), pp. 89ff.
39. Rosenkranz, pp. 29–30.
40. This was recommended by the medical doctor Frank, *System,* vol. 2, pp. 607–692.
41. Ernst Christian Trapp, *Versuch einer Pädagogik,* Theodor Fritzsch, ed., (Leipzig: Koehler, 1913), p. 31.
42. Janssen, p. 10.
43. Budde, pp. 196 ff., cf. 220ff.; Schlumbohm, *Kinderstuben,* pp. 312–315.
44. Budde, pp. 81ff.; for an example from the late eighteenth century, see Schlumbohm, "Constructing Individuality," pp. 36–37. Cf. Anne-Charlott Trepp, "Männerwelten privat: Vaterschaft im späten 18. und beginnenden 19. Jahrhundert," in Thomas Kühne, ed., *Männergeschichte–Geschlechtergeschichte: Männlichkeit im Wandel der Moderne,* (Frankfurt am Main: Campus, 1996), pp. 31–50, esp. 45–47.
45. Gotthilf Heinrich von Schubert, *Der Erwerb aus einem vergangenen und die Erwartungen von einem zukünftigen Leben: Eine Selbstbiographie,* (Erlangen: Palm und Enke, 1854), vol. 1, pp. 58–60, 62, 134, 189, 228, 241. Cf. Heinz D. Kittsteiner, *Die Entstehung des modernen Gewissens,* (Frankfurt am Main: Insel, 1991).

46. Habermas, pp. 373ff., makes this point, contradicting implicitly Budde, pp. 150ff., esp. 152.
47. Trepp, pp. 343–344, cf. 333ff., 345ff. For more examples of fathers and mothers keeping diaries on the development of their baby children see Irene Hardach-Pinke, *Kinderalltag: Aspekte von Kontinuität und Wandel der Kindheit in autobiographischen Zeugnissen 1700 bis 1900*, (Frankfurt am Main: Campus, 1981), pp. 171–172.
48. Budde, pp. 193ff., 220ff., quote 222–223. Cf. Hardach-Pinke, *Kinderalltag*, pp. 174ff.; eadem, *Bleichsucht und Blütenträume: Junge Mädchen 1750–1850*, (Frankfurt am Main: Campus, 2000).
49. Trepp, pp. 353–354. Cf. Gottfried Kößler, *Mädchenkindheiten im 19. Jahrhundert*, (Gießen: Focus, 1979), pp. 73ff.
50. Examples of the latter: Klöden, in Schlumbohm, *Kinderstuben*, p. 278; Hermann Enters, *Die kleine, mühselige Welt des jungen Hermann Enters: Erinnerungen eines Amerika-Auswanderers an das frühindustrielle Wuppertal*, (Wuppertal: Born, 1970), pp. 27–28, 30.
51. Schumacher, pp. 37–38.
52. See above note 18 and related text.
53. See the example of Otto van Eck in Baggerman's and Dekker's contribution to this volume.
54. English translation by Richie Robertson: Karl Philipp Moritz, *Anton Reiser: A Psychological Novel*, (London: Penguin, 1997).
55. Interestingly, this is not true in the case of Moritz, *Anton Reiser*.

Contributors List

Arianne Baggerman directs the research program "Controlling Time and Shaping the Self. Education, Introspection and Practices of Writing in the Netherlands, 1750–1914" in the Faculty of History and Arts at Erasmus University Rotterdam. She has published books and articles on writing, publishing, and reading in the seventeenth- to nineteenth-century Netherlands, including *Een drukkend gewicht. Leven en werk van de zeventiende-eeuwse veelschrijver Simon de Vries* (1993) and *Een lot uit de loterij: Het wel en wee van een uitgeversfamilie in de achttiende eeuw* (2001). Recently she published (with Rudolf Dekker) *Kind van de toekomst: De wondere wereld van Otto van Eck (1780–1798)* (2005).

Claire M. Busse is Assistant Professor of English at La Salle University. She is currently working on her book *Not Their Own: Children as Commodities in Early Modern Drama.*

Patricia Crain is Associate Professor of English at New York University. She is the author of *The Story of A: The Alphabetization of American*

Literature from The New England Primer *to* The Scarlet Letter (Stanford, 2000).

Rudolf Dekker teaches history at the Faculty of History and Art of the Erasmus University Rotterdam. His works include *Childhood, Memory and Autobiography in Holland from the Golden Age to Romanticism* (1999) and *Humour in Dutch Culture of the Golden Age* (2001). He has edited *Egodocuments and History: Autobiographical Writing in its Social Context since the Middle Ages* (2002), and *The Tradition of Female Transvestism in Early Modern Europe* (1989) with Lotte van de Pol. He collaborated with Arianne Baggerman on a book about the experiences and worldview of a Dutch boy during the 1790s, based on his diary: *Kind van de toekomst. De wondere wereld van Otto van Eck (1790–1798)* (2005). They also have edited a collection of essays: *Egodocumenten: Nieuwe wegen en perspectieven* (2004).

Jan Fergus, Professor of English at Lehigh University, has published extensively on eighteenth-century readership, drawing on provincial booksellers' records, as well as on Jane Austen. She has just completed a book-length study, *Provincial Readers in Eighteenth-Century England.*

Erica Fudge is Reader in Literary and Cultural Studies at Middlesex University, London, and is the author of *Perceiving Animals: Humans and Beasts in Early Modern English Culture* (Macmillan, 2000) and *Animal* (Reaktion, 2002), and is coeditor of *At the Borders of the Human* (Macmillan, 1999) and editor of *Renaissance Beasts: Of Animals, Humans and Other Wonderful Creatures* (Illinois, 2004). Her forthcoming monograph *Brutal Reasoning: Animals, Rationality and Humanity in Early Modern England* will be published by Cornell. She is associate editor for the humanities on the journal *Society and Animals.*

Andrea Immel is Curator of the Cotsen Children's Library at Princeton University. She has written essays, notes, and reviews on various aspects of the illustration, publishing, and reception of children's books from the late seventeenth to twentieth centuries. Her recent work includes the chapter on the children's books and schoolbooks of the eighteenth century in the forthcoming fifth volume of the *Cambridge History of the Book in Britain*. She is also a Senior Editor of the forthcoming *Oxford Encyclopedia of Children's Literature* and the general editor of the multivolume printed catalogue of the research collection at the Cotsen Children's Library to be completed in 2008.

Cynthia J. Koepp is Professor of History at Wells College, where she specializes in early modern European cultural and intellectual history. She is the coeditor (with Steven L. Kaplan) of *Work in France: Representations, Meaning, Organization, and Practice* (Cornell University Press, 1986) and has published essays on eighteenth-century political economy, on Diderot's *Encyclopédie,* and on attitudes toward work. Her current research focuses on the Abbé Pluche's best-selling *Spectacle de la nature* and the popular Enlightenment.

Michael Mascuch is an Associate Professor in the Department of Rhetoric at UC Berkeley. He is the author of *Origins of the Individualist Self: Autobiography and Self-Identity in England, 1591–1791* (Stanford, 1997). His current research focuses on the reformation of literacy and orality in the discourses of religion, science, and the novel in the early modern period.

William McCarthy, Professor of English Emeritus at Iowa State University, is coeditor of *The Poems of Anna Letitia Barbauld* (1994) and of a collection of Barbauld's poetry and prose (2001). He is writing a new biography of Barbauld, to be completed in 2007. He is also the author of a biography of Hester Thrale Piozzi.

Marianne Novy is Professor of English at the University of Pittsburgh, where she teaches courses in the Renaissance and in nineteenth- and twentieth-century women writers. She has written *Love's Argument: Gender Relations in Shakespeare* (1984), *Engaging with Shakespeare: Responses of George Eliot and Other Women Novelists* (1994), and *Reading Adoption: Family and Difference in Fiction and Drama* (2005). In addition, she has edited, most recently, *Transforming Shakespeare: Contemporary Women's Re-Visions in Literature and Performance* (1999), and *Imagining Adoption: Essays on Literature and Culture* (2001), a Choice Outstanding Academic Title. She is currently researching representations of outsiders in Shakespeare.

Jürgen Schlumbohm is a permanent fellow of the Max-Planck-Institute for History, Göttingen, and professor at Oldenburg University, Germany. He specializes in the history of family, kinship, childhood, and childbirth. His books include: *Kinderstuben: Wie Kinder zu Bauern, Bürgern, Aristokraten wurden, 1700–1850* (1983), *Lebensläufe, Familien, Höfe: Die Bauern und Heuerleute des Osnabrückischen Kirchspiels Belm in proto-industrieller Zeit, 1650–1860* (2nd ed. 1997) and *Geschichte des Ungeborenen: Zur Erfahrungs- und Wissenschaftsgeschichte der Schwangerschaft 17–20. Jahrhundert* (2002), which was coedited with Barbara Duden and Patrice Veit.

Jill Shefrin is a scholar in the field of games and pastimes in the history of education and childhood in eighteenth- and nineteenth-century Britain. She is currently preparing a descriptive bibliography and historical study of educational aids and pastimes published by the Darton firms (1787–1876). She was for many years a librarian with the Osborne Collection of Early Children's Books, Toronto Public Library, where she regularly curated exhibitions, including *"The Box of Delights: 600 Years of Children's Books."* (1995). She is a Research Associate in Arts at Trinity College, University of Toronto. Her lectures and publications include *"Such Constant Affectionate Care": Lady Charlotte Finch, Royal Governess, and the Children of George III* (2003) and *"Dearmerest Mrs. Dearmer": The Life and Work of Mabel Dearmer, 1872–1915* (1999).

Kristina Straub is Professor of Literary and Cultural Studies and Associate Dean of Humanities and Social Sciences at Carnegie Mellon University where she teaches eighteenth-century British studies and gender studies. She is the author of *Divided Fictions: Fanny Burney and Feminine Strategy* (1986) and of *Sexual Suspects: Eighteenth Century Players and Sexual Ideology* (1991). She is the editor of many teaching and scholarly editions of eighteenth-century British texts, as well as coeditor of *Body Guards* (1992) with Julia Epstein.

Michael Witmore is Associate Professor of English at Carnegie Mellon University, where he teaches Renaissance literature and culture. His research deals with the theatrical and cultural significance of "spontaneity" in early modern drama and performance. He is author of *Culture of Accidents: Unexpected Knowledges in Early Modern England* (Stanford, 2001) and a forthcoming monograph entitled *Pretty Creatures: Children and the Agency of Fiction in the English Renaissance* (Cornell).

Index

A

Abduction, 78, 94, 97 n. 12
    Cymbeline, 56
    Pericles, 57
Absent mother, 64, 65
Adult actors, 78, 91
    Alleyn, Edward, 79
    audience/actor relationship, 91–92, 94
Alphabet letters, 214, 272
    age at which a child learns to read, 269
    The History of Little Goody
        Two-Shoes, 215
        literacy/learning, 228, 235
        spelling lessons, 222
        universal availability, 231
        wooden blocks, 222, 225
The Anatomy of Melancholy, 26, 29; *see also*
    Robert Burton
Animals, 20–24, 27, 28–31, 35, 172, 225,
    226, 227, *309*, 310
    compared to peasants, 179 n. 14
    dog laughter, 22, 24, 25, 28
    reasoning ability, 21–22, 36 n. 6, 37
        n. 22
    witchcraft, 45, 229–230

Apprenticeship, 56, 75, 127, 129, 145, 310
    Compared to child actors, 13
Art of Teaching in Sport, 183; *see also* Lady
    Ellenor Fenn
Ariès, Philippe, 1, 2, 10,
Aristotle, 13, 20, 23, 27, 28, 31, 36 n. 6, 56,
    70 n. 3, 284
Aristocratic values, 171, 193, 199
    mother as teacher, 182–188, 191, 194,
        196, 261
    spiritual guidance for children, 189, 192,
        195
    spiritual guidance for servants, 133–134,
        142–143

B

Barbauld, Anna Letitia, 261, 272, 275
    Lessons for Children, 268–270
    Palgrave School, 266–267, 270–271
    poet, 266
    Protestant Dissent, 270
    teaching methods, 267–271
Batavian Revolution, 281, 283, 299
Beaumont, Francis, 80, 91–95, 101 n. 37; *see*
    also The Knight of the Burning Pestle

Beggary, 174, 217, 308
Birth-parents, 55–57, 59, 61, 67, 69
    idealized mother, 64–65
    resemblance, 62–63
Blood relations, 56, 60, 65–66, 70 n. 3, 95
Burton, Robert, 26, 29; *see also The Anatomy of*
    Melancholy

C

Calvin, John, 20, 29–30, 35
Chapbooks, 244–245
Charity schools, 127, 142–143
Child actor, 3, 13, 75, 52 n. 11, 79, 82,
    88–91, 93
    abduction, 78, 94, 97 n. 12
    audience/actor relationship, 82–85,
        87–88, 91–93, 95
    boy actors in female roles, 62
    choir schools, 97 n. 11
    inductions, 81-85, 92, 101 n. 37
    relationship with authors, 86–87
    Salomon Pavy, 75, 77–78
    as theater property, 75, 77–78, 80,
        86, 95
    unpaid workers, 77
    writs of impressmeent, 97, n. 11
Child minister, 12, 109–118, 120–122
    establishing credibility, 113
    Hatfield, Martha, 113
    Trapnel, Anna, 113
    Wight, Sarah, 12, 104
Child prophet, 114
Child servants, 127–128
Children possessed, 3, 13, 41–49, 53 n. 14,
    228–230; *see also* Throckmorton case
    Darling, Thomas, 43–44
    demonic forces, 3
    divine forces, 3, 107, 109–116, 123
    fits, 41, 43, 44, 46, 50
    Goody Two-Shoes, 229
    Samuels family, 41–45, 47–48
    Throckmorton children, 41–45
Children's contribution to family survival,
    310, 312, 314, 317, 322
Children's markets, 311
Children's work, 81
    acting, 3, 13, 77, 86
        celebrity, 80
        Pavy, Salomon, 75
    domestic servants, 128, 311
    gooseherd, 310
    herding cattle, 310, 312

picking berries, 312
ploughing, 307, 311
spinning, 310
stable boy, 310
toy-making, 310
Cleaver, Robert, 19, 23, 30, 34; *see also* John
    Dod, *Godly Forme of Household*
    Government
Conception of time, 283, 286
    cyclical, 283, 284
    linear, 283, 284
    punctuality, 286
    scientific debate, 285
Conventicle Act of 1664, 114
Cottage industry, 310, 322
Countess of Bute, 185–187
Critical Review, 182
Crusoe, Robinson; see also Daniel Defoe,
    245, 316

D

Darling, Thomas, 43–44, 51 n. 2
Darwin, Charles, 27,
Death rates, 56, 67, 69
De Beaumont, Jeanne-Marie Le Prince, 7,
    182, 187
    active mothering, 181, 185, 195
    aristocratic pupils, 183–184, 189–190,
        193, 194, 198, 205–206 n. 40
    importance of rank, 189, 194
    Magasin des adolescentes, 188, 191, 205
        n. 38
    Magasin des enfants, 182–183, 188–189,
        191–194, 200 n. 7, 204 n. 33
    Maps, 192, 197–198
    theories of education, 184, 188,
        190–194, 197, 209 n. 59
Defoe, Daniel, 134, 135, 137–138,
    140–143, 316
    The Family Instructor in Three Parts;
        I. Relating to Fathers and Children.
        II. To Masters and Servants. III. To
        Husbands and Wives, 128,
        130, 133
    Robinson Crusoe, 245, 253, 316
Diaphragm, 24, 27
Diary-keeping, 187, 281, 290, 321
    analogous to clock, 290
    in relation to time, 290–292, 299
    Pomfret, Lady, 183, 187
    Van Eck, Otto, 277, *278,* 293
De l'Épée, Abbé, 270, 273

Delft, 280–281, 289
    Van Eck, Otto, 281, 291, 293–294, 296
    watch inventories, 290
Dod, John, 19, 23, 30, 34; *see also* Robert
    Cleaver, *Godly Forme of Household
    Government*
Domestic servants, 13, 127
    analogous to children, 128, 130–134,
        142, 144, 145–146
    children as, 128, 311
    conduct manuals, 140–141, 146–147
        Domestic Happiness Promoted, 146
        *Footman's Friendly Advice to his
            Brethren in Livery, The*, 150
        Present for Servants, A, 146
        *Serious Advice and Warning to
            Servants, More Especially Those of
            the Nobility and Gentry*, 129
        Servant's Magazine, The, 147
    corrupt, 134
    dress of, 139–139
    Gay, Hannah, 105
    literacy, 129–130, 141, 144
    masters, 128–131, 142–143
        educational responsibility, 129–130,
            141–143, 145
        spiritual responsibility, 133–134,
            142–143
    sexuality, 138–139, 146
    theater, 145–146
    Trimmer, Sarah, 128–130, 133, 137,
        142–144, 146

E

Education of children,
    aristocratic, 181–184
    boys, 182, 184, 188, 194, 201 n. 11, 202
        n. 23, 206, n. 45, 209 n. 59
        Rugby School, 243, 246, 249, 254
    girls, 182, 184–199, 201 n. 11,
        203 n. 24
    role of the father, 159, 163–165
    role of the mother, 162–163
Educational advancement, 213
Enlightenment values, 7, 155, 177, 182,
    193–194
    faith in progress, 275
    learning, 213
        teaching practices, 261–262
        theories of education, 279
    rationality, 213, 268
    self-sufficiency, 213

Envangelical Protestants, 108, 111, 115, 121
    Scripture, 120
    Wight, Sarah, 113–114
*Exceeding Riches of Grace Advanced by the Spirit
    of Grace, in an Empty Nothing Creature,
    viz. Mistress Sarah Wight, The*, 104, 107,
    112, 116–117, 124; *see also* Henry Jessey
    recording of conferences, 106, 113
    religious practices, 103, 111, 108

F

Fairy-tales, 215, 219, 252
Female prophets, 108
Fenn, Lady Ellen, 182–183, 195, 197, 206
    n. 44, 210 n. 72
Feral child, 261
    mute, 271
    response to food cue, 271
    training the senses, 272
Finch, Lady Charlotte, 194–196, 206 n. 41,
    210 n. 75
Foster parents, 55, 56, 57, 58, 60, 64, 66–69,
    72 n. 20,
    child as gift exchange, 76
    child to solidify relationships, 76
Foucault, Michel, 5
French Revolution, 281, 283

G

George III, 194
Godly Forme of Household Government, 19;
    see also, Robert Cleaver and John Dod
Goldsmith, Oliver, 216, 252, 267; *see also The
    Vicar of Wakefield,*
Goody Two-Shoes, 216
    alphabet letters, 222–224
    animals, 225–226, 230
    orphan, 215, 217
    self-made, 229
    shoes as commodity, 218–221
    wealth, 226–228
    witchcraft, 228–230
Governess, 181, 183, 186, 192, 200 n. 5
    De Beaumont, Jeanne-Marie Le Prince,
        182, 187, 189, 194
    fictional, 184,
    French, 182, 198
    mother as, 188, 194
    royal, 194–195, 197
Guide to Grand-Jury Men, A, 43–44; *see also*
    Richard Bernard

H

Hale, Mathew, 46
Heredity, 56, 58–59
    resemblance, 62–63
High German, 315, 322
History of Little Goody Two-Shoes, The, 11,
    213, 243, 245–246, 249; *see also* John
    Newbery
    orphaned child, 217, 220–221, 252, 256
    poverty, 220
    rags-to-riches, 215
    reading instruction, 215, 222–223, 225
    witchcraft, 228–230
Hobbes, Thomas, 26

I

Induction, 81–82
    Antonio and Mellida, 80
    audience/performer relationship, 90
    creating instability, 85
    Cynthia's Revels, 80
    distinct from stage dialogue, 83
    Isle of Gulls, 80
    Knight of the Burning Pestle, The, 80
    Jack Drum's Entertainment, 80
    provoke audience sympathies, 82
    unscripted child actors, 83
Infants, 20
    laughter, 22, 28, 29
    reasoning ability, 21–22, 28
Itard, Jean-Marc-Gastard, 261
    analytical pedagogy, 272
    Pinel, Philippe, 271
    Séguin, Edouard 274
    teaching methods, 272–274
    Victor, 271–274

J

Jauffret, Louis-François, 158
Jessey, Henry, 104–112, 117, 123
    Baptist/Independent minister, 104
    Catechisme for Babes, 115
    Conventicle Act of 1664, 114
    Evangelicals, 113–114, 120
    *Exceeding Riches of Grace Advanced by the
      Spirit of Grace, in an Empty Nothing
      Creature, viz. Mistress Sarah Wight,
      The*, 116, 119, 124
    Wight, Sarah, 104, 107, 109, 114, 119
Jesus Christ, 27, 31, 116, 118, 122, 126 n. 23

Jigsaw puzzles, 192, 197–198, 209 n. 59
Jonson, Ben, 13, 75–76, 80, 82, 83, 86–88,
    96 n. 7
    on the death of his daughter, 76
    on the death of his son, 76
    Pavy, Salomon 75
        abduction of, 97 n. 11
        child actor, 77
        as a commodity, 77
        death, 78
        popularity, 79
        Cynthia's Revels, 84, 87–90
Joubert, Laurent, 23, 27, 29, 30, 33, 37
    experience of joy, 26
    false laughter, 24, 28,
    passion and laughter, 25
    physical effects of laughter, 24
    shared faculty, 25
    Treatise on Laughter, 37, n. 20

K

Kempe, William, 22
Knight of the Burning Pestle, The; see also
    Francis Beaumont, 80, 91–95,

L

Laughter, 22
    bastard, 25, 28, 31, 33
    belly laughs, 23
    children, 27, 34
        false, 28
        innocent, 28
    Christian, 30–32
    dog, 22, 24, 25, 28
    exercise, 32
    false, 24, 28
    infant, 22, 28, 29
        age of beginning, 27
        lack of judgment, 28
    Jesus Christ, 27, 31
    learning to laugh, 32–35
    link between body and mind, 23, 24, 25,
      26, 27
    Plato, 27
    religious, 32
    self-reflection, 26, 32
Learning
    educational play, 181, 183, 279
    geography, 182, 197–198, 266
    hands-on, 170–171
    history, 181, 197, 266

languges, 262, 266
opportunity for, 161
parent/child, 7, 162, 163–165, 181–188
philosophy, 182, 191
physics, 182
religion, 182, 262
scientific experiments, 167–168, *169, 170,*
scientific study, 182, 196, 201 n. 11, 266, 295
spelling, 222
study of nature, 156–158
writing, 268,
Lessons for Children, 268–270; *see also* Anna Letitia Barbauld
Life expectancy, 67
Literacy, 213, 221, 226
cultural capital, 214
relationship to property, 214, 224–225, 228, 230–232, 235 n. 6, 242 n. 47, 254
goods freely given, 224
inalienable, 225, 232
rewards, 213
shifts in meaning of property, 231
Locke, John, 155, 182, 184, 193, 273
awareness of time, 283, 285
concept of identity, 231
property, 220, 231–232
on shoes, 217
Some Thoughts Concerning Education, 217, 222
London servants, 134–139
Lost children, 15, 55, 67, 76
Low German, 315
Luther, Martin, 104

M

Magasin des enfants, 182, 188–189, 191–194, 204 n. 34, 37; *see also* Jeanne-Marie La Prince de Beaumont
Marprelate controversy, 81
Marston, John, 80, 82–83, 99 n. 22
Marxism, 6, 274
Master/servant relationship, 4, 127–131, 135, 143–148
discipline, 128, 134
education, 130, 133, 142
as family, 128–129, 133
friendship, 132–133
legal protection, 139–140
urban servants, 132, 134–136, 139, 141
Medicine, 33, 225

Memorization, 30, 264, 267, 269
Mischievous boys, 312, 313, 321
Mother as teacher, 162–163, 182–188, 191, 194, 196, 261, 315, 320
Mulcaster, Richard; *see also Positions*, 32–33

N

Newbery, John, 213, 223–225, 243, 245, 250, 255; *see also The History of Little Goody Two-Shoes*
patent medicines, 225
satirized by Samuel Johnson, 224
Nurse, 56–58, 67–69
Nurture vs. nature, 55

O

Original Stories, 183; *see also* Mary Wollstonecraft
Orphaned child, 58, 217, 221, 232
Goody-Two-Shoes, 9, 215
loss of affection, 217
loss of protection, 217
vulnerability, 217

P

Palgrave School, 267–268
Denman, Thomas, 271
Reformist politics, 270–271
Sayers, Frank, 267
Tyler, William, 267
Paulsen, Friedrich, 306
appreciation of nature, 307–308
children's work, 310–311
hierarchy of learning, 308
reading, 308, 315–317, 321
Parent/child relationship, 4, 55, 75, 128, 165, 194, 321
alienation, 56
infant care, 30
physical resemblance, 62–63
theatrical portrayal, 56–69
Perkins, William, 30, 31
Phonics, 269–270
Pinel, Philippe, 271
Plato, 25, 27
Play, 182–183, 196, 199 n. 1, 279
Pluche, Abbé; *see also Spectacle de la nature* 8, 153–154, 168–169, 170, 172, 176–177
philosophy of education, 155, 159, 160–161, 165

delight the eye, 167, 177
    father as teacher, 163–165
    freedom to learn, 166–167
    learn from the familiar, 156, 158
    mother as teacher, 162–163
    societal reformer, 171, 173–175
Positions, 32–33; *see also* Richard Mulcaster
Preindustrial Germany, 305
    books, 305, 308, *309*, 312,
        315–317, 321
    children's work, 307, 310–312
    hierarchy of learning, 308
    isolation of children, 318
    middle-class parenting, 318, *319*,
        321–322
    Paulsen, Friedrich, 306
        appreciation of nature, 307, 308
        books, *309*, 315–316
        learning by imitation, 312
        learning by participation, 308
        play, 310, 312, *313*, 318, 320, 322
        reading, 308, 315–317, 321
    peasant life, 11, 306–308, 310, 324 n.14
    physical exercise, 320
    socialization of children, 306, 307
    street life, 312–313, 318, 320, 322
    social structure, 307–388
Promfret, Lady, 188, 198, 203 n. 29, 204 n. 30
    De Beaumont, Jeanne-Marie
        Le Prince, 187
    diary entries, 187
    Royal family, 194–195, 198
*Pronounciation Taught as an Amusement by
    Means of Cuts by an Indulgent
    Grandmother*, 183
Property, 216, 220, 226, 229, 231
    Relationship to literacy, 214, 225,
        230, 254

R

Reformation, 2, 29, 35, 103
Reform Bill of 1832, 271
    education doctrine, 33
Renaissance worldview, 56
Restoration, 114
Rise of childhood, 305
    print media, 306
    verbal communication, 306
Robinson Crusoe, 253, 316
Royal children, 195–198, 210 n. 77, 211 n. 78
Rugby School, 11, 243,
    bookselling records, 244–245, 247, *251*,
        257 n. 3

class discipline, 246
Clay family, 244, 247, 249
History of Little Goody Two-Shoes, The,
    245–246, 249, 252, 254,
    isolation from family, 247, 250
    school culture, 246–248, 250

S

Satire, 81–82, 137–138, 215, 253
Séguin, Edouard, 274
Serious Advice and Warning to Servants, 129
Shakespeare, William, 15, 43, 55, 74 n. 36,
    96 n. 7,
    Cymbeline, 56, 58, 60–61, 64–65, 68
    imagery, 65
    parenthood, 56–58, 66–69
    Pericles, 56–59, 62, 65–66, 68–69
    Winter's Tale, 56, 60, 62–66
Social advancement, 213
Social subordination of children, 6, 10, 14
    child actors, 75, 81
Socrates, 26
Somers, William, 43
Spectacle de la nature, 8, *169, 170*, 175–178;
    see also Abbé Pluche
    dialogue style, 159
    entomology, 156, *157*, 158–159, 161
    experiments, 167–169, *170*
    geography, 160–161
    hands-on activities, 166, 169–170
    how-to book, 159
    importance of artisans, 172–173
    physics, 161
    social critique, 154
Stuart, Lady Mary, 185–186
Swift, Jonathan, 137–139
    Directions to Servants in General, 135

T

Theater companies, 77–78, 81, 85–86, 94–95,
    97 n. 11, 100 n. 32
    adult, 79, 81
    children's, 46, 52 n. 11, 77, 81–84, 95,
        99 n. 22, 101 n. 36
Thrale, Hester, 261, 272, 275
    broad-based subjects, 262, 264
    Children's Book, The, 262, *263, 265*
    mother-teacher, 262
    records of children's accomplishments,
        262, *263, 265*
    religious education, 262, 264

Throckmorton case, 43, 45, 48, 100 n. 30,
  100 n. 30; *see also* Children Possessed
    Samuels family, 41–45, 47–48
    Throckmorton children, 41–42, 47–50
      fits, 41, 43, 46, 48
      hearing voices, 42
      involuntary speech, 42, 46
      physical distress, 41–42
Timepieces, 288
    clocks, 287–288, 290
    railway timetables, 287
    sundials, 287
    watches, 277, 286, 289
      sign of good taste, 289
      status symbols, 278, 289
      temporality of life, 289
Toys, 166–167, 192, 310
Trimmer, Sarah, 128–130, 133, 137,
  142–144, 146
    *Easy Introduction to the Knowledge of
      Nature*, 195
    *The Oeconomy of Charity; or An Address to
      Ladies Concerning Sunday Schools*, 150
      n. 51
    *The Servant's Friend, an Exemplary Tale:
      Designed to Enforce the Religious
      Instruction Given at Sunday and Other
      Charity Schools*, 149 n. 24
Tutors, 181, 200, n. 5, 293
    De Beaumont, Jeanne-Marie Le Prince,
      182, 184, 187
    Goody Two-Shoes, 225

U

Unpaid workers, 77, 81
Unscripted child actors, 83

V

Van Eck, Otto, 277
    awareness of time, 278–280, 291,
      295–297, 299
    death, 280, 284, 297, 299–300
    Delft, 280, 281, 289, 290, 291, 293,
      294, 296
    diary-keeping, *278*, 290–294
    illness, 293, 295, 299
    parents' politics, 280
    routine, 14, 293–294
Vicar of Wakefield, The, 216, 252; *see also*
  Oliver Goldsmith

W

War of the theaters, 82
Whole language reading instruction,
  268–269
Wortley Montagu, Lady Mary, 185,
  203 n. 29
    importance of learning languages, 187
    importance of reading, 187
    self-educated, 186
Widdowes, Daniel, 20–21,
Wight, Sarah, 104–110, 117–118, 122
    child-minister, 109, 112–115,
      117–118
    Conventicle Act of 1664, 114
    divinely ordained, 109–111
    education, 111
    establishing credibility, 113
    *Exceeding Riches of Grace Advanced by the
      Spirit of Grace, in an Empty Nothing
      Creature, viz. Mistress Sarah Wight,
      The*, 116, 119, 124; *see also* Henry
      Jessey,
    Jessey, Henry, 105–109, 112, 115, 117
    physical afflictions, 106, 123
    relationship with mother, 105–106,
      122–123
    suicide attempts, 105, 123
    trained in the scriptures, 105
Witchcraft, 3, 41, 48–49, 50–51 n. 2,
  52–53 n. 14, 84, 228, 229–230; *see also*
    children possessed
    Bernard, Richard; *see also A Guide to
      Grand-Jury Men*, 43–44
    bewitched children, 13, 41, 43
    Darling, Thomas, 43–44
    fits, 41, 43, 44, 46, 4850
    involuntary speech, 42
    physical distress, 42
    Throckmorton children, 41–50; *see also*
      the Throckmorton Case
    trance-like states, 43
    Samuels family; *see also* the
      Throckmorton Case, 41–45
    Somers, William, 43
Witch hunters, 50
Witches of Warboys, 24, 41–43, 50 n. 2, 52
  n. 14; *see also* the Throckmorton case
    Samuels family, 41–45
    Throckmorton children, 41–45
Wollstonecraft, Mary, 183, 202 n. 16;
  see also Original Stories,
Wright, Thomas, 21–22, 25